REINVENTING MARXISM

Howard J. Sherman

Reinventing Marxism

The Johns Hopkins University Press
Baltimore and London

© 1995 The Johns Hopkins University Press
All rights reserved. Published 1995
Printed in the United States of America on acid-free paper
04 03 02 01 00 99 98 97 96 95   5 4 3 2 1

The Johns Hopkins University Press
2715 North Charles Street
Baltimore, Maryland 21218-4319
The Johns Hopkins Press Ltd., London

Library of Congress Cataloging-in-Publication Data will be found at the end of
this book.
A catalog record for this book is available from the British Library.

TO
Barbara Sinclair
with love

Contents

Preface   xiii

Acknowledgments   xvii

Part I. The Political Economy of History   1

Chapter 1. Why Reinvent Marxism?   3
  The Emergence of the New, Critical Marxism   4
  Marx and Critical Marxism   5
  The Soviet Union and the Old Marxism   5
  The Renaissance of Critical Marxism   7
  Radical Institutionalism   9
  Post Keynesianism   10
  Radical Economics   11
  Marxian Trends in the Social Sciences   11
  Why Should Marxism Be Reinvented?   12

Chapter 2. A Critique of Reductionism   13
  Psychological Reductionism   13
  *The Writings of Lewis Feuer: An Example of Extreme
    Psychological Reductionism*   13
  Psychological Reductionism and "Human Nature"   14
  Orthodox Economics and Psychological Reductionism   16
  Economic Reductionism   16
  The Economic Reductionism of Marvin Harris   16
  Economic Reductionism in Soviet Marxism   17
  The Critics of Soviet Marxism   19

G. A. Cohen's Economic Reductionism   20
Conclusions on Economic Reductionism   22
Conclusions on All Reductionism   22
Appendix
2A. Psychological Reductionism in Orthodox Economics   22

Chapter 3. The Relational Approach   29
Definitions   29
The Framework of Analysis   30
The Economic Process   30
The Social Process   33
The Relational Approach: First Approximation   35
Specific Interactions   37
Interactions between Ideas, Institutions, Relations,
    and Forces   39
The Sociology of Knowledge: The Evolution of Ideas   40
Social and Political Institutions   44
The Relations of Production   47
The Forces of Production   50
The Relational Approach: Second Approximation   51
Conclusions   52
Appendixes
3A. A Formal Model of the Relational Approach:
    First Approximation   53
3B. The Holistic Approach of Institutionalism   54

Chapter 4. The Historical Approach   56
Contemporary Orthodox Social Science and
    Historical Change   57
Soviet Marxism on Historical Change   58
Cohen's Economic Reductionist View of
    Historical Change   59
Historical Specificity   62
An Evolutionary Approach   63
Qualifications to the Marxian Historical Model   63
A Theory of Evolution with Qualifications   66
A Critical Marxian View of Forces and Relations   68
The Process of Socioeconomic Revolution   70
The Historical Approach as a Method   71
Questions, Not Answers   72
How Are the Relational and Historical
    Methods Connected?   73

Appendixes
4A. *Orthodox Economics and Historical Change*   74
4B. *The Institutionalist View of Evolutionary Change*   79
4C. *Backwardness and Uneven Development*   82

Chapter 5. A Critique of Individualism and
      Extreme Collectivism   85
Extreme Collectivism   86
Individualism   86
The Individualist Critique of Marxian Class Analysis   87
Mancur Olson's Critique of Marxian Class Analysis   90
A Post-Marxian Critique of Marxian Class Analysis   92
Myths about Marxian Class Analysis   93
Conclusions   94
Appendixes
5A. *Individualism and Orthodox Economics*   95
5B. *Individualist Methodology in Analytic Marxism*   101
5C. *Liberal Institutionalist Views of Individualism*
      and Class   106

Chapter 6. Class Analysis   109
Problems of Defining Class   109
What Is the Middle Class?   111
A Factual Analysis of the Middle Class   112
A Factual Analysis of the Working Class   113
A Relational Approach to Class Conflicts   115
Three Levels of Class Conflict in the Historical Process   116
Class Conflict in the Economy   120
Social and Political Class Conflicts   121
Ideological Class Conflicts   123
Questions, Not Answers   125
Conclusions   126

Part II. Political Economy: A Relational-Historical Approach

Chapter 7. Poverty, Inequality, and Exploitation   129
Poverty and Inequality   130
The Labor Theory of Value   130
The Traditional Marxian Theory of Exploitation   133
A Technological Reductionist View of Value
      and Exploitation   134
A Relational or Class Theory of Exploitation   136

A Historical Approach to Exploitation   140
Conclusions   141
Appendixes
7A. *Class Conflict in U.S. Labor Relations*   141
7B. *The Theories of Roemer and Sraffa*   145
7C. *Exploitation and Racial Discrimination*   146
7D. *Exploitation and Sexist Discrimination*   149

Chapter 8. Unemployment and Business Cycles   152
*Orthodox Economic Approaches to Unemployment
     and Cycles*   152
The So-called Falling Rate of Profit Theory   157
*The Historical Approach to Economic Crises and
     Business Cycles*   158
Stages, Trends, and Cycles   161
The Relational Approach to Crises and Unemployment   164
The Marxian Theory of Wage Cost (or Reserve Army)   165
*The Marxian Theory of Effective Demand
     (or Underconsumption)*   168
A Marxian Profit Squeeze (or Nutcracker) Theory   169
Adding Realism by Successive Approximations   172
Conclusions   175

Chapter 9. Democracy and Capitalism   177
Conservative Psychological Reductionism   177
Conservative Economic Reductionism   178
Soviet Marxism and Economic Reductionism   178
A Historical Approach to Government   180
A Relational Approach to Debates on Government   182
The Degree of Democracy   186
The Conflict between Capitalism and Democracy   188
The Effect of Politics on the Economy   191
Conclusions   192

Chapter 10. The Rise and Fall of the Soviet Union   193
A Historical Approach to the Rise of the Soviet Union   193
*A Historical Approach to the Soviet Transition,
     1917–1928*   194
The Political Institutions, 1928–1988   198
Soviet Forces of Production, 1928–1988   199
A Class Analysis of the Former Soviet Union   200
The Fall of the Soviet Union   205
Conclusions   210

Part III. The Critical Method

Chapter 11. Dialectics as a Critical Method   215
    Is Dialectics Important or Useless?   216
    Dialectics as a Relational-Historical Method   217
    The Relational Approach   219
    The Historical Approach   221
    Rejecting and Replacing the Law of the Unity
        of Opposites   222
    Rejecting and Replacing the Law of Quantity
        and Quality   224
    Rejecting and Replacing the Law of the Negation of
        the Negation   226
    The Process of Model Building   227
    The Method of Successive Approximations   229
    Conclusion: Questions, Not Answers   230
    Appendixes
    11A. The Early Evolution of Dialectics   230
    11B. G. W. F. Hegel, Nineteenth-Century Pioneer
            of Dialectics   231
    11C. Soviet Marxism: Dialectics as a System   235
    11D. Dialectics and Logic   240

Chapter 12. The Conflict of Paradigms   243
    Empiricism   244
    Rationalism   251
    The Dilemma and the Road to a Solution   254
    Materialism as a Relational-Historical Method   254
    Normal Science   255
    Revolutions in Science   257
    A Criticism and Amplification of Kuhn   259
    Revolution and Relativity   261
    John Dewey and Instrumentalism   262
    Conclusion: Questions, Not Answers   263
    Appendixes
    12A. Mathematics and Statistics as Rhetoric   264
    12B. Analytic Philosophy and Analytic Marxism   267
    12C. Phenomenological Marxism   268

Chapter 13. Determinism and Predeterminism   270
    Predeterminism   270
    Predeterminism and Soviet Marxism   272
    A Critique of Soviet Predeterminism   273

Free Will and Voluntarism   276
Existentialist Marxism   277
Determinism as a Relational-Historical Method   278
The Concept of Determinism   279
Cause, Effect, and Overdetermination   282
Conclusion: Questions, Not Answers   284

Chapter 14. Marxian Humanism and Liberal Humanism   286
  The Myth of Value-Free Social Science   286
  Orthodox Economics and Ethical Values   288
  Alternative Marxian Views of Ethics   288
  Is Marxism Contradictory?   292
  Marxian Humanism as a Relational-Historical Method   294
  Utilitarianism, the Standard of Liberal Humanism   296
  Marxian Humanism and Liberal Humanism   298
  A Relational Approach to Ethics   299
  The Historical Specificity of Ethics   300
  Which Side Are You On?   302
  Conclusion: Questions, Not Answers   305
  Appendixes
  14A. Institutionalism and Ethics   307
  14B. Conservative Biases in Orthodox Economics   308

Part IV. A Radical Program for the Twenty-first Century

Chapter 15. Reinventing Socialism   317
  The Paradigm of Marxism: A Weapon for Radical
    Political Economy   317
  Lessons of Soviet History   320
  Lessons of Yugoslav History   322
  Lessons of U.S. History   324
  The Historical Perspective: A Program for the Left   326
  An Immediate Program for the Left   327
  A Medium-Term Program for the Left   332
  A Long-Term Program for the Left   334
  Conclusions   336

References   339

Subject Index   359

Name Index   365

Preface

This book is designed to help change the status quo (which currently includes massive unemployment, poverty, discrimination, and other social diseases). If you like the status quo and side with the elite of the world, or don't care about human misery, this book will try to subvert and change your opinion.

Notes for an Autobiography of a Heretic

My father was a civil engineer who worked for the Santa Fe Railroad for some years. He then became a general contractor and business-man. He was quite wealthy at times but went bankrupt twice in his life. When he was young and poor he voted socialist, and when he was bankrupt he voted for the New Deal. But when he made a con-siderable amount of money he had no love for radicals and became a Republican. My mother was a traditional housewife with conven-tional views for most of her life, but at age sixty she began to paint, and she created a large number of quite unconventional paintings, which surprised my whole family.

I had a happy childhood, with no emotional or financial worries. My parents were Jewish, and I was brought up in a very mild and re-formed version of the Jewish religion, with the family going to temple only a few times a year. I did have to attend Sunday school at the temple and was class valedictorian; my speech—to about a thousand Jews—was entitled "Why I Am against Zionism." I became an agnos-tic at about age fifteen and was an atheist by sixteen.

The Second World War, and my revulsion at fascism and its sexist and racist views and behavior, made me a radical and a heretic. I have always hated any form of fascism or intolerance. At seventeen I was a delegate to the Progressive Party convention of 1948, which nominated Henry Wallace. My ideal was Paul Robeson, the great African American actor and singer. Because of its resistance to fascism, I was very sympathetic to the Soviet Union and the Communist Party for many years. After the Khrushchev "secret" anti-Stalin speech of 1956, which documented the evils of Soviet dictatorship, I became a democratic socialist.

I began my higher education with two years at the University of Chicago (where I was a political activist), then transferred to the University of California at Los Angeles (where I was a political activist) and received a B.A. in economics in 1950. Then I went to the University of Chicago Law School (where I was president of the National Lawyers' Guild chapter) and received a J.D. degree in 1953. Unfortunately, being a radical political activist in the United States was not easy in the 1950s. I passed the bar exam but was denied the right to practice law for political reasons. I was then drafted into the U.S. Army but was given an undesirable discharge for political reasons. As the result of a class-action lawsuit carried to the Supreme Court in a seven-year legal struggle, my discharge was changed to a general discharge under honorable conditions. After the army, I went back to school and got an M.A. in economics from the University of Southern California (where I was a political activist). Eventually, I went to the University of California, Berkeley (where I was a political activist), and received a Ph.D. in economics. With a formal education in law and economics, as well as an excellent informal education in politics, I have spent the rest of my life writing in the field of critical, or radical, political economy.

I was a heretic in more than political ideology. I believed in and campaigned for: democracy, socialism, communism, the metric system, phonetic spelling, atheism, racial equality, sexual equality, environmental quality, world government, a single world language, nudism (which I do not practice), vegetarianism (which I do not practice), and an end to white collars and ties (which I usually do practice). I have continued to believe in most of these issues and to crusade for them to the best of my ability. Though I am always willing to do other political activity, I have done most of my crusading through academic means, by lecturing and writing books and articles.

The Direction of My Research

The political-economic direction of my research may be divided into three categories, reflected in the titles of my previous books:

1. books on economic crises: *Macrodynamic Economics: Growth, Employment, and Prices* (1964); *Elementary Aggregate Economics* (1966); *Profits in the United States: An Introduction to a Study of Economic Concentration and Business Cycles* (1968); *Stagflation: A Radical Theory of Unemployment and Inflation* (1976); *Macroeconomics: Monetarist, Keynesian, and Marxist Views* (co-authored with Gary Evans, 1984); *The Business Cycle: Growth and Crisis in Capitalism* (1991);

2. books on comparative and socialist economics: *The Soviet Economy* (1969); *Comparing Economic Systems: A Political-Economic Approach* (co-authored with Andrew Zimbalist, 1984);

3. books on radical and Marxian social science: *Radical Political Economy: Capitalism and Socialism from a Marxist Humanist Perspective* (1972); *Economics: An Introduction to Traditional and Radical Views* (co-authored with E. K. Hunt, 1972); *Sociology: Traditional and Radical Perspectives* (co-authored with James Wood, 1979); *Foundations of Radical Political Economy* (1987).

The Style of This Book

Since I am attempting to contribute to the construction of a unified perspective for the social sciences and history, I have gone to great trouble to eliminate any technical economics jargon. Many economists write in the most obscure style in order to impress people with their profound knowledge, even when they have nothing to say.

Some radical and Marxian academics also succumb to the disease of profundititis. In the 1920s and 1930s, one important group of dissident Marxists, which made some major contributions, was known as the Frankfurt school. Since the Frankfurt school Marxists were rejected by the mass workers' parties and their constituents, they wrote mainly for the intellectuals. One sympathetic writer says that "those . . . who remained true to their cultural revolutionary ideals, paid the price of commitment not only in political inactivity, but also in an intellectual isolation that found expression in the inevitable tendency for their writing to become increasingly abstract and academic" (Brown 1973, 27). This condition remains true today, with their followers often mixing the mystic jargon of Hegel and Freud with current academic jargon.

A delightful example of this style is Herbert Reid's article "American Social Science in the Politics of Time and the Crisis of Technocorporate Society: Toward a Critical Phenomenology" (1973). If one gets beyond his lengthy title, one finds among his conclusions this gem: "As Merleau-Ponty recognized but as Enzo Paci made fully explicit, the temporal irreversibility and structure of needs and satisfactions is the permanent, precategorical structure of the life-world which provides the key to a political critique of the reification of time as an aspect of technistic alienation and alienated labor in industrial society" (1973, 215). The style of these writers makes them difficult to read and reflects their limited constituency but certainly does not prove them either right or wrong. This book, in contrast, strives to state its views as clearly as possible—even if that means that some radicals and most economists will refuse to read it.

The Scope of This Book

This book presents a Marxian view that is critical of conventional social science but is also critical of the old, Stalinist, Soviet Marxism. In the past few decades there have been hundreds of specialized monographs building the framework of a new, nondogmatic, critical Marxism. But there have been very few attempts in recent years to combine all these specialized contributions into a new, coherent paradigm, stating the new Marxism as a unity of all the social sciences. Obviously, no one is an expert in all of the social sciences, let alone history and the philosophy of science. Nevertheless, Marxism is a view that claims that a unified social science is the essential basis for specialized work, so a new, unified paradigm is long overdue. For better or for worse, the aim of this book is to present the basic framework of the whole field of Marxism.

Acknowledgments

I have received financial help on this book from the University of California, Riverside, Research Committee, to whom I am grateful. I am also grateful to various publishers and journals for the use of some materials from my own articles, even though I have completely rewritten the materials in every case. The articles are as follows: "Dialectics as a Method," *Insurgent Sociologist* (1976); "Technology vis-à-vis Institutions," *Journal of Economic Issues* (1979); "Marx and Determinism," *Journal of Economic Issues* (1981); "Marxism and Humanism," *International Journal of Social Economics* (1992); "The Historical Approach to Political Economy," *Review of Social Economy* (1993); "The Relational Approach to Political Economy," *Rethinking Marxism* (1994); "The Methodology of Critical Marxian Economic Theory," in Philip Klein, ed., *The Role of Economic Theory* (1994); and "Class Analysis," in Victor Lippit, ed., *Studies in Radical Political Economy* (forthcoming).

I owe a special debt of gratitude to Paul Baran and Paul Sweezy, both for their pioneering contributions and for the personal encouragement they gave me over many years. I thank Joan Noguera, Sandy Schauer, and Shirlee Pigeon for helping with typing. I thank the following students, who critiqued the book in several seminars: William Aviles, Melinda Brough, Philip Cormier, Carey Cress, Kenneth Fernandez, Jacqueline Fontana, Paul Forbes, Douglas Heumann, Thomas Kelly, Chris Lee, Stanley Mallison, Cyrus Masroori, Carolyn Rodriguez, Anna Samdalo, Alan Schmidt, Curtis Simon, Barbara Tallon, Vera Valdivia, and Paul Woodburne. I thank Anju Gupta for research help. Finally, I thank the following, who have read various articles incorporated in this book and/or parts of this book in various incarnations and whose constructive criticisms greatly improved my formulations: Lynne Babior, Ronald Chilcote, Steven Cullenberg, John B. Davis, Paul Diesing, William Dugger, Gary Dymski, David Fairris, John Fisher, John B. Foster, Mason Gaffney, Keith Griffin, Robin Hahnel, Michael Howard, Mehrene Larudee, Victor Lippit, Patrick Mason, Joseph Nogee, Robert Pollin, Atiq Rahman, Stephen Resnick, Warren Samuels, Linda Stearns, Marc Tool, Howard Wachtel, Barney Wagman, and John Willoughby. I have received a great deal of encouragement from my editor at Johns Hopkins, Henry Tom, and an enormous amount of help from my copyeditor, Joanne Allen. I claim full responsibility only for the mistakes that remain in the book.

PART ONE

The Political Economy of History

ONE

Why Reinvent Marxism?

In the last several decades it has often been said that Marxism is in crisis. When the Soviet Union and the Eastern European Communist regimes collapsed, it was said that this was also the end of socialist and Marxian theory. The old kind of Marxism, dominant for over half a century, was the official Marxism of the Communist parties and the former Soviet Union, so it will be called *Soviet Marxism* for brevity. The old, Soviet Marxism has indeed collapsed. Good riddance! It was a distortion of Marx's thought and was mainly designed to justify the Soviet status quo of dictatorship and extreme central planning.

As long as capitalism has problems, however, some sort of radical theory is urgently needed. Capitalism does indeed have problems, which include high levels of violence and irrationality reflected in crime, suicide, and wife and child abuse; discrimination against women and minorities; intense poverty and immense wealth; exploitation of workers; large-scale unemployment; and environmental destruction. This book shows how the decline of the old, official Soviet Marxian perspective has led to a new Marxism, which is unofficial, independent, profoundly democratic, critical of all existing societies, and critical of all old, rigid ideas. The new Marxism has often been called critical Marxism. *Critical Marxism* describes most contemporary Marxism as well as any term could, but any one term makes it sound like there is a single, new school. There are, however, many schools of thought in contemporary, non-Soviet Marxism.

One aim of this book is to present the wide range of opinions these new schools hold in common, while specifying the differences that exist on all important issues. Therefore, with the important exception of the official dogmas of the former Soviet Union, China, and the Communist parties, all of contemporary Marxism is simply called Marxism in this book. In other words, when the reader sees the word *Marxism* unadorned by some adjective, it means the new, critical, democratic Marxism, not the old, official dogmas of Soviet Marxism.

A new, critical kind of Marxism, as a part of radical political economy, may also be contrasted with the dominant, orthodox social science in all of its separate disciplines. *Orthodox* social science is defined as the dominant view in the universities; it may also be called conventional, traditional, or mainstream, and it contrasts with the unorthodox, radical, Marxian, and other dissenting views. As this book will show, contemporary Marxian political economy includes radical and Marxian views in all of the disciplines and attempts to put them into a unified whole. Contemporary conventional or orthodox social science, on the other hand, treats each discipline separately, in its own university department, with careful boundaries.

Because each orthodox social science is different from the others, an in-depth critique of them would require a full book on each one. There are, in fact, excellent radical descriptions of the history of thought in each discipline: in economics, see Howard and King 1989a, 1992, E. K. Hunt 1992b, and Mirowski 1989; in sociology, Schwendinger and Schwendinger 1974; in political science, Lustig 1982; in anthropology, Harris 1968; in history, Zinn 1970; and in psychology, Lichtman 1982. When discussing the viewpoint of any orthodox or conventional discipline, it is extremely important to remember that it contains many heterogenous elements. For example, the dominant orthodox economics contains not only conservatives but also many militant liberals. The basic approach may bias the dominant, orthodox disciplines toward a conservative defense of the status quo, but liberals often overcome that tendency, and a few radicals use orthodox social science methods to reach unorthodox, anticapitalist conclusions.

The Emergence of the New, Critical Marxism

Contemporary Marxism emerged out of the fight of radicals in many countries against both the old, Soviet Marxism and the basic assumptions of most conservative and liberal social science. Contemporary, non-Soviet Marxism has also been influenced by radical allies, such as radical institutionalism and radical Post Keynesianism in economics, as well as many allies in the other social sciences, including feminist theory and antiracist theory.

Marx and Critical Marxism

In the second half of the nineteenth century, Karl Marx (1818–83) and Frederick Engels (1820–95) established a critical perspective for political economy. Marx's writings were influenced by the misery of the urban working class in the industrial revolution, their increasing numbers in capitalist industry, and their increasing attempts to organize. Intellectually, Marx was influenced by the economics of the classical liberals Smith and Ricardo in England; the revolutionary vision of the French socialists; and the dynamic approach of the German philosopher G. W. F. Hegel. In each case Marx conducted a thorough critique to separate out their important advances from their ideological biases.

It has been shown (Stillman 1983) that Marx mainly worked through critique, as reflected in the titles of his books: *Capital: A Critique of Political Economy, The Holy Family: A Critique of Critical Criticism, A Contribution to the Critique of Political Economy, The Critique of Hegel's Philosophy of Right,* and so forth. Marx's critique of political economy "refers both to those thinkers who analyze the economic order and to the actual workings of the economic order, that is, to both theory and the reality it describes" (Stillman 1983, 253). Marx may be considered the first great user of critical method in the social sciences. There are, however, many things Marx did not discuss and many things that he got wrong. The first rule of contemporary, non-Soviet Marxism is that Marx's authority proves nothing.

The Soviet Union and the Old Marxism

The views of Karl Marx, as interpreted by various socialist leaders, dominated the socialist movement before the First World War. Another version of Marxism was advocated by the Communist parties when they split from the socialists after the First World War. When the Communists came to power in the Soviet Union in 1917, they faced terrible economic conditions, foreign hostility and intervention, 80 percent illiteracy, and a mostly peasant country in need of all-out economic development. As they developed the economy by Draconian measures, their Marxian views were quickly changed by the situation. The Soviet ruling class developed its own ideology, which it called

Marxism but which must be distinguished from all critical, democratic Marxism. (The development of the Soviet ruling class and its ideology is discussed in detail in part II.)

Under Stalin a bloody dictatorship killed its opponents, particularly those who tried to keep to a radical, pro-human, Marxism, and allowed no free speech or discussion. According to Gorbachev, the last head of the Soviet Communist Party, "In the past the Party recognized only Marxism-Leninism as the source of its inspiration, though the tenet was utterly distorted to suit the pragmatic needs of the day, becoming something of a collection of canonical texts" (Mikhail Gorbachev, quoted in Schmemann 1991, 1A). Thus, in Gorbachev's opinion, the Stalinist version of Marxism transformed it into a tool to defend the status quo of class relations in the Soviet Union. It seems incredible that a critical, democratic, humanist outlook could be distorted far enough to become an apology for Stalin's dictatorship, but there are truly no limits to human ingenuity. While U.S. textbooks glorified market capitalism and the U.S. political system, textbooks in the former Soviet Union glorified central planning and the Soviet political system. Thus, the Soviet Marxian outlook was one that would provide the optimal support and defense of the Soviet status quo.

The most well-known work of official, Soviet Marxism is Joseph Stalin's *Dialectical and Historical Materialism* (1940), which I quote briefly in the appropriate chapters. Stalin's views became dominant in all of the Communist parties. There is a detailed explanation of the official Communist view of social theory in Cornforth 1971b. A detailed explanation of the official Communist view of philosophy and methodology is contained in Cornforth 1971a; Gollobin 1986; and Somerville 1946. Soviet Marxism claimed to be monolithic and homogeneous. In reality, of course, thousands of Communist writers in a hundred different countries had different historical experiences and wrote many variations of the Soviet position. Some, written by poets or novelists, are remarkably passionate, and some, by top Soviet scholars or Communist scholars in other countries, are remarkably sophisticated.

The core of official Soviet Marxism was an approach that began with two, and only two, conflicting classes in capitalism: the working class and the capitalist class. The following chapters show that the Soviet view was based on alleged necessary and inevitable laws of the evolution of society. More precisely, chapters 2 through 6 show that Soviet Marxism had three features at its core. First, everything in society, from the ideology of racism to the behavior of the Supreme Court, can be reduced to an economic explanation. This economic reductionism was Soviet practice, although it was often denied. Second, the social process can only be understood in the light of the inevitable laws of history. Third, all analysis is based on collective entities, such as classes, which need not be justified in terms of individual behavior. Thus, Soviet Marxism tended to ignore individual motivations. Again, this extreme collectivism was denied in theory but was usually practiced.

In 1956 Nikita Khrushchev, head of the Soviet Communist Party, gave a famous speech—it was supposedly secret but actually was printed around the world—that attacked Stalin and Stalinism. That event, as well as the Yugoslav break with Stalin beginning in 1948, marked the beginning of the end of Soviet Marxism. From that time till its collapse at the end of the 1980s, the Communist world broke apart, until there were a large number of competing Marxisms, each the official line of a Communist party. From 1989 through 1991 the Communist regimes of Eastern Europe and the Soviet Union were overthrown, after which Soviet Marxism was no longer an official creed in those areas.

In fact the viewpoint of Soviet Marxism is now all but dead. It is mentioned in this book only briefly to help us understand how contemporary Marxism grew in reaction to it. A few of its ideas have lived on in some modern scholars. Yet critics of Marxism still view the old, dead Soviet version as an ideal straw man to knock down. Therefore, a leading independent Marxian writer, Paul Sweezy, notes: "One of the most urgent intellectual tasks of our times . . . is to rescue Marxism from the travesties that have been made familiar by bourgeois scholars and critics on the one hand and by mass social democratic and governing 'Marxist' political parties on the other. To a surprising extent, the versions of Marxism emanating from these seemingly antagonistic forces overlap or coincide" (Sweezy 1992, 56).

The Renaissance of Critical Marxism

The goal of this book is to rethink, restructure, and reinvent Marxism in order to make it a useful tool within critical or radical political economy. Since Marxian scholars disagree among themselves, the version of Marxism in this book is my personal view and should not be blamed on anyone else—though it will often be the majority view. On every issue, I note both a majority view and one or more minority views. My own view of Marxism as it is revealed in this book will surely be called non-Marxian by some other scholars. But it is utterly silly to spend any time on the semantic issue of whether something is or is not "Marxian," when there are hundreds of versions of Marxism—and hundreds of interpretations of Marx. The point of this book is not to interpret Marx. This is not another attempt to say what Marx really meant, so Marx is seldom quoted. Rather, this book is an attempt to develop a consistent and useful radical method of social analysis. If that goal is achieved, one may call it Marxian or radical or eclectic—or whatever one wishes.

From the weakening of Soviet Marxism in the 1950s until the present, numerous alternative views of Marxism, some old and some new, have been taken seriously and gathered influence. A listing will show the dizzying number of Marxisms that have flourished: Maoist Marxism; Trotskyist Marxism (e.g., the writings of Ernest Mandel); Yugoslav Marxism; Eurocommunism; the Marxian theories of Georg Lukács, Rosa Luxemburg, and Antonio Gramsci; Freudian Marxism; existentialist Marxism (e.g., the writing of Jean Paul Sartre); phenomenological Marxism; the Marxism of Herbert Marcuse and the Frankfurt school (which used the term *critical method* somewhat differently than it is used here); New Left Marxism (which resulted from the resistance to the Vietnam War); Marxian structuralism; Althusserian Marxism; Marxian feminism; Analytic Marxism; postmodernist Marxism; and even deconstructionist Marxism. Each of these contributed something to the contemporary Marxian approach and to the project of creating a consistent and sharp radical tool of analysis. In short, a renaissance in Marxian thought began in the late 1950s and has continued until today (for a clear road map of the various Marxian views, see Chilcote and Chilcote 1992). The old Soviet Marxism is mostly dead, but a critical, non-Soviet Marxism is flourishing.

A considerable number of the above theories are discussed at appropriate points throughout this book. For example, one trend in the new Marxism is the postmodernist trend. In the artificial language of postmodernism, one might say that the aim of this book is to deconstruct the old Marxism and reconstruct a new one. (The clash between the postmodernists and their enemy, the modernists, is discussed in part III.)

Contemporary, non-Soviet Marxism is much harder to define than the old, official, Soviet Marxism because orthodoxy has a particular position, while each unorthodox Marxian writer has a view that is to some extent unique. In this book, *Marxian* writers are defined as self-identified Marxian theorists who are not of the old, Soviet variety, so the category includes most of the various schools mentioned above. It is worth reiterating that the viewpoint of this book is meant to include all Marxian writers and does not represent an exclusive new school.

Contemporary Marxism has developed in part as a critique of both Soviet Marxism and orthodox social science, especially orthodox (neoclassical) economics. Critical Marxian social scientists have criticized Soviet Marxism for (1) reducing all explanation to economics, (2) a drastically simplified, two class notion of conflict, and (3) a claim that all history is predetermined and moves on a single path. Critical Marxian social scientists have also criticized neoclassical economics for tending (1) to reduce all explanation to psychological assumptions, (2) to base all theories on individual choice, and (3) to use an ahistorical, static, equilibrium analysis. All of these criticisms are investigated in detail in chapters 2 through 6.

The viewpoint of Marxism as a tool of radical political economy is developed in detail throughout this book, but a brief notion of its core concepts may be helpful to the reader. First, Marxism does not agree that society can be reduced to either psychology or economics; rather, society is seen as an organic whole whose intricate relationships must be investigated. Second, society is viewed as undergoing historical evolution, but not with any predetermined, inevitable goal. Third, Marxian analysis begins with the division of society into classes, but there are multiple classes, and every class action must be consistent with individual behavior.

Radical Institutionalism

While much of radical political economy derives from non-Soviet Marxism, U.S. radicalism is also heavily influenced by the institutionalist school begun by Veblen. Thorstein Veblen gave a thoroughgoing radical critique of orthodox economics and sociobiology. His followers today continue that critique in the pages of the *Journal of Economic Issues*. Most institutionalists are liberals who have a militant attitude toward reform of the capitalist system but are opposed to radical change and to radical views on many issues. Some excellent presentations of the whole range of institutionalist thought are Dugger 1989, 1992; Samuels 1980; Tilman 1992; Tool 1990; and Wilbur and Jameson 1983 and 1990.

In addition to liberal institutionalists, however, there are many radical institutionalists. The viewpoint of radical institutionalism differs from contemporary, non-Soviet Marxism in terms of terminology and the lack of explicit use of class analysis but is very similar in most respects (see Hunt 1979, as well as the very important book on radical institutionalism by Dugger [1989]). Because institutionalists have contributed much in the area of the social theory and methodological foundations of the radical viewpoint—and have influenced contemporary U.S. Marxism—they are discussed at many points in this book.

In the view developed in this book (discussed in detail in Dugger and Sherman 1994) radical institutionalism agrees with contemporary Marxism to a large extent on the first two core issues discussed above. First, the institutionalist view of society is holistic; that is, it sees society as a single organism with many aspects. Second, institutionalism is evolutionary in its understanding of society and history. On the other hand, few institutionalists, even radical institutionalists, agree with the centrality in social analysis of the Marxian concept of class, and they seldom discuss the notion of a drastic revolutionary change in the basic operation of society.

Post Keynesianism

Marxian political economy is also greatly influenced by the Post Keynesian school in economics. John Maynard Keynes was a member of the British establishment, but he shook orthodox economic theory to its roots. He attempted to demonstrate how a capitalist economy could generate massive involuntary unemployment over a long period of time. This was a radical departure from previous orthodoxy.

Keynes's views were interpreted conservatively by most economists, but the Post Keynesians have explored the more radical implications of Keynes. They have evolved a strongly antineoclassical methodology (see Pheby 1988; see also Robinson 1964). Their view of macroeconomics is completely opposed to the dominant U.S. eclectic mix of New Classical and New Keynesian theory. They build their macroeconomic theory on a foundation of understanding of economic concentration and the power of oligopolies (based in part on the works of the Marxian Michal Kalecki). Post Keynesians also include the followers of Pierro Sraffa, who critiqued the core of neoclassical theory and wrote a substitute. Their views are clearly presented in the *Journal of Post Keynesian Economics* and the *Cambridge Journal of Economics*. Excellent surveys of Post Keynesian economics include Arestis 1990; Arestis and Skouras 1985; Eichner 1988; Jarsulic 1988; and Sawyer 1989. Post Keynesian theory has heavily influenced my views of inequality and value theory as well as unemployment and business cycle theory in part II of this book, but since their methodology is very similar to the radical institutionalist methodology, I do not discuss it separately.

Radical Economics

In the late 1960s, the civil rights movement, the women's liberation movement, and the anti–Vietnam War movement produced a radical environment in the United States. Among other consequences, these movements led to a resurgence of radical thought in all disciplines. In economics it led to the founding of the Union for Radical Political Economics (URPE) and the *Review of Radical Political Economics* (for details of the evolution of URPE and the accomplishments of specific radical economists, see Gintis 1982; Sherman 1984; and Weisskopf 1982). Radical political economy in the United States has largely used a Marxian approach, but it has also been influenced by institutionalism, Post Keynesianism, feminist theory, antiracist theory, and others.

The substantive issues argued by radical political economists are discussed in part II of this book and were presented more fully in Sherman 1987 and in Sawyer 1989. The substantive issues on which radical economists have focused include poverty and exploitation, racial and gender exploitation, monopoly, environmental destruction, unemployment and inflation, and imperialism and underdevelopment. For recent radical environmental studies, see Grundman 1991; and Raskin and Bernow 1991. For general perspectives and methodology of radical economists, in addition to parts I and III of the present book, there have been two excellent Marxian presentations—Albert and Hahnel 1978; and Resnick and Wolff 1987—both of which influenced this book. For extensive discussions of radical microeconomic theory, see *Modern Approaches to the Theory of Value* 1990; see also King 1990, vol. 2. The focus of Marxian microeconomic theory is exploitation and class under capitalism. For a thorough discussion of radical macroeconomics and business cycles, see the survey in King 1990, vol. 3, as well as Sherman 1991. The critical focus of radical macroeconomics has been the question of how capitalism generates economic crises and business cycles.

Marxian Trends in the Social Sciences

A comprehensive radical political economy should include radical and Marxian scholars in economics, history and all of the social science

and humanities disciplines. Since the disciplines are kept institution-
ally separate, however, one must look at each of them separately. Fortunately, there is an excellent collection by Ollman and Vernoff, *The
Left Academy: Marxist Scholarship on American Campuses*, in three
volumes (1982, 1984, 1986), which summarizes all of these contributions. Volume 1 discusses radical and Marxian sociology, economics,
political science, philosophy, psychology, history, and anthropology;
volume 2 discusses radical and Marxian literary studies, art history,
classical antiquity, education, geography, biology, and law; and volume 3 discusses radical and Marxian feminist scholarship, African
American studies, Puerto Rican studies, chicano studies, Asian American studies, criminology, health and medicine, communications, and
social work. It is not necessary to repeat all of this here.

Why Should Marxism Be Reinvented?

The democratic and critical Marxian outlook as presented in this
book is based to some extent on all of the sources stated above, but
there are so many conflicting views that final responsibility rests on
my own choices. The Marxism in this book is not what all self-identified Marxian writers follow, because there is no agreed consensus, but
rather what the author recommends that they follow.

This journey through the past has provided the basis for answering
the question, Why should Marxism be reinvented? There are two
sides to the answer. First, the old, Soviet version of Marxism, which
was dominant in the world for many decades, is almost gone. Some
thought this would mean the end of Marxism; but the result has been
the flourishing of a new Marxism, the foundations of which were laid
by the painstaking work of hundreds of Marxian scholars over the
last forty years. Second, capitalism continues to show the same sick
symptoms of crisis, exploitation, discrimination, pollution, war, and
alienation. Therefore, a radical political economy is badly needed.

It is the argument of this book that the contemporary version of
democratic and critical Marxism provides the most important tools
for such a radical analysis of the ills of capitalism and for deciding
how to change it. Part I presents the core social approach of Marxism; part II applies that approach to political economy; part III examines the methodological problems of that approach; and part IV examines the policy stance of a critical and democratic Marxism.

T W O

A Critique of Reductionism

Some theories of society have tried to reduce all explanation to a single crucial factor, a magic key, one basic force that determines all else. Some have said that because human beings are conscious, human psychology explains everything. Others have said that because eating must come before thinking, economic factors explain everything.

Psychological Reductionism

The psychological reductionist view, prevalent in the nineteenth century, boasted such famous theorists as Sigmund Freud (for a well-written, sophisticated, and comprehensive comparison of Freud and Marx, see Lichtman 1982). The psychological reductionist view (also sometimes called psychological determinism or mentalism), which is still widespread, holds that society, including the economy, can be explained by ideas and psychology.

The Writings of Lewis Feuer: An Example of Extreme Psychological Reductionism

An example of extreme psychological reductionism is the view of the sociologist Lewis Feuer (1969), which attributes most modern social conflicts to the innate instinct of youth and students to rebel and destroy their fathers. Feuer finds student movements responsible for (1) the First World War, because a student assassinated Archduke Ferdinand (his chapter title is "The Bosnian Student Movement Blindly Provokes the First World War"); (2) Hitlerism, because a student assassinated a right-wing dramatist in 1918, which led to a repression and a heritage "transmitted to the Nazis"; (3) the Bolshevik revolution, because a student assassinated liberal Tsar Alexander II when he "was about to give a constitution"; (4) Stalinism, because students assassinated Stalin's friend Kirov in 1934; (5) the Second World War, because student pacifism in the 1930s reduced resistance to Hitler; (6) the Chinese Communist revolution, because "Mao's conflict with his father and its primacy as a motivation for his political ideas were typical of the Chinese students who emerged with him"; (7) the Cuban revolution, because for the student Castro "the United States became a surrogate father to be blamed"; (8) espionage and treason in America, because Ethel and Julius Rosenberg had a "reason-blinding passion of generational hatred [which] begot a corrupted idealism which led to treason"! Feuer claims students rebel because they have "intense, unresolved Oedipal feelings, a tremendous attachment to their fathers" (Feuer 1969, 51–58).

The radical historian Howard Zinn says of Feuer's psychological reductionism: "The value of Feuer's book is that, by carrying to absurdity what other social scientists do with more sophistication, it may awaken us to their methodological inanity" (1970, 164–65). Feuer's view has little relationship to most modern orthodox social science, but it does illustrate the absurdity of psychological reductionism when taken to an extreme.

Psychological Reductionism and "Human Nature"

It is an age-old view of the average person, as well as many philosophers, that the essential nature of human beings shapes society. To Aristotle it was "clear that there are *by nature* free men and slaves, and that servitude is agreeable and just for the latter. . . . Equally, the relation of the male and the female is *by nature* such that one is better and the other inferior, one dominates and the other is dominated" (Aristotle 1941, 1255). This view, which is an early variant of psychological reductionism, has been refuted on several grounds.

In the first place, the physical nature of human beings—our level of physical evolution—changes much too slowly to explain social evolution. Societies change in a hundred or a thousand years; significant changes in human physical makeup, including brain capacity, take at least a hundred thousand years. Therefore, social change cannot be explained by human nature.

In the second place, our psychological characteristics and behavior —what is usually meant by human nature—change as a result of socioeconomic changes. Humans are born into a functioning society and are shaped by that society, though our ideas, once shaped, certainly play an important role in future social development. Thus, modern "human nature" is very different from that of the ancient Athenian, even though there has been no perceptible evolution in humans' physical and mental capacities. The psychological "nature" of orphaned children brought up in the ghetto is similar to that of those born in the ghetto. A ghetto child orphaned and brought up from birth in an affluent family, however, shows all the cultural habits and aptitudes of the affluent.

A society's view of human nature is even influenced by its geographical location:

> In desert societies—including the American Southwest—water is so precious that it is money. People connive and fight and die over it; governments covet it; marriages are even made and broken over it. If one were to talk to a person who has known only that desert and tell him that in the city there are public water fountains and that children are even sometimes allowed to turn on the fire hydrants in the summer and to frolic in the water, he would be sure one were crazy. For he knows, with an existential certitude, that it is human nature to fight over water. (Harrington 1970, 373)

If the notion that there is an eternal human nature that cannot be changed and shapes society is a myth, why does this myth have such a long life? The answer is that such myths play an important role in helping to support the status quo. "If it is 'human nature' that determines the historical process, and if this 'human nature' is unalterable, then all attempts to achieve a radical transformation of the human character and of the foundations of the social order are necessarily doomed to failure" (Baran 1960, 6). For this reason, many conservatives work hard to perpetuate the myth of an eternal human nature.

Psychological reductionism has often been used to support the status quo. If all society is determined by ideas and if those ideas are determined by biological instincts (or by an eternal human nature), then it is impossible to change social institutions. Any basic political-economic change would be rejected by people's instincts or by human nature. In this view, all reformers and revolutionaries are building castles in the sand. In fact all psychological reductionist theories are one-sided and do not explain the origins or the reason for change in psychological attitudes themselves.

A very different view of human nature is held by those reformers, and even some radicals, who counter the conservative ideology of an evil, greedy, aggressive human nature with an ideology of an ideal, good human nature. With an ideology that human nature is essentially good, there will be utopia on earth, provided that capitalist repression is lifted. The utopian view of human nature is just as misleading as the conservative view. There is no evidence of either an eternally good or an eternally evil human nature, but only of a human nature that changes as institutions and structures and relationships change.

Orthodox Economics and Psychological Reductionism

Whereas Lewis Feuer is an example of an extreme reductionism that does not persuade many people, and arguments about eternal human nature are seldom heard in the social sciences, a very serious and often dominant view in economics has been another form of psychological reductionism. The evolution of orthodox economics with regard to its psychological reductionist aspect is detailed in appendix 2A, where it is shown that most orthodox economics reduces the explanation of all social phenomena, from prices to prejudice, to certain assumptions about subjective desires and preferences. These psychological preferences determine everything else, but the origin and changes of tastes and preferences are never explained. Thus, this theory is an incomplete theory of society and is misleading because it largely ignores the role of social structures and relations.

Economic Reductionism

Having examined psychological reductionism, let us now consider the opposite view: economic reductionism. Examples here include the extreme technological version of one school of anthropologists, the economic reductionism of Soviet Marxism, and the economic reductionism of G. A. Cohen.

The Economic Reductionism of Marvin Harris

Technological reductionism, the extreme form of economic reductionism, has been given a very thorough defense by the non-Marxian anthropologist Marvin Harris (1979). His approach is totally opposed to "numerous strategies that set forth from words, ideas, high moral values and aesthetic and religious beliefs to understand the everyday events of human life" (ix). His criticisms of psychological reductionism are very insightful. He sees all of society as determined by technological changes and neglects all feedback from ideas.

As an example of technological explanation, Harris shows in detail that Hindus refuse to eat cows not because of some superstition but because of the great economic need to use cows as beasts of burden and a source of milk and fertilizer. Harris is so extreme that he considers Marx a psychological reductionist because Marx concentrates attention on the human relations of production rather than on technology.

Although Harris's theory suffers from an extreme reductionism, parts of his *Cultural Materialism* are, nevertheless, marvelous to read because of the brilliant way Harris criticizes other views, such as Soviet Marxism, structuralism, sociobiology, and various forms of psychological reductionism. Furthermore, his concrete applications are delightful reading because he does not seem to follow his own narrow technological reductionism (see also Harris's wonderful book *Cows, Pigs, and Witches* [1974], as well as his amusing *Cannibals and Kings* [1977]). Perhaps Harris's very fruitful inconsistency is an indicator that extreme reductionism sounds silly and so really good authors do not stick to it.

Economic Reductionism in Soviet Marxism

Soviet Marxism argued for a type of economic reductionism, even though in general terms it frequently rejected economic reductionism (see, for example, Cornforth 1971b or Stalin 1940). According to the Soviet Marxian view, the economic base of capitalism determines a capitalist social superstructure. In Soviet Marxism the economic base was defined to include all forces of production (land, labor, capital, technology) plus all class relationships (e.g., the relation of the worker to the capitalist owner). The social superstructure included all ideas, social institutions, and political institutions.

The Soviet Marxian theorists usually used the metaphor of base (or foundation) and superstructure when referring to the relationship between economic structure and social or political institutions and ideas (see, e.g., Cornforth 1971b). This metaphor is misleading because it implies that the economic base determines the social superstructure but that the social superstructure has no effect on the economic base. Use of this metaphor reflected a tendency in Soviet Marxism to ignore the superstructure, which led to many mistakes. For example, it assumed that if the economic conditions of workers got very bad, workers would be in favor of socialism and there would be a socialist revolution. We now know that no such simple sequence follows a bad economic situation.

This view of base and superstructure has led some Marxian scholars to technological reductionism, the notion that technology by itself determines all social evolution. For example, John McMurtry takes the extreme position that "the productive forces are the moving power and ultimate determinate of human history" (1978, 71). Such technological reductionism suffers from the fact that it cannot explain technological change, since that is a given. It ignores the influence of ideas, political institutions, and group economic relationships on technology, so it is as incomplete a theory as psychological reductionism.

Since the base-and-superstructure metaphor is misleading, this book avoids it. The term *economic process* is used in place of what Soviet Marxian theorists referred to as the economic base. Similarly, what Soviet Marxists called the social superstructure will be called the *social process* when the view of most non-Soviet Marxian writers is explained.

The political implications of the economic reductionism of Soviet Marxism must be stressed. If economics determines everything, then the economic power of capitalists must always be dominant under capitalism, regardless of political form. Therefore, democracy under capitalism is a fraud because the capitalists always rule. Conversely, in the Soviet Marxian view, the Stalinist Soviet Union had a socialist economic base with workers as the only class, so its political superstructure was socialist and democratic! The Soviet Union was, according to this theory, the most democratic state ever seen. Furthermore, because changes in the forces of production continually happen, capitalism inevitably leads to socialism, regardless of people's opinions. These simplistic economic reductionist views were as one-sided as the opposite extreme of psychological reductionism.

A consistent economic reductionism claims (1) that economics determines everything else in society and (2) that nothing else in society determines the economic structure. Most of official Soviet Marxism was ambiguous on these two points, saying that the economic base "ultimately" determines everything else but that other factors may have some "reciprocal" effect on the economy (see Stalin 1940). These ambiguous statements, however, must either end up at a consistent economic reductionism or deny such reductionism entirely.

What is wrong with a consistent economic reductionism? First, a consistent economic reductionism must deny that ideas and political institutions affect economic processes. But in reality this influence may be seen every day. For example, politicians write laws that affect the economy. Second, it is not logically consistent because it cannot explain changes in the economic structure. Specifically, it cannot explain changes in technology, which must be explained in part by changes in science, that is, by changes in a set of ideas. Moreover, it cannot explain a socioeconomic revolution, because one step in the revolutionary process is the change in consciousness of the oppressed classes, but that is a change in a set of ideas.

The Critics of Soviet Marxism

The critics of Marxism followed the lead of the Soviet Marxian theoreticians by proclaiming almost unanimously that Marx was an economic or technological reductionist, and they implied that all Marxian scholars are technological or economic reductionists. They then proceeded to demolish this straw man. Listen to the critics:

Turner contends, "Marx began with a simple . . . assumption: Economic organization, especially the ownership of property, determines the organization of the rest of society" (1974, 79). Wolfson says that "*a priori,* Marx decided upon economic motivations as part of the materialist conception of history" (1966, 3). Danto argues, "Marx believed . . . that there is a one-way interaction between social processes and at least some psychological processes, so that what we think, and how we act, are to be explained by reference to our relations vis-à-vis the prevailing structure of production; and whatever it is that causes change in the structure of production, it is not something which is brought about by individual human action" (1965, 269). Another typical critic, Blanshard, asks: "Was it economics or was it religion that was behind the Crusades, the Inquisition, and the Reformation? Is it economics or is it religion that is behind the division of Ireland?" (1966, 331). Since contemporary Marxian social scientists do not reduce the explanation of these events to economics, the question does not hit the target.

Even some non-Marxian writers have argued that the critics are wrong to attribute to Marx such a one-sided view of social processes. Two mainstream U.S. sociologists, Berger and Luckman, state that an interactive, two-way view is probably the correct interpretation of Marx, and that it does away with most of the criticism of Marx as an "economic determinist."

> It is safe to say that much of the great "struggle with Marx" that characterized not only the beginnings of the sociology of knowledge but the classical age of sociology in general . . . was really a struggle with a faulty interpretation of Marx. . . . The essentially mechanistic rather than dialectic character of this kind of economic determinism should

make one suspect. What concerned Marx was that human thought is
founded in human activity . . . and in social relations brought about by
this activity. (Berger and Luckman 1966, 6)

In other words, in their view Marx's concept means that ideas do not
come out of nowhere and that all other aspects of human society are
conditioned by our productive activity. But Marx's method insists
that the investigator should always consider all the feedbacks as part
of a unified structure; that human activity shapes human thinking but
that human thinking also shapes human activity. Another incisive but
sympathetic critic of Marxism, Schumpeter, has written that

> the economic interpretation of history does not mean that men are,
> consciously or unconsciously, wholly or primarily, actuated by eco-
> nomic motives. . . . Marx did not hold that religions, metaphysics,
> schools of art, ethical ideas and political volitions were either reducible
> to economic motives or of no importance. He only tried to unveil the
> economic conditions which shape them and which account for their
> rise and fall. . . . of course men "choose" their course of action, which
> is not directly enforced by the objective data of their environments; but
> they choose from standpoints, views and propensities that do not form
> another set of independent data, but are themselves molded by the ob-
> jective set. (1950, 10–12)

So according to Schumpeter, human beings make their own history,
but only under certain objective conditions that influence their decision making. Marx's theory, called *historical materialism,* is not a
magic formula for deciding all things by economics but a directive to
political economists to spell out in detail all the particular relations
between economic processes and social processes in a specific historical situation. Thus in Schumpeter's view the Marxian theory does not
deny the role of politics or Catholicism but rather explains their importance in relation to a given economic structure.

G. A. Cohen's Economic Reductionism

The most sophisticated, careful, and elegant argument ever presented
for the view that Marxism is, and should be, economic reductionist or
even technological reductionist was presented by G. A. Cohen (1978).
The economic reductionist position was also supported from a Marxian view by W. H. Shaw (1978) and J. McMurtry (1978). (Cohen
himself later changed some of his views, but that is not relevant to the
argument.) Cohen's 1978 work undoubtedly proves that Marxism asserts that the economic process (including human relations as well as

technology) influences human ideas and institutions. But many critics of Cohen argue that he does not prove that Marxism does or should deny the influence of ideas and political and social institutions on the economic process.

Those Marxian scholars who have criticized economic reductionism or have criticized Cohen's arguments in great detail include Michael Albert and Robin Hahnel (1978); Alex Callinicos (1988); Jorge Larrain (1986); Stephen Resnick and Richard Wolff (1987); S. H. Rigby (1987); Jean Paul Sartre (1968); Derek Sayer (1987); Paul Sweezy (1992); Ellen Wood (1990); and Eric Wright, Andrew Levine, and Elliott Sober (1992). The debate has included how to interpret Marx as well as how to best understand society. This book does not focus on interpreting Marx, but it does consider the debate on how to best understand society.

What those opposed to Cohen have explained is that ideas and social and political institutions do influence the economic structure, and vice versa. Many contemporary Marxian and radical political economists have criticized the mechanical view that one factor determines others, as a cue ball hits other balls, and instead have emphasized that society must be viewed as an integrated whole.

Cohen presents a *base-superstructure thesis* to support economic reductionism. Cohen's base-superstructure thesis claims "that the structure of a society, 'the economic base,' explains that society's legal and political 'superstructure' and forms of consciousness" (Wright, Levine, and Sober 1992, 16; they do an excellent job of exploring Cohen's arguments in detail). Most Marxian social scientists agree with Cohen that the economic base does help explain the superstructure, but they also emphasize that one cannot explain the economic base without tracing the influence of the political ideas and scientific ideas.

Cohen also offers a *primacy thesis* to support technological reductionism. This thesis asserts "that the level of development and productive forces in a society explains the set of social relations of production, the 'economic structure' of that society" (Wright, Levine, and Sober 1992, 16). In Cohen's view, the technology will explain human economic relations. Cohen might argue that when the level of technology is too low for a worker to create a surplus beyond subsistence, it is not profitable to enslave anyone, so slavery does not exist. Similarly, Cohen might argue that slaves can only handle a simple technology, so slavery also would not be possible at a very high level of technology because slaves could not be trusted with aircraft or expensive computers or even tractors.

While Cohen is correct that technology sets some limits on human economic relations, surely the type of economic relations also affects technology. In the Great Depression the economic system and economic relations prevented the improvement of most technology for ten years. Thus it cannot be said that technology has primacy over human economic relations.

Conclusions on Economic Reductionism

The long argument over economic reductionism, in which hundreds of authors have taken part, has not reached any final consensus. The debate, however, has clarified the issues, and most Marxian scholars are now anti-reductionist. The view that the "economic base" completely explains the "social superstructure" and that there is no reciprocal effect is deficient because it cannot explain changes in the economic base. Furthermore, within the economic sphere, the argument that technology is primary and determines economic relationships (with no reciprocal effect) is deficient because it cannot explain changes in technology. Thus, both the base-superstructure and primacy theses must be discarded.

Conclusions on All Reductionism

All reductionism in the social sciences, whether psychological or economic, whether crude or sophisticated, lacks the ability to present a complete theory of society. Since it is always partial, it is always misleading.

Appendix 2A: Psychological Reductionism in Orthodox Economics

For the purpose of examining its methodology, the evolution of the dominant, orthodox economics may be very roughly divided into four stages: (1) classical political economy, (2) neoclassical economics, (3) Keynesian economics, and (4) the New Classical and New Keynesian economics.

Classical political economy, whose most well-known proponents were Adam Smith and David Ricardo, was dominant from about the 1770s till the 1860s (though it began to decline long before then). The classical economists were political economists in that their theories included politics, sociology, and history as well as economics in the narrow sense. They saw society as a unified whole. They discussed not only psychology but also technology and class relationships; they focused on the behavior of the capitalist, the landlord, and the worker as well as the streams of income to each of these classes.

Neoclassical economics dominated from roughly the 1870s until the 1930s. The neoclassical economists reduced all explanation of economic behavior to psychology, given certain resources and technology. Neoclassical theory began with certain assumptions about individual preferences and choices and considered how the individual (consumer, worker, or enterprise) optimized his or her utility (or firm profits) in the marketplace. According to neoclassical economics, the combined efforts of all individuals in the competitive process led to an overall optimal result, given the initial degree of inequality of ownership of resources. The focus was on psychology and optimization (reflected in increasingly complex mathematical models), certainly not on economic institutions or class relations.

The third stage in the evolution of orthodox economics, from roughly the 1930s to the 1960s, was the Keynesian revolution and its consequences. Both the classical and the neoclassical economists assumed that involuntary unemployment was impossible. In 1936, in the midst of the Great Depression, when U.S. unemployment was measured conservatively in the official statistics at 25 percent, John Maynard Keynes published a book explaining how the capitalist economy could and did give rise to large-scale involuntary unemployment lasting a considerable time. This theory, discussed more fully in part II, effected a revolutionary change in orthodox, conventional economics.

The relationship between Keynesian economics and neoclassical economics was, however, ambiguous. On the one hand, Keynes discussed aggregates (such as aggregate consumption and national income), whereas neoclassical economics had discussed only individual consumers and particular prices. On the other hand, Keynes did state some "fundamental psychological laws" and appeared to accept the neoclassical view of individual, psychologically given costs and prices. When Keynesian economics (or at least the standard interpretation of Keynes) was at its height, these ambiguities did not bother most economists. But eventually Keynes's neoclassical opponents charged that Keynesian aggregates and structural discussions were contrary to Keynes's alleged foundations in good neoclassical economics. Conservative economists attempted to construct a new macroeconomics consistent with neoclassical microeconomics.

From the 1970s to the 1990s, orthodox economics witnessed the initial dominance of a New Classical (or reborn neoclassical) set of theories. These theories, which promoted conservative policies that fit well with the conservative politics of the U.S. and British governments in the 1980s, constituted a whole new macroeconomics—including aggregate consumption, investment, and business cycles—based on a renewed neoclassical microeconomics of psychological preferences and choices with individuals maximizing or optimizing in the market. According to the New Classical theories—the monetarist, rational expectations, and real business cycle theories—markets will always clear and full employment will always be reached. Individual enterprises will achieve an optimal result for society if markets are allowed to function freely, with no government regulation (though of course government must enforce the laws of private property, which are taken as given).

The main focus of the dominant version of orthodox economics is on the maximization of utility by consumers and the maximization of profits by firms. Many new, important theories have emerged in the dominant, orthodox economics in the 1980s and 1990s, most of them opposed to various aspects of the older neoclassical economics and many of them with liberal policy implications. But before we turn to these new theories, it is important to emphasize that most textbooks—reaching millions of students, as well as most of the day-to-day practice of most orthodox, conventional economists—continue to be dominated by the neoclassical religion and the newer New Classical version.

For example, a leading orthodox elementary textbook by Paul Samuelson and William Nordhaus explains the basis of supply and demand in neoclassical terms: "A century ago economists hit upon the fundamental of utility; and it was from this analysis that they felt able . . . to derive the demand curve and explain its properties." They say that the customers buy a commodity because of its utility. They define *utility* as "the subjective pleasure, usefulness, or satisfaction derived from consuming goods" (1992, 411). They argue that relative prices (say, of tea and coffee) depend on the preferences of individuals. Thus, the explanation is reduced to psychology.

Many things in neoclassical economics change when one gets to the higher levels of theory, but this basic approach, which begins with psychological preferences and optimizing choices, remains dominant at all levels. Hal Varian, in a widely used text of graduate microeconomic theory, says the same thing in more complex language: "In the theory of a competitive firm, the supply and demand functions were derived from a model of profit-maximizing behavior and a specification of the underlying technological constraints. In the theory of the consumer, we will derive demand functions by considering a model of utility maximizing behavior coupled with a description of underlying economic constraints" (1992, 94). The model is still based on the psychology of consumers and firm owners. Thus psychological preferences are the basic building blocks of neoclassical theory. Varian calls preferences a "primitive" concept, which is a fancy way of saying that they are taken for granted and are not explained.

Neoclassical textbooks take the psychology of the individual as given in the sense that the authors do not explain it. The neoclassical economist assumes that individual preferences come from some place—perhaps they are innate—but never considers how society shapes those preferences. It is merely assumed that the highest goal of a well-functioning economy is to follow consumer preferences, wherever they may originate. And the main interest of consumers in life is to maximize utility. (One detailed and insightful Marxian analysis of neoclassical economics is Wolff and Resnick 1987.)

Neoclassical economists then proceed to show how consumer preferences in a capitalist economy do indeed determine the prices of commodities and the amounts produced—given pure and perfect competition and at least sixteen other unreal assumptions (see the careful account of these assumptions in Graaf 1967). All neoclassical textbooks reduce economics to supply and demand behavior. They further reduce demand to individual utility and supply to individual disutility, that is, work or the cost of supply. Thus neoclassical theory makes individual psychology the ultimate source of the value of commodities. The causation always runs from the individual psychology to the functioning of the economy. No neoclassical textbook ever asks whether economic relationships influence individual preferences. But surely it is worth asking the subversive question, Are we born with a demand for television sets, or do advertising and social conditioning have something to do with it?

Because neoclassical economics begins and ends with subjective psychological states, it does not examine the relationships between classes, nor does it concern itself with the bases of power in the government. An approach that ignores power and class interests is quite helpful in the defense of the status quo, because the status quo then appears to be the result of the automatic functioning of an impartial system that merely reflects human preferences. Neoclassical economics cannot explain why economic policy is as it is; it leaves that to the

sfs

political scientists. Neoclassical economics is economics but not political economy. (For an excellent discussion of the history of thought of
neoclassical economics, see Hunt 1992b.)

New Institutionalism and New Keynesian Views

The above description presents the view of neoclassical economics,
but some orthodox economists would say that some of these points
are no longer correct. For example, far more attention is paid to
changing institutions in the historical work of Douglas North (1990)
or the so-called New Institutionalism of Oliver Williamson. The New
Institutionalism and other new trends are described and analyzed in
an outstanding book by Christos Pitelis (1991) and in an essay by
William Dugger (1992, ch. 12).

The New Institutionalism does indeed provide more realism, because it pays attention to such institutional features as the cost of information and supervision inside the firm, the cost of transactions in
the market, and the cost of government regulations to the firm. This
goes well beyond earlier neoclassical explorations. Yet the neoclassical methodology is applied in the sense that, given these institutional
barriers, the psychologically based choices or optimization of profits
are still the center of attention. Thus, the New Institutionalists still
use the neoclassical methodology of psychological reductionism, even
though more institutional features are included as givens in the background (this point is spelled out in Miller 1993). Warren Samuels
concludes from a careful study of the New Institutionalist literature
on law and economics that "the new institutionalist approach is sub-
stantially conducted within the neoclassical paradigm . . . [including]
stable preferences [and] . . . the rational choice model" (1994, 8–9).

Another important new trend in orthodox economic theory is the
recognition that labor contracts do not enforce themselves, but must
be enforced. The neoclassical approach assumed that each factor of
production, including both labor and capital, interacted in the market, with each individual optimizing as best he or she could. After that
the market would automatically give to each individual an amount of
money (or other goods) equal to the marginal (or additional) product
added by the individual's own goods and services. The newer orthodox approaches use game theory to recognize and model the various
conflicts in the economy (see the micro aspects in Kreps 1990 and the
macro aspects in Mankiw and Romer 1991). This is an important advance in realism. It is still the case, however, that game theory models
assume certain psychological preferences and choices on the part of

individuals in an optimization process. Since they begin with individual psychology, such theories may still be reasonably called psychological reductionism.

The various approaches of the New Keynesians represent a third important trend in high-level orthodox theory. They contradict the classical and neoclassical notion that all unemployment is voluntary and show certain causes of involuntary unemployment. One such cause is traced in what is known as *efficiency wage theory,* of which more will be said later (see the presentations of efficiency wage theory in Ackerloff and Yellen 1986; Mankiw and Romer 1991; and Weiss 1990). What is important about all of the New Keynesian approaches, including the efficiency wage theory, is that they, like Keynes, allow for equilibrium below full employment.

The notion that the economy may not adjust to full-employment equilibrium is again a major step toward realism in orthodox economic theory. While the New Keynesians are antineoclassical in that substantive sense, they are proud that they still follow the neoclassical methodology. Thus they stress the neoclassical microeconomic foundations of their macroeconomic theories. Included in those microeconomic foundations are the same sort of psychological assumptions, leading to a process of utility optimization for individuals. That optimization process is the same one that is present in all neoclassical theory. It is not unreasonable, therefore, to characterize New Keynesian theories as being psychological reductionist, a point spelled out in detail in DeMartino 1993.

Another interesting new trend in orthodox economics is the postmodernist view. Postmodernists have challenged one main aspect of the fundamental methodology of neoclassical economics and of most orthodox economics: They do not believe that economics is a purely neutral, positive science. On the contrary, they point out the extremely biased rhetoric used to make arguments in economics. This view is discussed in part III. So far, however, the orthodox postmodernists have accepted without debate that economics is mainly about individual psychological choice, so it appears that they remain psychological reductionists.

To summarize, many (though not all) orthodox textbooks remain tied to the neoclassical theories, and all of them are tied to the neoclassical methodology of psychological reductionism. A large percentage of all orthodox economists still use and teach the older theories. In the period since 1970 there have been major advances at the highest levels of orthodox theory. But even at the highest levels orthodox theories are almost all psychological reductionist—and proud of it.

To reiterate, the weakness of psychological reductionism is that it cannot explain psychology itself or any changes in human psychology that do occur. Thus it will always produce incomplete and misleading theories, though neoclassical economic theories that are nevertheless subtle, sophisticated sounding, and elegant.

THREE

▬▬▬▬

The Relational Approach

This chapter attempts to leave behind the false dichotomy posed by psychological and economic reductionism in order to present a complete social theory, the *relational approach* to political-economic analysis. It is part of what Marxian social scientists have called *historical materialism,* though that term has, unfortunately, become associated with economic reductionism. Briefly, the relational approach treats society as a unity, so it does not speak of individual things or factors, but of relations and processes. It does not investigate psychology and technology as isolated phenomena, but only in relation to each other. For nonreductionist Marxian writers, concepts such as class cannot be defined by any criteria except relational ones. So a slave or slave owner cannot be understood separately, as a lone individual, but only as part of a social relationship.

Definitions

This section begins with very simple conceptualization, but it must be understood that the concepts in any complex analysis will be expanded, modified, and reworked many times in the course of the whole discussion. In Marx's *Capital,* for example, the definitions are not clear-cut and set once and for all, but slowly emerge and change in increasingly complex approximations to reality: "Viewing the world as devoid of the clear-cut classification boundaries that distinguish the common sense notion, Marx could not keep a definition of one factor from spilling over into everything. For him, any isolating definition is necessarily 'one-sided' and probably misleading" (Ollman 1971a, 25). The lesson is not to stop trying to state precise definitions but to realize that every definition is tentative and must be made more precise and more comprehensive as the investigation proceeds. For example, the religious ideas and the institutions of the Catholic Church are inseparable in reality, but each must be clearly and separately defined for purposes of analysis.

The Framework of Analysis

Any society may be divided into two parts: the economic process and the social process. As shown in figure 3.1, the social process is the entire noneconomic part of society, which includes ideas as well as social and political institutions.

These definitions are used here because they are useful for analysis in social science. Whether these definitions follow Marx is highly controversial. It does not matter, however, whether the definitions follow Marx; what matters is whether they are useful in a critical or radical analysis. For example, the followers of the traditional Soviet Marxian view called the economic process the *economic foundation* or the *economic base,* while the social process was called the *social superstructure.* This terminology was biased toward economic reductionism because the terms imply that a base or foundation is somehow more important than a superstructure. The term *process* is used for both social and economic activities in order to remove that bias.

From these definitions, one important identity is:

$$\text{SOCIETY} = \text{ECONOMIC PROCESS} + \text{SOCIAL PROCESS} \qquad (3.1)$$

This identity indicates that the division is exhaustive, so for the purposes of this analysis all of society falls in one of these two processes. Some phenomena, such as language, may be perceived to be part of both, but for a given analysis one must decide in what category to put each relevant phenomenon. One should also remember that all of the divisions specified here are for analytic purposes only; since both processes are part of a larger process, they have no independent existence apart from each other.

The Economic Process

The economic process, in turn, may be divided into the *relations of production* (also called *productive relations*) and the *forces of production* (also called *productive forces*). Thus, by definition, another identity can be written as follows:

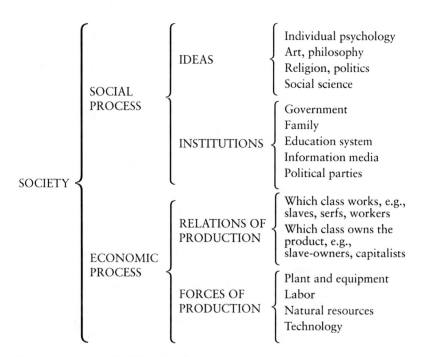

Figure 3.1. Framework of Social Analysis

ECONOMIC PROCESS = PRODUCTIVE RELATIONS +
PRODUCTIVE FORCES   (3.2)

We must now define the controversial concepts on the right side of the above equation.

The *forces of production* are the factors operating in the productive process. The forces of production comprise human labor, plant and equipment, land and natural resources, and technology. The number of workers available depends on population, laws, and sociological attitudes about who should work. The amount of plant and equipment depends on what was produced up to the present, but it also depends on the rate of depreciation, that is, wear and tear and obsolescence. The availability of land and resources is reduced by use and erosion but is expanded by new geological discoveries and by technological improvements in the recovery or use of materials.

"Technology can be defined quite narrowly as tools, less narrowly as the material arts, and much more broadly as knowledge about how to do things" (Samuels 1977). The broadest definition is used here. Technological improvements in turn affect the education and training levels of labor, the quality of plant and equipment, and the usefulness of natural resources. For example, before its use as a fuel was known, coal was just dirty, useless black lumps.

Neoclassical economics tends to think of the forces of production as the only component of the economy. It views the forces of production as a set of inputs combining together through voluntary contracts, with little or no discussion of concrete institutions, class relationships, and specific historical setting. Radicals, on the contrary, emphasize not only the forces of production but the relations of production as the heart of political economy. The *relations of production* are the interconnections between groups of human beings in the process of creating goods and services. This definition must be taken very broadly to include not only class relationships but also many other aspects of the labor process, the relations of debtors and creditors, the distribution of income and wealth, and so forth.

Most Marxian historians find that throughout recorded history societies have been made up of a major exploiting class (which also ruled politically) and a major exploited class (which was also subordinate politically). On the other hand, most contemporary Marxian writers stress that there always have been numerous other classes, either remnants from previous economic processes or new groups beginning to arise and foreshadowing a new economic process. Of course there have been some very primitive classless societies, and there may again be classless societies in the future, so Marxian writers do not see class as an inherent feature of all possible societies. Thus, the relations of production are nothing but class relations in any class-divided society, but they may describe cooperative relationships in a classless society.

Except in primitive societies, however, the productive relations of all known societies do describe the interconnections of classes of humans in the production process. Class is a relationship. Classes are defined by their relation to other classes in the productive process, either as exploiters or as exploited. Note that the concern here is with actual economic relations, not the legal rules that correspond to them, which are part of the social process. The productive relations may be summed up in the answer to two questions. Which class does the work of society? For example, under slavery all labor was done by slaves, under feudalism labor was done by serfs, and under capitalism labor is done by legally free workers. Which class owns the means of production and the product? Under slavery, the slave owners owned the land, the slaves, and the product of the slaves' labor.

Under feudalism, the church, the nobility, and/or the monarch possessed the land and the product of the land, except what was produced on the small plots worked by the serfs on their own time. Under feudalism, the serf was not owned directly but was bound to the land. Most serfs also owned some instruments of production and had the right to possess and use some land for themselves. The serfs also had the duty to work on the lord's land for many days, often two hundred or more per year.

Under capitalism, the capitalist class owns the means of production, the entire product, and the profit resulting from the worker's labor. Of course, this description of the rights of the capitalist class is abstract and greatly oversimplified. In the United States most ownership of the means of production is lodged in corporations, not individuals. Yet the corporation itself is owned by individual stockholders; that is, they own its equity after the debts are subtracted from the assets. The profit goes to the corporation, but then most of it is usually distributed to the individual stockholders. The worker under capitalism is not bound to one job, but may look elsewhere, is free to take a job at any wage, and is free to be fired and starve.

The Social Process

Since everything that is not included in the economic process is by definition included in the social process, it is an extremely broad concept. The social process includes both ideas and social and political institutions. Thus:

$$\text{SOCIAL PROCESS} = \text{IDEAS} + \text{INSTITUTIONS} \qquad (3.3)$$

The ideas in the social process include all the socially significant attitudes, such as racism, sexism, or patriotism. The social process also includes all the viewpoints in the social sciences, such as neoclassical economics, radical political economy, or sociobiology. Furthermore, the category "ideas" in the social process includes individual psychology, which according to most Marxian scholars is *not* given at birth, but arises from our interactions with other human beings and is part of the social process. Margaret Mead's work in anthropology provided strong evidence that the typical psychology or character of men and women (such as passivity or macho behavior) is determined purely by their cultural or social environment (1971).

The social process also includes many types of institutions and processes. Most obvious is the political process, comprising the legislature, the executive, the political parties, the courts, the prisons, the armed forces, and the police. The education process tries to institutionalize the process of learning. The media—including newspapers, television, movies, and literature—further attempt to shape our thinking. In the medieval period, religious institutions were the primary spreaders of ideology. The family is another institution that shapes young minds to certain views and behaviors. Each of these institutions, as well as the ideologies spawned by them, change drastically in each historical period.

The dichotomy between the social process and the economic process includes all the phenomena in the society, but it is not meant to be either rigid or unchanging. The framework is designed as a useful tool, and the tool may be changed when the task is changed. Where a particular aspect of society belongs is often not clear and may change with the problem. For example, Marxian theorists had a lengthy controversy over whether language was part of the social process or part of technology; but language has aspects of both, so which is stressed depends on the problem. Knowledge of biology might normally be considered part of technology, but when Hitler's Germany distorted biology to create a racist outlook, biology could be considered as part of the social process. No framework can consider in advance the place of every aspect of society; the important issue is whether the framework is clear enough and spotlights important enough distinctions to be a useful tool of social analysis. (This view of definitions and frameworks is compatible with institutionalist instrumentalism [see Dewey 1939], but it is also compatible with a Marxian view of dialectics [see part III].)

When most Marxian political economists speak of the theory or model of some pure economic process (such as a pure capitalist economy), they call it a *mode of production.* When most Marxian scholars speak of an actual country, say Germany, they call the actual process a *social formation,* which may include a number of modes of production. It is often important to distinguish between a pure model and the process as it is found in reality. For example, the former Soviet Union was mainly centrally planned, but it always included many decentralized aspects. In the United States, the South before the Civil War was mainly characterized by a slave mode of production, but one could not understand it without recognizing that it existed within a capitalist context, since it was surrounded by a capitalist country and its international trade was with capitalist countries.

No pure models exist in reality. Pure models may be used legitimately in an analysis or deceptively in propaganda. It is legitimate to consider a simple model that leaves out many complications when it is only the first step in an increasingly realistic analysis. It is deceptive when someone assumes that the U.S. economy has pure and perfect competition and then concludes with a policy prescription that says that the economy is perfect and thus no reforms are needed. It is legitimate to compare pure and perfect models of capitalism and socialism. It is deceptive to compare a pure and perfect model of capitalism with the actually existing "socialist" economy of Cuba; it is equally deceptive to compare a pure and perfect model of socialism with actually existing U.S. capitalism.

When radicals speak of capitalism in the United States, they are speaking of the dominant mode of production but not the only mode of production. If there are several modes of production within a society, then there will be many different classes, reflecting the different modes of production. Thus, all present-day societies reveal many different classes within the setting of a complex web of different modes of production with different degrees of importance (see the detailed discussion of this point in Ruccio and Simon 1986).

The Relational Approach: First Approximation

The *relational approach* is defined as an approach that begins with relationships in society rather than with individuals or things. For example, one must understand both slave and slave owner within the relationship of slavery. One cannot define *slave* without defining *slave owner,* nor *slave owner* without *slave;* the terms have no meaning separately. Moreover, no social theory can explain slaves without explaining slave owners, and vice versa. Similarly, one cannot understand debtors without understanding their relation to creditors, nor landlords without their relation to tenants. People can only be understood within the matrix of social relations. Understanding the psychology of an individual slave is impossible until one understands the relation of slavery.

The relational approach can best be understood as two approximations at two levels of abstraction. The first approximation is at a fairly concrete level of analysis. In this first approximation the relational approach asserts that society must be viewed as an integrated whole containing certain relationships or interactions. This approach is thus very different from the focus on isolated factors presented in reductionist approaches. The key relationships are spelled out in the next several pages. The second approximation, discussed later in the chapter, considers the limitations of this first approximation and presents the issues at a higher level of abstraction.

In the relational approach (first approximation) not only does technology determine ideas but ideas determine technology at the same time. It is thus very different from the one-way causation characterizing those approaches that reduce everything to psychology or those that reduce everything to technology. The relational approach maintains that society is to be seen as a unified organism, not a set of isolated spheres, so social scientists should always begin with interactions or relationships.

Relational thinking pervades all Marxian and radical social science (see, e.g., the excellent work by Ollman [1992]). It is worth noting, however, that except in economics, the idea of society as an integrated whole has long been part of the orthodox social sciences. Orthodox economists, in contrast, normally consider the economy as if it were totally isolated from the rest of society. Only at the end of their economic analysis do they consider, for example, what the impact of government might be on the economy, without ever looking at politics and economics as an organic whole. But the greatest orthodox anthropologists, political scientists, and sociologists, such as Max Weber or Talcott Parsons, have long had some kind of integrated vision of society.

The dominant sociological view in the 1950s and 1960s was *structural functionalism,* which emphasized the unity of society. If the family was constructed so that men were dominant and women subordinate, structural functionalism explained how this structure functioned to help preserve and stabilize society. The main differences from the Marxian view were the assumption that there was no class conflict and the related assumption that the preservation of a stable status quo was the goal of the social sciences (see Sherman and Wood 1989, 18–23).

As an example of the Marxian use of the relational approach, throughout the three volumes of *Capital* Marx repeatedly asserts that capital is not a thing but a relation. He explains that it is wrong to think (as neoclassical economists do) of capital as physical machinery because that is not its most important aspect. What is important is that capitalist wealth used in the production process can command the labor power of workers. Thus, *capital* stands for a relationship among human beings, though it is expressed in financial and in physical terms.

The reductionist approach always talks about X influencing Y, as if

X and Y were totally separate and as if there were a one-way causal relationship between them. The relational approach, however, emphasizes that in reality (1) no part of society is separate from the rest and (2) all of the aspects of the social process interact with many-sided causation and interaction. In that sense, it is always misleading to say only that X influences Y or, if one prefers mathematical terminology, that X is a function of Y. It will always be more correct to say that X and Y, such as politics and economics, interact and affect each other. The relational approach has been used and further explained in various ways by many Marxian writers, including Michael Albert and Robin Hahnel (1978); Alex Callinicos (1988); Jorge Larrain (1986); Stephen Resnick and Richard Wolff (1987); Jean Paul Sartre (1968); Derek Sayer (1987); Paul Sweezy (1992); Ellen Wood (1990); and Eric Olin Wright, Andrew Levine, and Elliott Sober (1992). Some of these writers emphasize concrete interactions between aspects of society, A and B; but others, such as Resnick and Wolff (1987), emphasize the higher level of abstraction, where A and B are not considered separate at all (as discussed below).

Specific Interactions

Concretely, as a first approximation to reality, Marxism says that (1) the economic process influences, causes, and determines the social process, while (2) the social process influences, causes, and determines the economic process. This first approximation makes clear that there is an interaction, not a one-way causation.

In the broad sense used above, there is plenty of evidence that the economic process, including human relations of production as well as forces of production, does influence, cause, and determine the social process, ideas and social and political institutions. For example, the birth control pill, a technological innovation, has profoundly changed human sexual views and behavior. Some basic technological advances, such as the use of fire or writing, affected practically every aspect of the human social process. In addition, one's position in the relations of production, such as whether one is a slave or a slave owner, shapes one's way of thinking as well as one's style of life. In the United States today there is an enormous difference between the viewpoint of a frequently unemployed worker and that of a millionaire corporate executive.

One qualification is necessary: our social process is partly determined by the economic process, but it is also partly determined by its own evolution. For example, our literature is influenced by the socioeconomic environment, but it is also influenced by the whole history of literary technique. Similarly, the ways lawyers and judges speak are mostly determined by previous legal cases, yet changes in the economic process obviously influence the content of legal developments. Thus, the social process is determined in part by the evolution of the economic process but also by its own evolution. Using mathematical terminology, one of the basic points of historical materialism is just this: *the social process is partly a function of the economic process and partly a function of the past social process.*

A second statement of the relational approach used by nonreductionist Marxian writers is that the economic process is influenced, caused, and determined by the social process. For example, ideas affect politics, politicians make laws, and these laws certainly affect economic and property relationships. Similarly, ideas are the stuff of science, and science is surely one influence on technology. Moreover, some political ideas lead to revolutionary activity, which may eventually change the economic system.

The previous economic process also influences the present economic process. For example, political-military conditions in the Second World War set the stage for the atomic bomb, but previous technological advances were also crucial in its construction. To sum up this point, another basic point of historical materialism is: *the economic process is a function of both the social process and its own past.* If one recognizes that both statements are true simultaneously, that is about as close as any one can get—in formal, mathematical language—to the relational view that social and economic processes interact and determine each other.

The most frequent objection to the relational approach is that since the social and economic processes constitute the whole of society, to say that they interact amounts to saying that everything affects everything. Several of the authors mentioned above as holding a relational view have been accused of merely restating this useless truism. A closer reading of the work of all of these writers indicates that they had something much more substantial in mind. Each of these authors—as well as this book—makes the point that within the entire social matrix one must highlight the key relationships, as every political economist has done.

It is perfectly true that to say that *all* relations must be spelled out before any conclusions can be reached would be paralyzing and harmful. The task of a political economist, however, is to overcome that trap, to find the most important relationships and highlight them. If we focus on the most important, relevant sets of relations, it is possible to make correct conclusions without specifying all of the infinite details of our society.

What are the specific contributions of the relational approach? In other words, what makes contemporary Marxian political economy distinct? First, the relational approach does give a basis for rejecting any kind of reductionism, and since reductionism has plagued the social sciences for more than a century, that is a useful accomplishment.

Second, Marxian social scientists do specify the most important relations; that is what hundreds of specific Marxian (and other radical) studies have done. The next part of this chapter specifies some of those relations. Moreover, part II applies this approach to the main questions of political economy.

Third, chapter 4 explains how the interactions discussed here lead to a unified theory of historical change. Fourth, chapters 5 and 6 focus on what Marxian social scientists take to be the most useful entry point to all relations, namely, class relations. A proposal of where to start in understanding any society is a very substantive and distinctive contribution (as Wolff and Resnick [1987] emphasize). Thus, the use of the relational approach does lead to a clear specification of the most important relations in a dynamic context.

Interactions between Ideas, Institutions, Relations, and Forces

Up to this point, my analysis has been on the very general level of the economic process and the social process. A clearer understanding, however, requires an examination of more concrete concepts. The social process, as I have said, may be divided into *(a)* ideas and *(b)* social and political institutions. The economic process may be divided into *(a)* relations of production and *(b)* forces of production. Thus

SOCIETY = IDEAS + INSTITUTIONS + RELATIONS

+ FORCES (3.4)

Each of these four categories is part of an integrated social whole. Thus, one may formulate four relationships to explain each of these four variables in terms of the others. Although they are all related to one another, it may be useful to highlight the main relationships and formalize the approach as follows:

Ideas are a function of social and political institutions, productive relations, productive forces, and previous ideas. (3.5)

Social and political institutions are a function of ideas, productive relations, productive forces, and previous institutions. (3.6)

Productive relations are a function of ideas, political and social
institutions, productive forces, and previous relations.   (3.7)

Productive forces are a function of ideas, political and social
institutions, productive relations, and previous forces.   (3.8)

A mathematical formulation of this approach is presented in appendix 3A, and the relationships are pictured in a simplified form in figure 3.2.

This formalized relational approach (first approximation) is useful for focusing our attention on a systematic method of examining society. Later, however, the more advanced form of relationalism will emphasize that this simple, formal approach is only a rough approximation to the relational view of society as an integrated whole.

The Sociology of Knowledge: The Evolution of Ideas

A comprehensive sociology of knowledge would explain how ideas are influenced by (1) the evolution of social and political institutions, (2) the evolution of the relations of production, and (3) the evolution of the forces of production but also (4) the previous evolution of ideas.

Ideas and institutions interact within the social process. A painter's work will be influenced in part by the past history of painting but also by political events, such as wars, or by changes in family relationships. So our ideas are influenced by the past history of ideas but also by changes in social and political institutions.

Ideas battle among themselves through human protagonists, but not in some impartial arena where the best always win. Ideologies are not identical with class relations, but they are used as weapons by a class if they aid its survival; if not, they often remain insignificant. The dominant ideas will be those that ultimately are most useful to the ruling class. There is a confused notion that Marxism means that each class simply learns from its own work conditions and always votes in its own interest. On the contrary, Marxism emphasizes that the ideas of the ruling class are dominant in normal times and that the dominance is achieved through the use of all of the social and political institutions, as shown below. If a different class had the dominant ideas, that class would be able to change society to fit its interests (as happens in social revolutions).

The ruling ideology is not imposed by any magical means, but through the control of the media, schools, churches, government, and jobs. Workers are taught an ideology of harmony to cover the facts of

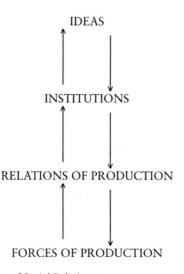

Figure 3.2. The Dynamics of Social Relations

oppression. The ideologies of racism and sexism similarly justify and help continue types of oppression. Male and female are socialized by the family and all the other institutions of society to fit certain stereotypes, and it is therefore no surprise that most do fit the stereotype. Stereotyping begins at birth with a blue ribbon for boy babies and a pink ribbon for girl babies.

Ideology also plays a role in war. In a piece called the "War Prayer," Mark Twain satirized the process by which the ideology of patriotism has been used to get people to fight bloody wars. In these wars, according to Marxian historians, workers of one country slaughter workers of another country to make the world safe for imperialist or neocolonial profit making.

Ideological conditioning is so pervasive that Herbert Marcuse, in *One Dimensional Man* (1964), argued that it is completely dominant, and he concluded that revolutionary change is almost impossible. That conclusion does not follow, because drastic, new experiences can shake people loose from social conditioning and the spell of the ruling ideology. When African Americans in the early 1960s came alive to their situation and to the possibilities of change, they acted through legal challenges and demonstrations to effect that change. In the late 1960s students and youths protested the Vietnam War in enormous demonstrations that did have some effect eventually. In the late 1960s and early 1970s women became more conscious of their oppression—

as a result of their experience in the civil rights and antiwar movements as well as their changing economic status—and were able to
wrest many reforms from the male ruling class.

In a similar way, in most periods most social scientists are conditioned by society to follow the dominant conservative paradigm without much thought about it. Social scientists do pursue new theoretical
analysis for many individual reasons, including the pure love of theoretical games and puzzles, the desire for more money and prestige or
job security at a university, and, for some, such as Marx or Keynes,
the desire to improve society. Most social scientists, however, do
routine work, expanding and making more elegant the dominant paradigms. Only in a very unstable period, such as the 1930s, will socioeconomic problems and conflicts result in a major reform of the
dominant theory, which was the case with the emergence of Keynesian economics. Only in a period of social revolution, such as the
French or the Russian Revolution, will drastic change result in an
overthrow of the dominant paradigm.

Example: The Reproduction of Economists

One interesting example of how people's ideas are conditioned by society is the manner in which the viewpoint of neoclassical economics
is reproduced by one generation of economists after another. Graduate schools of economics take bright, mostly liberal students who are
interested in policy and make them into people who play games and
write elaborate mathematical and mostly conservative theories. A survey by Colander and Klamer (1987) of 212 graduate students at
Chicago, Columbia, Harvard, Yale, Stanford, and MIT found that 47
percent considered themselves liberals, 12 percent radicals, 22 percent
moderates, and only 15 percent conservatives, although the average
student was a twenty-six-year-old male from an affluent home.

They found that most beginning students want relevant, policy-
oriented courses and thus are very unhappy with "the heavy load of
mathematics and theory and a lack of relevance of the material they
were learning" (Colander and Klamer 1987, 96). Most of the students
thought it was very important to read history and political science but
had no time to do so. Colander and Klamer concluded that these
broad-minded entering students were transformed by graduate education, which "is succeeding in narrowing students' interests" (98).
They quote the view of Robert Kuttner (who is himself summarizing
many critics, from Vasily Leontief to John Kenneth Galbraith): "Departments of Economics are graduating a generation of *idiots savants,*

brilliant at esoteric mathematics, yet innocent of actual economic life" (95).

In fact, 36 percent of the students express great interest in political economy when they enter. Yet by graduation a majority perceive that success in economics requires that they be good at technical problem solving and excellent in mathematics; only a minority think that a thorough knowledge of the facts of any specific field of economics is very important. So they come to believe that economics is a game in which deep knowledge of institutions is secondary. The basic finding is that most graduate students are dissatisfied because they feel that reality and policy have been ignored in order to concentrate on mathematically precise but unreal theorems. This finding has been confirmed by an extensive study of the American Economic Association's own Commission on Graduate Education in Economics (see Newlon 1991).

The aim of the conditioning is not merely to move them from policy to mathematical game playing but also to change their ideological views. One evidence of conditioning is the differences between the attitudes of students at Harvard and at Chicago. Although some of the differences are due to student choice of Harvard because it is liberal or Chicago because it is conservative, the rest are due to their training. Thus, at Chicago 49 percent strongly agree that "neoclassical economics is strongly relevant to the problems of today," but only 9 percent at Harvard strongly agree. Seventy percent of the students at Chicago but only 15 percent at Harvard strongly agree that "a minimum wage increases unemployment among young and unskilled workers." On the other hand, 44 percent at Harvard but only 6 percent at Chicago strongly agree with the liberal view that "the market system tends to discriminate against women." And 54 percent at Harvard but only 16 percent at Chicago strongly agree with the liberal statement that "the distribution of income . . . should be more equal." Finally, "rational expectations" is considered an important assumption by 59 percent at Chicago but only 14 percent at Harvard and none at MIT! So one must conclude that the different graduate schools have profound effects on the students' ideologies.

Colander and Klamer conclude that "the likely reason for students' transformation into technique-oriented individuals is that most of them aspire to academic jobs. They know that tenure depends on publication in the right journals" (Colander and Klamer 1987, 108). It should be emphasized that the transformation is not merely from policy to technique; it is also an ideological transformation. The two issues are linked by Locke Anderson, who shows "how useful abstract theory is for protecting the rich and powerful against the misguided jealousies of the poor and the weak" (1987). Students do not mind learning math and statistics, he says, but they do object to the lack of relevance.

Anderson points out that the American Economic Association was founded by dissidents and even socialists but that pressures on universities began to eliminate these views by the first decade of the twentieth century (when there were some spectacular violations of academic freedom). He notes that students are conditioned in a process in which "graduate study is conducted by leaders of the profession, who select and train students in their own image. Most graduate training at the doctoral level is done in a small number of rather similar departments whose faculty interests define what comprises 'excellence' in an economist" (46). The students are brainwashed by courses and do what they have to do to pass exams, please a dissertation adviser, get a position, get tenure, and get salary increases. "So the varied and talented people who enter the economics profession go to the university 'and they all come out the same' as Pete Seeger sings" (46).

Social and Political Institutions

It is the hypothesis of this chapter that in order to understand any set of institutions (e.g., the legal system), one must explain these institutions by (1) the ideas of the society, (2) the class relations of the society, (3) the forces of production of the society, and (4) the past history of such institutions. An extreme psychological reductionist view, in contrast, holds that a rational thinker, some great man (never a great woman), sits in his quiet study and devises governmental institutions and laws for the good of all. This conservative apologia for the status quo is surpassed only by the religious thinkers who believe that all governments and laws are divinely ordained.

The materialist view of Karl Marx contends that: "legal relations as well as forms of the state are to be grasped neither from themselves nor from the so-called general development of the human mind, but rather have their roots in the material conditions of life" (Marx [1859] 1904, 11). Marx stresses that all political institutions, of which the legal system is a good example, are determined by economic relations and forces (though elsewhere he notes the impact of ideas once they are taken over by the ruling class). Many Marxian political economists have emphasized that political institutions have a certain degree of autonomy from the economic process in capitalism. One of the most interesting writers in this area is the non-Marxian sociologist Theda Skocpol (e.g., 1979), who emphasizes—and perhaps overemphasizes—the semi-independent role of the governmental apparatus in social revolutions. In the terms of the relational framework there is a strong influence on political institutions by ideas and by past political institutions.

Example: The Legal System as an Institution

In the Marxian approach, the political and economic variables determine the legal process. According to Marxian social scientists, the outcomes of legal processes are determined by the conflict between the needs and requirements of the most powerful economic class (or classes) and the needs and requirements of other classes. Nonruling classes, including the oppressed, may sometimes affect particular laws through political pressure. Once established, laws and the state apparatus act in a kind of feedback mechanism to reinforce the political and economic process of the status quo. When, however, this legal process tries to maintain the economic status quo while fundamental realignments of economic power are occurring, then it must attempt to hold back economic changes. For example, by the late seventeenth and eighteenth centuries feudal regulations of commerce and the monopolies granted by the British and French kings were fetters on industrial and commercial development. Eventually the obsolete feudal governmental process could only be swept away by revolution.

Changes in legal institutions are determined by changes in political ideas, class relations, and productive forces. The forms of legal change are also affected, however, through the internal development of the legal profession. Only in this last fact—that lawyers and courts do develop the forms of the law along lines that have some basis in precedents—does the psychological reductionist view grasp one aspect of this evolution.

An excellent book by Tigar and Levy (1977) shows in great detail how our present laws of contract and property evolved as the result of class conflicts. In the early medieval period the law recognized only the personal obligation of serf to feudal lord. The early merchants and traders had to fight for the idea of an enforceable contract between equals (though the two parties to a contract are seldom equal). The medieval law did not recognize the right to own property; it only recognized the right to possess property, but only as long as the possessor did his or her duty to a higher feudal lord. Capitalists had a long struggle before they succeeded in enshrining in the law the idea of private ownership of property. In fact private ownership was not fully won until after the French Revolution of 1789 proclaimed it.

Based on the laws of contract and private property are the criminal laws that enforce repression by the state against those who would violate private property or contract rights (see Gordon 1971). Under capitalism, if a man or woman steals a loaf of bread, he or she is guilty regardless of the need of the person or of his or her family. One can certainly imagine a better society in which anyone would be thought criminal who would prevent a starving man or woman from taking whatever he or she needed to stay alive, or a society in which all necessities were free. And what about the laws that make it a crime to force a hospital to care for someone at gunpoint but do not make it a crime for a hospital to turn away a sick woman with no money? Such are the legal consequences of a process built upon the foundations of private property.

Crimes by the poor are usually punished with much harsher sentences than are crimes by white-collar or more affluent citizens. The report of the president's crime commission concluded that "the poor are arrested more often, convicted more frequently, sentenced more harshly, rehabilitated less successfully than the rest of society" (President's Commission on Law Enforcement and the Administration of Justice 1968, 87). This 1968 statement remains true today (see Reiman 1990).

The effects of class relationships thus stand out very clearly in law enforcement practices and in procedures in both civil and criminal courts. The actual inequality in the legal process (caused by economic inequality) is concealed in the formal legal equality. Both the billionaire, such as Ross Perot, and the poor African American worker, such as Rodney King, have the same formal rights in court and with the police, but Ross Perot is given a police escort and Rodney King is given a police beating. As Anatole France put it, "In its majesty the law of the French Republic allows neither the millionaire Rothschild nor the Paris *clochard* [beggar] to sleep under the bridges of the Seine" (quoted in Deutscher 1971, 97).

Aside from the social deference to the one and the prejudice against the other, there is also the enormous difference that the millionaire can employ the best possible lawyer. The wealthy can keep even an open-and-shut case against them stalled in the courts for many years. Yet the poor lose many, many cases against them—whether brought by the police or the landlord or the bill collector—even when they are totally in the right under the laws of capitalism, simply because they have no money with which to fight the case.

The vast majority of the lower-income victims of the legal process lack the financial resources to hold out for a trial, and most (70 percent in the United States) are forced to plead guilty in order to avoid lengthy detention before their case comes to trial (see Lefcourt 1971, 501). Moreover, in the pretrial period, the rich are always able to be released on bail, while the poor are both unable to raise a considerable bail and more likely to have a high bail set because they are not "respectable" citizens. (The best discussion of the U.S. legal process is in Reiman 1990, *The Rich Get Richer and the Poor Get Prison*. For a clear presentation of the main cases see Ginger 1977.)

The Relations of Production

What determines the class relations of production? It is the hypothesis of this chapter that the relations of production are determined by (1) the ideas of society, (2) the political and social institutions of society, (3) the forces of production, and (4) the previous history of class relations. For the last two thousand years, the relations of production between groups of human beings, such as the relations between slave and slave owner or between worker and capitalist, have been class relations in most societies. Marxian social scientists believe that it is also possible to have a new society with cooperative, nonclass relations.

From a Marxian viewpoint, these class relations are the starting point in analysis of society (see, e.g., Resnick and Wolff 1987). This view is very far from technological determinism. It is the human relations in the economic process that directly affect human social and political institutions and thought. The relations of production are themselves determined by the other main processes of society, as noted above.

To understand the internal evolution of the economic process, we must clarify especially the relationship between the relations of production and the forces of production. The question is sometimes asked whether the relations of production (including class conflict) are more important than the forces of production (including technological progress), or whether the opposite is true. From a relational perspective, one can only say that they interact, each being a particular function of the other. One can then look at specific examples of these functions. For example, slavery has a functional relation to technology in the sense that it usually is found in agricultural societies, after the hunting and gathering stage but before the industrial stage.

On the other hand, technology under slavery has a functional relation to the slave relationships of production. Slavery holds back the use of complex tools, because the slaves will damage them or use them as weapons. Slavery also holds back invention, because all work and all practical use of technology is considered a fit occupation only for slaves.

Example: Sharecropping Relations

As an example of the evolution of the relations of production, consider the relations between sharecropper and landlord in the U.S. South after the Civil War. There was an all-pervasive ideology of racism, which had originated as an apologia for slavery but continued as a justification for the exploitation of African American sharecroppers.

The political institutions were rigged against the African American by the Hayes-Tilden compromise of 1876. By that compromise, the northern industrialists and their Republican Party kept control of the federal government, but the southern landowners and their Democratic Party were given the southern state governments. The federal army withdrew and the Ku Klux Klan rode over the countryside, while Jim Crow segregation laws replaced the slave code.

In this context, sharecropping was a convenient way to make use of the relatively skimpy means of production left in the South. Given the lack of equipment and technology as well as the prohibition of slavery, large-scale agricultural enterprise was not feasible. Moreover, sharecropping was a compromise between the ex-slave's desire for independence and the ex–slave owner's desire for continued control.

There was a very close tie and mutual influence between the relations of sharecropping and the forces of production. On the one hand, these relations could not rise above existing forces and were constrained by them. On the other hand, the particular class relations of sharecropping held back technological progress. An interesting economic history by two non-Marxian economists, Ransom and Sutch (1977), demonstrates in detail how the class relations of sharecropping held back the development of technology as well as the amount of capital in the southern agricultural process for many decades. On the one side, the sharecropping tenant had only a one-year lease, so he or she could be forced to pay a higher amount for the land or be pushed off it entirely if it were improved. "Not surprisingly, the tenant insisted on maximizing the value of the current crop (to half of which he was entitled) and showed little interest in long-run investment prospects from which he would be unable to benefit unless he were allowed to continue to work the farm" (101).

On the other side, the landlord would continue to own the land, so one would think the landlord might be willing to pay for improvements. "Yet, since the landlord would receive only half of the benefits of investments in the quality of his farm, his incentive to make such outlays would be reduced. Only if the return expected was worth twice what it cost would the landlord find a particular investment to his advantage" (102). To these disincentives must be added the debt peonage process. Since the sharecropper was almost always in debt to the local merchant, it was necessary that the sharecropper plant only the safest cash crop, namely, cotton. The complete dependence on cotton further restricted the technological possibilities for improving agricultural productivity. The combined effect of these two relations of production—sharecropper-landlord relations and debtor-creditor relations—held back the forces of production in the South for many miserable decades. It need only be added that these relations were reinforced and supported by the ideology of racism, which further held back the economic progress of African Americans in many ways, for example, by allowing them little or no education.

Example: Class Relations and Computers

A good contemporary example of how the relations of production may hold back technological development may be seen in the computer industry. In the United States, within a process of intense competition for private profit, the computer industry tries very hard to prevent certain programs from being copied. Most programs for microcomputers are sold on disks that can ordinarily be copied. The copying and spreading of computer programs facilitate the spread of knowledge and allow research to make faster progress. Because the companies selling computer programs wish to maximize their profits, however, they do all they can to prevent copying and thus the spread of knowledge of these programs. Thus, the profit motive of the capitalist class may sometimes reduce the flow of useful information and hold back some kinds of economic progress.

In the music industry, the digital audiotape (DAT) would allow individuals to copy music at home at the same level of quality as commercial music. This, of course, might reduce the profits of the recording companies. An insightful article (Horner 1991) reveals the attempts to prevent individual use of this new technology. It concludes, "Fearing a monumental loss in sales of prerecorded music, record companies attempted to sabotage new technology to reduce the output of music" (449).

More generally, the large corporations have always made use of monopoly power to hold back the introduction of new products when they might make existing capital or some existing products obsolete. Similarly, Thorstein Veblen often commented that corporations cut back or "sabotage" production in every recession, reducing production to raise or protect profits (Veblen [1922] 1962).

The former Soviet computer industry likewise suffered limitations, but they were different because they were caused by different relations of production. From 1928 to about 1989 the Soviet Union had public ownership of almost all industry, so all computer programs could easily be copied without concern for profits. But there was also a political dictatorship, which controlled the means of production. The leaders of that dictatorship were dedicated to the prevention of the spread of dissident views. Therefore, they tried to prevent the unauthorized spread of copiers, computers, and even typewriters, and they drastically limited the number of authorized users.

The Forces of Production

Having examined the determination of ideas, social and political institutions, and class relations of production, we have only to examine how the forces of production are determined. The forces of production are directly affected by class relations of production, but they are also affected by institutions and ideas, as well as the previous evolution of technology.

Example: Nuclear Energy as a Force of Production

In order to have nuclear energy, it was necessary to attain a certain level of knowledge of scientific ideas. But the science of nuclear energy did not develop in a vacuum. It depended partly on the organization and resources of the educational process and partly on the motivation and resources of the large corporate research divisions. Atomic energy was developed, however, mainly by the U.S. government in its crash program to build an atomic bomb in the Second World War. Under capitalism, one result of wars has been widespread improvement in technology. On the other hand, depressions have prevented progress in technology (as was most painfully obvious in the Great Depression).

The Relational Approach: Second Approximation

The preceding sections spell out a set of general relationships (formalized in the four equations from 3.5 to 3.8) as the basis of historical materialism. This first approximation to the Marxian relational approach, however, faces a severe problem. Based on key relationships, Marxism asserts that each society is unique and historically specific. Marxism insists that because each society is unique and specific, it has its own laws of movement. If each society has its own unique laws of movement, then there can be no universal laws applying to all societies or to all historical periods.

Therefore, the four statements discussed and exemplified in the above sections must be reinterpreted. They cannot be taken as a set of laws or a set of universal answers. Some Marxian theorists have spoken of historical materialism as such a set of universal answers and have caused much confusion. The variables that we have examined in depth are the key variables, but we must understand their role differently than was implied in the first approximation.

In a critical, nondogmatic view of historical materialism, the relational approach states a guide to research, a set of questions that are useful to investigate. Some might say that if it does not give answers, the relational approach is a waste of time. On the contrary, if one can suggest the best questions to ask, then one has conquered the main obstacle in, and made an important contribution to, the social sciences. That is the claim made for Marxian historical materialism and its relational approach. Each reader must decide if the approach is useful for his or her problems, but the questions discussed here have proven useful to many social scientists.

As a nondogmatic approach to social problems, the relational method teaches some important lessons by suggesting the right questions to ask. These questions suggest the best way to examine any social issue; the questions are based on the previous experience of social science. One cannot prove that a method or approach, or a suggestion to ask certain questions, is true or false. One can only ask, Is the relational method, this set of questions, useful and fruitful for social analysis?

So what are the questions that nonreductionist Marxian social scientists claim it is useful to ask? Let us begin with explanation of ideas. The relational method suggests that one ask the following questions in order to examine a set of ideas. As an example, let us examine the ideas of racism and sexism. (1) How are these ideas (racism and sexism) influenced by the social and political institutions (such as laws prohibiting discrimination)? (2) How are these ideas influenced by the class relations of production (such as the fact that most African Americans have low-paying jobs or are unemployed)? (3) What influence is exerted on these ideas by changes in the forces of production (such as invention of the birth control pill)? (4) What influence is exerted on these ideas by past ideas (such as U.S. popular notions of democracy and equal opportunity)?

To examine a social or political institution (such as the U.S. Congress), the relational method suggests asking: (1) How is the institution shaped by class conflicts (such as the fight over the capital gains tax)? (2) How is the institution influenced by ideological conflicts (such as the argument over abortion)? (3) How is the institution changed by technological innovations (such as the invention and spread of television)? (4) How are the forms and procedures of the institution affected by its own past behavior and tradition (such as the right to filibuster in the Senate or the Speaker's power in the House)?

To examine class relationships (such as those of slavery in the South), the relational method suggests asking: (1) How have the relationships been influenced by ideology (such as racism)? (2) How have the relationships been influenced by social and political institutions (such as the pre–Civil War legal system of the South)? (3) How have the relationships been influenced by the forces of production (such as the invention of the cotton gin)? (4) How have the relationships been affected by previous class relationships (or how was sharecropping affected by previous slavery in the South)?

Finally, if one wishes to understand the forces of production (such as the computer), the relational method suggests that one ask: (1) How is this force of production affected by ideas (such as the scientific ideas that led to computer technology)? (2) How is this force of production affected by social and political institutions (such as the patent laws)? (3) How is this force of production affected by class relations (such as relations of secretaries to bosses)? (4) How were the present forces of production (computers) affected by previous forces (such as typewriters)?

Conclusions

Marxism rejects the reduction of explanations in the social sciences to any one isolated factor, such as psychology or economics. As a first approximation the relational approach examines a series of key relationships in society and looks at society as an integrated whole comprising such relationships. This approach is good enough for most concrete studies. But if it is pushed to its logical extreme, it is flawed. Marxian social scientists believe that each society in history has its own unique relationships and its own unique laws. Thus, if these statements are taken as rigid, given universal laws, they are either incorrect or meaningless, vague generalities. A second approximation, using the same key variables, states that the relational approach consists of questions, not answers. These questions are a guide for research rather than a fixed dogma.

Appendix 3A: A Formal Model of the Relational Approach: First Approximation

A formal model of the main social identities and interactions may be stated in a series of equations.

The symbols are defined as follows: X = society, E = economic process, S = social process, I = ideas, N = (noneconomic) institutions, R = relations of production, and F = forces of production.

The identities are:

Society equals economic process plus social process, or

$$X = E + S \tag{3A.1}$$

Economic process equals relations of production plus forces of production, or

$$E = R + F \tag{3A.2}$$

Social process equals ideas plus institutions, or

$$S = I + N \tag{3A.3}$$

Substituting (3A.2) and (3A.3) in (3A.1), it follows that society is composed of ideas, (noneconomic) institutions, relations of production, and forces of production, or

$$X = I + N + R + F \tag{3A.4}$$

The above equations are illustrated in figure 3.1.

The behavioral relations are:

Ideas are determined by noneconomic institutions, relations, forces, and previous ideas, or

$$I_t = f^1(N_t, R_t, F_t, \text{ and } I_{t-1}) \tag{3A.5}$$

where t is a time period and f is a function.

(Noneconomic) institutions are determined by ideas, relations, forces, and previous noneconomic institutions, or

$$N_t = f^2 \,(I_t, R_t, F_t, \text{and } N_{t-1}) \qquad\qquad\qquad (3\text{A}.6)$$

Relations of production are determined by ideas, noneconomic institutions, forces, and previous relations of production, or

$$R_t = f^3 \,(I_t, N_t, F_t, \text{and } R_{t-1}) \qquad\qquad\qquad (3\text{A}.7)$$

Forces of production are determined by ideas, noneconomic institutions, relations, and previous forces, or

$$F_t = f^4 \,(I_t, N_t, R_t, F_{t-1}) \qquad\qquad\qquad (3\text{A}.8)$$

This model is a useful shorthand reminder of the basic relationships suggested by the Marxian theory of society as seen in the first approximation to the relational view. The chapter shows, however, that these propositions cannot be interpreted as a set of laws. They are reinterpreted in a second approximation as a list of variables to be related through the appropriate questions.

Appendix 3B: The Holistic Approach of Institutionalism

The Marxian approach may be clarified at this point by comparing it with the institutionalist approach. Institutionalist views of the most basic socioeconomic relationships—how economy and society interact—are quite similar to the view of nonreductionist Marxism. William Dugger, a leading institutionalist, writes that he favors "holism," which is the view that "economies are integral parts of larger societies and cultures" (1992, xx). There is no perceptible difference between Marxian relationalism and institutionalist holism.

More specifically, what is the opinion of institutionalists with regard to the relation between economic and social processes? Warren Samuels, another leading institutionalist, writes: "The received doctrine in the Veblen-Ayres tradition of institutionalism maintains that progressive technology may be juxtaposed to passive and inhibitive institutions . . . and, second, that technology is the primary . . . force in economic and social evolution" (1977, 873). But Samuels states forcefully that all of the more sophisticated versions of the institutionalist doctrine totally reject technological reductionism as "untenable." For a rigid technological reductionism Samuels substitutes an interaction and tension between technology and institutions, showing that each is a function of the other. "Apropos the dualism that institutions are a function of technology, and technology is a function of institutions, technological change creates opportunities and necessities for new property and other rights. Technological change is a function of research and development efforts which are a function of power process-cum-capitalized expectations, both of which are a function of property and other rights" (884).

In Samuels's terminology, institutions are a function of technology, while technology is a function of institutions. This terminology is quite different from the Marxian terminology. But the sense of it is no different than the Marxian perception of an interaction between economic and social processes.

F O U R

The Historical Approach

The dominant paradigm in the ancient and medieval periods, when social and technological change was very slow compared with what it is in the present, asserted that *no* basic changes ever could or should occur. "The world in which even the most intelligent men of olden times thought they lived was a fixed world, a realm where changes went on only within immutable limits of rest and permanence, and a world where the fixed and unmoving was . . . higher in quality and authority than the moving and altering" (Dewey [1920] 1957, 54). This viewpoint led to purely static social analyses in praise of the structures that were in existence, which would exist eternally. It is still reflected in the popular saying "There is nothing new under the sun" and in the even more pessimistic saying "You can't change human nature."

In the early capitalist period, when the overthrow of feudalism was still fresh in mind, the leading analysts recognized the reality and desirability of past change but thought that humanity had now reached the perfect, or "natural," order. "Ricardo thought of social organization as something that had changed materially in the past, but had reached maturity and would not change materially in the future" (Mitchell 1937, 207). Since institutions were fixed, social scientists could concentrate on narrower issues. "Ricardo, taking for granted the social relations of his time . . . centered the economist's attention on price, both commodity and factor price" (Hamilton 1970, 60). Most present-day social scientists admit the possibility of general institutional change but still concentrate in practice on narrow problems in a fixed society. Only a few conservatives, such as the sociologist Robert Nisbet, cling to the position that "change is . . . *not* natural, not normal. . . . Fixity is" (1969, 270).

The opposite view holds that social history "is of an endless maze of relations and interactions, in which nothing remains what, where, and as it was, but everything moves, changes, comes into being and passes out of existence. This primitive, naive, yet intrinsically correct conception of the world was that of ancient Greek philosophy, and was first clearly formulated by Heraclitus: everything is and also is not, for everything is in *flux*, is constantly changing, constantly coming into being and passing away" (Dewey [1920] 1957, 26). This primitive view of change has sometimes led to the incorrect, extreme notion of a law of constant change. Thus the sociologist Ralf Dahrendorf asserts that "all units of social organization are continuously changing, unless some force intervenes to arrest this change" (quoted in Coulson and Riddell 1970, 70).

This extreme assertion of continuous change is just as lacking in content or precise meaning as its opposite. There certainly have been major social changes in the past, but that fact does not justify the much more absolute statement that change always has and always will occur everywhere. If the statement just means "things change," it is a meaningless truism, so it teaches no useful lesson. If it means that change occurs so quickly that social science cannot make any meaningful statements, then it is wrong and harmful to the process of understanding.

It is meaningless to ask whether there is absolute change or absolute stability. The question is, What kinds of relations and conflicts may lead to what kinds of changes? In the Marxian view, social scientists "do not need to pay a little more attention to change, or even a lot more, nor do they need to make change, as opposed to order, their basis of analysis. Rather they need to make groups of people in interaction over time in social structures their basis of analysis" (Coulson and Riddell 1970, 71). The Marxian historical analysis explores and asks questions about the process of change based on relations among processes but makes no universal statements about change.

Contemporary Orthodox Social Science and Historical Change

In the 1950s, at the height of the Cold War, there was very little evolutionary analysis in the orthodox social sciences or even in history. There was instead a view called *functionalism,* showing the general laws of how societies function efficiently (see Martindale 1965). In anthropology a small group used evolutionary analysis, but they were treated as outcasts and considered possibly subversive (the evolutionary and nonevolutionary anthropology theories of that time are discussed in an excellent history by Marvin Harris [1968]).

Why was evolutionary social analysis considered subversive in the 1950s? Of course it sounded a bit like Marxism, but that was not the main reason. Evolutionary social theories may be considered subversive because they show that society has changed from one type in the past to a drastically different one in the present, and they imply that evolutionary change will produce a different society in the future. These particular biases seem to be part of ancient history because most of the social sciences have changed and become extremely different since the 1950s. (More recent trends in each of the social sciences and their relation to Marxian thought are discussed in Ollman and Vernoff 1982, 1984, and 1986.)

The most resistance to evolutionary and historical analysis has been in orthodox economics. In the long period of neoclassical dominance, from the 1870s to the 1930s, almost all orthodox economists concentrated on theories of equilibrium and adjustment to equilibrium rather than on evolutionary change in economies. Not only did neoclassical economics focus solely on equilibrium via the market mechanism but it contended that the economy automatically reached a full-employment equilibrium. Most orthodox economists—but not all—still concentrate their attention on analyses of economic equilibrium, excluding the notion of systematic evolutionary change.

On the other hand, there has been a sharp struggle by John Maynard Keynes, his immediate followers, and the New Keynesians today to overthrow the idea of automatic adjustment to full employment. Contrary to the neoclassical tradition, the Keynesian tradition explains how an equilibrium may occur at a point far below full employment. The concept of equilibrium in economics, from the earliest classical views to the contemporary New Keynesian school, along with examples of how it has affected economic reasoning, is discussed in appendix 4A.

Soviet Marxism on Historical Change

Soviet Marxists under Stalin insisted on a simple, unilinear view of rigidly similar evolution in all societies. In a typical Soviet Marxian text, Keiusinen claimed: "All peoples travel what is basically the same path. . . . The development of society proceeds through the consecutive replacement, according to definite laws, of one socioeconomic formation by another" (1961, 153). In the Soviet view, every society must pass through slavery, feudalism, capitalism, socialism, and communism. The alleged laws mentioned by Keiusinen were, of course, economic laws. According to Keiusinen, it is a basic law that the forces of production must inevitably continue to accumulate. On the other hand, class relations are frozen, because the ruling class refuses to change relationships that are to its benefit. Sooner or later the forces of production outgrow the narrow confines of the existing class relations. This is a contradiction within society and must inevitably lead to a revolutionary change, regardless of human desires.

The simplistic view that there is the same predetermined, unilinear progression in every society is, in the view of critical Marxian social scientists, incorrect and inadequate. Economic forces of production do not determine anything by themselves; they are part of the process of change. Moreover, it will be shown below that the qualifications to the view that all societies progress in the same way include different rates of change, different time lags between variables, occurrences of retrogression to previous modes, occurrences of jumps over supposed stages, and diffusion from one society to another. For these reasons, development is better envisioned as uneven rather than smooth (see appendix 4C).

The confusing approach of Soviet Marxism led to many attacks on Marxism as a belief in inevitable laws of history. One such attack on Marx was made by Karl Popper. "Popper argues that since Marx's whole theory of historical materialism rests upon the assumption of autonomous accumulation of the means of production as a universal law of history, the theory of historical materialism is defective at its roots and cannot pass for genuine science" (Hudelson 1990, 49). On the contrary, most contemporary Marxism does not advocate any universal laws of history, but only specific tendencies within given systems. Most present-day Marxism certainly does not make it a universal law that the means of production are always expanding and improving. On the contrary, modern research stresses that the class relations of production often hold back accumulation and technological improvement, with long periods of stagnation or retrogression.

Cohen's Economic Reductionist View of Historical Change

The most careful analysis and defense of the old, economic reductionist, linear view of the evolutionary process was given by G. A. Cohen (1978). He based his analysis on quotes from Marx, such as the following:

At a certain stage of their development, the material forces of production in society come in conflict with the existing relations of production, or—what is but a legal expression for the same thing—with the
property relations within which they had been at work before. From
forms of production of the forces of production, these relations turn
into their fetters. Then comes the period of social revolution. With the
change of the economic foundation, the entire immense super-structure
is more or less rapidly transformed. (Marx [1859] 1904, 12–14)

But Marx's words, while provocative and interesting, have been subject to many different interpretations, so no time will be spent here interpreting Marx; only the substantive points will be argued.

Following Wright, Levine, and Sober 1992, Cohen's analysis may
be divided into six theses.

   1. The compatibility thesis. The compatibility thesis says that a certain level of productive forces is only compatible with a certain type
of productive relations, and vice versa. The compatibility thesis may
be true when extreme limits are considered. Feudal relations were
compatible with medieval European technology, but would they be
compatible with computer and assembly-line technology? Would
complex feudal relations be equally compatible with the primitive
technology of a hunter-gatherer society? Would democratic socialism
be compatible with the level of Russian technology in 1917? It should
be stressed, however, that there is no one-to-one correspondence.
There is a wide range over which various class relations may be compatible with a single level of technology. Similarly, a wide range of
technology is compatible with a single set of class relations. The extent of these ranges is an empirical question.

   2. The development thesis. The development thesis says that "the
productive forces tend to develop throughout history" (Cohen,
quoted in Wright, Levine, and Sober 1992, 23). The development thesis is overstated as an eternal absolute, since there have been societies
in which the forces of production did not develop. Cohen argues that
it is rational human nature that always pushes for development. This
is a type of psychological reductionism, so it is not compatible with
the economic reductionism of most of his argument. The whole point
of Marxism is that the productive forces will develop if, and only if,
class relations are appropriate, so development does not always take
place.

   3. The contradiction thesis. The contradiction thesis says that
"with sufficient time, the productive forces will develop to a point
where they are no longer compatible with the relations of production
under which they previously developed" (Cohen, paraphrased by

Wright, Levine, and Sober 1992, 25). The contradiction thesis is true as a syllogism, but only if its assumptions are true. If (1) the forces and relations are only compatible in a range, (2) the forces always develop, and (3) the class relations do not basically change, then, of course, the forces and relations will be incompatible at some time. One cannot argue with a syllogism, but the assumptions are questionable when they are stated so universally. As a universal statement, Cohen's thesis is contrary to actual, messy history, as well as to the specificity on which historically-oriented Marxism insists (as shown below). Empirical research indicates that most previous societies eventually self-destructed or stagnated. It is unwarranted speculation, however, to extend these factual findings about many previous societies to a universal law that includes present and future societies. That depends on whether all of Cohen's assumptions are fulfilled in each case.

4. *The capacity thesis.* The capacity thesis says that a new class will have the capacity or power to overthrow the old class relations. The capacity thesis is not necessarily true because there might not be a new class with power to overthrow the system. In the case of the capitalist class, new forces under feudalism led to the growth of the capitalist class and its power. Under capitalism, the working class grows, but how much power does it have? Is it able to organize? At what point does it have this capacity? The questions are legion and will be different in each social system.

5. *The revolution thesis.* The revolution thesis says that the class with the capacity to overthrow the old regime will actually do so and will set up a new relationship. The revolution thesis assumes that the new class has not only the capacity but also the desire to overthrow the system. The tension between unchanged class relations and a rising potential for development of forces may lead to that desire. But all of recent history has shown just how questionable any assumptions about the desire or consciousness of classes, particularly the very heterogeneous working class, are.

6. *The optimality thesis.* The optimality thesis says that the new class relations will be optimal for economic development at the present level of the forces of production. The optimality thesis is certainly questionable. Some revolutions have led to rapid economic development. On the other hand, the Mongols under Genghis Khan and the Nazis under Adolf Hitler caused regression to come to certain societies after a revolutionary change.

It turns out that all such attempts to define universal and inevitable movements of history are easily contradicted by specific historical facts. A very cautious argument by Wright, Levine, and Sober concludes that in a defensible version of historical materialism, "epochal historical change is [1] still rooted in material conditions, . . . [2] it still has directionality, . . . and [3] changes are still actualized through class struggle, . . . but [4] there is no longer any claim to the inevitability of specific transitions" (1992, 90). G. A. Cohen's spirited and elegant defense of the old viewpoint on historical change has helped clarify the issues, and the critics of Cohen have explained the issues very thoroughly.

Historical Specificity

So far, this chapter has considered and criticized the ahistorical equilibrium approach as well as the notion of a predetermined, inevitable, unilinear path of historical development. In the Marxian historical approach each socioeconomic process must be examined as it changes and must be seen in the light of the given milieu at a particular time. The specific relations and evolution of each society and the social process within it must be examined within the context of the social evolution of the whole world. Thus, every social science issue is viewed as having a historical dimension.

Not only social, political, and economic institutions but also individual psychology can only be understood in a specific historical context. "The principle of historical specificity holds for psychology as well as for the social sciences. Even quite intimate features of man's inner life are best formulated as problems within each specific historical context" (Mills 1961, 163). The most devastating institutionalist critique of universalism, as well as the best statement of the need for historical specificity, is contained in C. Wright Mills's *Sociological Imagination* (1961); an early Marxian work on the subject was Frederick Engels's critique of Herr Eugen Dühring, *Anti-Dühring* ([1878] 1966).

In the historical approach to Marxian political economy each idea or situation must be viewed in its changing, historical context. For example, if the issue is how much religious tolerance was advocated by John Locke, then one should *not* ask a static question that compares him with some absolute standard, such as, "Was he tolerant of atheists?" Rather, one should ask the dynamic question, "Was he moving ahead of his day and age by urging toleration for all Protestant sects?" Similarly, freedom of contract was a very progressive cause against feudal restrictions on contracts, but freedom of contract became a reactionary idea when it was offered as an excuse for unrestricted child labor in the nineteenth century.

Following the method of historical specificity, Marxian scholars seldom try to say anything about labor in general; that is, their goal is not to discuss those characteristics that are the same in all societies. Thus, instead of discussing the laws of supply and demand for labor in general, most Marxian political economists speak of wage labor under capitalism, slave labor under slavery, and so forth. Thus, both definitions and laws are bounded by the specific historical constraints of a given system. For example, Marxian historians have emphasized how feudalism differs from capitalism in each aspect. Under capitalism, there are close interactions between politics and economics, but under feudalism (or in the Soviet Union) economic power and political power were fused. Thus, the nature of the state was very different under feudalism than under capitalism. Even the concept of class must be defined somewhat differently if we are to understand the feudal estates in contrast to modern classes.

An Evolutionary Approach

Although each mode of production is unique, the relational and historical methods are applicable to all class societies and, in different ways, to preclass societies. A law of political economy must be specific to one set of class relations, but the process of change can be approached in somewhat the same way in all societies. In spite of all the specific differences between societies, there are some common features to the basic process of evolutionary and revolutionary change in society, so it applies to many different social issues and many different societies (just as Darwin uses the same approach to myriad different issues in biological evolution).

Qualifications to the Marxian Historical Model

In addition to his technological reductionism, a major problem with G. A. Cohen's approach is that he provides one fairly rigid model of evolution and does not deal with the many exceptions and qualifications, which is necessary if the model is to be realistic. A very careful summary of Marx's manuscripts finds that "the general theory of historical materialism requires only that there should be a succession of modes of production, though not necessarily any particular modes, and perhaps not in any particular predetermined order" (Eric Hobsbawm, introduction to Marx [1857] 1964). As Hobsbawm indicates, many areas of the world have not followed the linear progression that Cohen's theory would lead us to expect. Moreover, the various modes of production are never met in pure form. A crude understanding of Marxism can easily lead to a lengthy discussion of pure capitalism, as if it really existed. Real social formations always contain elements of other systems or modes of production. For example, in the mid-nineteenth century the United States had not only had a capitalist mode of production but also a slave mode of production as well as an independent small farmer mode of production.

Most Marxian social scientists emphasize that human societies have followed many different evolutionary roads. Some very specific qualifications to any general scheme must be stressed that indicate that evolution is *not* continuous and *not* linear. While G. A. Cohen may recognize each of these qualifications, he does not consider them in his theory, and some may contradict his theory.

1. *Incremental changes and revolutionary changes.* Evolution includes both incremental changes and jumps, as well as major qualitative changes. Qualitative changes include not only major reforms but also revolutionary changes, as in the French Revolution of 1789 or the Russian Revolution of 1917.

2. *Differences in timing.* Even similar stages of evolution will be found at different times in different places. For example, civilizations arose independently and by somewhat parallel evolution in China and in Peru, but at quite different times.

3. *Retrogression and progression.* There are cases of retrogression from one stage back to an earlier stage. The decline of the Roman Empire was accompanied by a real decline in knowledge, communication, and commerce over large areas. Hitler's fascism moved Germany backward from a capitalist democracy to a dictatorship resembling feudalism in some respects. The Mongols destroyed a number of civilizations and sent these areas back to earlier forms of society.

4. *Time lags.* There are all kinds of complex time lags in the evolutionary process, so changes are seldom uniform or complete. Although enormous slave plantations came to dominate ancient Roman agriculture, large numbers of small peasant farmers continued to fight for existence for centuries. Although a few hundred corporations dominate the U.S. economy, millions of small business people and farmers persist in trying to eke out an independent living. Moreover, changes in economic or class conflicts are not reflected immediately or directly or automatically in ideologies. Thus various superstitions and religions (such as Christianity) appear to persist for centuries after the

societies that produced them have vanished. Actually, although their name and some ceremonies may remain the same, these religions are greatly modified in form and content by succeeding social conditions.

   5. Diffusion and internal evolution. Many of the political and economic transformations in human history did not happen through the internal evolution of one society, but through diffusion from a different society. Diffusion of social relations or technologies or ideas from one society to another has occurred in many ways, for example, through conquest, colonialism, trade, and missionary work. The Roman Empire spread its mode of production and ideology to many previously primitive economies. In the medieval period the Europeans learned a great deal of technology and culture from their trade relations with the Arabs.

   G. A. Cohen's Marxian model tends to look only at internal evolution caused by the conflict of endogenous factors. Neoclassical economics, along with similar schools in some of the other social sciences, tends to see change caused only by exogenous factors or diffusion from external sources. In all actual cases there are both internal and external causes, both evolution and diffusion. The Roman Empire was weakened by its own internal conflicts, but it fell because barbarian tribes around it jumped in to carve it up as soon as it weakened. A business cycle expansion is weakened by its own internal tensions, but it is usually pushed into actual decline by some external event that would not have caused a decline before it was vulnerable.

   What is perceived as internal or external, endogenous or exogenous, depends solely on the limits of the model or theory used to explain something. For example, if a theory took into consideration all of Europe in Roman times, including the internal development of the barbarian tribes, then their behavior would no longer seem to be external or accidental to the story of the Roman Empire, but would appear to be internal and necessary to the story of European development. Similarly, a model of the U.S. business cycle may take Japan and Europe as external, in which case their behavior is treated as exogenous shocks accidental to the model. But if one takes a model of all of the developed capitalist countries, then it is natural for the investigator to view the degree of synchronization of business cycles as an internal development of the model.

   A model can always include any set of human relations as internal to it. Thus, government can be viewed as external to the economy, but it can also be viewed as part of the political economy. Given the natural environment, all social evolution is internal if, and only if, the unit under analysis is all of human society. If all human society is included in a model, only those who believe in supernatural deities will look to an exogenous explanation of change.

Diffusion also opens the possibility for some societies to jump over stages that their neighbors passed through. Primitive as well as slave-type economies have been brought suddenly to capitalism through conquest or other contact, though economic relations in the colonies of capitalist countries are of a deformed and usually stagnant type of capitalism. Primitive and feudal societies were brought straight to an alleged socialism in parts of the Soviet Union and China. Diffusion may also bring retrogression to a stage that a society has already passed through. In West Africa the disruption caused by slave traders reduced some affluent commercial areas to more primitive agricultural forms.

6. *Conflict in ideology, and politics, and economics.* To the extent that G. A. Cohen discusses class conflict, he stresses it only at the economic level. It will be shown, however, that class conflict occurs at three levels: the production or economic level, the level of political or social institutions, and the ideological or psychological level. Thus an understanding of class conflict itself requires one to go beyond technological or even economic reductionism. Class conflict will be shown to have a key role in historical change.

A Theory of Evolution with Qualifications

In spite of all the qualifications listed above, it is still correct to speak of a process of social change through stages of evolution. The analogy of Marxian with Darwinian evolution may even be extended to the selection mechanism. Marxian scholars discuss social evolution through competitive selection. This perspective, however, is very different from the conservative Social Darwinism, which claims that an individual who is at the top of society financially (such as Ross Perot) is necessarily fitter or better than the poor. In contrast, in the Marxian view individual wealth is largely a function of existing class relations and financial inheritance.

Using the historical approach, Marxian social scientists do expect the best-adapted mode of production to be more likely to survive in the very long run, provided that civilization on the earth is not destroyed in a nuclear war or an environmental disaster. That society will probably survive which is best adapted to the fullest development of both technology and human potential. The phrase *best adapted,* however, must be defined very carefully. When the Mongols wiped out the Persian civilization, they were no doubt stronger and better adapted to that environment in a military sense, but the destruction of Persia did mean the end of a flourishing cultural activity for a long period. Similarly, that the Soviet system lost out to U.S. capitalism reflects the weakness of the Soviet system but does not prove the superiority of the U.S. system in any ethical or cultural sense.

To speak of the evolution of society is only to say that change occurs through understandable mechanisms in patterns that are repeated in a rough way many times. The result is that social scientists can understand how one form of society may lead to another. This does not mean that every society goes through the same stages; rather, different forms of society result from different cultures and different external influences.

A concrete Marxian study of the socioeconomic stages in early human history concludes from a lengthy investigation of the archaeological and anthropological facts that "it is not in the least surprising that the development of societies observed in different parts of the Old World, to say nothing of the New, should exhibit divergence rather than parallelism. This conclusion does not invalidate the use of the term 'evolution' to describe social development." In fact one can still use the analogy between social and organic (biological) evolution because "organic evolution is never represented pictorially by a bundle of parallel lines, but by a tree with branches all up the trunk and each branch bristling with twigs" (Childe 1951, 166). Of course there are a great many differences between the processes of socioeconomic evolution and organic evolution, but "to admit this is not to deny cultural evolution, to deny that cultural change is an orderly and rational process that can be understood by the human intellect without invoking any necessarily incalculable factors and miracles. On the contrary, it can be described in general intelligible formulae . . . there is no need to assume supernatural interpositions" (175, 179).

Using the relational-historical approach, Marxian historians do *not* claim that there is an inevitable march of "progress" to "better" societies, an idea that originated with eighteenth-century liberalism. Social evolution does not necessarily mean progress in any sense, but only better adaptation or a better ability to survive under the given conditions. Only if one defines progress in a peculiar way to mean nothing but adaptation can one speak of evolution bringing progress. A society better adapted for survival may still be poorer in art or culture or humanist values, so one should not speak of progress in a general sense as inevitable.

One might think that such a framework, with all its qualifications, would be considered a truism by any reasonable social scientist. Yet one set of institutional pressures and ideological commitments led some Marxian theorists to speak of universal and unilinear evolution. A different set of institutional pressures and ideological commitments has led some conservative social scientists to deny any validity to the concept of social evolution, believing that the status quo should and will exist forever.

Because most Marxian writers assert that the best-adapted economic system has a higher probability of survival, in this very limited sense critical Marxian social scientists tend to be guardedly optimistic concerning the direction of present history. The competitive evolutionary process between societies only operates over a long time span, and nothing guarantees that civilization as a whole will survive if there is a nuclear or environmental disaster. Within a society, there is some probability that a class may survive and dominate if it is best adapted to the conditions of the society. These, however, are longterm probabilities and tendencies based on experience of the past competition of groups and societies, *not* inevitable laws describing what will happen. Marxism is, thus, "a theory that did acknowledge overall directionality to historical change, but rejected the view that directionality implies a unique path and sequence of events" (Wright, Levine, and Sober 1992, 79).

A Critical Marxian View of Forces and Relations

Many social scientists think that all talk about a tension between productive forces and class relations is a strange Marxian aberration. But shorn of the mystic language about inevitable contradictions, these concepts can be powerful tools for understanding complicated social processes.

In the present society, technology is improving by leaps and bounds. There is incredible growth in the numbers and quality of computers, robotics, and spaceships to the moon, all of which would have seemed utterly fantastic not so long ago. On the other hand, society continues to have obsolete socioeconomic relations generating enormous unresolved problems, including poverty, unemployment, drugs and alienation, starvation in some regions, and continuing wars.

How many times do we ask ourselves how it is possible to go to the moon while it is impossible to solve poverty? Surely this shows a tension between our enormous productive capabilities and our present class relationships. If this tension is not removed, then an internal process moves society toward conflict and confrontation. In the Marxian historical view, this tension is a major cause of class, racial, national, and gender conflicts. The Marxian view that the tension between productive forces and class relations leads to conflict and change remains a powerful tool. It requires the many qualifications given above, but it is the basic tool for achieving an insightful grasp of the social sciences.

Several examples of the use of this tool can be considered. One example is the fact that the forces of production stagnated under Roman slave relations for centuries. There were many reasons, including the lack of incentives for slaves, the lack of interest by the slave owners in anything relating to production, and the lack of mass purchasing power for greater production. Another example is that toward the end of feudalism, the class relations held back agricultural and industrial advance. Two thorough and excellent discussions of the issues may be found in Hilton 1975 and Ashton and Philpin 1985; see also the pioneering work by Dobb (1946).

Robert Brenner asked how feudal class relations held back the feudal forces of production. "The inability of the serf-based agrarian economy to innovate ... is understandable," he says, "in view of the interrelated facts, first, of heavy surplus extraction by the lord from the peasant and, second, the barriers to mobility of men and land which were themselves part and parcel of the unfree surplus-extraction relationship" (in Ashton and Philpin 1985, 31). Even when there was a strong market demand, the peasant had no excess income to spend on improvements, while the lord found it easier to make additional profit by squeezing the peasant, who was prevented from moving. Brenner points out that even in areas where there were similar market forces and similar demographic trends, the results were very different if the class relations were different. Finally, he shows how actual changes in class relations were caused by the class conflicts engendered by this tension-filled situation.

As another example, it has been shown in detail how sharecropping (the relations of production) held back technology in southern agriculture (the forces of production) for decades (see Ransom and Sutch 1977).

One very important example is the fact that in every upswing of the capitalist business cycle many economists see only harmony and endless prosperity. They are then astounded to see—and this always happens—the economy go into a downspin. Marxian political economists, however, look beyond the apparently harmonious upswing of the cycle to find a slow increase of tensions or disproportions. For one thing, there are disproportions between expanding productive capacity and restricted consumer demand—and consumer demand is limited by class relations. Thus radical political economy, using the tools of Marxism, is not surprised when each period of prosperity is followed by a recession or depression. Without the Marxian relational and historical approach, it is very difficult to achieve this integrated understanding of the cycle of boom and bust. Institutionalist work on the cycle has used a similar holistic and evolutionary method, which is best seen in Wesley Mitchell's magnificent pioneering work on business cycles (in several books, cited in Sherman 1991).

Finally, the best recent example of how the relations of production may hold back the forces of production was the dramatic slowing and collapse of the Soviet economy. The growing tension in the Soviet economy led to class conflict (for a detailed discussion, see ch. 10).

Because many conventional social scientists are overly impressed by what appears to be stable and dominant in present society, they seldom look deeply into new and opposing trends. Thus they usually assume major change to be impossible and are always surprised even by small changes in social relations, not to speak of comprehensive revolutions. Few conventional social scientists predicted the large-scale activism of the sixties, nor did they expect it to lead to vast changes. In contrast, according to Paul Baran, "What is . . . central to the Marxian position is the capacity and willingness to look beyond the immediately observable facts and to see the tree of the future in the tiny shoots barely perceptible in the present" (1959, 11).

The Process of Socioeconomic Revolution

Although the revolutionary process remains controversial, most Marxian writers are in agreement about a few points (see, e.g., Callinicos 1988, 94). First, if productive forces develop while class relations remain unchanged, then the forces will eventually be inappropriate to the existing class relations. Second, the result is a crisis of some sort, which is often reflected in stagnant or declining productive forces. Third, this tension may then result in class conflict. This class conflict will be reflected only in part in direct economic form; it will also be reflected in political and social conflict and in ideological conflicts. These political and social conflicts may be expressed as religious, racial, gender, or national conflicts, and the racial or gender conflicts may develop an independent life, exacerbating the class conflicts. Fourth, the outcome of the class conflict will depend on the exact nature of the interests and power of a multitude of classes. Marxism argues that under the right circumstances, as in Russia in 1917 and 1991, a revolution will result from individual and class behavior.

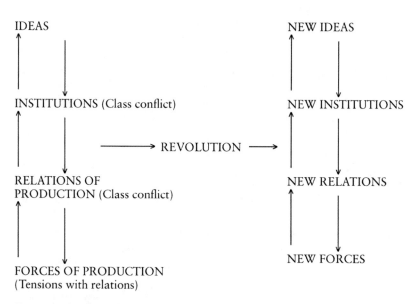

IDEAS   NEW IDEAS

INSTITUTIONS (Class conflict)   NEW INSTITUTIONS

        → REVOLUTION →

RELATIONS OF   NEW RELATIONS
PRODUCTION (Class conflict)

             NEW FORCES
FORCES OF PRODUCTION
(Tensions with relations)

Figure 4.1. Conflict and Revolutionary Changes

(The difficult issues concerning collective behavior and the importance of class are discussed in the next two chapters.)

The typical picture of the revolutionary process is depicted in figure 4.1. This figure shows four levels of conflict in an existing society.
There is the basic tension between the existing class relations and the
productive forces. Then there are class conflicts within the economy
(e.g., strikes), political conflicts, and ideological conflicts. Together
the three levels of class conflict lead to a revolution at some point.
The revolution produces new ideas, new political institutions, and
new class relations. This new society allows the productive forces to
grow. If the new society is still a class-divided society, there will again
be a class conflict, but it will be different from the old type of class
conflict.

The Historical Approach as a Method

Like the relational view, the historical aspect of the critical method is
better seen as a methodological suggestion for approaching problems
than as a set of laws. As Engels put it, "Our conception of history is
above all a guide to study, not a lever for construction [of universal
laws] after the Hegelian manner" (quoted in Rigby 1987, 104). The

reason for this viewpoint is that if one treats the historical approach as a set of laws of evolution, there is a dilemma. If we take historical specificity seriously, a set of political and economic or historical laws applies only to one specific mode of production. If, on the other hand, one attempts to generalize these laws for all times and places, then they must be unspecific, vague, truisms. The dilemma is perceived to be this: either the laws of history are very limited and specific or else they are general but fairly meaningless. Neither horn of the dilemma gives us a useful historical materialism.

Stalinist Marxism took the second horn of the dilemma, stating the laws of historical materialism in a vague enough manner that people were deceived into thinking that they were meaningful statements applying to all societies. G. A. Cohen also follows the second horn of the dilemma, except that he tries very hard to make the laws precise though still universal. This is an impossible task, and his attempts have resulted in an outpouring of criticism.

Paul Sweezy (1992) takes the first horn of the dilemma, saying that the laws of historical materialism apply only to capitalism. A number of other theorists have agreed with Sweezy's view; for example, Gottlieb (1987) argues that historical materialism applies only to the era of competitive capitalism, so his interpretation is even narrower than Sweezy's.

Neither horn of this dilemma, however, is acceptable. One certainly does not want a set of vague truisms, since they really do not say anything. On the other hand, to say that historical materialism applies only to capitalism is a very limiting sort of conclusion. Hundreds of Marxian and radical studies of noncapitalist societies have made good use of the Marxian approach. Those studies indicate the usefulness of applying the Marxian method to noncapitalist societies. If historical materialism applies only to capitalism, then does that mean that Marxian social scientists have no method for understanding the history of the former Soviet Union? That would be an unwelcome and unnecessary limitation. (The method is applied to the evolution of the Soviet Union in part II below.)

Questions, Not Answers

The historical approach as seen by critical Marxists does not give specific answers; it states neither vague, general laws nor precise, specific laws. According to the historical, or evolutionary, method of Marxian political economy, one should ask the following important questions. The broadest question would be, How is this political-economic system, and each part of it, evolving? One should not assume that any problem in political economy can be handled as if it were static unless one finds that the dynamic, historical issues are insignificant. It is the thesis of this method that historical issues are extremely significant for almost all issues of political economy.

Besides the general questions—how a society evolved, what its present evolution is, and where it is likely to go—the historical approach to political economy suggests some far more specific questions:

1. What are the present class conflicts? Class analysis is seen as the entry point and central focus of all social analysis.

2. What racial, gender, or nationality conflicts exist?

3. Are there at present tensions or incompatibilities between the productive forces and class relations?

4. How are class conflicts (and other conflicts) being played out in the political sphere and in social organizations?

5. How are class conflicts (and other conflicts) being played out in the ideological sphere? How are changes in ideology affecting such conflicts?

6. Are these conflicts nonrevolutionary, or may they be leading toward revolution?

7. If there were to be a revolutionary change, what might be the new ideologies, institutions, and class relations? How would race and gender issues be affected?

8. What trends, what incremental changes, are presently occurring that may cause major changes in the future?

9. What incremental changes led up to major changes of the past?

10. If a major change or revolution has just occurred, what changes will it cause in previous trends?

How Are the Relational and Historical Methods Connected?

In physics, space and time are discussed as two aspects of the universe within a unified space-time theory. In the social sciences, relations at a given time and historical changes should be discussed as two aspects of a unified relational-historical approach. A proper understanding of relationships (including conflict relations) at a given time should lead to an understanding of the future process of change. An understanding of past processes of change is necessary for an understanding of present relationships. So there can be no contradiction between these two approaches. A false dichotomy is sometimes asserted because present relations are assumed to be static and ahistorical, while history is assumed to be reductionist and nonrelational. If one accepts these false assumptions, one can then state an apparent dichotomy between present relationships and history. Such a dichotomy, however, is false and misleading because relationships should be seen in a historical context, while historical change must be explained by conflict in relationships.

Appendix 4A: Orthodox Economics and Historical Change

The attitude of orthodox economics toward historical change has varied over the four stages of its evolution—the classical stage, the neoclassical stage, the Keynesian stage, and the New Classical and New Keynesian stage.

Stage 1. Classical Economics and Historical Change

The classical economists, such as Adam Smith, often discussed history. Their attitude, however, was that precapitalist societies were all tending toward the laws of capitalism, which were natural laws that would continue to hold forever once in place. Thus, if there had been evolution, it had now ended.

In classical economics there was some confusion between the laws of precapitalist economies and those of capitalism. For example, classical economists were well aware of the prevalent use of barter in most earlier societies, but they seemed to think that the capitalist system could still be treated as if it were a barter economy. They argued that money was merely a "veil" over the exchange between two commodities. Thus money played no active role. Therefore, the hoarding of money could not cause a lack of aggregate demand, because the underlying reality was that commodities were exchanged for commodities.

The classical economists made extensive use of the idea of equilibrium. They believed that competition would always bring about the proper adjustment to any change in supply or demand and thus equilibrium would always be restored.

In the very long run, the classical economists thought that the capitalist economy would reach an optimal situation, so there would be no further changes. There would be long-term static equilibrium. The population and the labor supply would also be in equilibrium, and there would be full employment. Obviously, such a view is contrary to a theory of continuing evolution.

Stage 2. Neoclassical Economics and Equilibrium

Neoclassical economics, beginning in the 1870s, greatly refined the notion of equilibrium. Alfred Marshall, for example, spelled out the conditions for short-run, medium-run, long-run, and very long-run equilibrium. The neoclassicals thought in terms of fixed psychological characteristics giving rise, through a process of individual optimization in the market, to universally applicable laws. Thus the notion of a historical or evolutionary approach died out completely. The neoclassicals fought hard and succeeded in defeating the German historical school, which had advocated an evolutionary approach. Neoclassical laws were often expressed as mathematical models, assumed to be applicable anywhere.

Equilibrium may be defined as follows: "A market or set of markets is in equilibrium if the agents participating in that . . . market(s) have no cause to alter their plans (how much they desire to buy and sell)" (Weeks 1989, 36). Equilibrium in one market is called *partial equilibrium,* while equilibrium in all markets, including feedbacks from one market to another, is called *general equilibrium.* The equilibrium type of analysis assumes that the economic world is mostly in balance or that it is adjusting back to balance by marginal or incremental changes after some exogenous shock. This approach is far from the notion of evolutionary change as the central point of analysis. Paul Samuelson notes that a neoclassical equilibrium theorist "naturally tended to think of models in which things settled down to a unique position independently of initial conditions" (quoted and discussed in Mirowski 1989, 390).

It has been said that in neoclassical economics human psychology "is universal and eternal, existing more as a fact of nature than as an historical product" (Amariglio, Callari, and Cullenberg 1989, 427). In other words, the neoclassical paradigm reduces all political economy to individual choices (based on preferences, resources, and technology) but ignores the role of specific social institutions in creating social evils. "In short, to base an analysis on the common factors and relationships that permeate any (and all) human society is to take the focus of analysis away from the specifics of the given social order, with its particular forms of privilege and oppression" (Horowitz 1971, 8). Because neoclassical economics has an equilibrium approach and is founded on given psychological preferences, it is ahistorical and nonevolutionary.

Example: Alfred Marshall

Since in the neoclassical view the alternative to market equilibrium is chaos, only small incremental changes may be made. In the 1890s, the motto of the father of neoclassical economics, Alfred Marshall, was "Nature makes no leaps," and he believed that society could not and should not make leaps either. A progressive in his day, Marshall was strongly in favor of liberal incremental reforms, but he did not believe that more drastic changes were possible. Lekachman comments that in this paradigm "economics becomes the ally of minute incremental change. The 'system' is realistically accepted" (Lekachman 1973, 306).

Example: Lord Robbins

In the 1930s, leading neoclassical economists still argued, in the midst of the Great Depression, that equilibrium analysis of profit and utility maximization could be applied to any society, no matter what its institutions were like. Thus the eminent neoclassical theorist Lord Robbins attacked "the view that the laws of Economics are limited to certain conditions of time and space, that they are purely historical in character" (1935, 80). Robbins argued that in every society there existed (1) land, labor, and capital and (2) rational marginalist optimization behavior by consumers and producers. The specific institutions of slavery or feudalism or primitive clan ownership do not change the marginal laws at all, in his view. Thus Robbins claimed: "No one will really question the universal applicability of such assumptions as the existence of scales of relative evaluation, or of different factors of production" (81). He claimed that one could draw very important conclusions from such universally valid assumptions.

Stage 3. The Keynesian Revolution

John Maynard Keynes shook the economics establishment by declaring that capitalism could create large-scale, involuntary unemployment. This was a revolutionary change from the former classical and neoclassical position that the economy will always adjust, automatically and more or less rapidly, to equilibrium at full employment. Since Keynes presented his argument during the Great Depression, when 25 percent of all U.S. workers were unemployed (according to the understated official data), his more realistic view and suggested cure was accepted with enthusiasm by many economists and even many political leaders.

Although Keynes's conclusion was shocking to neoclassical economists, it was presented in a form and a methodology that most economists thought was compatible with neoclassical methodology. Keynes argued strongly that full employment was not automatic and that involuntary unemployment would often be the case. But Keynes explained unemployment as an equilibrium situation below full employment. The standard U.S. Keynesian interpretation of Keynes in the 1950s and 1960s strongly emphasized the adjustment to equilibrium. The standard Keynesianism of this period was similar to the neoclassical approach in stressing both psychological laws and an equilibrating process.

Stage 4. The New Classical and New Keynesian Approaches

The New Classical approach, which became dominant in the 1970s, reverted to the earlier neoclassical approach in all of its glory, with a few new wrinkles. Not only did it begin with individual psychology but it stressed the optimization process leading to markets clearing at equilibrium. Even more than the neoclassical economists, it emphasized the rational calculations of individual psychology. It attacked Keynes for supposedly ignoring neoclassical microeconomics, so it urged an emphasis on the neoclassical foundations of macroeconomics. A few examples will give the flavor of their methodology.

Example: G. C. Archibald

A similar argument to that of Lord Robbins was made fifty years later by the orthodox economist G. C. Archibald, who stated that the economic problem consists of scarce resources and insatiable needs. He concluded that this problem "is universal: it transcends times and space, political or social organization. . . . From the universality of the economic problem, it also follows that if the theory of the firm proves to be a useful . . . portion of the theory of allocation . . . in a . . . capitalist context, so it must be in a Communist context; there must be a Soviet analogy" (quoted in Sawyer 1989, 19). In fact the operation and problems of the Soviet economy were totally different from those of any capitalist economy (see ch. 10).

Example: Hal Varian

In his widely used graduate textbook Varian describes equilibrium in a single market. He says that "when there were many economic agents each had an incentive to act as a price taker. Given prices each agent could then determine his or her demands and supplies for the good in question. When the price was such that supply equaled demand, the market was in equilibrium in the sense that no agent would desire to change his or her actions" (1992, 135). He then moves from this partial equilibrium, in one market, to general equilibrium, in all markets.

Varian states a universal analysis of supply and demand leading to equilibrium that can be applied to Neolithic cave dwellers, Egyptian pharaohs, feudal nobility in France, Soviet commissars, and modern English financiers. The point is that the New Classical approach sees competition in the marketplace as a natural product of any set of rational human beings, whereas Marxian and institutionalist writers see it as a product of particular socioeconomic institutions and relations. In the New Classical view, "The 'market' represents rationality per se, outside any specific social context" (Amin 1990, 11).

For example, New Classical theory assumes that individuals freely choose their occupations on the basis of their given preferences (see examples and quotations from neoclassical and New Classical economists in Marglin 1989). In the Marxian view, individual workers are forced by their circumstances to work or starve, and their choices are very limited. A survey shows that, given a choice, only one in four blue-collar workers (or one in six unskilled steel workers) would choose the same occupation again (Marglin 1989, 97). Of course preferences are not eternal, but are produced by specific historical conditions.

Example: Gordon Tullock

The New Classical analysis has also been applied to the legal system. If one assumes that the economy is in equilibrium and that it rewards individuals according to their marginal product, then it follows that the emphasis should be on improving the efficient functioning of the present system. It then follows that crime should be punished in the most efficient manner. Thus in examining the legal process, Gordon Tullock (1971) argues for more "efficient" justice, which means speeding up the legal system by removing due-process safeguards, ignoring the necessity of such safeguards for minimal protection of the poor. He makes this argument on the basis of a universal view of both the economy (in which every individual has maximized utility) and the law, which disregards specific institutional constraints such as the inability of the poor to make equal use of legal processes.

The New Keynesian Approach

The New Keynesians have increased the realism of orthodox economics by reintroducing the concept of involuntary unemployment and the reasons for it. The New Classical economists argued that the concept of involuntary unemployment was unnecessary because there was no reason for it to exist, except temporarily at times of adjustment. But the New Keynesian explanation of unemployment still involves an optimization process leading to an equilibrium at below full employment. Thus, although some of the New Keynesians' substantive theories are new, their methodology reverts to the earlier standard U.S. Keynesian variant of the 1950s. It should be noted that one of the new procedures for dealing with problems is game theory. The procedure may afford some new insights, but it still begins from purely psychological assumptions, considers a process of individual optimization, and arrives at equilibrium. (The standard use of game theory is presented in Kreps 1990; for the New Keynesian view of it, see Mankiw and Romer 1991.)

Appendix 4B: The Institutionalist View of Evolutionary Change

Long ago, Thorstein Veblen, the founder of institutionalism, attacked neoclassical economics because it "confines its interests to the definition and classification of a mechanically limited range of phenomena. Like other taxonomic sciences, hedonistic economics does not, and cannot, deal with phenomena of growth except so far as growth is taken in the quantitative sense of a variation in magnitude, bulk, mass, number, frequency" (reprinted in Hunt and Schwartz 1972, 178).

Veblen points out that neoclassical economists apply their classifications in a timeless manner, seeing only a little more or less of each quantity in entirely different eras and societies. Veblen claims, for example, that for neoclassical economics, "a gang of Aleutian Islanders sloshing about in the wrack and surf with rakes and magical incantations for the capture of shell-fish are held, in point of taxonomic reality, to be engaged on a feat of hedonistic equilibration in rent, wages and interest. And that is all there is to it. Indeed, for economic theory of this kind, that is all there is to any economic situation" (Veblen, in Hunt and Schwartz 1972, 178–79).

According to Veblen, most neoclassical economists do admit that some varieties of qualitative changes, such as depressions or recessions, do take place, but they view them as caused by external factors, such as wars, plagues, or stupid governmental mistakes. What almost all neoclassical economists seem to hold in common, according to institutionalists, is the impossibility of explaining qualitative social changes by previous internal (or endogenous) quantitative changes. They either deny qualitative changes or see them as externally caused. For example, both unemployment and inflation are seen by pure neoclassicals only as adjustments back to equilibrium after an external shock.

One of the most thorough institutionalist explanations of the evolutionary approach is by David Hamilton (1970), who begins by noting that "the eighteenth century viewed social forms as fixed in nature and what change took place was at most a quantitative one within fixed limits set by a natural order of things" (19). He contends that all economists agree on the need to study change but that neoclassicals tend to use a static, quantitative, or mechanical approach rather than an evolutionary one. He claims that neoclassicals resist the study of social evolution because (1) they evolved from classical economics, which was founded before the theory of evolution became popular; (2) they want quantitative precision, which is difficult to achieve in the study of broad historical changes; and (3) there are vested interests that pressure social scientists not to advocate evolutionary theories. He asserts that institutionalism, by contrast "is Darwinian, not Newtonian. It is evolutionary, not mechanical" (117).

Similarly, Alan Gruchy attacks the purely equilibrium economics of the neoclassical paradigm (see, e.g., Gruchy 1947, 4). "The institutionalist, on the other hand, considers change to be part of the economic process . . . a process of cumulative change" (Hamilton 1970, 17). Institutionalists have made a major contribution to political economy by viewing economic change as the result of internal processes, not external accidents. Institutionalists allow for qualitative changes or jumps in society. Of course liberal institutionalists usually focus on reforms, whereas radical institutionalists consider both reforms and revolutionary changes.

Example: Gardiner Means

The controversy over the possibility of jumps or qualitative changes versus equilibrium with incremental changes is not merely an abstract debate among philosophers; it bears directly on the everyday work of economists. Gardiner Means, a militant liberal institutionalist but not a radical, argues that prices are set artificially by monopolies and that monopoly prices are maintained to some degree in recessions. He contends that firms with monopoly power move prices only in jumps, not smoothly, as might be predicted if all prices were competitive (1972, 292–306). He attacks a conservative study by Stigler and Kindahl (1970), which tries to show that monopoly does not have much effect on prices. This neoclassical study comes up with price movements that are quite smooth but admittedly quite different from the price movements calculated by the Bureau of Labor Statistics for the same products.

Stigler and Kindahl used statistical procedures to smooth their price series. Means comments:

> This artificial smoothing of the frequency and size of the actual price changes in the underlying data covers up the actual rigidity and quantum jumps which are characteristic of administered [oligopolistic or monopolistic] prices. Yet the authors cite Alfred Marshall's famous dictum that *natura non facit saltum* in support of their contention that the greater smoothness of the National Bureau indexes as compared with the corresponding BLS indexes ... is evidence favorable to the greater validity of the National Bureau indexes. ... In this day of world-wide knowledge of earthquakes, quantum mechanics and biological mutations it is somewhat quaint to offer the view that "nature does not like jumps." It is hardly a reason for not facing up to the implications of the price jumps in the actual data or the challenge to classical theory which they present. (1972, 305)

This example by Gardiner Means makes clear the necessity of examining both qualitative and quantitative types of change—and using both types of analyses.

Warren Samuels (1977), writing in the institutionalist tradition, says that "economic development is a function of the pressure of technological change against the inertia of traditional modes of organized behavior (institutions or power structure ...). Economic growth is a product of the conflict of the instrumental logic of technology *vis-à-vis* resisting forces" (873). This institutionalist description shows how conflict between technological innovations and rigid, class relations may lead to evolutionary change.

Samuels, like Veblen, refers to the conflict between groups when he says, "The key is the tension between old and new ways of doing things . . . but especially as to who is able to do what, that is, between conflicting interests. . . . This tension may and often does take the form of conflict between established interests and new interests seeking realization or legitimacy. . . . Moreover, institutional change means distributional change" (1977, 882, 885).

Although the terminology is very different, this formulation is quite similar to the Marxian view. One difference is that Samuels would say that conflicts over power between groups are not the same as class conflicts. Samuels speaks of conflict as "the necessity to remove institutional constraints on industrial efficiency" (1977, 874). So institutionalists agree with the Marxian view that there is a need for a historical, evolutionary approach. Moreover, Marxists and institutionalists agree on the use of a holistic, or relational, approach. Most institutionalists differ from Marxists (1) by ignoring class conflict or by seeing it as power conflict and (2) by ignoring the consideration of revolution in favor of intensive study of reforms. Marxists differ in a number of ways from liberal institutionalists but have very few differences with radical institutionalists.

Appendix 4C: Backwardness and Uneven Development

A mechanical approach to development tends to see it as smooth, straight, continuous, progress measurable by quantitative methods. The "most advanced" may be suddenly overtaken by the "most backward."

In a way that is analogous to biological evolution, a society may evolve in a very specific and overspecialized manner until it fits into a special niche in one environment. Just as the polar bear is beautifully adapted to the arctic environment, so too is Eskimo society adapted to that environment and no other. This principle of overspecialized evolution may be applied, not just to one tiny corner of the world, but to a dominant and apparently stable species or society. In its day, the saber-toothed tiger appeared to have completely adapted to its environment, but it was overspecialized: it could not withstand relatively small changes in the environment, and it could not rapidly make any further evolutionary changes. In an analogous way, some dominant societies have become rigid in their social relations and have reduced their rate of cultural progress by freezing into specific niches. Obvious examples include the ancient Roman Empire or the British Empire of the modern period. "The more specialized and adapted a form in a given evolutionary stage, the smaller is its *potential* for passing to the next stage" (Harding et al. 1960, 97). Just as the saber-toothed tigers vanished, so may obsolete societies decline and fall.

In contrast, the society that is less rigid, undifferentiated, and "backward" economically may sometimes spurt forward to pass the previously more "advanced." Japan is an example: although its economy was devastated and chaotic after the Second World War, it became a leading industrial power in less than twenty-five years. Similarly, the backward frontier society of the early-nineteenth-century United States rose with incredible rapidity to the industrial forefront. Sudden spurts by previously less developed societies also occurred in Japan in the 1870s, Germany in the 1880s, and Russia in the 1930s. Certainly, in this respect some nineteenth-century Marxian theorists were wrong in their expectation that England would take the lead in the socialist revolution. They were casually considering the broad sweep of history by which mature capitalism may lead to socialism on a world scale, but they were neglecting the specific road of evolution in different areas. In fact, it almost never seems to be the case that the most advanced country of one stage becomes the leader in the next stage. On the contrary, some previously less developed country often leaps ahead when there are major upheavals.

As Lenin was fond of pointing out, capitalism had spread as a system all over the world, but it could then be broken at its weakest link (tsarist Russia), and this most "backward" country could then jump ahead. Lenin argued (for example, in his pamphlet *Imperialism*) that it was a general rule that capitalist countries develop at uneven rates, both between countries and over time. He thus predicted revolution where capitalism was quite weak. This was the case in Russia, where a mostly foreign capitalism was imposed in isolated spots within a vast ocean of still semifeudal relations in agriculture.

Another who explored the potential power of "backwardness"— and the danger of being the leader—was Thorstein Veblen ([1915] 1945). In his book on Germany, he showed how it had an advantage over England at a certain point—the late nineteenth century—because it did not have a vast investment in antiquated machinery. It could, and did, begin from scratch to build with the latest borrowed technology a brand new industrial plant. This ability was demonstrated again by Japan and Germany after the Second World War.

Similarly, Egypt was the first to discover and widely use a form of writing, but it got stuck with nonphonetic hieroglyphics, while others forged ahead to create and use phonetic alphabets. Likewise, when Egypt and Persia reached their peaks and stagnated, the young civilization of Greece went far beyond them. And the then barbarian Rome eventually went far beyond Greece in many ways. When Roman slavery declined, the barbarian Germans and the Arabs made the advance into a much more productive feudalism. "If . . . we consider the discontinuity of advance and the relatively greater potential for advance of the backward areas over the more developed as normal . . . in evolution, then that aspect of the rise and fall problem is not a problem" (Harding et al. 1960, 108).

Another example of the process of uneven (or zigzag) development came in late feudalism. As late as the sixteenth century, England was among the weakest areas in economic development. Italy, Flanders, and France were all more developed, but the very strength of their medieval institutions, with collaboration between some feudal lords and merchants, made further capitalist development difficult (see Nef 1940). Likewise, it was the *strength* of the existing slave state in the Eastern Roman Empire (Byzantium) that prevented the rise of a more progressive feudalism there, as happened in the declining Roman Empire.

FIVE

A Critique of Individualism and Extreme Collectivism

With respect to the relationship between the individual and society, there have been two extreme and incorrect viewpoints in the history of social analysis. The dominant view in the United States has been what is commonly called *individualism,* the concept that all socioeconomic explanation must begin with individual behavior. The individualist method is usually found in tight association with psychological reductionism, so that individual behavior is assumed to result from individual psychology. We have already examined the reduction of every phenomenon to psychology, but we must now examine the specific form of reductionism that claims that everything can be explained in terms of individual thoughts and individual behavior.

At the other end of the spectrum are those who sometimes seem to treat nations and classes as existing without any individual parts or having a reality above and beyond individuals. These writers, who may be labeled *extreme collectivists,* seldom find time to discuss individual motivations or behavior. The extreme collectivists also practice a form of reductionism in the sense that they explain everything in terms of groups or structures, seeing no need to consider individual thinking and behavior.

Both of these extreme reductionist viewpoints—reduction of all explanations to individuals or reduction of all explanations to groups or structures—have had great impact on social scientists as well as on large numbers of the general public, translating into political behavior.

Extreme Collectivism

Some followers of the philosopher G. W. F. Hegel appear to argue that a totality, such as a country or a class, exists above and beyond its individual components. This is not the dominant position of present-day non-Soviet Marxian scholars; rather, it is the position defined above as *extreme collectivism*. Suppose, for example, that someone said, "The working class is antiracist because it knows that racism attempts to divide and weaken the working class." That extreme collectivist position would be incorrect because it treats the collective known as "the working class" as if it were a single entity with a single view. Yet in the United States, for example, the working class includes African Americans and whites, poorly paid workers and highly paid professionals, men and women. Each of these groups has its own interests, its own psychology, and often its own behavior. The actual behavior patterns of each group often differ from the assumed homogeneous behavior patterns of the whole working class.

Contemporary, critical Marxian writers reject the notion that the working class is a superhuman entity. Perhaps one could find examples of an extreme collectivist view of the working class in some of the most popular propaganda of some of the old Communist parties, but it has never been the view of serious Marxian scholars.

Rather than Marxism, the most common example of extreme collectivism in the modern world is nationalism. A nationalist claims that to be patriotic is to love one's country, right or wrong. This makes a country sound like a real living entity rather than a collection of individuals. When Serbs have killed Croats or Croats have killed Serbs, they have been treating their ethnic group as a real living collective. Thus an attitude of extreme collectivism has often been part of preparation for war, which is legalized murder.

Racism is another form of extreme collectivism. The mighty green race is superior to the lowly purple race. Such statements always assume that the whole race thinks and acts together, or at least that the individual members all act in exactly the same way.

Individualism

There have been historians who have attributed all important events to the whims and biases of individuals. Many studies of Stalin purport to show that Stalin, with his warped personality, caused much of the evil in Soviet society. Such an analysis hides or distorts the real problems that existed in Soviet institutions. Chapter 9 shows that

Stalin did not cause the problems of Soviet society: rather, he reflected its deep problems, weaknesses, and conflicts.

Similarly, there are those who attribute crime to the individual attributes of criminals, drug use to the preferences of individuals, and suicide rates to the choices of individuals rather than to the structure of the society that gives rise to these problems. There have been historians who have argued that women's rights activists pushed for women's rights because they were lesbians. Some historians have contended that the abolitionists pushed for the abolition of slavery because of their peculiar personality traits. (For examples of many of these types of historical analysis, see the excellent critique in Zinn 1970.)

Suppose an economist subscribed to an extreme form of individualist methodology. Such an economist might look for the causes of unemployment in the preferences and choices of the unemployed. Perhaps these workers lack confidence. Or it might be argued that individual workers lack good information, so they go searching for better jobs when none are available. Such an economist would believe that workers chose unemployment for various reasons and thus would not feel that it was necessary to investigate the structure of the U.S. economy to find out why the inner dynamics of capitalism might cause unemployment.

Appendix 5A explores the history of individualism in the actual economic theories of economists, from the classical economists to the New Keynesians. Appendix 5A shows that one thing the contending schools of modern orthodox economists have in common is an allegiance to individualist methodology. For example, aggregate consumer spending must be explained by the choices of individuals. The problem is that a rigorous acceptance of extreme individualism rules out analysis of class relations and structural problems, as discussed below.

The Individualist Critique of Marxian Class Analysis

Class analysis begins with relationships between groups rather than with isolated individuals. In contrast, the individualist method asserts that all phenomena of society are explainable only in terms of individuals and their beliefs. According to Jon Elster, an advocate of individualism, "Methodological individualism is the view that all institutions, behavior patterns, and social processes can be explained in terms of individuals only, their actions, properties, and relations" (1986, 22).

The supporters of the individualist method actively attack the relational approach, though they confuse it with extreme collectivism. Thus the well-known individualist philosopher Karl Popper attacks Marxism and the

> theory that the social sciences study the behavior of social wholes, such as groups, nations, classes, societies, civilizations, etc. . . . . This view must be rejected as naive. It overlooks the fact that these so-called social wholes are very largely postulates of popular social theories rather than empirical objects; and that while there are, admittedly, such empirical objects as the crowd of people here assembled, it is quite untrue that names like "the middle class" stand for any such empirical groups. . . . Accordingly, the belief in the empirical existence of social wholes or collectives . . . has to be replaced by the demand that social phenomena, including collectives, should be analyzed in terms of individuals and their actions and relations. (1959, 281)

Popper does a service in criticizing extreme collectivism, which has sometimes made glib or mystic accounts of social wholes greater than their individual parts. But it was noted above that such extreme collectivism is completely different from the position of most Marxian social scientists.

Popper is correct that a class does not exist beyond its "individuals and their actions and relations." He is correct that Marxian political economists must always prove that the majority of individuals in a class are motivated in a certain direction in order to say that a class is motivated in that direction. But most Marxian theorists contend, contrary to Popper, that the relations of all individuals in a properly defined class have something in common. Thus, the concept of class is a meaningful concept. Marxian political economists define each class such that all of its individual members are in roughly the same relation to other classes. For example, in the pre–Civil War South the individuals in the slave and slave owner classes were on average the same in terms of individual biological characteristics (such as average brain capacity) but totally different in terms of their average socioeconomic behavior and most of their ideological beliefs. So a nonclass view of the South at that period would be deficient. Thus, contrary to Karl Popper's belief, the concept of class is both necessary and fruitful in political and economic research in any class-divided society.

Not only are social statistics about groups meaningful but they often result in valid predictions. How is that possible if each individual psyche is so unique? The answer is that the individuals in the groups studied, such as all industrial workers or all African American voters, have the same objective relationship to society in some one aspect. The fact that the relationship is the same produces a meaningful statistical average; otherwise, all such statistics would be useless. For example, on the issue of rent control one can predict the majority response of all landlords and the majority response of all tenants. There will obviously be many exceptions, with some exceptional landlords advocating the tenant side and vice versa. These exceptional responses usually exist because other relationships are more important for these individuals than the one under study. Thus, the landlord-tenant relationship may be overshadowed for some individuals by differences in race, family background, education, geography, and so forth.

Literally everything in the environment goes into shaping our psychologies, so each individual is unique. Yet on any social issue a large proportion of people having the same relation to society will share the same attitude. Most of the deviations will be predictable to the extent that people's other social relationships are known. Concentration on human relations is important because in the social sciences what is termed an *explanation* does not merely describe isolated, alleged facts. A social explanation must link the phenomenon under analysis to other related and already known phenomena. A social analysis expands our knowledge of interconnections or patterns. Understanding society does not mean piling up isolated, individual facts; "understanding or interpretation is a matter of the ordering of . . . facts; that is, determination of their relations" (Dewey 1939, 511). Based on an understanding of these interrelations, one can predict or deduce other social phenomena.

The individualist approach, in contrast, results in abstract discussions of the economics or sociology of isolated individuals (such as Robinson Crusoe on his island). Those who view society as an amorphous collection of such isolated individuals overlook the fact that "society does not consist of individuals; it expresses the sum of connections and relationships in which individuals find themselves. It is as though one were to say: from the standpoint of society there are neither slaves or citizens: both are men. Rather they are so *outside* society. To be a slave or to be a citizen are social determinations, the relationships of Man A and Man B. Man A is not a slave as such. He is a slave within society and because of it" (Marx [1858] 1973, 77).

To speak of the psychology of an individual slave without examining his or her relation to the class of slaves and to the class of slave owners is to understand nothing, not even the slave's psychology. Can anyone believe that a Roman slave or a southern sharecropper

snatched from the cradle and brought up as an emperor or a billionaire would have the same psychological characteristics as an adult
that he or she would have had if this had not occurred?

Conservatives sometimes speak as if alcoholics, "delinquents,"
drug users, and "the poor" were isolated individuals, separate from
each other and separate from the rest of society. Thus each individual
drug user may be labeled as an unusual social deviant who has chosen
drugs, whereas the problem is a particular set of social relationships.
Conservative politicians contend that the unemployed are unemployed because they are lazy or lack confidence in their ability to get
work. The individualist analysis obscures the fact that the problem is
caused by society. Similarly, conservative politicians tell us in speech
after speech about those individuals who have chosen crime, as if it
were not a social problem.

Most Marxian social scientists examine the system as well as the
individual (see Ollman 1973, 504). Thus for Marxism, poverty is not
a problem of failed individuals but one caused by the capitalist economy (see Bluestone 1972; Gordon 1972; and Wachtel 1972). Moreover, it is the class relationships of capitalism, and not the victimized
individuals, that create the widespread frustration and alienation
leading to alcoholism, drug use, and crime (see Bandyopadhyay 1971).

The relational approach sees all problems as interconnected in a
social whole, though the whole is composed of individuals. In this
sense Marxian scholars may be called *holists*. *Holism* means that we
try to grasp the whole forest as well as the individual trees. But as
Karl Popper points out, someone who tries to claim that the forest as
a whole exists without or independently of the trees is talking nonsense. Popper is correct about extreme collectivism but not about the
use of holism by Marxian (and institutionalist) political economists.
A careful holism, which sees both the forest and the trees, clarifies and
emphasizes this aspect of the relational view. Holists frequently refer
to society as an organic whole, which is a useful metaphor as long as
one does not mistakenly claim that society does this or that. Neither
society nor history does things; people do.

Mancur Olson's Critique of Marxian Class Analysis

An extremely important twist to the argument of individual versus
collective behavior was given by Mancur Olson and the enormous literature that has commented on his thesis (see citations in Barbalet
1992). Olson argued that an individual may have interests opposed to
his or her class interests that prevent class action. For example, from

an individual point of view, should a worker participate in a strike? Suppose an individual worker stays home in comfort and safety while all other workers go on strike and win the strike. The worker who stays home will still benefit. This problem, which has become known as the *free rider problem,* is a problem for all movements. Even if I believe that it is necessary to take collective action to protect abortion clinics so that women have the right to choose, I may still believe that it is unsafe for me to protect clinics and that others will do it for me.

The obvious problem for Olson's brilliant concept is that it proves too much. If each individual really calculated in this way, then one could "prove" that there would never be strikes or revolutions. The false conclusion follows from an approach that takes for granted certain false premises. It assumes that individuals are isolated from society, or above society, and therefore are able to calculate dispassionately about social processes. The contrary relational approach asserts that we must understand individuals within the reality of a tight web of social relations.

Obviously, each individual does make some calculation about his or her behavior in each situation. But one immediate qualification is that in many situations people react habitually to certain stimuli without any rational calculation. For example, in recent years the ethnic fighting in Eastern Europe, especially in Yugoslavia, has not been the result of rational calculation of benefits by most individuals; rather it represents deeply ingrained and conditioned responses.

When people do calculate rationally, the calculation is quite complex. What safety or comfort do I gain by not participating in a revolution taking place in my country? The presumed benefit of personal safety must be balanced against the benefits a successful revolution may bring. If I were a Jew living under the fascist occupation of Warsaw in the Second World War, or a black African living in South Africa under apartheid, the dangers of participating in a revolution might be far outweighed by the dangers of allowing the system to continue. Thus, I may find it rational to participate even when I know that my particular contribution may or may not make any difference.

Marxian social scientists have done numerous studies of the conditions under which the individuals constituting a class will have the subjective desire to make a change and will decide that it is rational for them to participate in the movement (see, e.g., Callinicos 1988, 184). Most of these studies have found that under the right circumstances, the decision to participate in a revolution is rational and has been made (as in Russia in 1917 or 1991).

Barbalet (1992) argued that Olson distorted the Marxian position when he attacked Marxism for not paying attention to these problems of collective action. In the first place, most non-Soviet Marxian writers agree with Olson that a majority of the individuals in a class must recognize their class interests and subjectively decide to follow them; otherwise, the mere fact that a class has an interest in changing a system will have no effect. Note that both Olson and most critical Marxian political economists contradict G. A. Cohen's (1978) assumption that if a class has the power to make a revolution and its long-term interests require a revolution, then that class will make a revolution.

In fact, Barbalet argues that the Marxian analysis satisfies those "rational" requirements for collective behavior laid down by Olson: "By sympathetically bringing Olson to bear on Marxian class theory, the problem of movement from a class-in-itself [class interests] to a class-for-itself [individual consciousness of class interests], from structure to action, is redefined. The problem of class formation or action in this context concerns the manner in which small or intermediate groups at the point of capitalist production might federate into a large, mobilized group" (1992, 466). Thus modern radicals have acknowledged the importance of Olson's questions and have integrated them into their own relational approach.

A Post-Marxian Critique of Marxian Class Analysis

Post-Marxism is a school that assumes that all of Marxism consists of the (now dead) views of Stalinist Marxism. It presents most of the usual criticisms of Marxism, but in a modern terminology, while claiming not to be anti-Marxist. (For an excellent, critical discussion of Post-Marxism, see Wolff and Cullenberg 1986.) One representative of this view is Doug Brown (1992). Brown contends that there is a crisis both for theories of class and in the reality of class. He argues (1) that class is still relevant but of declining importance and (2) that there is in the present period more "heterogeneity, pluralization, and individualization" among workers.

Brown contends that in the Post-Marxist outlook "there is no particular consciousness a wage earner should have by virtue of his or her relationship to the means of production" (548). All nonreductionist Marxian social scientists would agree that workers' consciousness will differ somewhat according to race, ethnicity, or gender. That does not mean, however, that class relationships have no effect on consciousness. (Chapter 6 shows that class does play a vital role.)

Brown claims that there are truly divergent interests within the working class related to race, gender, and skills. He finds that the technological revolution of the last two decades has meant increasing differences in workers' skills, leading to differences in life style and consciousness. Most Marxian theorists would agree that the working class is very heterogenous and diversified in both skills and attitudes. That does not mean, however, that workers do not have a common, hostile relationship with corporations. Brown himself concludes that "class is still relevant, but given the fragmentation of postmodern capitalism, it has become less relevant" (551). A hypothesis examined in chapter 6 is that class analysis is still very relevant to political economic analysis.

Myths about Marxian Class Analysis

Some critics of Marxism say that in the Marxian view there are only two classes, that the two classes are always in violent confrontation, and that the capitalist class has absolute control of the government— an easy straw man to refute. For example, one liberal sociologist says that Marxism simply "assumes" that "inherent in the economic organization of any society—save the ultimate communistic society—are forces inevitably generating revolutionary class conflict. . . . Conflict is bipolar, with exploited classes under conditions created by the economy becoming aware of their true 'interests' and eventually forming a revolutionary political organization that stands against the dominant, property-holding class" (Turner 1974, 79). On the contrary, the Marxian approach does not a priori assume the class struggle, but concludes that it exists on the basis of very extensive empirical research. Nor does any non-Soviet Marxian scholar say that class conflict is always bipolar.

In a similar criticism of Marxian class analysis, a neoclassical economist claims that "the dialectic framework of that theory prescribed not only that there be two (and only two) basic classes, but that they exist in sharp antagonism to one another" (Balinky 1970, 38). Marxian class analysis, however, makes use of a multiclass model. The only exception is in a few abstract economic models where a two-class model may be used as the simplest approximation for mathematical convenience, but it is normally made clear that this assumption is unrealistic and will be changed in more realistic models. Even neoclassical economists often use a model in which "labor" and "capital" are the only classes, for both income distribution and growth problems.

Joseph Schumpeter argues that the Marxian view exaggerates the antagonism between capitalists and workers: "To any mind not warped by the habit of fingering the Marxian rosary, it should be obvious that their relation is, in normal times, primarily one of cooperation and that any theory to the contrary must draw largely on pathological cases for verification" (Schumpeter 1950, 19). *In normal times* the subjective view of most workers certainly favors cooperation. In that respect, Schumpeter is certainly correct—and most Marxian writers would agree. There are even cases of great affection of workers for a boss; a secretary may identify with the boss even if the boss exploits the secretary.

In normal times the Marxian approach emphasizes that the majority of the working class sees no alternative to the present system. That was true of most people for most of the period of the Roman Empire and for most of the period of feudalism, and it is equally true for most of the period of capitalism. In normal times the ideology of the ruling class is clearly dominant. Certainly, there are often strikes, class-oriented arguments over taxes, and propaganda for and against unions, but these routine class conflicts are not seen as conflicts between classes by most people. Only in revolutionary, non-normal times is there a mass response to revolutionary ideas; only then do class conflicts sometimes become apparent to all.

Another often repeated myth about Marxian class analysis was restated in a book by a liberal institutionalist, Wendell Gordon, who attacked all radical and Marxian social scientists, but particularly my own work, for "an almost-relished desire for polarized conflict between the bourgeoisie and the proletariat or between the Establishment and 'the people'" (1973, 180). This is the most peculiar criticism of all because it confuses the desire for conflict with the fact of conflict. Marxian political economists find class conflict to be a fact; their goal is to end class conflict and establish a harmonious society. Unlike some conservative theorists, such as Mosca and Pareto, who claim that we can never end the division of society into the mass of poor people and the ruling affluent elite, Marxian scholars do foresee an end to class conflict.

Conclusions

Neoclassical economics assumes that everything in society can be explained at the individual level, particularly by the psychology of individuals. We have seen that this type of reductionism is subject to all of the weaknesses of any type of reductionism. We have also seen that the implications of the individualist method tend to strengthen the status quo. We have found extreme collectivism to be another form of reductionism, reducing all explanations to structures or groups, without consideration of individuals.

Some of the myths that surround Marxian class analysis have been cleared away. All those using the individualist method attack the approach of extreme collectivism, which treats collective entities as if they were somehow above and beyond the individuals that compose them. The accusation has been made—by neoclassical economists, by Post-Marxists, and by many others—that all Marxian social scientists take a position of extreme collectivism as well as economic reductionism. This, however, is a myth because most present-day Marxian writers are completely opposed to both economic reductionism and extreme collectivism.

The critique of individualism and extreme collectivism has so far been very brief. Readers who are interested in a more in-depth critique will find it in the appendixes to this chapter.

Appendix 5A: Individualism and Orthodox Economics

Once again, it is worth recalling that orthodox economists have quite varied opinions and that the dominant opinion has changed over time.

The Classical Period (1770s to 1860s)

The classical economists often discussed nations and classes as well as individuals. Much of classical economics talks about the landlord class, the working class, and the capitalist class, who earn rent, wages, and profit from land, labor, and capital. The classical economists were not extreme collectivists, nor were they extreme individualists.

The Neoclassical Period (1870s to 1930s)

Neoclassical economics always began with the psychology of individuals: the individual consumer maximizes his or her utility based on his or her individual preferences. In that sense, individualism has already been implicitly discussed as part of psychological reductionism, but it is so important that it is worth considering it as analytically separate from the other two pillars of neoclassical economics—psychological reductionism and an ahistorical equilibrium approach.

Example: Robinson Crusoe

Robinson Crusoe was a fictional character who spent much of his life shipwrecked on an island. Many neoclassical economists used Crusoe as the perfect example of how an individual allocates his or her time and material resources so as to maximize his or her utility. Stephen Marglin comments that "the basic idea of mainstream economics that the world can be modelled as a group of Robinson Crusoes who live each on his own island maximizing utility and meeting to trade with each other is not only a simplification but a fundamental distortion of reality" (1989, 92). Such a picture, in which individuals with sets of given preferences meet to trade in the market on an equal basis, ignores the differences of power among groups, such as workers and capitalists. Marglin spells out in great detail how this approach distorts relationships in the labor market, making it appear as if an individual worker met a giant corporation on an equal basis.

Example: Individualism and Who to Blame

Based on the individualist approach, many conservative neoclassical economists tend to blame the victim for all economic problems. For example, the so-called search theory provided an individualist theory of voluntary unemployment. Search theory argued that unemployment is merely the voluntary movement of workers, who leave a job to hunt for higher pay. The search theory argued that workers often have misinformation leading them to believe that better jobs are available when that is not true, so workers voluntarily quit their present jobs to look for new ones (Alchian 1969). This extreme individualist theory is far from the facts of the real world: when General Motors fires fifty thousand workers in a single week, that is not voluntary unemployment.

Another example of the neoclassical theory blaming the victim is the theory's belief that the individual worker chooses how much education to get (balancing it against leisure time). So lack of training and lack of education are due to the preferences of the individual. The truth is that the number of years of education correlates with family income.

According to the neoclassical theory, the individual worker competes in the labor market against all other workers. That competition results in each worker's being paid according to the marginal product he or she produces. Thus, if there is perfect competition in the labor market, a worker who receives less than the average wage must be producing less than the average worker produces (whether due to lack of training, biological inheritance, or some other reason). It follows that the working poor (who work full-time but still get low wages) and all those with lower than average wages (such as women and African Americans) are poorer than others because they are less productive. If the individual is equally productive with other individuals, then competition assures equal wages. The entire approach is unrealistic in the extreme because the choices of workers are actually very limited.

Example: Individualism and Power

If one begins and ends an analysis with individual maximization of utility, then there is no place for consideration of the economic power of a giant corporation or the conflict between various groups. John Kenneth Galbraith, in his presidential address to the American Economic Association, pointed out that because of its lack of recognition of power or conflict, neoclassical economics "offers no useful handle for grasping the economic problems that now beset the modern society. . . . Rather, in eliding power—in making economics a nonpolitical subject—neoclassical theory . . . destroys its relation with the real world" (1973b, 2). Galbraith argues that realistic political economy died when neoclassical theory became "economics" and left "politics" for political scientists.

Example: Individualism and Democracy

By using a purely individualist approach to the expression of democratic will, Milton Friedman claims that the political market of a democracy is defective in that a minority wastes its votes, whereas the economic market of capitalism is a perfect democracy in that each individual gets exactly what his or her votes (dollars) will buy. "That is why the economic market is so far the only mechanism available that provides real individual democracy" (1974, 104). So it is real individual democracy when the billionaire Ross Perot has 3 billion "votes," while a low-paid worker may have only six thousand "votes." The whole socialist critique of political democracy under capitalism is that some people can use enormous wealth to make their opinions dominate the political sphere.

The Keynesian Period, 1930s to 1960s

Keynes makes some gestures toward individualism, as in his fundamental psychological law of consumption, but Keynes is best known for his introduction of aggregates into orthodox analysis. Before Keynes, there was no such thing as aggregate consumer demand in most orthodox analysis. Before Keynes, neoclassical economics was content to discuss only individual consumer demand, both because of its individualist methodology and because of its belief in full-employment equilibrium. In order to explain aggregate involuntary unemployment, Keynes found it necessary to analyze aggregate consumer demand, aggregate investment demand, aggregate government demand, and aggregate foreign demand (net exports). Once these new concepts came into common use, they forever changed economics. Universities no longer taught "economics": they began to teach separate courses in *microeconomics,* the study of individual units, and also *macroeconomics,* the study of aggregate national categories.

Even during the Keynesian period, neoclassical economics continued to dominate the microeconomic theory of prices and wages. Furthermore, neoclassical economists began to branch out in an imperialist endeavor to influence all areas of social science. The most important of these attempts during the Keynesian period was that of Gary Becker.

Example: Individualism, Racism, and Sexism

Gary Becker's imaginative application of neoclassical economics to racism and sexism fully combines all the basic neoclassical assumptions. He begins with the psychological preferences of the individual, rather than human socioeconomic relationships, and he uses an ahistorical analysis of optimal equilibrium. Becker takes as given the subjective preferences or tastes of individuals. He does not limit these individual preferences to goods and services, but extends the category of preferences to include sexual and racial prejudices. Thus he writes: "Discrimination and prejudice are not usually said to occur when someone prefers looking at a glamorous Hollywood actress rather than at some other woman; yet they are said to occur when he prefers living next to whites rather than next to Negroes. At best calling just one of these actions 'discrimination' requires making subtle and rather secondary distinctions" (1957, 5). Becker's individualist approach takes racist prejudice against African Americans or sexist prejudice against women to be the same as an individual's preferring apples to oranges.

Becker's individualist argument assumes as given the preferences or prejudices of individual racists and sexists. But such prejudices are not fixed by something in human biological makeup: they are inculcated by social conditioning. Thus one type of society might prefer Cadillacs and TV sets and white males, but another type of society might prefer bicycles and folk dancing and African American females. Our preferences are made, not born. Second, Becker assumes that all preferences should be allowed because every individual is equal in power and the result is an optimal equilibrium. On the contrary, in the present society one small group of white males holds most of the political and economic power. That economic power is used to promote continued prejudice and continued exploitation against women, minorities, and all workers.

The New Classical and New Keynesian Period, 1970s to the Present

As the New Classical period began, the neoclassical method was applied to everything and anything. First and foremost, it was claimed that Keynesian aggregate concepts themselves must be given foundations in an individualist, psychological, and equilibrium analysis. Thus, aggregate consumer demand was explained, not in terms of class behavior and the income distribution between groups, but solely by hypotheses about how individual consumer psychology works toward optimization (for example, in the "permanent income hypothesis" of Milton Friedman).

This attempt at individualist foundations for macroeconomic aggregates began in part in the Keynesian period, but it later became so dominant that some beginning graduate theory courses in "macroeconomics" never discussed any aggregate concepts, only theories of individual optimization. In this way, the New Classical economists tried to restore the neoclassical dominance in the field of macroeconomics that had been created by Keynes. They succeeded in telling another generation of students that aggregate involuntary unemployment is impossible for more than a brief period of adjustment to equilibrium. Many New Classical economists in this period continued Becker's program, of extending their analysis to other areas, such as environmental issues and welfare issues.

Example: Individualism and the Environment

A critique by Peter Soderbaum (1990) argues that the usual neoclassical approach to environmental problems limits itself to the purely individual economic costs of environmental destruction. Neoclassical economists examine only individual costs even when doing cost-benefit studies of environmental impacts of new projects. Soderbaum contends that this is totally inadequate because environmental problems require an interdisciplinary approach to the entire environment, not just to costs clearly allocated to individuals. Such a report should not merely emphasize economic factors such as dollar cost (which can be apportioned to individuals); it must also consider the biological impact on nature as well as the biological impact on human beings.

Example: Individualism and Human Welfare

New Classical economists tend unconsciously to accept the economic status quo, mainly by acceptance of an individualist methodology reflected in the technical apparatus at the heart of so-called welfare economics. New Classical economists are trained to search for the competitive equilibrium that will be optimal for all individual consumers and individual producers. New Classical welfare economics sees any departure from this mythical point of social harmony as hurting everyone through the loss of efficiency. According to the New Classical rule called Pareto optimality, improvement beyond the present point is defined to mean movement to a new point where some people may be better off but no one individual will be worse off. This rule is accepted because individualist economics knows no way to balance possible gains to many individuals against losses by a single individual. In this view, there is no criterion other than the individual's utility; therefore, the present institutions and distribution of wealth are assumed to be among the given facts. The technical argument is that no two individuals have the same psychology, so an additional dollar has a different utility to different individuals. In pure New Classical welfare economics, "interpersonal comparisons are verboten" (Lekachman 1973, 307).

For example, New Classical welfare economists would say that there is no "scientific" way to tell if total utility or happiness would be improved by taking $1 million from a billionaire (a Ross Perot or a Du Pont) and, by so doing, giving $1 to each of 1 million unemployed workers. Since there is no way to compare different individual income distributions, so-called welfare economics takes the income of each individual as given and concentrates all its energy on the goal of "efficiency" (Pareto optimality in the jargon of economists).

It follows, according to most New Classical welfare economists, that class conflict over income redistribution must always be destructive, because some individual is losing. To put the point most strongly, based on these criteria, it would be impossible to prove that a slave society would be better off if it abolished slavery. While the slaves would be better off, the slave owners would be worse off, and who can calculate the subjective pain of losing slaves? (For the most thorough critique of neoclassical and New Classical welfare economics, as well as an alternative radical or Marxian view, see Hahnel and Albert 1990.)

New Keynesian Theory

As noted in earlier chapters, the New Keynesians have also done much new theoretical work within the neoclassical methodology, but they have come to very different conclusions from those reached by New Classical economists. In particular, the New Keynesians have shown various ways that equilibrium may be below full employment, generating involuntary unemployment.

For the purpose of this chapter, however, it must be noted that all of these new theories continue to use an individualist methodology. They have changed their analysis of macroeconomic issues and some of its policy conclusions, but they are proud of doing it within the accepted individualist and psychological reductionist methodology.

Appendix 5B: Individualist Methodology in Analytic Marxism

Most of this chapter deals with the individualist assault on class analysis by conservatives and liberals, but there is also a heated debate concerning these issues within contemporary Marxism. It centers around the school that calls itself Analytic Marxism. According to Eric Olin Wright, Analytic Marxism is "the systematic interrogation and clarification of basic [Marxian] concepts and their reconstruction into a more coherent theoretical structure" (1985, 2). If that were the complete description of Analytic Marxism, then I, together with all good Marxian scholars, would be a member of that school. To the extent that Analytic Marxists argue that (1) nothing (including Marxism) should be taken on faith and (2) one must pursue social analysis rigorously with a careful methodology, they are in agreement with, and part of, the general stream of all independent, critical Marxian and radical writers.

Unfortunately, Analytic Marxism is split because some members oppose, while some members espouse, an individualist approach or methodology. Eric Olin Wright says he is an Analytic Marxist, but his main work is on class. So it is not surprising that Wright himself is

opposed to the reduction of class to individuals, and he is opposed to
the basic assumption of methodological individualism: "If Marxist
class analysis is to advance, it is essential that it develop what is sometimes called 'micro-foundations,' but this does not imply that all of
the causal processes in class theory can be adequately represented at
the level of individuals and their interactions" (276). Wright is concerned about the dogmatic assertions by some extreme collectivist
writings that classes are super entities, but unlike other members of
the school, he accepts the common-sense criticism of the extreme collectivist position without going to the other extreme of individualist
methodology (see Wright's critique of individualist methodology in
Levine, Sober, and Wright 1987). People such as Wright, who hold a
nonreductionist relational view of class, should simply be called
Marxists, because nothing distinguishes them as a school.

The individualist methodology of some leading Analytic Marxists
involves *rational choice theory,* the notion of determination by individual preferences as stated in New Classical economics. In defending
Analytic Marxism, Thomas Mayer says, "Explanation in the social
sciences should start with the assumption that social actors are selfish
and rational" (1990, 421). In fact Analytic Marxism has also been
called rational choice Marxism, individualist Marxism, or even—by
its enemies—neoclassical Marxism. Jon Elster, who calls himself an
Analytic Marxist, advocates the rational choice theory, which, he
says, assumes "that structural constraints do not completely determine the actions taken by individuals in a society" (Elster, quoted in
Callinicos 1988, 78). If this merely means that people make choices
based on all of their social constraints, it is a platitude; but if it means
that preferences are formed by something outside all of the relations
of society, then it is wrong.

Elster attacks an extreme collectivist methodology, which he claims
is held by Marxian social scientists, saying: "Methodological collectivism . . . assumes there are supra-individual entities that are prior to
individuals in the explanatory order" (Elster 1985, 6). Of course there
are no supra-individual entities, such as classes or nations, that are
prior to individuals; but nonreductionist, critical Marxism does not
hold this view. Classes are composed of individuals, so how can they
be prior to individuals? Elster takes the extreme position that everything can be reduced to individuals and their preferences. In talking
about individual preferences, he sneaks in social relations to explain
individuals by his assumption that individuals live in society.

Perhaps the Analytic Marxist who takes rational choice theory to the furthest extreme is Adam Przeworski, who contends that people actually exercise individual preferences to choose the class to which they wish to belong (see Przeworski 1985). For example, Mrs. Jones owns land but also has work skills, so she may choose whether to be a landlord or a worker. Przeworski's view is discussed below along with the similar view of John Roemer.

John Roemer is one of the most important Analytic Marxists (see Roemer 1986). Roemer is a radical and argues for democratic socialism, but he believes in a psychological reductionist, individualist, ahistorical, equilibrium methodology. Roemer claims that "methodological individualism and the equilibrium method are essential for Marxist analysis" and, further, that "aggregate behavior must fundamentally be explained as the consequence of individual utility maximization. . . . the most convincing . . . explanation of a social phenomenon is one . . . that explains the phenomenon as the result of individuals pursuing their interests, as they perceive them, subject to the constraints they face" (1989, 378). According to the most sympathetic interpretation, this is a tautology; he is merely insisting that collective behavior can always be traced back to individual behavior. But all the rest of Roemer's writings, when they are subjected to an analytic dissection (as fitting for Analytic Marxism), indicate that he goes much further than this tautology and arrives at the usual individualist method of neoclassical economics. (Note that Roemer also uses an ahistorical equilibrium method, which was criticized in chapter 4.)

Roemer agrees with Przeworski that individuals are free to prefer and choose to be in whatever class they wish: "An agent can sell his labor power, use it to work in his own shop, and/or purchase the labor power of others" (Roemer 1989, 390). Note first the terminology: he uses the neutral term *agent,* as if people were not born into a capitalist or worker or other class, and he uses *his,* apparently assuming that all agents are men. He has conveniently forgotten the social constraints mentioned by him in the previous quote. He says that an agent can choose to work in his or her own shop, but where does this person get the money to buy the shop? He says that a person can choose to purchase the labor power of others, but where does the person get the money to do so? Could an unemployed person make a rational choice to buy a shop and employ others? In many examples, Roemer assumes that individuals own certain productive assets, but this assumption sneaks in the basic class relations of capitalism. He claims that his model of individual choice produces classes as a result of choice, but actually it assumes class relations (and the government to protect capitalist property) when it allows "agents" those choices.

The strongest criticism of individualist methodology in the 1970s came from John Roemer, who stated a stark contrast between two methods: "The classical economists and Marx placed *society* at the center of the economic system and the individual on the periphery. Neoclassical theory reverted to a Ptolemaic error by placing the individual at the center" (1978, 148, reprinted in the excellent collection by King [1990]). So the strongest critic of the later Roemer is the same Roemer before his conversion! In fact Roemer's description of Marxism ("the individual on the periphery") sounds more like economic reductionism and extreme collectivism than a careful nonreductionist Marxism, so perhaps his later self was merely reacting against the dogmatic position of his earlier self.

One of the early Roemer's criticisms of the later Roemer's position is quite trenchant. He points out that constrained optimization by rational individuals is the main neoclassical tool, but "the economic problem for the . . . worker is not one of constrained optimization. Workers' income is sufficiently small that their discretionary choice is trivial, their training and social position is not such as to provide a real latitude in choice of job. What choice the worker does encounter is of no real consequence—beer versus wine, auto assembly versus warehouse work" (1978, 151). Note that this point strongly undercuts the notion that workers can rationally choose what class they wish to belong to.

Two critics of individualist Analytic Marxism note that it is reacting not merely against an extremist dogma but also to the attractions of being in the dominant viewpoint: "A specter is haunting Marxism, the specter of respectability" (Anderson and Thompson 1988, 215). In the long period of a rising tide of conservative ideology in the 1970s and 1980s, the social sciences drifted away from the radicalism of the 1960s. The direction, unconscious in most cases, was toward the legitimacy, respectability, and material benefits associated with the dominant viewpoint in each of the social sciences. This is a normal happening in every reactionary era. It will be reversed only when new mass protest movements give intellectuals a new impetus.

Three other critics state that Roemer's Analytic Marxism includes a psychological reductionism in that it traces everything to the level of individual preferences, but individual preferences are not explained and are prior to the system: "The historical formation of intentions is presumed to take place prior to economic behavior" (Amariglio, Callari, and Cullenberg 1989, 424). But this psychological reductionism is not obvious, because "the agents who comprise the economic structure are endowed initially with those attributes which are functional to the system of exchange" (423). So the socioeconomic system appears to be formed from individual intentions and behavior, but those intentions are really assumed to be such as will produce exactly that system. (For Roemer's various implied assumptions, see the detailed exposition in Devine and Dymski 1991.)

An insightful critique of Analytic Marxism by E. K. Hunt concludes that "in their efforts to make Marx scientifically rigorous, they have rejected as unscientific nearly every tenet of traditional Marxism. One person's *rigor* appears as another person's *mortis*" (1992a, 92). Another critic points out that Analytic Marxism was in part a reaction against extreme collectivism or structuralism but that the Analytic Marxists went to the other extreme of denying the importance of class relations of production, the basis of Marx's political economy (Wood 1989; see also Lebowitz 1988).

Howard and King point out that "Marx claims (rightly) that the characteristics of individuals (such as their preferences), the degree of technological sophistication, and property rights are all highly interdependent. Roemer's neoclassical methodology . . . treats them as independent" (1989b, 401). Individual choices guide Roemer's whole system. According to Howard and King, neoclassical economists "have always prided themselves on . . . showing how the performance of economic systems may be derived from choices, or from the exogenous determinants of these choices (preferences, technologies and endowments)" (403). It is true that economic reductionism often reduces everything to economic factors and ignores individual choices, while Roemer reduces everything to individuals and their choices. Howard and King ask, If one can reduce the social sciences to individual psychology, why doesn't Roemer go further to reduce psychology to biological components and then reduce biology to physics?

The critics of individualism cite three limitations to individualist methodology: (1) the very concept of an individual differs in different societies, so the individual is socially constructed; (2) some things are better explained by structures or processes, without direct reference to individual choices; and (3) individuals do not always react "rationally in the narrow neoclassical sense" (Howard and King 1989b, 408). They emphasize that opposing individual choice to social process, as Roemer and Elster do, is a false dichotomy because individuals only exist within society.

Appendix 5C: Liberal Institutionalist Views of Individualism and Class

Liberal institutionalism is a sort of halfway house between neoclassical individualism and Marxian class analysis. The liberal institutionalists make every argument against neoclassical individualism made earlier in this chapter, but they also attack Marxian class analysis. Both institutionalist and Marxian scholars might be called moderate or mild collectivists in that they see groups and classes as existing and important, but not above and beyond individuals.

At the present time, John Kenneth Galbraith is perhaps the most important follower of the liberal version of the institutionalist viewpoint. Galbraith is very perceptive and incisive in his denunciation of the neoclassical view that individuals control the market and the political process and that optimum utility results. "In the neoclassical view of the economy a general identity of interest between the goals of the business firm and those of the community could be assumed. The firm was subject to the instruction of the community, either through the market or the ballot box. People could not be fundamentally in conflict with themselves" (Galbraith 1973b, 6). Contrary to the neoclassical view, Galbraith says: "There can no longer . . . be any separation by economists between economics and politics. When the modern corporation acquires power over markets, power in the community, power over the state, power over belief, it is a political instrument" (Galbraith 1973b, 6). It should be stressed that the view that corporations have "power over the state" is close in substance (though different in terminology) to the Marxian view that under capitalism the long-term interests of the capitalist class normally prevail in the state.

The most thorough discussion of power in institutionalism states that "it is the structure of power . . . which governs whose interests are to count for resource allocation, income and wealth distribution" (Samuels 1979, iii). Samuels locates power primarily in the giant corporations: "Whether one refers to the typical manufacturing industry as oligopolistic . . . or by some other term, the great bulk are dominated by a relative . . . handful of firms" (Samuels 1979, iii). He contrasts this realistic institutionalist picture of power and conflict with the neoclassical view of individual consumer sovereignty over the economy and individual voter sovereignty over the state. Samuels notes that the institutionalist view implies corporate power and a lack of social harmony. This view is very similar to the Marxian view, though it is stated in different terms.

Another well-known liberal institutionalist says flatly, "Institution-alists take conflict rather than harmony as their point of departure in economic analysis" (Gruchy 1973, 623). Again, this sounds like Marxism, but while liberal institutionalists are very critical of the neoclassicals, they also distinguish their position from the Marxian view. In the liberal institutionalist view, "The neo-Marxians have a dualistic theory of the economic system that reduces everything to a contest between two classes, the capitalists and the proletariat. In contrast, the neo-institutionalists have a pluralistic theory of the economic system that reduces everything to a struggle among a number of competing power groups. Furthermore, there is nothing like the Marxian concept of class struggle in the neo-institutionalists' analysis of the functioning of the class system" (Gruchy 1984, 551). Reduction to two classes is a myth, since the view of most contemporary Marxians is completely opposed to such reductionism.

A difference does remain, however, between Marxian and liberal institutionalist writers concerning whether power is exercised by multiple interest groups or through class conflict. While conservative economists tend to see only harmony, liberal institutionalists certainly do recognize some conflicts among many different interest groups. For example, two liberals attack conservatives for not seeing plural interests in a battle over the emission of pollutants: "The combatant parties include the manufacturer . . . responsible for the emissions . . . and the affected parties; . . . the neutral party is the federal government" (D'Arge and Wilen 1974, 362). These two liberals assume without evidence that the government is neutral and above class conflict. Similarly, they assume that social scientists are above class conflict. Therefore, they propose as a solution "a reasoned noncommittal or neutral review of the evidence by a public official or member of the scientific community" (364). They also suggest the "establishment of an impartial body whose sole function is the gathering and processing of pertinent information. . . . such an agency should be immune or indifferent to the pressures of conflicting parties" (367). Unfortunately, this view paints a too pleasant and naive picture of both the government and the academic community. They should look at various state pollution boards' day-to-day decisions in favor of business interests.

In a similar liberal critique of the Marxian class analysis, Galbraith maintains that "the modern state is not the executive committee of the bourgeoisie, but it *is* more nearly the executive committee of the technostructure" (1973a, 172; see also the critique of Galbraith in Sweezy 1973). Galbraith defines the technostructure as a group composed of scientists, engineers, advertising people, lawyers, and coordinators. Surely, someone should break the news to the DuPonts and the Ross Perots that it is not they, but their hired engineers and legal experts, who really control their corporate empires and that it is really the middle-class technostructure, and not the wealthy, who control the U.S. government. Certainly, some managers control their firms to the detriment of small stockholders, but those managers are mostly large stockholders themselves. So the capitalist class still controls capitalism and still wields power in the government.

The weakness of the liberal position can be seen best in the reforms and tactics proposed by the liberals. Galbraith proposes to pass laws to regulate monopoly by educating the voters to "the public interest," but doesn't every voter have some class interest? According to Galbraith, the most vital reform in Congress "is for a congressional budget committee" (1973a, 299). He speaks as if another congressional committee would change the balance of class forces. In fact the budget process has been reformed in the direction Galbraith specified. But the continuing budget crisis reveals that the problem is the class interests of the rich, who have profits and capital gains, versus the poor and middle-income groups, who have labor income. The problem is not the lack of congressional committee processes but the conflict between class interests, which sometimes are reflected partly by political conflicts.

It must be stressed that institutionalists are a very heterogeneous group, ranging from liberals to radicals, with a densely packed spectrum of views in between. It is important to note, moreover, that the school of radical institutionalists, beginning with the radical Thorstein Veblen, has challenged each of the liberal views and has presented quite opposite views. The clearest presentation of modern, radical institutionalism is by Dugger (1989, 1992). It is clear from Dugger's books that radical institutionalists continue to use the language of power rather than class, but that they are open to consideration of class when it seems useful to the study of power relationships.

Class Analysis

C lass analysis may be seen as the most important substantive application of the relational-historical method. It is the key entry point into Marxian social science.

Problems of Defining Class

According to the individualist view, "The concept of class, and that of 'discontinuity' (class struggle) are eliminated and replaced by notions of classes and strata which have status, power, and prestige. In this conception there is a continuous scale" (Colfax and Roach 1973, 62). The individualist concept of class, now discarded by most social scientists, described a class (say the upper middle class) as having a little more income, a little more status, and a little more prestige than the class below it, so the criteria were continuous and quantitative. In contrast, the Marxian definition is based on qualitative differences. In the Marxian view, each class stands in a different relation to the means of production and other classes, so some classes may exploit others.

A Marxian analysis of class relations begins with a relational definition of class. A class is not defined by more or less of some set of characteristics, but by its relation to another class in the production process. There is no eternal elite and no eternal underclass. Rather, a class relationship is specific to one mode of production. Of course there may also be nonclass societies. There are two excellent discussions of the problems of defining class by Marxian writers: Wright 1985 and Resnick and Wolff 1987. This analysis draws on their insights, though it does not follow either one on some issues.

Definitions and concepts of class have important political implications. For example, if there are only two classes in capitalism, and if capitalists are always dominant over workers in politics, then the only way to make basic changes in class relations is by a revolution. If after a socialist revolution only the working class remains and it runs the government, then there must be perfect democracy by definition. Soviet Marxism tended toward these conclusions in its popular propaganda.

Of course one can formulate any definition as long as it is constant during a discussion. Moreover, somewhat different definitions of class will be useful for tackling different problems. In an abstract model of exploitation, two classes are sufficient to clarify the main issues. Marx used such a model in volume 1 of *Capital,* but he made it perfectly clear that this was a simplification of reality: "The actual composition of society . . . by no means consists of only two classes, workers and industrial capitalists" (1968, 493). Present-day Marxian social scientists use a multiclass model when they ask concrete political or historical questions. In fact neoclassical economists also use an abstract, two-factor model—of labor and capital—to explain the simplest case of distribution of income. There is nothing wrong with such simplification unless it is used to draw policy conclusions, for which a more realistic model is necessary.

In discussing any real historical case, such as the origins and development of the French Revolution, one must use a definition that will grasp the very complex multiclass conflicts that shaped this event. The same multiclass analysis will be necessary in an examination of a budget battle in the U.S. Congress. In terms of the understanding of politics and tactics by the Left in modern capitalist countries, a two-class concept of reality is a disaster. There is no homogenous working-class majority, so class coalitions are necessary tactics, and a Marxian analysis must include "the middle class," as discussed below.

Marxian class analysis, if used properly, can be a very helpful tool in democratic politics. It forces political analysts to go beyond personalities and ask what class interests are involved in each issue. In the contemporary Marxian view, this requires a very complex analysis of the many classes and class strata. Marxian analysis exposes the fact that political democracy under capitalism is limited by the awesome power of money and wealth, which makes the playing field very uneven.

Because it is based on a class analysis, Marxian research leads to the conclusion that there will be a very limited political democracy unless democracy is extended to the economy. According to class analysis, a high degree of economic democracy—the control of the economy by the people through democratic processes in national, state, local, and enterprise elections—is the only firm foundation for a vibrant political democracy.

What Is the Middle Class?

Any class analysis of the United States must define and explain the middle class because most U.S. citizens, when they think of class at all, think of themselves as middle class. Barbara Ehrenreich poses the issues: "Karl Marx predicted that capitalist society would eventually be torn apart by the conflict between a greedy bourgeoisie and a vast rebellious proletariat. He did not foresee the emergence within capitalism of a vast middle class that would mediate between the extremes and create a stable social order. But with the middle class in apparent decline and with the extremes diverging further from each other, it would be easy to conclude that the Marxist vision at last fits America's future" (1991, 203, from a set of very amusing and provocative essays). For the objective data on the "decline of the middle class" in recent decades, see the exceptionally thorough study by Winnick (1989).

One hundred years ago most of the United States was composed of small farmers and small business people. Since most of these small, family enterprises did not hire anyone, their owners were neither capitalists nor workers from a relational point of view. Both groups certainly could have been called middle class. Today those two categories are tiny remnants.

There is, however, a new set of groups that could be described as middle class, including managers and professionals. There is a widespread debate among Marxian scholars over exactly how to categorize these new groups. Since they are all in a relation of employee to employer, one could argue that they are all workers, albeit white-collar, higher-income, salaried workers. Or one could characterize them by their degree of dominance and power, or by how close they are ideologically to capitalists or to workers.

Eric Olin Wright suggests that managers and professionals are in a somewhat contradictory class position. On the one hand, they are not ordinary workers in that they have more power, prestige, and income; they tend to identify ideologically with the capitalist class; and they often are in positions of power or control over other workers. On the other hand, they are still paid employees and may have a far lower income than their capitalist employers. Managers dominate workers and can tell workers what to do, yet they must also do as they are told.

Professionals do not own the means of production, must sell their labor power for a salary, and must take orders on the job, so they might appear to be workers from a relational viewpoint. Yet they also have a different relationship to other workers and to the corporation. Professionals have a wide degree of independence and control over their immediate environment. Wright argues that professionals are like ordinary workers in that they do not own the means of production, but they "have interests opposed to workers because of their effective control of organization and skill assets" (1985, 87). In assuming that professional experts have power because of their "skill assets," Wright is asserting that the sale of one's skills may put one in a position to exploit others. When it is stated so strongly, this notion that exploitation of others may occur through the exchange of one's skills in the market, is contrary to the Marxian view that exploitation results from control over the production process. The view that exploitation can be explained by individual exchange in the market is contrary to the relational methodological approach and is valid, if at all, only within the neoclassical paradigm.

Taken to a lesser extreme, however, Wright's point that people are sometimes placed in contradictory positions between capitalists and workers has a large measure of common sense to it. It is not important whether these groups are described as strata of the working class, as middle classes, or as being in contradictory positions. Behind these verbal differences is an important issue that may be stated as follows: For tactical political purposes as well as scholarly understanding, we need to recognize that in some situations some of these groups will gravitate toward a procapitalist consciousness, based on some procapitalist interests arising from their unique relationships to production and other classes. Yet in other situations they may gravitate toward working-class consciousness, based on some pro–working-class interests in their relationships to production and other classes.

A Factual Analysis of the Middle Class

The above theoretical analysis of the middle class poses the issues but leaves the answers very vague because the nature of the middle class is partly an empirical issue. Given the relational framework, we may examine the empirical results by Wright (1985), bearing on the relation of the present middle class to other classes, but see also the interesting collection of criticisms of Wright in Wright 1989.

Wright (1985, 194–96) finds that the "bourgeoisie," living primarily on property income, make up 2 percent of the economically active population (all data here are rounded). The "petty bourgeoisie," that is, people who are self-employed but have no employees, make up 7 percent. Small business persons, that is, employers of only a few people, constitute 6 percent, managers 12 percent, and supervisors, 17 percent. Experts and technical workers constitute 16 percent. Finally, wage workers, manual and nonmanual workers as well as productive and nonproductive workers, make up 40 percent of the active working population.

According to Wright (1985), capitalist countries have different degrees of inequality. In Sweden the income of those in the 95th percentile was only three times that of those in the 5th percentile of income receivers. In the United States, in contrast, the difference was 13 to 1, one of the more unequal among capitalist distributions of income. The extreme differences in income and wealth in the United States mean that there is greater polarization and a relatively smaller middle class in the United States than in a country like Sweden.

A Factual Analysis of the Working Class

Part of the confusion in the United States over who constitutes the middle class comes from confusion over who constitutes the working class. A few facts will help clarify our theoretical understanding of the working class. Remember that Wright found 40 percent of the active working population to be clearly in the category "worker," even leaving aside all self-employed and all levels of managers, supervisors, professionals, and technical experts.

Nonmanual, white-collar workers might be considered middle class, but Wright's study finds that their attitudes, incomes, and productive relationships are actually quite similar to those of blue-collar workers. At least, white-collar workers are far more similar to blue-collar workers than the current myths would indicate. Also, within the working class Wright (1985) finds no evidence of much distinction between manual and nonmanual workers, either in consciousness or in income. Nor does he find any evidence—in attitudes, behavior, or income—to indicate that the division into productive and nonproductive workers is a useful empirical division for workers. Note that he generally defines nonproductive workers to be in retail sales, finance, insurance, and government—a controversial definition.

Very important for a clear class analysis is the point by Wright (1985) that workers' attitudes are shaped far more by their previous work experiences than by their present work experience. Thus all workers have the common experiences of being forced to sell their labor power in order to live, being subordinate at the work place, and having no control over the use of the surplus. But previous experiences may differ in many ways, for example, by race and gender. Thus, a woman who has been previously limited to housework will have a somewhat different attitude than a woman who has worked at paid labor all her life. Finally, workers may be pulled in different directions by *(a)* holding jobs at two different levels, *(b)* living with someone whose job is at a different level or even in a different class, and *(c)* going through rapid changes (for example, from student to assistant professor to tenure).

When Marxian researchers go beyond theory to fact, what is the relation of class to race and gender? Wright (1985, 192–201) finds that women make up a majority of the working class! In other words, women constitute 61 percent of unskilled workers and 53 percent of all workers. Yet women make up only 30 percent of small employers, 32 percent of managers, and 26 percent of skilled workers. In the active economic population, 57 percent of white women, 78 percent of African American women, 69 percent of African American males, but only 27 percent of white males are workers. It is fascinating for a class analysis that among the dominant group of white males, more are in the middle strata (or new middle classes, if you will) than are in the "worker" category, at least according to Wright's definition. On the other hand, among the active economic population only 10 percent of white women are managers, along with only 8 percent of African American men and only 6 percent of African American women, but 17 percent of white males are managers and supervisors. Finally, two-thirds of all unskilled workers are women and African Americans.

It should be remembered that not all employment is in the private sector. In the United States, 18 percent of all ordinary workers and 30 percent of all experts are hired by federal, state, and local governments. Thus a very significant portion of the labor force is employed in the public sector. Any model of the United States as a pure capitalist economy is wrong.

In 1980, according to Wright (1985, 235), income in the United States rose by class as follows: unskilled workers had a mean income of $11,161; skilled workers, $16,034; supervisors, $23,057; small employers, $24,828; managers, $28,665; and the bourgeoisie, $52,621. Note that income derives from one's class position, but class is not defined by income. The finding that ordinary workers reported unearned (or property) income of only $363 annually, but managers reported unearned income of $1,646, is especially important. Thus, the average worker has very little stake in the present system of class relations, but the average manager owns enough income-producing property to have a significant stake in the capitalist system, and, of course, top managers of large firms have a large amount of unearned income.

A Relational Approach to Class Conflicts

The relational method emphasizes the need to look at human beings not as isolated individuals but as part of groups that are related to one another and sometimes in conflict. Marxian theorists do not argue that conflict must always exist in society, but they do insist that the question should always be asked, Are the class relations of this society antagonistic ones? Are there other conflicts as well?

Contemporary Marxian scholars have explored not only class conflicts but conflicts between big business and small business, racial conflicts, gender conflicts, nationality conflicts, and environmental conflicts, as well as how all of these are related in a given society. The critical method of Marxism, which asks relational questions, specifically questions about antagonistic relations, provides a useful approach for examining each of these conflicts.

Nothing in nonreductionist Marxism says that class conflict is the only conflict or even that it is always the most important. Class relations and class conflict are considered to be the best point for beginning to understand the structure of any class-divided society. Unless one understands the socioeconomic process of a society, one cannot understand race, gender, or nationality within it. Once one has found and examined class conflicts, however, the critical method of Marxism insists, one must then study separately racial, gender, and nationality conflicts. Of course one must examine how each of these conflicts is affected by class conflict, but one must also examine how class conflict is affected by racial, gender, and nationality conflicts. As one example of class and economic process affecting race, at the time of the 1992 Los Angeles riots (which were perceived in the media solely in racial terms) 43 percent of all African American youths in the riot area aged sixteen to nineteen were unemployed, which surely explained much of the rage and frustration. As one example of race affecting class, the riots in Los Angeles led to an outcry for more help for the inner cities, which may benefit all poor people, not just the African American poor.

Three Levels of Class Conflict in the Historical Process

Marxian writers using the relational method argue that it is wrong to speak as if one only had to pay attention to the economic level of class conflict. They insist on a careful investigation at three levels, each of which must be considered in reaching a proper understanding: (1) the purely economic level, (2) the level of political and social institutions, and (3) the ideological level. Because of these different levels of class conflict, class is a concept that unites the Marxian approach in anthropology, economics, history, political science, and sociology (see the discussion of this point in Elliott 1979; see also Miliband 1990). Because class is a central Marxian concept, it is the reason that Marxian scholars frequently stray into various related disciplines. In fact they should stray as often as possible, since most real-world problems are multidisciplinary given that there is only one society with many interrelated aspects.

At the economic level, a class is defined by its relation to other classes and the means of production. Marxian social scientists should ask the question, Who controls the means of production, and who works with the means of production? The question must also be asked whether one class (or classes) may exploit others, while one class (or classes) is exploited. Marxian researchers answer that in every class-divided social formation such exploitation in the process of production does exist. Wolff and Resnick make the careful statement that "classes are . . . defined as groups of persons who share the common . . . position of performing surplus labor [such as workers] or of appropriating it from the performers [such as capitalists] or of obtaining . . . shares of surplus from the appropriators [such as financiers]" (1986, 98). The Marxian historian G. E. M. de St. Croix comments that class is "the way in which exploitation is embodied in a social structure. By *exploitation* I mean the appropriation of part of the labour of others" (1981, 51). The Marxian concept of exploitation is at the heart of Marxian class analysis. By definition, exploitation occurs when one class appropriates without payment the surplus labor of another class.

Most Marxian researchers divide the work day—whether in a system of slavery, feudalism, or capitalism—into the necessary labor time and surplus labor time. Necessary labor time is that working time that goes to feed, clothe, and shelter the worker, while surplus labor time is that time during which products are produced beyond the necessary amount. Even under slavery, the slave is given food, clothing, and shelter, but Marxian historians point out that the slave also works beyond the amount needed to produce the daily necessities, providing surplus labor to the slave owner. Similarly, under capitalism the worker not only does necessary labor for his or her own necessities but continues to work much longer, providing surplus labor to the capitalist. Thus it is their role in the production process as exploiter or exploited that defines the capitalist class and the working class.

Slave economies and capitalist economies are similar in the fact of exploitation, but what distinguishes these two types of class economies? Marxian political economists stress that the differences between different class societies are based on the form of exploitation or appropriation of surplus labor. Marx wrote that "the essential difference between the various economic forms of society, between, for instance, a society based on slave labor, and one based on wage labor, lies only in the mode in which this surplus labor is in each case extracted from the actual producer, the laborer" (Marx [1867] 1965, 217). Thus, the mode of extraction of surplus labor (the form of exploitation) by one class of another is for Marxian writers the determining feature of the entire mode of production. For example, under slavery the slave can be bought and sold like any other tool of production, but workers under capitalism may voluntarily change jobs and make a new contract, so they can be fired, but they cannot be sold to another capitalist.

Since class relations are the key defining feature of each mode of production, it is easy to see why Marxian social scientists treat class relations of exploitation as the place where one should start in doing social science research. An intensive empirical study by Miliband found that "class conflict remained the most important, indeed the absolutely central, fact in the life of advanced capitalist societies" (1991a, v).

Similarly, in a debate led by Robert Brenner on the transition from feudalism to capitalism, Brenner argued against historians who gave priority to many other factors, such as trade or demographic trends. "For Brenner and for many Marxist historians, the issue of class exploitation and class struggle is fundamental for understanding essential aspects of the medieval economy" (R. H. Hilton, in Ashton and Philpin 1985, 5).

The relation of classes to the means of production is not simply a question of ownership (or the laws in which ownership is embodied). Some Marxian theorists have used property ownership as the main criterion for class, but the real issues are the power to exploit (rather than just ownership) and the control of the means of production (rather than just the legal rights of ownership). The laws defining Roman slavery were preceded by the conquest and enslavement of peoples, so the exploitation of slaves rests on these socioeconomic bases.

Under capitalism, we usually speak of ownership of capital as a defining characteristic of capitalists, but it is the control, not the legal ownership, that is important. More generally, it is not the laws of ownership but the power to make decisions in the enterprise that is crucial. Thus a manager without ownership may nevertheless have control of the means of production and, consequently, the power over workers that goes with it. Moreover, the manager may be able to determine his or her own salary, which will then incorporate much profit or surplus labor. In this respect, corporate capitalism does differ from individual capitalism, where there is only one owner or a few partners.

Perhaps the best example of how legal forms may not reflect power was the former Soviet Union. All of the means of production in the Soviet Union were owned by the state for many decades. It was argued that the working class (or the whole people) controlled the state. The argument that the whole people owned the means of production was used to support the statement that there were no classes and no exploitation in the Soviet Union. In fact a small elite class had political control of the Soviet Union, which meant control of the state, which in turn meant control of the means of production. The Soviet ruling class used that control to set their own salaries, so the salaries of the Soviet ruling class did contain surplus labor extracted from the Soviet worker. In this sense, the former Soviet ruling class had much in common with the U.S. ruling class. On the other hand, the unity of political and economic control made the Soviet ruling class quite different from the U.S. ruling class.

A second level of class conflict is within the political structure. Marxian researchers using a class analysis recognize that there is a close relationship between politics and economics. That relationship has been closer in some social formations, such as the Soviet Union, than in others. As a result in the last few decades some Marxian scholars have argued that political domination should be part of the definition of class. They wish to integrate the concept of the ruling class with that of the exploiting class; they may even argue that domination is a more important concept than exploitation. While accepting the fact that political domination is important and directly affects the economy, to include political domination within the definition of class would give rise to much confusion. One can argue that something is important without muddying the analysis by including it in every definition.

Class consciousness may be defined as the ideological view of the majority of a class, including its self-identification and its understanding of itself. Using the relational approach, Marxian writers consider consciousness and ideology to be a vital part of the social process. If one class has an objective conflict with another but no one in either class has any knowledge or belief in that conflict, then for all practical purposes the conflict does not exist. Only if a class has conscious knowledge of itself does that consciousness affect history. In that sense, class consciousness is a decisive issue. But that does not mean that one should complicate the definition of *class* by adding the ideological factor. In an analysis it is clearer to first define *class* objectively and then ask what ideology the class holds.

In a similar fashion, in recent decades many Marxian theorists have talked about including nationality, race, or gender in the definition of class because these distinctions have proven to be so important for our understanding. Indeed, Marxian feminists have shown how to use both class and gender as powerful tools of analysis; while Marxian writers concerned with racial problems have shown how an understanding of both class and race is an equally powerful tool of analysis. Again, the analysis will be clearer if race, gender, and nationality are handled as separate concepts from class, even though the relationship is extremely close in many cases. The importance of the issue should not be confused with its definition. Marxian social scientists have always traced the effects of class on politics, consciousness, race, gender, and nationality. Most Marxian researchers have now begun to trace the effects of each of these upon class and upon each other.

Eric Olin Wright has set out the main properties of the Marxian concept of class. First, it is relational, relating each class to all others and to the means of production. It must be stressed that the Marxian concept of class is *not* based on incremental, gradational, or quantitative measures, such as income, but on the qualitative differences in relations between groups. Second, it is an antagonistic relation. Of course there may be harmony at times, there may be compromises, and all the classes are interdependent in one social formation at a given time. Classes are antagonistic in the sense that "the welfare of the exploiting class depends upon the work of the exploited class"

(Wright 1985, 75). Note that this flow of surplus to the exploiting class distinguishes exploitation from oppression. The relationship of oppression may also exist, but it is not a defining characteristic of class. Third, the relationship is based on the process of exploitation. For example, there is a causal relation between the riches of the feudal lords and the poverty of the feudal serfs (though exploitation does not always result in poverty). Fourth, the exploitation is based on the relationship of groups in production, not ideology, legal ideas, or power. Such a definition is a powerful tool because it can be used to define modes of production and to understand the change from one mode of production to another.

Class Conflict in the Economy

The U.S. class structure reveals a small class of capitalists in conflict in different ways and different degrees with professionals and managers as well as with the large class of workers (plus the unemployed, the small farmers, etc.). Marxian researchers using a relational-historical approach see a whole spectrum of classes, though there may be polarization on some issues in some periods. One critic of Marxism claims that the greatest "distortion of the facts is seen in Marx's polarization theory. It may even be true that the number of classes has become smaller, but modern society has certainly not been reduced to two classes" (Dupre 1966, 211).

No serious Marxian scholar claims that there are only two classes in modern capitalism: there are many classes and strata. There has been polarization, however, in two significant ways. In 1840 the small farmers and small businessmen and independent professionals constituted perhaps 90 percent of the populace. Today those groups constitute only 7–8 percent, while more than 80 percent of Americans are in the position of being employed by others. This employed group includes, of course, both poor and well-paid, both low-status and prestigious, both manual and mental workers, both professionals and nonprofessionals, both supervisors and supervised.

Because of this objective polarization into the relationship of employees and employers, the main political issues, such as unemployment benefits or capital gains taxes, are also polarized around capitalist interests versus workers' interests. This is true even though the category "employee" includes many strata that may be called classes, as well as different race, ethnic, and gender groups. Issues involving farmers or small business exist but are more peripheral and may be seen as one of many secondary conflicts in society.

Within the productive process, there are several varieties of class conflict. The conclusion of Marxian economic theory is that capitalists exploit workers by extracting profits from the values created by the workers' toil. Workers resist this exploitation by individual slowdowns, by tossing monkey wrenches in the productive process in many ways, and by organized activity such as collective bargaining and strikes. In many industries the collective arm of the workers, the union, meets the collective arm of capital, whether a single monopolistic giant or a trade association, head-on. The strength on either side, modified by supply and demand conditions, determines the split between wages and profits. Obviously, these class conflicts are neither random nor accidental; they are internal to the normal working of the productive process.

These class conflicts are partly reflected in and partly intensified by workers' alienation. Workers are alienated from their product by capitalists, who own it and sell it at a profit, thus exploiting the workers. Workers are alienated from their work because each worker does only a tiny, routinized part of the whole job. Workers are alienated not only from capitalists but also from each other as the result of competing against each other in the labor market.

Many radicals of the 1960s (such as Erich Fromm), basing themselves on the young Marx's *Economic and Political Manuscripts of 1844*, stressed subjective alienation as the main basis of class struggle, replacing the objective alienation of product and jobs caused by capitalist exploitation. The mass of poor and often unemployed workers, particularly minorities and women, tend to be most conscious of objective economic alienation through exploitation and unemployment. The better-paid and more fully employed workers, particularly professional workers, are more aware of subjective alienation caused by competitive pressures and dictatorial authorities over them. Most Marxian scholars stress that *both* subjective and objective types of alienation are present to some degree in all jobs under capitalism. The alienation results from the class conflicts within capitalist relations of production.

Social and Political Class Conflicts

Class conflict at the productive level is often mirrored in and modified by class conflict within all social and political institutions. For example, when Californians debated a proposition to permanently cut the progressive state income tax, it was attacked by the American Federation of Labor–Congress of Industrial Organizations and other working- and middle-class organizations; but it was supported by California's Manufacturers Association, Builders Association, Farm Bureau Association, Real Estate Association, and Chamber of Commerce. Obviously, neither the defense nor the attack was random, but represented class interests. Similarly, universal health care is supported by the labor unions and by most middle-class groups, but it is opposed by the U.S. Chamber of Commerce, the Business Roundtable, and most other business organizations. This second level of class conflict includes political struggle for control of the government. Control of the government, or what most Marxian theorists would call control of the state, is the most essential issue of this level of class conflict. (For a thorough handling of this issue, see ch. 9.)

There are also class conflicts within and about education. The ruling group in society always wishes to use the education system to convince people that the present socioeconomic system is the best possible system. Boards of education and regents or trustees of universities mostly enforce policies designed to support the status quo, partly because the regents and trustees of universities tend to be capitalists themselves, or lawyers who represent capitalists. For example, for a long time the University of California regents were all white, all male, all elderly, and all millionaires—a description that still fits the majority of regents. Of course schools and universities are also supposed to prepare students for jobs in the economy. How well they do that is a complex issue in itself (see Bowles and Gintis 1975, which emphasizes that education tends to reproduce the class structure of students' parents).

Religion has also been an area of class conflict according to Marxian analysis. For example, the English Civil War of 1648 was fought under the guise of religious issues, but there is ample evidence that the armies were actually arguing about class relationships in England (see Hill 1961). In the medieval period, religious power could not be separated from political power and economic power because the Catholic Church was the largest landowner in Europe and exercised direct political power over its estates. In present-day Poland the church is still one of the important political actors. In the United States, right-wing religious groups oppose all rights to abortion, just as they once opposed all contraception. The religious Right has made use of these social issues to gain political power, which has then been used to support the economic status quo, among other goals.

The media in the United States represent an area of class conflict. Publishers are generally members of the capitalist class, so they automatically tend to support the economic status quo; they approve of big business but see unions as threatening. On the other hand, reporters are generally middle or working class by background, and they are working for wages themselves. Thus, there tends to be some tension over every class-related issue in every large newspaper company. It should be added, however, that reporters are forced to sell stories, so sensationalism is a normal bias, often hurting progressive goals even more than direct class bias. For example, political scandals are a lot more fun than political issues.

The family in the United States often transmits class attitudes from one generation to the next. The nature of the family is different in societies with different class relations. For example, under slavery a slave-owner husband treats his wife as a possession, though usually as a very important possession to be kept isolated from all other men. Families belonging to different classes are also different. Thus, the family of a slave is very different from the family of a slave owner. The slave woman may be used sexually by the slave owner. Moreover, the slave family is more transient, because any member of the family may be sold at any time.

The type of gender discrimination in a society is affected by the class relations, but it also affects class relations. For example, it is no accident that the South refused to ratify not only the Women's Suffrage Amendment to the U.S. Constitution but also the Equal Rights Amendment. The South has also always been the least unionized region of the United States, mostly because of racial prejudice but perhaps partly because of its particular heritage of gender prejudice. Both racism and sexism may divide and weaken unions. There is a very complex and tangled relation between race, gender, and class in most societies (see Sherman 1987, ch. 5).

Ideological Class Conflicts

The third level of class conflict is manifested in clashing ideologies, as well as the impact of those ideologies on society. Of course in reality it is hard to separate institutions, such as the Catholic Church, from ideology, such as Catholic theology. Similarly, it is hard to separate the institution of slavery from the ideology of racism, or the Republican Party from its ideology. Yet it is very useful to separate each of these for analysis. One question that may then be asked is, How closely is each institution related to the ideas circulating in it, and exactly what are those relationships?

There are very real conflicts between ideologies. Examples include the arguments between those for and against taxation of capital gains, between feminists and sexists, and between the defenders of ecology and the growth-at-any-cost school. Moreover, each of these ideologies develops with more and more sophistication and elegance. At least there are more and more sophisticated arguments on both sides in academia; politicians, such as Ronald Reagan, may state the arguments very crudely.

The path of development of each opposing idea is partly determined by the battle with its opposite. Yet these internal developments of ideologies are not independent of class relations; they both highly influence and are highly influenced by the course of class relations. Thus the fact that prevention of pollution could cause loss of profits for powerful corporations has a great deal to do with the promotion of conflicting ideologies on pollution. On the other side, the surge of interest in ecological protection was related to the involvement and activist training of intellectuals in the civil rights and antiwar movements of the 1960s.

It should be noted that no class in history has ever had a simple, narrow, materialistic ideology that valued things simply because they were profitable to that class. On the contrary, the majority of members in each class usually believe that the desires of their class represent the good of the whole of society. Thus, the bourgeoisie did not lead the French Revolution on the basis of what was good for their own economic interests, but as a crusade for liberty, equality, and fraternity (or the brotherhood of all men). Similarly, the bourgeoisie in the American Revolution did not argue about keeping their profits but contended that they fought for life, liberty, and the pursuit of happiness.

The Marxian analysis contends that the ideas of the ruling class will normally be the dominant ideology because (1) they control economic power, (2) they control the flow of information, and (3) most people assume that what is will always continue. But Marxian social scientists also note that the ruling ideology is subject to attacks from other classes depending on the degree of social disequilibrium. Callinicos maintains that rulers do not always succeed in convincing most people that their ideology is correct but that they are usually successful in convincing most people that it is impossible to change the present situation, and he presents survey data supporting this view for the United States (1988, 137–47). One reflection of the belief that nothing can be changed might be the fact that the U.S. electorate certainly does not vote in favor of alternatives to capitalism and about half of the electorate does not vote at all.

Wright's findings on attitudes also reinforce our understanding of class and ideological conflict. Wright (1985) finds that there is no automatic class consciousness but that consciousness is affected both by class and by many other variables. He made use of a large-scale survey based on interviews in which a score of +6 meant 100 percent pro-worker and a score of –6 meant 100 percent anti-worker. His survey found both skilled and unskilled U.S. workers at +0.8, while U.S. managers were at –1.5 and the bourgeoisie were at –1.3. Thus, class does affect attitudes, though not in any simple, complete fashion.

In Sweden, where there are strong trade unions and a powerful socialist party, the same survey found skilled and unskilled workers at +2.7, the bourgeoisie at –2.0, and managers in between, at –.7. Thus the conflict between class attitudes was much stronger in Sweden than in the United States. Class consciousness in the United States is also affected by degree of unionization, previous class background, unemployment, gender, race, income level, amount of unearned income, and home ownership. From his survey of the United States and Sweden, Wright concludes that "the data support the thesis that the underlying structure of class relations shapes the overall pattern of class consciousness. . . . [But] the level of working class consciousness in a given society and the nature of the class coalitions that are built upon these class relations are shaped by the organization and political practices that characterize the history of class struggle" (278).

Some of Wright's political implications from these findings are worth noting. Since a majority for socialism must include intermediate groups as well as "workers," as he defines them, it is necessary for the Left to stress not only immediate material advantages for workers but also long-term advantages for most people, including better health care, an end to militarism, a better environment, and less alienation, that is, programs appealing to both workers and professional groups, both poor and middle-income groups.

Questions, Not Answers

No one has discovered any eternal laws that apply to classes or to class conflict in every society. On the contrary, class relationships are strikingly different in different social formations. Therefore, there are no easy and general answers concerning class. Using the relational-historical method, Marxism does suggest what questions to ask. Being able to say what questions are most likely to be fruitful is saying a lot in the social sciences, where that is often the most difficult task.

The relational approach instructs us to begin with questions about group relations, while the historical approach tells us that these relations are specific to each mode of production. Therefore, in each social investigation, a Marxian analysis must begin by asking the question, What, if any, are the class relations? Are the relationships all relationships of conflict? of harmony? Or do the relationships involve both harmony and conflict in varying degrees? If there is class conflict, what are the types of class conflicts? Are there economic, political, and ideological class conflicts? Are there conflicts within classes? Are there racial, gender, and/or nationality conflicts? Are there conflicts between developers and the ecology movement? How are the nonclass conflicts related to class conflicts in the society?

Conclusions

Note that the questions about class conflict in a given social formation are a subset of the questions (asked in chs. 3 and 4) about relations in a historical process, not a new and different approach. In other words, the most basic points in the Marxian approach—which was designed as a weapon for radical political economy—remain: (1) replacement of psychological or economic reductionism by a relational, or holistic, approach to social analysis and (2) replacement of a static, equilibrium approach by a historical, or evolutionary, approach. Thus, the approach of Marxism—and of most radical social scientists—may be called the relational-historical method. One can apply that method to myriad problems, in which the most important beginning point is the analysis of class. The analysis of class, rather than individual psychology, is the entry point to all social, political, and economic analysis. Once the class relations of a society are understood, one can then proceed to explore race, gender, environment, and all other problems. Class relations are the logical starting point from a Marxian view; but it is meaningless to ask what the most important relation is, except at a given political moment.

PART TWO

Political Economy
A Relational-Historical Approach

SEVEN

Poverty, Inequality, and Exploitation

P art II attempts to show how the relational-historical approach is actually applied in Marxian political economy. It does not, however, attempt to present a complete Marxian political economy because that task has filled thousands of books and articles (for a bibliography of the most important contemporary Marxian political economy, see Sherman 1987). Only four major issues are introduced in these four chapters: poverty and exploitation, unemployment, the state or government, and the sad history of the Soviet Union. Each issue is presented very briefly here in order to show only how the relational-historical approach may be applied to each of them as a means of building a useful radical political economy. These chapters lay the foundations for detailed studies of political economy, but they are by no means complete expositions of the subjects.

What is distinctive about the Marxian view is that it attributes poverty and inequality not to individual psychological differences but in large part to the institutionalized system of exploitation. Exploitation may be defined roughly as the appropriation by one class of the product of labor of another class. The literature on exploitation is vast, so no definitive study can be attempted here. The goal of this chapter is merely to introduce the reader to the issues and to explain why the old Marxian view on this subject must be rejected in favor of the newer Marxian relational-historical approach to exploitation. The chapter moves from a traditional Marxian view to alternative views and concludes with a relational, historical, and class approach to exploitation.

Poverty and Inequality

What most concerns U.S. Marxian social scientists is the vast poverty and inequality in this richest of all nations. For some decades, 15 percent to 17 percent of all citizens of the United States have been living under the official poverty line. The poorest 40 percent of income recipients get only about 16 percent of all U.S. income, whereas the wealthiest 5 percent of U.S. taxpayers have been getting over 17 percent. The richest 2 percent of all families own 71 percent of all privately held corporate stock, so this is one measure of the capitalist class. Another index of the capitalist class is the fact that those making more than a million dollars a year made more than 75 percent of their income from property ownership, in the form of profit, rent, and interest. On the other hand, almost all the income of the poorest 40 percent of U.S. citizens comes from labor, in the form of wages and salaries. Finally, the income of the capitalist class, that is, property income, including profit, rent, and interest, constitutes more than 28 percent of all U.S. income (Sherman 1987; for a detailed study, see Winnick 1989).

The Labor Theory of Value

Traditional Marxism begins with a theory of value or price (called the *labor theory of value*), which it proceeds to apply to a theory of profits and exploitation. According to traditional Marxism, the value of any commodity in a capitalist economy is determined by the amount of labor embodied in it. By *labor* is meant not only the present, living labor of workers but also the past labor embodied in the plant, equipment, and raw materials used up in the process of production.

The argument is as follows: Suppose we examine an economy in which each producer is an independent unit, doing his or her own work, hiring no one, and being hired by no one. He or she may produce farm goods or hunt for animals or do handicraft work.

To begin with the simplest case, let us assume that each producer also makes his or her own machinery and mines raw materials from scratch, à la Robinson Crusoe. In this case, it is almost a platitude that products exchange according to the labor each expends. Adam Smith used an example in which some people hunt beaver, while others hunt deer. If it takes, on the average, twice as long to catch a deer as to catch a beaver, then a deer-catcher will demand and receive two beavers for one deer (or twice as much "money" for a deer as for a beaver).

If exchange does not take place at prices proportional to the labor embodied in the products, there will be adjustment to that level. Suppose a situation in which the market rate of exchange is only one for one even though twice as many labor hours are expended on catching a deer as on catching a beaver. Such a situation is known as *disequilibrium*. Then the hunters will switch over to catching beaver, because it takes only half the time, yet the reward is equal. As hunters quit catching deer and the supply of deer in the market decreases, competition for the smaller supply must force a rise in the price of deer, until one deer is exchanged for two beavers. Only then will an *equilibrium* exist; that is, it will be equally profitable to catch a deer or a beaver, so that there will be no further switching. Thus, when the system comes to rest, the ratio of prices in exchange will equal the ratio of labor hours expended.

If it is necessary to purchase equipment from others, such as a bow and arrows, the answer is still basically the same. The bow and arrows will be exchanged according to the labor that went into making them. If the bow and arrows are offered at a price relatively greater than the labor time bestowed on them, the hunters may go back to making their own bows and arrows. Still, the bow and arrows must be included in the price of deer at the labor cost of making them, regardless of whether they are made by the hunter or by someone else.

In the modern case, suppose a society that regularly uses money and is "capitalist" in the sense that there is private ownership of productive facilities, that the goal of production is private profit, and that capitalists are free to hire and fire workers. In this case, the capitalist supplies capital in the form of factories and equipment, while workers supply the labor power needed for production (here we ignore other classes). The final product must sell for a price equal to the total labor put into it, including the present labor of production plus the labor that went into producing the factories, raw materials, and equipment that were used up in the productive process.

The argument is essentially the same as in the simple economy of independent producers. Suppose the capitalist tries to sell (or exchange) the product at a higher relative price than is proportionate to the labor in it. Then other capitalists can produce it for less, either for themselves or to sell in competition with the capitalist. In other words, if the price is above the labor value, so that a profit above average is being made, other capital will flow into the industry and increase its supply until by competition the price falls to the level of its total value in terms of labor hours. Yet the capitalist can at least obtain that price because no one can produce the product for less. If the price should fall below the value in terms of labor hours, profit will be below average, capital will flow out, and supply will drop. In the long run, competition will force the price back up to its full value in terms of labor hours, and only then will equilibrium be reached.

The labor theory of value remains simple only if a number of qualifications are assumed to hold. Traditional Marxism makes these assumptions. First, the theory applies only to labor expended under the usual contemporary technological conditions. If a person produces an automobile by hand that is identical with those produced on an assembly line, the product will still have a value equal only to the labor necessary to produce it in the usual mass-production process.

Second, there are constant average costs of production over the whole relevant range. As long as costs per unit are constant, a higher demand does not affect the labor expended per unit. If there were increasing costs of labor per unit as output rose, then a change in demand would change the value of the product in terms of labor hours.

Third, the product must have a utility; labor expended on useless objects does not count. Note, however, that although utility must be present for any value, it does not determine the quantity of value produced. Utility may be a factor determining demand, but if it is assumed that supply and demand are now balanced and equal, then the quantity of value must be determined by something else, namely, the labor expended. In other words, the demand will determine the distribution of labor among industries and the amount of each product, but it cannot affect the relative price or exchange ratio of products because, according to the second assumption, a change in scale does not affect the cost per unit.

Fourth, expenditure of more skilled labor will count as some multiple of an hour of average labor expended. The labor expended in "producing" the more skilled worker, including, for example, the education and training of an engineer, is greater than that expended in producing an ordinary worker. Therefore, he or she passes on to the product a greater value per hour.

Fifth, it is assumed, as a first approximation, that living human labor and inanimate objects (congealed labor) are used in the same ratio in every product. Otherwise, prices will not be proportionate to labor values. (There is a vast literature on this issue, discussing exactly how labor values are transformed into prices in the general case; see, e.g., Lichtenstein 1983.)

Sixth, it is assumed, as a first approximation, that there is pure and perfect competition, with no monopoly power. Monopoly power will cause prices to deviate from labor values.

Seventh, it is assumed, as a first approximation, that aggregate demand equals aggregate supply; that is, there is no excess supply of goods, no unemployed labor, and no idle capacity. A lack of demand would cause prices to drop below long-run equilibrium.

Eighth, it is assumed, as a first approximation, that government spending, taxation, and production are negligible and that there are no government regulations, except the rules of private property and contract.

Ninth, it is assumed, as a first approximation, that all the world is one capitalist nation with a free flow of labor and trade and capital. In reality, international relations may affect domestic wages and prices in many ways.

Obviously, many of these assumptions are unrealistic. That does not prove that the theory is wrong, only that it would be extremely complex if the general case were presented.

The Traditional Marxian Theory of Exploitation

Traditional Marxism stated, according to the labor theory of value, that commodities derive their value solely from the labor put into them in the production process. Workers were paid only according to the labor expended on their necessities. Profit is the *surplus value*, or the residual of the worker's product that remains after the worker is paid. Traditional Marxism argued that the capitalist normally makes his or her profit by selling the product at its value, which is the amount of labor embodied in it. The capitalist makes a profit because he or she has bought the worker's power to labor, the worker's *labor power*, at its value, which is the labor embodied in the necessities of life given to the worker as wages. The profit results because there is a difference between the value of what the worker produces and the value of the worker's necessary consumption.

The wage of the worker, or the value of his or her labor power, is determined by the labor expended in producing the worker. That labor includes what is necessary for his or her food, clothing, shelter, and education, as well as the food, clothing, shelter, and education of his or her family (under the conditions and traditions of the given time and place).

The worker's labor embodied in the final product, however, is much greater than the labor that is required to keep the worker functioning. In other words, a worker produces far more in a day than the wages paid to keep him or her alive and functioning. In traditional Marxian terms, the value produced is much greater than the *necessary value* to pay for the worker's own subsistence. This difference is profit, or *surplus value,* which reflects the objective fact of surplus labor expended by the worker and appropriated by the capitalist.

A Technological Reductionist View of Value and Exploitation

One group of Marxists call themselves orthodox, though others call them fundamentalist, meaning that they accept Marx's *Capital* as fundamental and unchallengeable truth. This group includes Willi Semmler (1982), Anwar Shaikh (1978), and John Weeks (1981). They restate the traditional labor theory of value as an inexorable economic law of capitalism, but in a very sophisticated, complex mathematical format.

The view is economic reductionist in that prices, profits, and wages are determined by impersonal economic forces and not primarily by class relations. The theory is stated in terms of the technology of commodity production: the value of any commodity is the inherent amount of socially necessary labor embodied in the commodity at the present level of technology. Thus, Weeks even claims that Frederick Engels "completely misconstrued Marx's value theory" (1981, 8). He claims that Engels emphasized that class conflicts determined profit and wage levels and, therefore, income distribution. Weeks maintains that Engels was wrong because wages and prices are given by the law of value, not human relations.

The technological reductionist argument on exploitation is this:

1. All commodities are exchanged at their long-run value, which is the amount of labor time necessary to produce the product (given the assumptions listed above).

2. Human labor power (the capacity to work) is a commodity under capitalism, sold in the market. Like all other commodities, it is bought and sold at its long-run value, which is the amount of labor time necessary to produce the worker.

3. Capitalists extract from labor power the expenditure of labor for a given number of hours. Those hours worked may number—and do under capitalism—far more than the hours required to produce the value of the worker (i.e., wages). So the difference between the value of the worker (wages) and the value of the product (price) is the surplus value (or profit) going to the capitalist.

This argument is very formal and reduces the explanation to a technological one. It is not firmly rooted in institutional and human relations. Thus, from a relational view, the argument is flawed. One problem is that labor power is not a usual sort of commodity. Labor power may be called a commodity if one wishes; that is a semantic or definitional question. But whatever it is called, labor power is very different from the usual capitalist commodity in some very important respects relevant to this argument (see Bowles and Gintis 1981). It is true that labor power is similar to the usual capitalist commodity in that it is bought and sold in the market—which causes workers much misery when they are unemployed.

Yet labor power differs from most things called commodities in several ways. First, in a pure capitalist system all other commodities are produced by capitalists. Workers are not produced by a capitalist assembly line. Workers are not produced in a factory as other commodities are; most of the labor going into the production of a worker is the unpaid love and care of a family.

Second, all other commodities are sold by capitalists in market exchanges governed by impersonal supply and demand. Not only is workers' capacity to work (or labor power) not produced by capitalists but it is not sold by capitalists. The worker's power to labor is sold by millions of workers—though capitalists, once they have bought labor power, may sell services. So the supply conditions of labor power are totally different from those of all other commodities bought by capitalists.

Third, in the case of all other commodities, there is no need for the seller to be present when the commodity is used or consumed. The worker, however, must be present when labor is used, so the worker may or may not agree to a certain speed of production. A machine has a specific, technologically given maximum speed, but the intensity of labor by workers depends not only on their ability but also on their conscious attitudes and social relationships.

For all of these reasons, it is not the case that the value of labor power automatically equals the number of hours put into the production of the worker. Labor power cannot be viewed as a separate thing, with a certain value given exactly by technology, but must be viewed as a relationship (as shown below).

The fact that labor power differs from other commodities means that even if one accepts the labor theory of value for other commodities, the technological reductionist version of the labor theory of value does not explain the value of labor power (wages). If the Marxian theory is to be persuasive, the value of the worker's labor power must be explained in some manner other than that of the traditional or technological reductionist version. (See appendix 7B for the approaches of Roemer and Sraffa.)

A Relational or Class Theory of Exploitation

A relational theory of exploitation recognizes that the value of the worker's labor power, and hence the degree of exploitation, is determined by human relationships. These relationships cannot be reduced to either individual psychology or technologically determined labor hours. For example, the traditional Marxian approach assumed that workers produce at the average technologically given productivity per hour. But in reality productivity per hour is a variable, dependent on the strength of workers versus the strength of capitalists. Thus, in the relational view one may generalize that the average value of labor power is determined by the relationship between capitalists and workers under given conditions of supply and demand. Both the relationship and the conditions must be spelled out and analyzed in a systematic fashion.

Two determinants of the degree of exploitation of labor are the real hourly wage and the productivity of labor. All other things being equal, exploitation will be greater if the hourly wage is lower and less if the hourly wage is higher. All other things being equal, exploitation will be greater if the productivity of labor is higher and less if the productivity of labor is lower. What determines the real wage and productivity?

The real hourly wage is determined by the industrial conflict between capitalists and workers, within the production process of capitalism, under certain economic conditions of supply and demand. Appendix 7A notes some of the highlights of class conflict in U.S. labor history in order to show how relative class power has influenced the degree of exploitation.

What exactly are the conditions of demand and supply that affect hourly wages? The conditions under which the wage bargain is struck include (1) the demand for labor. Given the level of technology, the demand for labor is a function of the demand for goods and services. But the demand for goods and services depends not only on national income but also on the class distribution of income between workers and capitalists (see Sherman 1991, ch. 5). The degree of exploitation also depends on (2) the supply of labor, which is a function of population growth (which is different under different class relations) and rates of labor participation. The supply of labor is affected by child labor laws, retirement provisions, relations of men and women, and everything else that affects the desire or necessity for paid labor positions.

The hourly wage also is affected by (3) the excess supply of labor, reflected in the unemployment rate; (4) the worker's fallback position in the event of unemployment, which includes the level of unemployment benefits and welfare benefits (which in turn reflect class power); (5) the power of workers through their labor unions, reflected in rates of unionization, especially in key firms and key industries; (6) the degree of monopoly power by business over prices and the degree of monopsony power by business over wages; (7) the power and tactics of capitalist governments, including recognition and regulation of unions and enforcement of fixed labor contracts, all of which reflect class power relationships; and (8) international events, including both shifts of economic power (such as Japan versus the United States) and wars.

The productivity of labor is a central issue in industrial conflict. Capitalists try to speed up production, which workers usually try to resist. The conditions affecting the outcome of this conflict include the same eight conditions discussed above plus three others. In the long run, (9) productivity is very much influenced by technology, which is itself partly influenced by government policies, reflecting class relations. In the short run, (10) the productivity of both machinery and labor will depend in part on the degree of capacity utilization, reflecting the business cycle. Finally, (11) productivity is in part affected by the amount of effort per hour (intensity of labor).

The intensity of labor is itself a result of class conflict (see Bowles and Gintis 1981). Even if a contract is signed for wages and hours, that still leaves the intensity of labor each hour on the job as something that will be decided by conflict. In some circumstances, the conflict may be very peaceful, and some normal standard may emerge as more or less acceptable to all parties. At other times and places, conflict over the intensity of labor may escalate to any level. The clearest understanding of battles over the intensity of labor may be seen in Charlie Chaplin's film *Modern Times*. No one who has seen that film can ever forget Charlie working on the assembly line and trying to keep up with his job as the assembly line moves faster and faster. Charlie has to keep moving further and further along the conveyor belt, until finally he reaches the end and is about to be sucked into it.

In other words, once the wage level is determined, the question is what determines the labor expended per worker. Both the "orthodox" Marxian and the neoclassical view just assume that a worker's labor power is bought for a given number of hours and is expended at average intensity in that period. When one admits that the intensity of labor is not a technologically given fact, but is governed by the labor-capital relationship, then it is necessary to discuss the importance of different intensities of labor.

But what determines the intensity of labor? A machine will work at a certain maximum load for the lifetime of the machine, as determined by technology. Workers, however, are not machines and may work faster or slower than the average, resist speed-up, and go on strike. The fact that a worker's labor power is bought for eight hours does not determine the intensity of labor expenditure per hour.

The average intensity of labor is determined by capitalist attempts to increase intensity and workers' resistance to speed-up. There is a large literature on the ways used by capitalists to speed up work with a given technology (see Braverman 1974). For example, bosses use the technique known as Taylorism, which includes precise measurement of minimum job times and setting of norms. The success of capitalist speed-up depends on many of the same factors that determine wages. If there is a weak union and high unemployment (so that workers feel threatened by job loss), then it is possible to intensify labor expenditure per hour. If there is a strong union and full employment, workers may successfully resist speed-up. Thus, labor intensity is determined by relative class power under given conditions of supply and demand.

Part of the class conflict over exploitation is waged in the legal arena. There have been momentous conflicts over child labor laws, laws for minimum wages and maximum hours, and laws that have recognized or restricted union activity.

Of course, there is also an ideological conflict over exploitation of workers. For example, at present there is continuous argument over what is a "special interest," with all politicians claiming to fight special interests. But some media and some politicians define special interests to mean workers' unions, women's organizations, or African American civil rights organizations. On the other hand, some liberal and radical politicians define special interests to be the major corporations as well as the banks and the savings and loan industry. While everyone is against the special interests, it turns out that some (such as former President Ronald Reagan) define special interests as the interests of workers, women, and minorities (who together constitute the vast majority of the people). Others (such as African American leader Jesse Jackson) define special interests as the interests of a small, powerful, capitalist minority. The perception of which group is a special interest will affect the passage of labor laws, which influence the degree of exploitation.

There are also conflicts over race and gender that affect the degree of exploitation. The wonderful film *Salt of the Earth* (made by the Mine, Mill, and Smelter Workers Union) illustrates dramatically how race and gender affect issues of exploitation and interact with them. For example, in the film there is an injunction preventing the miners from picketing, so the Mexican American women in the mining town take over the picket line against Anglo police, while their husbands have to learn how to mind the babies. In the U.S. South, racism was long used very effectively to divide workers and thus prevent unionization. In some areas of the country, unions of high school teachers have been weakened by sexist males' refusing to cooperate with women teachers. There is also a large literature, mostly by radical economists, explaining how women and minorities have often been shunted into an inferior, secondary labor market in which the wages are low and the chances for advancement are nil. In other words, there is one labor market for highly paid white males and another for poorly paid minorities and women.

Conflicts over the budget that clearly affect the rate of exploitation occur in Congress every day. For example, if taxes are to be raised or lowered, one must always ask whose taxes are to be raised or lowered. Are they those of the rich or those of the poor, those of workers or those of corporations? When spending is debated, one must always ask who is getting the money. Is it a subsidy to rich tobacco-producing corporations or an extension of unemployment benefits?

Finally, class conflict over exploitation has an international aspect. Multinational corporations based in the United States may own mines in South Africa. Thus, they will do all they can to weaken the mining unions in South Africa. For many decades, one method was to support the system of apartheid, which prevented black and white workers from associating with each other in many ways. As long as black workers got the worst jobs and housing, while white workers got somewhat better jobs and housing, workers' unions could be kept weak and divided. This system increased the profits of U.S. corporations investing in South Africa. A large amount of the literature on imperialist penetration of other countries in search of maximum profits is presented in Sherman 1987, ch. 9.

A Historical Approach to Exploitation

In the Marxian relational view, the basis for exploitation lies in the particular class relations of a given social formation. The type of exploitation would be different in every different set of class relations. The exploitation of slaves is a very different process from the exploitation of workers under capitalism. Even in one social formation, the exact mechanisms of exploitation change over time as the class relations of that social formation evolve. Appendix 7A shows concrete examples of this evolution.

Exploitation is not an eternal condition; it changes in various ways at various times. There is no equilibrium condition, but a changing matrix of forces, with some constant features within each mode of production. But changes are not limited to gradual, incremental reforms. There are also revolutionary changes in the mode of exploitation. Marxian historical analysis provides the hope that exploitation may even be altogether abolished some day.

The changing form of exploitation means that it is a more obvious fact in some societies than in others. Under slavery, it is obvious that slaves are forced, by threats or by violence, to produce a surplus over their own subsistence, a surplus that goes to the slave owners. Under feudalism too it is obvious that serfs are coerced, by tradition, religious ideology, and the threat or use of violence, to produce a surplus by working on the feudal lord's land, a surplus that goes to the feudal lord.

Under capitalism, it is not obvious, but it is still true, that workers are coerced. Under capitalism, the coercion is by economic necessity (though the legal rules of the game are backed by force). The economic necessity forces workers to work for the boss at a wage that is less than the value of their output. That surplus over what is paid to the workers is profit. Since the profit comes from the workers' labor, the process is defined by the Marxian theory as exploitation.

Under the institutions of private property, capitalists control the means of production and the jobs for workers. Workers, who lack the capital to create their own business, are free to take a job or starve. Today, workers may also go on welfare or receive unemployment compensation at a low income and a degrading status. The relations of private property—supported by tradition, ideology, law, and force—as well as the threat of unemployment if one does not work within those relations are the glue that holds the system of capitalist exploitation in place.

Prices, wages, and profits reflect a system of relations in which workers are paid a certain wage, but the entire product is sold by the capitalist at whatever price it can command in the market. Consumer demand is based on the class income and class behavior of those receiving labor income and property income. The very meaning and amount of prices, profits, and wages are determined by these relations, not merely by technical conditions. For example, in the 1980s the cost of production of a product was lower in South Africa than in the United States, even when the technology and machinery were the same, because unions were suppressed, prejudice divided workers, and the state was used to oppress the majority of workers. So the prices of products, wages of workers, and profits of capitalists are the result of a certain set of class relations, certain rules of the game, certain social institutions—and not merely the technical conditions of production.

Conclusions

The institutional setting, that is, the capitalist relations of production, provides the limits within which class conflict determines wages, prices, output, and profits. Given the conditions of demand and supply (including the level of unemployment), class conflict determines wages, the intensity of labor, and the output per worker. Under capitalist institutions and normal relations of class power, the labor going into the output of the worker will be greater than the labor going into the bundle of goods that constitute the worker's wage, thus producing surplus value or profit.

The changes in the socioeconomic system that are necessary to eliminate poverty, exploitation, and inequality are discussed in part IV.

Appendix 7A: Class Conflict in U.S. Labor Relations

To avoid the notion that this discussion of exploitation is a purely abstract exercise, it may be useful to provide some more concrete historical examples. Here we will use the general questions of the relational-historical approach to exploitation as tools for understanding some brief highlights of the actual history of class conflicts in U.S. labor relations.

Before the Civil War, the relationships of the U.S. economy were still dominated by rural, agricultural production and small business; there were few large concentrations of workers. Consequently, unions were weak and usually short-lived. After the Civil War, U.S. capitalism expanded rapidly into the South and the West, industry became large-scale, and enterprises with large numbers of workers became commonplace. At the same time, working and living conditions were miserable. For example, in New York City in the 1860s thousands of little girls and boys worked from 6:00 A.M. until midnight and were paid only three dollars a week. These conditions led to the spread of individual unions and national federations.

The National Labor Union was a militant federation in the 1860s and 1870s. It was unusual in that it admitted large numbers of professionals and other middle-class individuals. So it turned away from unionism to reform and then quickly died away. In the 1870s and 1880s, the Knights of Labor expanded rapidly because of a major, long-term depression combined with much police brutality toward strikers. After one strike in which police killed twenty men, women, and children, the *New York Tribune* wrote about the strikers: "These brutal creatures can understand no other reasoning than that of force and enough of it to be remembered among them for generations" (quoted in Boyer and Morais 1970, 69). Anyone could join the Knights, so its middle-class character eventually turned it to currency reform and opposition to all strikes, which led to a rapid decline in membership.

The American Federation of Labor (AFL), formed in the 1880s, was at first quite militant and socialist-oriented. The preface to its first constitution stated: "A struggle is going on in the nations of the world between the oppressors and oppressed of all countries, a struggle between capital and labor which must grow in intensity from year to year and work disastrous results to the toiling millions of all nations if not combined for mutual protection and benefit" (quoted in Boyer and Morais 1970, 90). But the AFL soon gave up the struggle between capital and labor. It became a "business union," trying to win incremental wage increases, paying no attention to larger issues, having highly paid leaders with no militancy, and trying hard to compromise with business.

The biggest and bloodiest strikes of this period were fought by independent unions. The American Railway Union struck the railroads in 1894 but was defeated with violence when the U.S. Army came in to move the trains on the excuse of "protecting the mail." In the early 1900s, the Western Federation of Miners struck against miserable conditions in the Colorado Rockefeller-owned mines but was defeated by the state militia, who used machine guns on some miners' camps. In 1912 a strike by women and children against long hours and low pay in the textile mills of Lawrence, Massachusetts, was led by the Industrial Workers of the World, a radical labor federation.

In the Great Depression, during the thirties, wages fell by one-third, while one of every four workers was unemployed. The AFL did little, and it even opposed unemployment compensation. Again, independent unions led some militant strikes. One example was the strike of the International Longshoreman's Union on the West Coast in 1934. When the union first tried to bargain with the employers, the employers simply fired all the union leaders. Eventually, about thirty-five thousand maritime workers were out on strike, the center of the strike being the Embarcadero at the port of San Francisco. On July 3, 1934, the police decided to break the mass picket lines to allow scabs to work. One reporter wrote: "The police opened fire with revolvers and riot guns. Clouds of tear gas swept the picket lines and sent the men choking in defeat. . . . Squads of police who looked like Martian monsters in their special helmets and gas masks led the way, flinging gas bombs ahead of them" (quoted in Boyer and Morais 1970, 285). But this was only the preliminary. The pickets returned on July 5 (known as Bloody Thursday), and they were joined by many young people from the high schools and colleges as well as by hundreds of other unions' members. The police charged, using vomiting gas, revolvers with live ammunition, and riot guns. Hundreds were badly wounded, and two workers were killed.

The pickets finally were driven away, and the employers thought they had won. But many union locals, as well as the Alameda Labor Council, called for a general strike. In spite of a telegram from the president of the AFL forbidding any strike, the workers of San Francisco launched a general strike to support the maritime workers and in protest against the killings by the police. The general strike was amazingly successful: "The paralysis was effective beyond all expectation. To all intents and purposes industry was at a complete standstill. The great factories were empty and deserted. No streetcars were running. Virtually all stores were closed. The giant apparatus of commerce was a lifeless, helpless hulk" (newspaper report, quoted in Boyer and Morais 1970, 287).

During the general strike, labor efficiently allowed into the city emergency food and medical supplies but nothing else. Thousands of troops moved into the city, but there was no violence; labor simply refused to go to work. The general strike lasted until July 19, when the local AFL officials, refusing to hold a roll-call vote of the central labor council, announced that a majority of the council had called off the strike. The employers, worried about another strike, raised the wages of the longshore workers to ninety-five cents an hour.

Then in 1935 John L. Lewis, head of the United Mine Workers, led an exodus of the most militant unions out of the AFL to form a new federation, the Congress of Industrial Organizations (CIO). The CIO engaged in many strikes, used many socialists and Communists as organizers, fought the employers tooth and nail, and spread very rapidly. The CIO supported Franklin Roosevelt and the New Deal, which legalized unions (forcing elections when enough workers petitioned), legislated minimum-wage and maximum-hour laws, and began the social security system. Because of labor militancy and a supportive government, unions grew from 11 percent of all employees in 1930 to 32 percent of all employees in 1950.

In the late 1940s and early 1950s, unions came under attack by Senator Joe McCarthy, by the House Un-American Activities Committee, and by new antilabor laws. The Taft-Hartley Act of 1947 weakened unions in many ways, including the institution of an anti-Communist oath for union officers. In the hysteria of those days, for example, Clinton Jencks, an organizer in the Mine, Mill, and Smelter Workers Union, was accused of not admitting to being a Communist, tried in a farcical trial, and sentenced to five years in prison. During the many years of trial and the appeal, Jencks suffered personally and the union suffered through the loss of his services. Eventually, after much time, expense, and agony, the U.S. Supreme Court held that much of the "evidence" was insufficient and unconstitutional. Jencks later became a radical economist and taught labor economics.

In the face of such witch hunts, coupled with the Cold War ideology, the CIO tossed out its ten most militant left-wing unions in 1949 and merged with the AFL in 1955. The new AFL-CIO compromised with big business, received some gains for its workers in return for pledges not to strike, and supported the Cold War. As a result of the decline in militancy, coupled with the anti-union labor laws, the unions steadily lost strength. Union membership fell from 36 percent of all nonagricultural workers in 1955 to only 17 percent in 1993. This decline has drastically reduced the bargaining power and influence of labor.

This decline does not mean there are no more class conflicts in the economy. For example, the *Los Angeles Times* reported that "striking meatpackers, who have twice blocked roads leading to the George A. Hormel and Co.'s main plant, 'totally took over' when the plant opened Saturday, and one person was arrested, authorities said" (*Los Angeles Times* 1986, 9). The struggle of labor versus capital continues, but with less violence than in the 1930s.

What lessons does the violent history of U.S. labor relations have for the analysis of society? First, if one wishes to analyze a particular issue, such as the tendency of the real wage to decline in the last two decades, then it is necessary to understand the historical evolution of labor and capital relations leading up to the last two decades. Second, to understand the situation at each historical stage, one must begin with the general relationships between the classes at that stage, what has sometimes been called the *social structure of accumulation* at that period. Specifically, one should begin with the stage of development of the organization and consciousness of the opposing classes, because that will determine their relative power (given the surrounding circumstances). Third, one should ask, How does the power, organization, and consciousness of the opposing classes affect

1. the wage bargain?

2. bargaining over health, safety, and other working conditions, including intensity of labor?

3. achievements of reform movements, such as the minimum-wage law or the enactment of unemployment compensation?

4. the ideological climate, with respect to the attractiveness of work, the desirability of unions, and many other issues?

5. the degree of environmental degradation by business in search of profits (see the excellent introduction to environmental issues in Foster 1994)?

This brief case study in class analysis begins to show the usefulness of a relational-historical method.

Appendix 7B: The Theories of Roemer and Sraffa

In addition to the labor theory of value Marxian approaches have included John Roemer's individualist approach and Piero Sraffa's technological approach.

In neoclassical theory, individuals choose their jobs according to their personal preferences. Since all exchanges are freely made and no one is coerced into working, and since each worker is paid according to what he or she adds to the product, the concept of exploitation does not exist for neoclassicals under pure competition. Even in the most recent orthodox game theory approaches, exploitation is not considered (see Kreps 1990).

Although the neoclassical theory does not consider exploitation, a few Marxian theories have used neoclassical tools (psychological preferences, individual choice, and an equilibrium mechanism) to

argue for a theory of exploitation. John Roemer (1982) has formulated a theory of exploitation in exactly such neoclassical terms. His
theory shows how those who own property may use the exchange
mechanism to "exploit" those who do not own property. It is useful
to show that one can explain some form of exploitation even within a
neoclassical outlook, but since the use of a psychological, individualist, and ahistorical approach leaves this theory with very weak foundations, it is not considered further here.

Piero Sraffa (1960) provides a consistent theory of prices that
solves some technical problems that Marx never solved. The technical
details are not important here (for a clear explanation of this difficult
theory, see, e.g., Hunt 1992b; Lichtenstein 1983; or Sawyer 1989).
Sraffa explained quantitatively how to measure the net value of a
commodity (above the value of the raw materials and depreciation
embodied in it). He used as a measuring stick a representative commodity with average quantities of capital and labor. Therefore, Sraffa
did not explain exploitation. Sraffa did succeed in giving a systematic
explanation of prices that is consistent with Marx's theory of exploitation and constitutes a severe criticism of the neoclassical theory.
Some Marxian writers believe that Sraffa gives a good basis for
Marxian economics.

Although his measurement of value is technological, he deliber-
ately avoided a technological solution to the division of income between workers and capitalists apparently because he believed that
class conflict was the key to that division. He provides no explicit theory of the distribution of income. At any rate, Sraffa did not go into
the question of exploitation, so we must construct our own explanation (though it need not be inconsistent with his theory).

Appendix 7C: Exploitation and Racial Discrimination

This appendix illustrates the basic mechanisms of discrimination that
are used against minorities. For simplicity, we will limit our discussion to African Americans in the United States, but the mechanisms
apply, with some differences, to discrimination against all minorities.
(Some excellent works on racism are Bonacich 1980; Boston 1988;
and Reich 1980.)

A Historical Approach to Racial Discrimination

Before the Civil War the South had a slave mode of production. Almost all African Americans in the United States lived as slaves on

plantations in the South. A minority of whites were slave owners. The majority of southern whites were poor farmers, who had some privileges over African Americans. Racist attitudes and discrimination were the rule.

After the Civil War, capitalist industrialists dominated the United States, but they left the South to white landowners, who were allowed to regain dominance by the use of force and violence. The violence continued, with a remarkable number of lynchings all the way up to the 1950s. In that stage of capitalism most African Americans remained as sharecroppers in the South under the domination of landowners, merchants, and moneylenders. Racist laws prevented African Americans from voting, from receiving a good education, and from integration with most of the economy. In 1890, 88 percent of all African Americans were still employed in agriculture or domestic service, and by 1930 this figure had only dropped to 66. Even in 1940, 75 percent of African Americans lived in the South, mostly in rural areas (see Baron 1985, 19).

All of this changed during the Second World War, when millions of African Americans moved to manufacturing jobs. By 1960 more than 40 percent of African Americans lived in the North and 73 percent had jobs in manufacturing. The new economic environment allowed African Americans to unite in the civil rights movement. Under the pressure of that movement, the Supreme Court began to lift racial restrictions in 1954, and Congress passed new civil rights laws in the mid 1960s that removed the obstacles to voting and made job discrimination illegal. The result was formal equality under the law, which has resulted in a growing African American middle class of managers and professionals. Most African Americans, however, remain in the lowest income categories, with twice the rate of unemployment of whites, a much higher rate of poverty, and a much lower percentage receiving a higher education.

Most white workers are in what is called a *primary labor market*, in which there are good, permanent, high-paying jobs that offer possibilities of advancement. Most African American workers are in a *secondary labor market*, characterized by temporary, marginal jobs, no chance of advancement, and a much greater chance of unemployment.

A Relational Analysis of Racial Discrimination

Marxian social scientists conclude from the history of discrimination that the forms of racial discrimination are determined by the socioeconomic system and racism is closely entwined with class relationships. Most societies in which one class has been exploited by another have also exhibited racist attitudes. The Marxian hypothesis is that racism has had two effects: (1) it has helped to divide those who are exploited politically by setting majority against minority; and (2) it has supported an increase in the exploitation of minority workers at the same time that it has helped to continue the exploitation of majority workers.

In the South before the Civil War, because of racism, poor whites would not have dreamed of uniting with the slaves, so there was no opposition to the white slave owners' control. In the 1890s the Populist Party was very strong for a short time because it was supported both by African Americans and poor whites. The ruling class consciously used racism to split and destroy the Populist Party. Racism was also the excuse for the poll tax, which prevented both African Americans and poor whites from voting.

The South remained a conservative bastion for many decades, until voting by African Americans finally began to change it. During that time the solid South voted against constitutional amendments to outlaw child labor, to give the vote to women, and to give equal rights to women. In the first part of the twentieth century, when the Socialist Party was strong in the North, racism prevented it from getting a foothold in the South.

On the economic front in the United States, racism has always been used as an excuse to pay African Americans and other minorities a lower wage than other workers. It has also operated to weaken the strength of organized labor. Its effect in weakening labor can be seen most obviously in the fact that trade unions have always been weakest in the South, with the result that wages of both white and African American workers have been lowest in the South. Thus, although the system of capitalism itself is the cause of exploitation, racism has been used to increase the rate of exploitation of both minority and white workers.

Looking beyond the case of African Americans, it should never be forgotten that the most horrifying use of racism in the twentieth century was against the Jews in Germany. Adolf Hitler told German workers that all of their troubles were caused by Jewish bankers. He told German industrialists and bankers that all of their troubles were caused by Jewish Communists. When Hitler took power, he outlawed the socialists and Communists, killed millions of Jews, and made war on all of the allegedly inferior, non-German peoples of other countries.

Appendix 7D: Exploitation and Sexist Discrimination

There are many similarities between racism and sexism. Both claim that one group is inferior to another, and both result in increased exploitation and oppression of the allegedly inferior group. (An excellent book on sexism and the struggle for women's rights was written by Barbara Sinclair Deckard [1983].)

A Historical Approach to Sexist Discrimination

In most primitive societies women gather fruits and vegetables, while men hunt. Usually the food supply contributed by women is more reliable than that contributed by men. It is not surprising, therefore, that the status of women and men is roughly equal in most primitive societies.

This situation changes dramatically with the advent of slavery. Under slavery male warriors conquer other groups and turn them into slaves, who become the property of the male slave owners. Male slaves do the heavy agricultural work, which is the basis of most slave societies. The male slave owners exploit the women slaves in both economic and sexual terms. It is common for the male slave owners to have several mistresses or even several secondary wives.

The wife of a slave owner is treated as property, but as very valuable property, especially if she is beautiful by the standards of that society (and standards of beauty have differed remarkably among societies). As valuable property, she is often idolized in literature, but the reality is that she is kept isolated from other men, as well as from outside social and political processes, and usually receives little education. She is primarily a sexual object, kept "pure" to produce legitimate male heirs. Since the man may have sex as often as he wishes with slave women, while his wife may receive the death penalty for sex with a slave, there is a blatant double standard. This general description of women under slavery applies equally to ancient Greece and Rome and to the southern United States before the Civil War, even though the specific forms of social life were different.

In the early western United States, men and women had to work together on isolated farms, both doing very hard work to survive. The result was a considerable degree of equality between man and woman. As capitalist industry became dominant in the United States in the last half of the nineteenth century, it brought increased equality to women in the South but reduced equality in the West. Among the working class, men and women both worked long hours, but women's work was often at home, where they would cook and clean, take care of the children, and also sometimes do sewing or work at some other craft that could be sold. Some working-class women worked in factories and then did additional work at home. In the harsh conditions of early manufacturing, men often spent their checks on drink and went home to abuse their wives.

In the middle and capitalist classes, women did somewhat less work than women of the working class, but unless they were rich enough to have servants, they still did an enormous amount of housework. The husband, however, was the one who owned property and business. Under the laws as late as the 1870s all income earned by women automatically went to their husbands. In the event of a divorce, women had no right to property; in fact, women did not even have the right to keep their children. Women had no right to vote and were not supposed to have anything to do with politics. Women who worked got much lower wages than men. Most women received no education. While the subordination of women was much less absolute than under slavery, it was still very clear and taken for granted.

When industrialization and urbanization became widespread and there was greater affluence, women demanded greater rights. It took a hundred years of struggle to get the vote for women. It was many more years before laws were finally passed in the 1960s to guarantee equal wages and equal educational opportunities for women, laws that women are still fighting to enforce. Middle-class women have gotten closer to economic equality in some professional spheres, but the great mass of working women still work for lower wages than men.

Relational Approach to Sexist Discrimination

This brief historical outline shows the close relationship of sexist discrimination to class structure and socioeconomic organization. Men are not born with the sexist view that women are inferior. Both racism and sexism are learned prejudices. They are learned through all the channels of information, including the media, the educational system, and the churches. After years of struggle against sexist images, most women are still stereotyped in movies and television. The media are big business, and they are run for profit by the capitalist class. Since wealth rules to a high degree in politics, education, and religion, ruling white male capitalists are in effective control of most of these channels of information.

Sexist prejudice, like racist prejudice, is useful and profitable to white male capitalists. As women have entered the labor force in large numbers, they have continued to be paid much lower wages. Most women workers are segregated in a low-wage job ghetto, including clerical workers, nurses, and salespeople. A disproportionately low percentage of women work in highly paid jobs such as those of doctors, lawyers, or business executives.

Furthermore, in those occupations that are largely female, though men's wages are slightly higher than those of women, even the men have lower wages than elsewhere given their qualifications. Why do both men and women get less pay than their qualifications would indicate in these areas? One reason is that women can not get into some of the other areas, so they provide an oversupply in these areas, driving down the wage rate. Another reason is that sexist prejudice weakens unions where men and women must work together. Thus, men often do not allow women equal leadership opportunities in a union, and unions often do not pay attention to the special demands of women, so women reciprocate by not joining or supporting them.

The South is a good example of a place where sexist prejudice has joined racist prejudice to prevent unionization. The South is also a good example of a place where both racist and sexist discrimination have been used to weaken liberal and progressive political movements. White males in the South vote overwhelmingly conservative, even when this is exactly contrary to their objective interests as relatively poorly paid workers.

In conclusion, it should be stressed that the ideologies of racism and sexism have a strong impact on class relations, but class relations also have a strong impact on these twin ideologies.

EIGHT

*Unemployment and
Business Cycles*

T his chapter explores theories of unemployment and business cycles from various points of view, ending with contemporary Marxian views. The Marxian views are distinguished by their relational and historical approach. A comprehensive theory of unemployment and business cycles cannot be presented in one chapter but requires a book (see, e.g., Sherman 1991). Here there is only space to summarize the main theories, note a few of the empirical findings, and give special attention to the methodology used by the different theories.

Orthodox Economic Approaches to Unemployment and Cycles

The orthodox theory of unemployment and business cycles has evolved through various stages, beginning with the classical economists.

Classical Economics and Say's Law

All of the major classical economists—except Thomas Malthus— accepted Say's law. J. B. Say, writing around 1800, argued that any supply to the market automatically generated an equal demand so there would be equilibrium at full employment. Supply meant output, which entailed the payment of wages, rents, interest, and profits, all of which would be spent to buy an equal amount of commodities. Thus, in the aggregate there would be relatively rapid adjustment of demand to any new supply. Supply and demand could differ for individual goods for various reasons, but aggregate discrepancies could only last a short time. According to this theory, therefore, there would be equilibrium at full employment. No involuntary unemployment was possible for any length of time in the aggregate. It was recognized that temporary unemployment could result from temporary shocks to the economy, such as wars or plagues or floods.

The classical economists also tended to think of the aggregate capitalist economy in the same way that they thought of medieval economies, where there was very little use of money. Those economies operated by barter, so a pig brought to market was both supply and demand. In fact the classical economists emphasized that money was only a veil over the exchange between two commodities. Obviously, in such a barter economy there could be no lack of aggregate (monetary) demand. Therefore, if capitalism is interpreted in this ahistorical, nonmonetary fashion, then general unemployment—as opposed to partial unemployment in one industry—is not a problem.

The Neoclassical Approach to Unemployment and Cycles, 1870s to 1930s

Neoclassical theories of unemployment will be shown to start from psychological preferences, individual choices, and an equilibrium mechanism.

One reason why unemployment is such a mystery to so many professional economists is the ahistorical, equilibrium approach, which is most extreme in Say's law. According to the neoclassical economists, Say's law "proved" that aggregate demand and aggregate supply would always be harmoniously adjusted by the marketplace, whether on Robinson Crusoe's island or in the modern U.S. economy. Say's law prevented neoclassical economists from accepting even the possibility of aggregate lack of demand. Thus, they could have no analysis of general, involuntary unemployment because it could not result from the workings of the economy, but could only be a temporary deviation from equilibrium caused by *external shocks*.

External shocks have been defined by various neoclassical economists to include sunspots, wars, waves of psychological pessimism, or mistakes by government in regulating the money supply. The shocks considered are almost all from the supply side, except for preference changes that may change demand from one good to another, but change from one commodity to another does not create a lack of aggregate demand.

Neoclassical analysis focuses on incremental adjustments back to equilibrium by the economic system. The assumption of equilibrium as the normal condition of a competitive capitalist economy rules out internal causes of the cyclical booms and busts of capitalism. On the contrary, according to the neoclassical view, all cyclical recessions and depressions—from which the United States has suffered some thirty-seven times—are caused by external shocks.

By starting from psychological preferences, neoclassical theories conclude that all unemployment is voluntary. The argument is that people freely choose every economic activity in which they participate. Unemployment is just another economic activity. So unemployed workers chose leisure over paid work. Discussing individual preferences avoids having to deal with aggregate problems and gives completely different policy answers. If the problem is individual choice of unemployment, then no government action will do any good.

The Keynesian Period, 1930s to 1960s

Although some of the neoclassical theories had useful elements in particular sectors, they all still relied too heavily on Say's law to give a satisfactory explanation of the massive unemployment of the 1930s. Thus many economists were receptive to the theory of John Maynard Keynes (1936), which systematically destroyed Say's law and provided a unified theory of the aggregate behavior of the economy. For several decades no respectable economist endorsed Say's law, though almost all respectable economists had done so in the earlier period, from about 1800 until 1930.

Keynes's theory explained how it is possible for a capitalist economy to suffer from a lack of effective demand. The deficient demand leads to involuntary unemployment. Keynes tells much of the story in terms of national aggregates, including aggregate consumption, aggregate investment, aggregate wages, and aggregate profits. Such aggregate concepts were a sharp departure from the purely individualist approach of neoclassical economics. Like many other pioneers (including Marx), Keynes was ambiguous on some points of methodology because he spent much effort trying to disentangle himself from the old neoclassical paradigm. On the one hand, his aggregate concepts often were not adequately traced back to individual motivation, so they have been criticized for extreme collectivism. The neoclassical theorists seized on this alleged extreme collectivism to argue the need for going back to individualism.

On the other hand, Keynes retains some of the terminology of psychological reductionism. Thus, he talks about a fundamental psychological law of consumer behavior. He calls the ratio of consumption to income the "propensity to consume," as if it were determined by purely psychological preferences. Both the psychological reductionism in his terminology and the alleged extreme collectivism in some of his aggregate concepts are relatively minor aspects of Keynes's successful revolution against neoclassical macroeconomics. His followers, the Post Keynesians, have overcome these early ambiguities.

More significantly, Keynes still included neoclassical notions in the sense that he described adjustment to equilibrium. The very important difference is that for Keynes the equilibrium will often be below full employment, and there is no assurance that it will ever move to full employment. Yet the equilibrium approach did mean that Keynes was not historical or evolutionary.

The New Classical and New Keynesian Period, 1970 to the Present

Most New Classical theories hold even more tightly to the neoclassical methodology than did the neoclassical business cycle theories of the 1930s. Some famous New Classical theories of economic crises and cyclical unemployment are actually called equilibrium theories—for example, Robert Lucas's "equilibrium theory of the business cycle" (see Lucas 1975)—so they obviously do not deal with the historical evolution of the economy. It has been said that an equilibrium theory of the business cycle is actually a contradiction in terms. The problem is that the system is never at a full-employment equilibrium, but must be understood as it has evolved, along a bumpy, nonequilibrium road.

Moreover, the New Classical economists hold strongly to Say's law, although in new more complex versions of its mechanism. Much research of this period assumes that there is no lack of aggregate demand and so the problems must come from the supply side. Thus, an article in the *American Economic Review* assumes that the causes of instability are limited to "supply shock and relative fiscal, money, and preference shocks" (Ahmed et al. 1993, 335). The term *preference shocks* refers to changes in consumers' preferences among commodities but not to problems of aggregate demand.

The New Classical economists took the individual-preference approach to its logical extreme. For example, Lucas says that in order "to explain why people allocate time to . . . unemployment we need to know why they prefer it to all other activities" (1986, 38). But it is utterly unrealistic to think that workers choose unemployment in some voluntary sense. When a recession hits, millions of workers are fired within a few months. When General Motors fires fifty thousand auto workers, it does not give them any choice.

It is assumed in almost any textbook of the New Classical period—such as Samuelson and Nordhaus 1992—that unemployment means that the wage is too high. Unions or governments have imposed such a high wage that firms do not demand enough labor for full employment. If only wages were lowered, there would be full employment.

But this analysis ignores the point made most strongly by John Maynard Keynes (though Marx makes the same point) that when the wages of all individual workers are cut, aggregate consumer demand declines. When Paul Samuelson was a militant Keynesian, back in the days of his first edition, 1948, he made this point and said that neoclassical economists were guilty of the fallacy of composition. In other words, since neoclassical economics looks only at individual firms, it assumes that cutting wages has a negligible effect on the demand for the firm's product. For example, it is true that cutting the wages of shoe workers in one firm may have no significant effect on the demand for shoes. But if all wages in a nation are cut by 10 percent, then aggregate consumer demand will be significantly affected.

As another example of the individual-preference approach, New Classical explanations of aggregate consumer behavior merely sum up the actions of individuals each of whom is assumed to maximize his or her psychological utility. The use of individual preferences as ultimate building blocks by New Classical economics has had a profound effect on theories of aggregate consumer demand, limiting them to summing up individual psychological behavior. When John Maynard Keynes (1936) pioneered this field, he talked about psychology, but he also considered the objective facts of income distribution—as did Marx.

Some Marxian and Post Keynesian economists have put forth theories of aggregate consumer demand based on the class or functional distribution of income among consumers (see Sherman 1991). These radical theories of consumer demand form one basis for political movements for redistribution of income in capitalism or even for revolutionary changes to produce a new income structure. But New Classical economics rules all such theories out of order by examining only the individual preferences, which are said to form the micro foundations of aggregate theories.

Thus, the dominant New Classical consumption theories, the Permanent Income Theory and the Life Cycle Hypothesis, are purely individualist and therefore ignore institutions and class relations, which makes these theories quite inadequate (see Green 1984). Since individual preferences are taken as given, they are never explained. For this reason, it has been said that New Classical microeconomics has no macro foundations (see Hodgson 1986).

Finally, there is the New Keynesian variant of orthodox economics. This view follows Keynes in that it does not assume Say's law. It has had the salutary effect that fewer and fewer orthodox economists accept Say's law. Involuntary unemployment is explained by the New Keynesians in many ingenious ways. For a thorough presentation of the *efficiency wage theory* and other ways of explaining involuntary unemployment, see Ackerloff and Yellen 1986; Mankiw and Romer 1991; and Weiss 1990.

Although the New Keynesians conclude that the economy may fall below full employment, it is still an equilibrium result. Moreover, as the New Keynesians state implicitly or explicitly, their approach is still one of basing the foundations of aggregate economics on theories of individual psychological preferences and choices.

The So-called Falling Rate of Profit Theory

Those who proclaim themselves to be orthodox Marxists (and whose critics call them fundamentalist or dogmatist) explain all of aggregate capitalist phenomena, from trends to cycles, on the basis of the so-called *falling rate of profit theory.* For example, John Weeks claims that Marx's work is characterized by the "central role of the law of value and its most important manifestation, the tendency of the rate of profit to fall. This interpretation of Marx's work . . . can be called . . . 'orthodox' Marxism" (Weeks 1981, 7).

In this allegedly orthodox view (whose orthodoxy is denied by many scholars), economic crises are caused by a decline of investment, which is caused by a falling rate of profit. Why should the rate of profit fall? In this view, all profit is derived from the living labor of workers. Suppose the rate of exploitation—the ratio of surplus labor to living labor (or, roughly, the ratio of profit to wages)—remains the same. Then the total amount of profit per worker remains the same. The rate of profit, however, is defined as the ratio of total profit to total costs. Costs include not only the costs of employing living labor (called wages here) but also the costs of using plant and equipment.

Suppose a new technology leads to a higher ratio of machinery to living labor in the production process. In John Weeks's view, the rate of profit depends on both the rate of exploitation of workers and the ratio of machinery to labor. This allegedly orthodox theory stresses that profit comes only from living labor. If the rate of exploitation of labor and the ratio of machinery to labor remain the same, then the rate of profit remains the same. But if the ratio of machinery to worker rises, while the rate of exploitation of workers remains unchanged, then the rate of profit will decline.

There is an extensive literature criticizing this theory on both empirical and theoretical grounds (see Sherman 1972, app. 2), so very few Marxian economists still accept it. The falling rate of profit theory is discussed here only because it is an excellent example of economic reductionism in one Marxian tradition. In this theory, technological change leads to economic change. The economic change causes a crisis, which only then leads to class conflict and revolutionary change.

Note that the basic explanatory factor is technology. Moreover, human or class relations play no role in the decline of the profit rate. The emphasis is on the ratio of plant and equipment to labor hours, not class conflict. The theory deals with abstract economic forces in a mechanical way, not with human relationships. In this sense, the theory is a clear example of technological reductionism. Since the abstract economic forces act by themselves without reference to individual desires or behavior, it may also be called an example of extreme collectivism.

The Historical Approach to Economic Crises and Business Cycles

Most Marxian, Post Keynesian, and institutionalist economists criticize Say's law. Say's law, an assumption made by both the classical and neoclassical economists, denied the very possibility of insufficient demand or general unemployment. All New Classical, monetarist, and supply-side economists still believe in Say's law, so they do not believe in crises of general unemployment. They acknowledge only temporary deviations from equilibrium, caused by external shocks such as incorrect government policies. Thus the argument over Say's law is anything but academic.

The important point here is that one main Marxian criticism of Say's law is the historical one that it is an unwarranted generalization from consideration of earlier and simpler societies. Three characteristics of the aggregate economy have changed from feudalism to capitalism. Taken together, these three allow for the possibility of the modern type of economic crisis or business cycle. First, a central feature of feudalism was that commodities were produced for the use of

an isolated manor, whereas under capitalism commodities are produced to be exchanged. Second, the isolated feudal manor produced
commodities because the feudal lord decided they were necessary for
the manor, whereas in capitalism commodities are produced only if
there is the expectation of profit from exchange. Third, feudalism
used barter, whereas capitalism uses money. We must now examine
why each of these characteristics makes a difference in terms of the
possibility of crises and cycles.

First, it is characteristic of the modern capitalist economy that almost all production is directed solely toward its sale in the marketplace. This was hardly ever true of earlier societies. In very primitive
economies the collective unit of the whole tribe carries on production
for the collective use of the whole tribe. In such primitive economies
there can be no question of overproduction of commodities; that is,
aggregate demand can not be less than aggregate supply.

Even in the ancient slave empires and in medieval feudalism, the
basic production unit was the plantation or manor, which produced
mostly for its own self-sufficient existence. In some cases the economic
unit may have sold a small surplus, but that was usually not a vital
part of its operation. In some of these societies—such as ancient
Rome—there was also a large, though not vital, trade in luxury goods.

In all these earlier societies, since most production was for the immediate use of the economic unit itself, the phenomenon of overproduction was impossible. Thus, the carpenter on the feudal manor
would not produce more wagons than the manor would use. It was
quite different when Henry Ford produced millions of autos, not for
the use of Ford workers, but for sale in the market. It was certainly
possible that Ford could produce many more cars than could be sold
at a profit in the market. Furthermore, if Ford found that he could not
sell so many cars at a profit, then he would have reduced his production, and some Ford workers would have been unemployed.

A second characteristic of capitalism is that the sole motivation for
production is the private profit of the capitalist. Production is not
merely for exchange in the market but for exchange at a profit in the
market. Each individual enterprise makes its own plans on the basis
of its own estimate of whether it will obtain a private profit by production. It follows that false profit expectations may lead the aggregate of all firms to produce more (or less) than the market will buy.
If more is produced than can be sold at a profit, private enterprise
will fire workers and reduce its investment spending, thus leading to a
depression.

A third characteristic of modern capitalism is the regular use of money. The defenders of Say's law always spoke as if money were only used as a lubricant in the process of exchange between two commodities. They held that the "essential" features of the capitalist economic process were the same as in a barter economy. In a barter economy, if a farmer brings a pig to market, the pig is his or her supply to the market, but it is also his or her demand in the market. Thus, in a barter economy every supply of goods to the market is at the same time a demand for other goods.

In a barter economy there may be too much of a single commodity and not enough of another, but there cannot be an excess of aggregate supply over demand. While many features in a money economy are the same as in a barter economy, there is an important difference: Because money not only is a medium of exchange between commodities but may be withdrawn from exchange and stored away for an indefinite time, it is possible to have a monetary income in the capitalist economy that is hoarded and not immediately respent for the equivalent supply of products. In more modern terminology, the velocity of money may decline (i.e., people and firms may spend money more slowly), so there is a decline in the spending flow in the market. As a result, the capitalist economy can suffer from a lack of effective demand; that is, those who have the desire to purchase goods may not have the money to buy them, while those who have the money may not choose to spend it at this time.

Although overproduction seems a strange and even absurd epidemic, its ravages among its millions of human victims are nonetheless very real. Under capitalism, not only are thousands of factories idle, gathering dust, but millions of workers are involuntarily idle, gathering frustration. In the Great Depression, according to official government statistics, one out of every four U.S. workers was unemployed. Yet official statistics drastically understate unemployment by ignoring discouraged workers who no longer try for a job.

Official unemployment data also ignore the involuntary reduction of hours to a few hours a week for many of those part-time workers who still have a job. In the 1930s, for example, this part-time unemployment, or less than full-time employment, was probably visited on another 50 percent of all workers. The remaining 25 percent suffered drastic cuts in wage levels. People traveled from place to place looking for work, subsisting on private handouts or food from government soup kitchens (for the human reaction to the Great Depression, see Terkel 1970).

After the Second World War there were no major depressions for two decades, in part because of the high level of military production.

Periodic "minor" depressions did continue in the 1950s and 1960s, with full-time unemployment of "only" 6–8 percent of all workers, including much higher percentages of unemployed women, black, brown, young, and elderly workers. In 1975 unemployment rose to 9 percent officially, but if we add "discouraged" and involuntary part-time workers, it was actually about 16 percent. In 1982 unemployment rose to over 10 percent officially (or about twelve million workers unemployed), with two million "discouraged" workers and several million involuntary part-time workers. From 1990 to 1992 the official unemployment rate was 8–9 percent. Thus, a high level of unemployment has occurred in every recent recession.

Stages, Trends, and Cycles

There is nothing wrong with using an equilibrium approach as a first, simplistic approximation to a full, realistic analysis. For example, Keynes's analysis of involuntary unemployment at equilibrium is an enormous improvement over the previous neoclassical analyses. Moreover, Marx clearly uses an equilibrium analysis of a very simplified model in the first volume of *Capital*. In that volume, unemployment appears mainly as a factor helping capitalists keep a stable long-run wage at a level that will create profits. Furthermore, in volume 2 of *Capital* Marx discusses what would be a long-run growth path for capitalism, with equilibrium at each period, though he also indicates why that is impossible.

It is necessary, however, to recognize the severe limitations of an equilibrium analysis, the distortions it creates, and the inaccurate policy conclusions that would flow from it if one went no further. Keynes does go further in his chapter on the trade cycle in the *General Theory*, providing notes for a dynamic approach to the cycle without reference to equilibrium. Similarly, Marx discusses cyclical dynamics in a nonequilibrium context in many sections of volume 3 of *Capital*.

Marxism uses three levels of historical and evolutionary analysis in examining economic crises and cycles: stages of history, stages of capitalism, and stages of each business cycle. The stages of history refer to the different types of economic processes or modes of production in history. Thus. in U.S. history at various times and places there have been (1) the primitive collectivist mode of production of native Americans; (2) the slave mode of production in the South; (3) an independent, noncapitalist, farming mode of production in the West; and (4) the capitalist mode of production. None of the first three modes of production show the typical business cycle phenomena. Only capitalism generates business cycles, though the capitalist business cycle did have effects on the other modes of production whenever they coexisted. Thus, the Marxian analysis of economic crises is historically specific to a particular mode of production.

All Marxian political economists acknowledge that capitalism is not constant over time but changes in important ways as it evolves into different stages. At an early stage the U.S. economy was underdeveloped, had mainly independent farming and slave relations, was on a very small scale, and was mainly agricultural. In that stage the U.S. economic cycle was not self-generated, but was dominated by the British business cycle.

Later, the U.S. economy became an example of advanced capitalism, with industry dominating, a large working class, urban rather than rural workers, large-scale enterprise, and a high degree of monopoly power in the economy. Still later, the U.S. economy is now heavily influenced by a very large government sector with heavy taxing and spending. For a complete, thorough, and interesting description of the stages of U.S. economic history, see DuBoff 1989.

There is very little agreement among Marxian writers about exactly how to divide U.S. history into stages, one main reason being that how one divides historical stages depends on exactly what question is asked. Different questions or different problems emphasize different aspects of the socioeconomic system. Therefore, they establish a different periodization. One prominent set of stages has been established by the school known as the Social Structures of Accumulation, according to which each structure leads to differences in class power, which lead to differences in profitability for capitalists. For example, the members of this school describe the "rise and subsequent demise of a postwar social structure of accumulation" after the Second World War (Bowles, Gordon, and Weisskopf 1986, 132). In brief, they find a stage of strong capitalist power, with workers made compliant by prosperity, and high capitalist profits. This period was followed by a stage of declining capitalist power, pressure by workers, and declining capitalist profits (see Bowles, Gordon, and Weisskopf 1990).

The 1950s and 1960s might be called the Most Pleasant Stage of U.S. capitalism from the viewpoint of the U.S. capitalist class and much of the population, although less pleasant from the viewpoint of women and minorities. In this Most Pleasant Stage (1) the U.S. economy had a good rate of growth; (2) real wage rates had a strong upward trend; (3) the U.S. balance of trade was positive; (4) unions were quite strong; (5) the U.S. economy had far higher productivity of labor than any other economy; (6) the dollar was very strong, U.S.

banks ruled the financial world, and the United States was the largest creditor nation; and (7) contractions were relatively mild, and unemployment was relatively low.

In the period since the early 1970s all of this has changed. This period has been a Dismal Stage, marked by (1) low rates of economic growth, (2) declining real wage rates and stagnating family income (see the discussion of this startling fact of U.S. life in Peterson 1993); (3) a negative balance of trade in every year since 1970; (4) declining union strength as a percentage of all workers since about 1955; (5) a U.S. rate of productivity rising much more slowly than those of most other industrialized countries; (6) a weakening dollar, increasing financial strength in many other countries, and the United States being the largest debtor nation; and (7) much stronger contractions and rising unemployment. The average level of unemployment in each cycle has been rising since the 1960s. Most of these points are spelled out in great detail in Sherman 1991 and in the literature on the social structure of accumulation, cited above.

Within the historical context of a given mode of production, and a given stage within that mode of production, the third level of historical evolution is the dynamics of change within each business cycle. Each business cycle is unique because the historical context keeps changing. Yet there are certain constants as long as capitalism exists. In particular, the sequence of events in each cycle remains much the same even though the length and intensity of cycles changes drastically, ranging from the Great Depression to the minor cycles of the 1950s. Wesley Mitchell divided each business cycle very roughly into four stages—recovery, prosperity, crisis, and depression (for details, see Sherman 1991, ch. 2). Yet Mitchell, no less than Marx, emphasizes the differences between cycles as long-run trends lead to new stages of capitalism. Mitchell explains in great detail how each stage of the business cycle evolves into the next stage. Marx made the same point, though with less rigor because he planned to write a whole separate volume on cycles. Thus, the stage called "prosperity" (in terms of capitalist profits) has a slow accumulation of tensions and distortions that lead to a stage of "crisis." On the other hand, the "depression" stage witnesses a slow accretion of changes that eventually may lead to a recovery.

The complex relation between long-run change and cyclical change sometimes leads to confusion regarding trends and cycles. A trend is an index of long-run change. Some analyses have treated trends as completely separate from cycles, using mechanical means to separate the two for separate analyses. There is nothing wrong with separating the two types of change for analytic purposes, provided their relation is kept firmly in mind. Growth under capitalism comes in the form of cycles, so the real world does not separate trends from cycles. A trend, such as rising unemployment or falling real wages from 1973 to 1990, is the joint result of both long-run pressures under capitalism and the effects of the business cycle.

On the other hand, a business cycle, such as the weak but long expansion from 1982 to 1990, is a result of both long-run trends and the usual cyclical forces. In brief, a complete theory of the business cycle must explain both the regularities observed in all cycles and the unique character of each cycle in the context of economic evolution. In this context, a trend reflects the rate of growth from one cycle to another, taking each cycle as a single average point. Similarly, a complete theory of a given trend, such as the rising national debt, must include the effect of the business cycle on it.

The Relational Approach to Crises and Unemployment

In looking at unemployment, modern orthodox economics begins with individuals with given psychological preferences engaging in an optimization process in competition with others, leading to some point of full-employment equilibrium, which is disturbed only by external shocks. In contrast, Marxian theories in the relational-historical approach view capitalism as a single, unified socioeconomic system with class relations as central, and they find the dynamic of capitalism itself to be the cause of economic crises. A relational approach must take human relations seriously, so most Marxian theories place class relations at the heart of their analysis of the business cycle.

Remember that class relations are reflected at the economic level, the level of the government and other institutions, and the level of ideology, so all of these must eventually enter the analysis. It will be shown specifically how class affects both consumption and investment, not to speak of government behavior. Also, international relations must be brought into any realistic analysis. It is useful, however, to begin with a simpler picture, one that concentrates only on the most essential relationships. A detailed discussion of the business cycle on all these levels of relationships, as well as formal models, and a thorough empirical analysis are contained in Sherman 1991.

Three Marxian theories are summarized here: a wage cost theory, an effective demand theory, and a profit squeeze theory. The reader should note that all three (1) deal only with the internal evolution of the cycle, taking the mode of production and the stage of capitalism as given in the first approximation; (2) make the class relations of capitalism a key feature; and (3) find the cause of the cycle of boom and bust in the internal dynamics of capitalism.

The Marxian Theory of Wage Cost (or Reserve Army)

All Marxian economists agree that investment is the key factor in the business cycle. It fluctuates far more than consumption, and it is the only way to get economic growth and more jobs. All Marxian economists also agree that the most vital determinant of investment is profit. The expected rate of profit on a new investment is the motivation for that investment, while total profits are a main source of investment funds as well as the basis for obtaining credit from financial firms. Profit may be affected by costs as well as by demand for commodities.

The first theory considered here is one in which rising wage costs cause a reduction of profit, which leads to less investment and an economic downturn. There is a Marxian as well as a conservative version of the wage cost theory. Some conservative theorists put the whole blame for cyclical depressions on rising wages. The conservative solution—which is pleasing to business—is to hold down costs, particularly wage costs. Those who emphasize the rising costs of labor claim that more employment can only come as a result of cutting wages. According to one standard textbook, "The general solution to involuntary unemployment is a reduction in real wages until the amount of labor demanded equals the amount supplied" (Leftwich and Sharp 1974, 249). The notion of solving unemployment by cutting wages conveniently ignores the fact that lower wages mean less demand for consumer goods, which makes it harder for capitalists to realize their profits. Both Marx and Keynes emphasized this fact.

Nevertheless, some radicals agree that every depression is the result of low profits caused by high wages and/or less labor productivity. Thus, two radicals, citing the *Wall Street Journal* as their source, say, "Knowledgeable observers of the labor scene have pointed directly to an increasingly obstreperous labor force as an influence on the decline in productivity during the expansion" (Boddy and Crotty 1975, 8). Like the conservatives, Boddy and Crotty argue that high employment levels lead to a militant, or "obstreperous," labor force, which causes higher wages and lower productivity, thus causing a crisis by lowering profits. Marx called the unemployed workers the "reserve army of labor." Because Boddy and Crotty stress that the "reserve army" of labor declines in the boom, leading to higher wage costs, which cause lower profits, their theory may be called the reserve army theory or the wage cost theory.

The Marxian wage cost cycle theory has been spelled out systematically by Goldstein (1985). First, he shows that every cyclical expansion is characterized by accumulation of capital and extensive investment, leading to a declining rate of unemployment. In other words, unemployment declines as output rises in every expansion. Second, he claims that the falling unemployment strengthens the bargaining power of labor, so that there are rising hourly wages and a declining rate of productivity growth. If hourly wages rise faster than productivity, the share of labor in national income must grow (or, in traditional Marxian terminology, the rate of exploitation will drop).

It is important to note that current Marxian wage cost theories all emphasize that the share of labor in income will not rise immediately. As soon as an expansion starts, unemployment begins to decline. But there is still a very high rate of unemployment, so employers can still draw more workers from the reserve army of unemployed without paying higher wages. Furthermore, as unemployment declines, it takes some time for this to become clear to all parties. Thus, the subjective attitudes of workers and capitalists change rather slowly, with a time-lag.

At the beginning of expansion, workers are still very worried about their jobs, while employers are still confident of getting all the workers they wish at the going wage. Only after a long time-lag do workers recognize that they are in a better bargaining position than in the recession, and after an even longer time-lag employers finally admit that it is harder to hire new workers at the prevailing wage. Only toward the end of the expansion do workers become more militant and capitalists begin to retreat. At that time, the increased bargaining power of labor leads to rising wages and declining productivity (as workers successfully prevent speed-up).

So far, the story from the reserve army viewpoint has emphasized (1) declining unemployment (due to expansion of output) and (2) rising wage costs. Those are the two facts most essential to the theory; the rest of the theory merely spells out the effects of those two alleged facts. If wage costs are rising and productivity is sluggish, then the share of labor in total income must be increasing. By definition, the *labor share* is the ratio of labor income to all production (wages/product), which equals the hourly wage rate (wages/hours) divided by productivity (product/hours).

Third, if the whole product is divided between labor and capital, then a rise in the labor share must mean a fall in the profit share.

Fourth, if the profit share of output falls, then, all other things being equal, which they usually are not, the rate of profit must decline. Thus, there is at the end of expansion a falling rate of profit, which in this theory is due to rising wage costs. Fifth, when the rate of profit declines, investors get worried and lower their investment. Less investment means fewer jobs, less output and income, less purchasing power, and recession.

Of course, in a recession all of these steps reverse themselves, giving rise to an eventual economic recovery. Very briefly, in a recession (1) unemployment rises, labor militancy declines, and labor bargaining power declines; (2) wages slowly fall, and eventually productivity rises, so, after a time-lag, the labor share falls, while the profit share rises; (3) causing a rising profit rate; (4) which leads to a rising amount of investment.

Some of the assumptions of the wage cost (or reserve army) theory may be—and have been—challenged. There is no argument about the first hypothesis: unemployment does fall in expansions and rise in contractions (see Sherman 1991, ch. 3). The second assumption, that the wage share will move opposite to unemployment, has been criticized on several grounds. In most business cycles both unemployment and the wage share move downwards for most of the expansion, while both unemployment and the wage share move upward during contractions. Furthermore, econometric tests show that there is no significant correlation between unemployment and the wage share (after correcting for autocorrelation [see Sherman 1991, ch. 8]).

The third assumption is that a rising wage share (or falling profit share) must mean a falling rate of profit. This does not follow logically from any reasonable definition of the rate of profit. It may happen if all other things remain constant, but that is unlikely. Suppose profit is defined as revenue minus cost. At the aggregate level, revenue equals consumption plus investment spending (if we examine only the private domestic economy). Cost will include both labor cost (wages, salaries, and so forth) and material costs (the depreciation of the plant and equipment as well as the cost of replacing raw materials used up). Thus, if wage costs rise, they may be offset by rising revenue from consumption and/or investment. Wage costs may also be offset by falling material costs. In the case of this theory, since it is assumed that wage costs are rising, it must also be assumed that aggregate consumption spending is rising. The rising consumption from wage income may offset the rising wages. The fourth assumption, that rising profits and rising profit rates will lead to more investment, is certainly true (see Sherman 1991, ch. 6).

The theory has some important insights, but it reduces all explanation of the cycle to just one factor: rising wages caused by falling unemployment accompanying rising output. This economic reductionist approach, hanging the whole explanation on just one factor, is common to many business cycle theories, but it leaves one with an incorrect understanding of the relationships involved. The exclusive concentration on costs of supply leaves out the entire dimension of demand. Rising wages lead to rising consumer demand, which must enter the picture.

The Marxian Theory of Effective Demand (or Underconsumption)

Many early theories of underconsumption argued naively that workers were not paid enough wages to buy back all they produced, resulting in a lack of consumer demand and hence a recession or depression. Such theories were incomplete or inaccurate and were criticized by many theorists, including Karl Marx.

Present-day Marxian theories of effective demand are quite different, spelling out exactly how class relationships affect the economy through their effect on demand. According to the Marxian theory of effective demand, first, in every expansion of the economy the share of labor in the national income declines (or in traditional terminology, the rate of exploitation rises). It is an empirical fact that the labor share does decline for most of every expansion (see Sherman 1991, ch. 8). It tends to lead the cycle (or turn before the peak), but it normally turns after the rate of profit turns. The reason that the labor share falls for most of the expansion is that productivity rises much faster than wages. Under the institutions of capitalism, the fact that productivity increases does not automatically mean that workers get higher wages, because the product belongs to the owners of the corporation. Higher wages are held back by fixed labor contracts, by employer resistance, and sometimes by government complicity with employers.

Second, the falling labor share tends to lead to a falling ratio of consumption to national income (called a *falling propensity to consume* in Keynesian language). The reason is that workers consume approximately 100 percent (or at least a very high proportion) of their income, while capitalists consume a much lower proportion of their income. The rich have plenty of income to meet their normal consumption standards, so they do not increase their consumption much when their income rises. Capitalists save more than workers and may or may not use their savings to invest. It is an empirical fact that the average ratio of consumption to income (or propensity to consume) declines in the expansion and that it is correlated with the falling labor share (see Sherman 1991, ch. 5). Thus, as the expansion progresses, the total consumer spending rises more and more slowly.

Third, investment is a function of profit expectations, which are determined largely by expected consumer demand. When consumer demand begins to grow more and more slowly, profit expectations also begin to stagnate, until the result is a decline in investment. A capitalist producing shoes, for example, invests in new plant and equipment if, and only if, there is an expectation that consumer demand will grow to be sufficient to purchase the product of the new plant. The decline in investment leads to a recession.

In the recession, all of these processes are reversed. First, the labor share begins to rise because wages fall more slowly than productivity. Second, the rising labor share eventually leads to a rise in the ratio of consumption to income, which means that consumer demand stops falling. Third, the signs of a stronger consumer demand lead to improved profit expectations. Better profit expectations lead to more investment, which causes an economic recovery.

The effective demand theory may be criticized as follows: First, the story told about a falling wage share, though broadly true, leaves out the important factor of changes in unemployment. Second, other variables than income and income distribution will have some effect on consumption, particularly the factors affecting consumer credit. Third, consumer demand certainly affects profits, but so do other things, including all types of costs. One cannot get out of a recession merely by raising wages; while this helps demand, it also raises capitalist costs. This theory, like most business cycle theories, is reductionist in the sense that it concentrates on just one factor. That factor is lack of consumer demand, caused by a falling wage share. The important insight is that consumer demand does affect profits. The most important thing overlooked is that costs also affect profits.

A Marxian Profit Squeeze (or Nutcracker) Theory

The wage cost theory is one-sided because it ignores demand. The effective demand theory is one-sided because it ignores costs. A profit squeeze theory must reflect both demand and costs. One cannot squeeze an orange from one side only because it rolls away; and one cannot logically explain a profit squeeze without looking at both the factors limiting demand and the factors increasing costs.

Three giants of business cycle theory—Karl Marx, John M. Keynes, and Wesley Mitchell—all recognized the two-sided character of the problem facing capitalists. John Maynard Keynes focused on the *marginal efficiency of capital,* which is roughly the expected rate of profit from a new investment. The expected rate of profit depends on the expected stream of revenue from the investment minus the expected stream of costs of the investment. But expected values depend on present and past experience, so we must concentrate on the present and past factors affecting the rate of profit.

Wesley Mitchell explained the evolution of profit rates over the cycle in terms of demand over the cycle and costs over the cycle. Mitchell spelled this out in enormous empirical detail, giving us a picture of the institutional causes of the business cycle that is a basic guide for anyone wanting to understand it.

Karl Marx pointed out that the capitalist must first extract profit (or surplus value) from the worker. "But this production of surplus value is but the first act of the capitalist process of production. . . . Now comes the second act of the process. The entire mass of commodities . . . must be sold. If this is not done, or only partly accomplished . . . the laborer has been none the less exploited, but his exploitation does not realize as much for the capitalist" (Marx 1907, 286).

Profits, therefore, may be squeezed from two directions at the peak of expansion. First, profits are squeezed by rising costs of production, which may prevent creation of surplus value. Second, profits are squeezed by limited demand, which may prevent realization of surplus value. Some Marxian economists—in the wage cost theory— emphasize only the capitalist's problems in producing surplus value. On the other hand, some Marxian economists—in the effective demand theory—emphasize only the capitalist's problems in selling the product or realizing surplus value. Any complete crisis theory must explain both sides of the nutcracker that squeezes capitalist profits at the cycle peak.

In the beginning and middle of the expansion phase of the cycle, output and capacity utilization are rising. The percentage of capacity that is utilized by capitalists is a good indicator of overall demand and perhaps the best single indicator of the stage of the cycle. What other important things are happening according to the profit squeeze theory?

First, as output and capacity utilization rise, the share of labor in national income steadily drops. The share of labor is, in fact, inversely correlated with output and capacity utilization, though some of the movement of the labor share is also explained to a lesser degree by the rate of unemployment with a considerable time-lag (see Sherman

1991, ch. 8). Expansion of output and better use of capacity means rising productivity outstripping wages. The contrary effect on the labor share of falling unemployment is felt only near the peak.

Second, consumer demand is determined by the amount of national income but also by the distribution of income between labor income and property income (see Sherman 1991, ch. 5). The fact that in mid-expansion the labor share is declining means that income is shifting from poor workers to rich capitalists. Since workers consume all their income, while rich capitalists consume only part of their income, the shift in income distribution from worker to capitalist means a decline in the average amount of consumption per dollar of income. For this reason the growth rate of consumption declines further and further, till it is very low before the cycle peak.

Third, on the cost side, labor income is rising, but it is rising more slowly than national income (or more slowly than profit income). Therefore, labor costs are not cutting into profits. One cannot, however, ignore material costs. Material costs include the depreciation of plant and equipment and the using up of raw materials. The third major assumption of this theory is that the prices of raw materials rise much faster than the prices of finished goods. This phenomenon was noted long ago by Wesley Mitchell (and even earlier by Marx) and is confirmed in modern data (see, e.g., Sherman 1991, ch. 10). Thus, on the cost side, costs per unit do not rise more than output because of labor costs, but they do rise more than output at the end of expansion because of rising raw material costs.

Fourth, profits and profit rates both rise rapidly in early expansion and more slowly in mid-expansion; then they usually decline before the cycle peak (see details in Sherman 1991, ch. 12). Profits equal revenue minus costs. In a capitalist economy, consumer demand is the largest single source of revenue. In early expansion consumer demand is rising very sharply. By late expansion (for reasons given above) consumer demand is rising very slowly.

The cost of raw materials rises very slowly in early expansion but rises faster than the price of final output in late contraction. Therefore, profit is squeezed between stagnant revenues (from limited consumer demand) and rising costs (from rising raw material prices). It is for this reason that profits and profit rates begin to decline in late expansion.

Fifth, investment is a function of profits and profit rates (see Sherman 1991, ch. 6). Rising profit rates increase expectations for future profits from new investment. Rising total profits provide a fund for reinvestment as well as an important asset to show banks when a firm wishes to borrow. The facts show that investment rises rapidly in early expansion, then decreases its rate of growth, reaching its peak at the cycle peak. To understand investment behavior, the political economist refers to profit behavior. The decline of profit rates and total profits in late expansion causes, after a time-lag, a decline in investment. The decline in investment always is at the cycle peak because it means less job generation, less income, and the beginning of recession.

These five steps slowly reverse themselves during the downturn. In the initial crisis, costs are still high, while demand drops precipitously, so profits and profit rates are subject to rapid decline in the crisis period at the beginning of every recession. What happens as the recession continues? First, the share of labor in national income begins to rise because wages decline very slowly, while productivity declines more rapidly; and the influence of rising unemployment will not act strongly enough to depress the labor share until toward the end of the recession. Second, the rising labor share leads to a rising average ratio of consumption to income (i.e., a rising propensity to consume). This causes consumption to fall more and more slowly, until it reaches a floor.

Third, raw material costs do not decline much at first, but they eventually begin a rapid decline, so that their ratio to output prices is reduced. Fourth, because of both the rising propensity to consume and the falling ratio of raw-material prices to finished goods prices, profits and profit rates recover toward the end of the recession. Fifth, with the recovery of profits and profit rates, expectations become optimistic enough to bring about a rise in investment. This results in increased output, employment, and income, so the recovery begins.

Adding Realism by Successive Approximations

The discussion so far has presented a rigorous and consistent theory of the mechanism whereby capitalism always tends to produce instability in the form of a business cycle of boom and bust. But there has been no discussion so far of (1) money and credit, (2) the effect of monopoly power, (3) the international spread of business cycles, and (4) the role of government. Each of these four vital aspects of the political economic system must be discussed and integrated with the description of the basic causes of the business cycle; only then will we have a truly unified, relational picture of the mechanisms of the unstable capitalist system.

Money and Credit

The existence of money and credit, according to both Keynes and Marx, is one reason why Say's law is incorrect. Hence, the existence of money and credit is a precondition of business cycles. But what is their role in the business cycle? During an expansion, the extension of credit to consumers and to investors means that demand grows more swiftly than it otherwise would have without credit, thus heating up the expansion and perhaps postponing the downturn. Why does credit expand so fast in an expansion? The fact is that because jobs and profits are increasing, consumers, investors, and financial institutions are all optimists.

Do money and credit cause a cyclical downturn or upturn? The answer seems to be that they generally have only a small effect in actually initiating a downturn. Toward the end of expansion, the interest rate rises; in fact it continues to rise until after the peak. So it does have some negative effect on profits, but it is only one factor added to the story told above. Once the contraction begins, however, the refusal of credit to many potential consumers and potential investors results in a worse contraction than there otherwise would have been, that is, a deeper and longer depression. The reason why credit drops so drastically in a recession is that consumers, investors, and financial institutions are all pessimistic in their expectations, for which they have good, objective reasons. Toward the end of a contraction the interest rate drops considerably, reducing costs, raising industrial profits, and possibly encouraging new investment. In both expansion and contraction, the profit rate reaches a turning point before any financial factors, so they probably react to it. The causation thus runs from the economy, through the profit rate, to the financial system, even though the feedback of the financial system may have an enormous impact. A detailed factual and analytic account of the financial side of the business cycle may be seen in Sherman 1991, ch. 14.

Monopoly Power

Those industries that have a high degree of monopoly power react to recession with constant or rising prices. The profit rates of those industries fall relatively less than those of other industries. Industries with monopoly power, however, tend to have larger declines in output and employment than other industries. Smaller firms in less concentrated industries tend to experience much greater declines in prices and profits but lesser declines in output and employment than the more concentrated industries. Thus, the existence of monopoly power means that the behavior of corporate profit is quite different in the more concentrated sectors than in the less concentrated sectors, so one should consider these sectors separately if one is to understand the business cycle really well. It appears that the existence of monopoly power distorts the response to recession, making output and employment results worst in the concentrated sector, while prices and profits drop most precipitously in the less concentrated sector. Monopoly power thus probably makes downturns worse than they would otherwise be. For a detailed factual and analytic discussion of the relation of monopoly power to the business cycle, see Sherman 1991, ch. 15.

The International Spread of the Business Cycle

Business cycles spread from one country to another through three different mechanisms. First, when a country goes into a contraction, its imports go down, because imports are based on national income. But if the United States imports less from Mexico, the Mexican economy may go into a recession. Second, if a country goes into a contraction, other countries are less willing to invest in it. For example, if the U.S. economy suffers a recession, then Japanese investors will be less willing to invest in the United States. But if enough countries are in recession, then Japan will have an excess of capital that cannot be invested, so Japan may have a recession. Third, there are many financial ties between countries. For example, if the U.S. stock market plunges, then the Japanese stock market may react with its own downward slide, as happened in October 1987. If the government of Brazil cannot repay a loan to the Bank of America, the Bank of America will suffer losses and may go bankrupt.

Generally, in the 1950s and 1960s the U.S. economy went through a number of small recessions, but Western Europe and Japan continued to grow, though the rate of growth of most countries usually declined during the U.S. recession. In the seventies, eighties, and nineties the economies of the United States, Western Europe, and Japan were far more synchronized. When all of them were in recession at once, they tended toward cumulative downward pressures. When all of them expanded at once, they tended toward cumulative upward pressures. The reason for the increased synchronization was increased international interaction through trade, investment, and finance. For further detailed analysis and factual description, see Sherman 1991, ch. 16.

The Role of Government

Neoclassical economists think of government as a dumb monster that is outside of the economic system and inflicts shocks on the system every now and then. Marxian and other radical political economists think of government as an integral part of the capitalist socioeconomic system. Thus, whenever the capitalist economic system expands, the government responds in a certain way. It responds the same way in every peacetime expansion; war situations are quite different.

During the average peacetime expansion the U.S. government usually expanded its spending, but at a very slow pace (slower than economic growth). At the same time, taxes grew at least as fast as national income, usually faster. Because some taxes are progressive in nature, they take more revenue at higher income brackets, so their proportion rises with increases in income. Since spending grows slowly and taxes grow rapidly, the usual pattern is a reduction of the deficit during expansions; there was even a surplus in the 1950s and 1960s. This means that the usual effect of fiscal actions is fairly depressing, or much less stimulating, by the end of the expansion. Monetary policy also tends to expand in order to accommodate growth in early expansion but becomes more wary and depressing by late expansion.

In a contraction the process reverses itself. The U.S. government is forced to increase spending for items such as unemployment compensation. At the same time, taxes decline at about the same rate as national income. Since spending is rising rapidly and taxes are falling rapidly, the deficit increases in contractions. More deficit spending tends to stimulate the economy at the bottom of the recession. Monetary policy comes under political pressure to also help stimulate the economy at the bottom of a contraction.

None of this means that government is the cause of the business cycle. In earlier periods of U.S. history, the government was much too small to affect the economy. Federal spending was only 1 percent of gross domestic product in 1929. Thus the business cycle existed long before government had much effect on peacetime cycles. Now it certainly has an effect, so its impact must be added to the basic story.

Conclusions

Since their approach is individualist, equilibrium-oriented, and psychologically reductionist, most orthodox economists (but not all) view the economy as operating at equilibrium, subject to external shocks, which cause people to make certain choices according to their preferences, including voluntary unemployment. Since their approach is relational, historical, and class-oriented, most Marxian political economists (1) see an integrated whole of the international capitalist political economic system, so (2) they see the system evolving cyclically with long-run growth according to its internal dynamics. Those dynamics are such, given capitalist class relations, that they cause every expansion to end in crisis, downturn, and widespread involuntary unemployment. The changes in the socioeconomic system that would be necessary to eliminate involuntary unemployment are discussed in part IV.

NINE

Democracy and Capitalism

One possible view of the relationship between democracy and capitalism sees the former determining the latter. A popular view in the U.S. media assumes that the voters determine the government, with all voters having equal power; then the government passes laws that determine the economic system in the interests of the majority.

Perhaps no reputable theorist now subscribes to this view, but during the Cold War at least one political scientist, Arnold Rose, asserted that the "power structure of the United States is highly complex and diversified (rather than unitary and monolithic), that the political system is more or less democratic. . . , that in political processes the political elite is ascendant over and not subordinate to the economic elite" (Rose 1967, 492).

In arguing for the proposition that the United States is democratic in nature, Rose found it necessary to emphasize that political power is to a large degree independent of and superior to economic power. The reason for this insistence is that economic power is distributed in an extremely unequal manner. If political power exactly followed economic power, the degree of inequality would leave little to be called democracy.

Conservative Psychological Reductionism

Rose's view is one form of psychological reductionism. The most popular form of psychological reductionism today is the view that the political ideas of individuals determine the economic system, and not vice versa. It is based on the individual psychology and alleged rational choices of the voter and the politician. The psychology of voters determines the political sphere, and the political sphere determines the economic sphere. This is a one-way process, so it reduces the socioeconomic system to psychology. By excluding any effect of the economic process on the political process, it leaves out a very important part of reality. It ignores the role wealth and money play in the political process, a role that is discussed below.

Conservative Economic Reductionism

Another popular viewpoint in the U.S. media equates capitalism with democracy. According to this view, if it is granted that the political system and the economic system are indeed two different things, then the capitalist economic system is the only possible foundation for political democracy. This view argues that in a capitalist economy every person is independent, while a centrally planned economy makes everyone dependent on a huge and arbitrary bureaucracy.

Whatever one thinks of central planning, it is hard to accept the notion that everyone in capitalism is equally independent. It is true that everyone has the formal right to leave a job and start a business. But one needs money to start a business. Most workers have little or no savings (and large debts), so most workers are very dependent on keeping their job. This limits their freedom, because if they are fired for loudly expressing unpopular views, they will join the ranks of the unemployed.

This second popular view is economic reductionist in a way because it says that the political system (political democracy) is fundamentally shaped by the economic system (capitalism). One major criticism of such a view is that so many capitalist countries have had political dictatorships, such as Nazi Germany or Franco Spain or Pinochet's Chile.

Soviet Marxism and Economic Reductionism

The Soviet Union and the Communist parties controlled by it argued for economic reductionism, but they came to a conclusion that was opposite that of conservative economic reductionists. They argued that any government is controlled by the dominant economic class. All Marxian political economists recognize that one cannot study political power without studying economic power, and vice versa. The most vulgar and dogmatic Soviet Marxian ideologues, however, took the extreme view that economics determines everything and that politics is completely subordinate.

Soviet Marxism argued that in capitalism the economy is controlled by the capitalist class. Therefore, the capitalist class exercises its economic power to gain complete control of the government. Workers are the vast majority, but they have no say in the government, so the capitalist government is a dictatorship of the capitalist class. The two classes—workers and capitalists—are in conflict, but the capitalists are always able to use the government against the workers.

On the other hand, in the old Soviet Marxian view, under *socialism,* defined to mean the Soviet model, the economy is controlled by the working class. Therefore, in the Soviet Union the working class controlled the government because economic power controls political power. Since a large majority of the population were industrial or agricultural workers, the Soviet government was thus democratically controlled, according to the Soviet view.

No Marxian scholar any longer takes such a simplistic view, but it was a very influential view for a very long time. According to many modern interpreters, Marx himself had a very sophisticated and complex view of political sociology (see Avineri 1968; Carnoy 1984; Draper 1977; and Szymanski 1978), but that is not an issue debated here. What is important is the great difference between the old Soviet view and non-Soviet Marxian views.

First, whereas the old view saw only two classes under capitalism, the critical Marxian view sees a multitude of middle classes. Whereas the Soviet theory pictured a unified capitalist class, the critical approach describes strife between factions of the capitalist class. Whereas the Soviet theory assumed automatic capitalist domination of the government, critical Marxism finds a complex, many-sided class conflict that may sometimes lead to major reforms helping middle classes, workers, and farmers.

Second, where the old Soviet Marxism assumed that capitalist governments bear a one-to-one relation to the economic interest of "the capitalist class," non-Soviet Marxism shows that governments do have a certain limited autonomy from the dominant class and that politics represent a tangled skein of long-run and short-run interests of a wide variety of different classes and different factions within classes.

Third, governments have functioned not only to protect the interests of the rulers against the ruled but also to further certain common interests of all classes. For example, in ancient Egypt it was necessary to control the Nile and irrigation. Of course there was also the Egyptian ruling class's need to hold down and repress the slave class in order to exploit the slaves' labor. All U.S. government functions today still have these two aspects: common functions for the community and class functions for the ruling class. For example, the building of highways serves the whole community, but the decision about which highways and how many highways is largely determined by the profit motives of the automobile industry and the construction industry, both of which maintain huge lobbies at the federal and state levels.

Fourth, some of the old Soviet Marxian writers argued as if the capitalist class directly runs the government of capitalist countries. The non-Soviet Marxian view, in contrast, emphasizes that the actual day-to-day running of the government is usually left to a specialized group of politicians, employed in the same way that engineers are employed, so that capitalist control is indirect. Nor is the control exercised by a conspiracy, but by the internal dynamics of the whole system and its institutions.

A Historical Approach to Government

The institution of government is not eternal. The institution of government as we know it did not exist in very primitive societies, and it may change drastically at some time in the future. Marxian social scientists hope that a day will come when there will still be a government, but it will use no force because there will be no class conflicts.

All Marxian writers are very critical of those theorists who insist that there always has been and always will be an elite of rulers and an oppressed mass of ruled. Contemporary, critical Marxism takes seriously the findings of anthropology that many primitive societies are built around the extended family or clan and have no government in the modern sense, and certainly no police or other repressive forces. Marxian anthropologists argue that there was not a repressive state, because there was no class division. In some very primitive societies people were elected for temporary leadership of community functions, but there was no need for repression because there was no exploited class.

Moreover, contrary to the view that government in a democracy merely reflects all of the voters' views in some equitable manner, government does not balance all interests and reach an equilibrium. Rather, different interests fight out battles in the political sphere, and the winners determine policy. In the political arena under capitalism, for example, farmers fight for certain policies, such as cheap loans or subsidies; sometimes they win, but sometimes they lose.

The form of government has changed many times in history, especially when there have been changes in class relationships. Thus, the ancient Roman government was controlled directly by the slave owners, but in the modern capitalist government the capitalist class usually has the greatest influence through indirect means. In feudal society the landlord ruled both the economy and the functions of government and repression. Capitalists rule the economy, but they usually do not directly rule in the government. More commonly, capitalists support politicians who will protect their interests. The politicians may not themselves be capitalists, but often they are lawyers or other hired hands of the capitalist class.

In the Soviet case there was government ownership of the whole economy and central planning of all economic activity, so the governing group was inevitably identical with the ruling economic group. Since the Soviet economy was centrally controlled, whoever ruled the government ruled the economy. In that respect, the Soviet government was like the feudal landlord, having both economic and political power.

In addition to changes in the basic class relations of a society, there are stages within a given social formation that lead to major changes in government policies. During the years of expansion following the Second World War, the capitalist class in the United States was willing and able to continue to increase the real wages of workers. Moreover, the capitalist class in that period fought only rather feebly against the fairly progressive government policies toward redistribution of income from rich to poor, though that policy was always rather limited. When times became much more difficult for the United States after about 1970, not only were higher wages successfully resisted but government distribution policies turned markedly against labor.

Examples of the new stage of confrontation were the tax laws initiated by the Reagan and Bush administrations. More precisely, from 1977 to 1990 all types of federal taxes as a percentage of income rose for the poor and the middle class but declined for the rich. There was a linear correlation from tax increases to tax decreases as the income bracket increased. Specifically, this is apparent if one examines the data for each decile (or tenth) of taxpayers. So, from 1977 to 1990 the poorest tenth of income receivers (the lowest decile) paid a tax increase of 28 percent. There were tax increases of 12 percent for the second lowest decile, 10 percent for the third decile, 3 percent for the fourth, 2 percent for the fifth, and 1 percent for the sixth decile. But the more affluent population enjoyed tax cuts. There was a tax decrease of 2 percent for the seventh decile, 3 percent for the eighth, 2 percent for the ninth, and a very significant 7 percent decrease for the top decile. Moreover, the top 1 percent of income receivers enjoyed a huge 23 percent decrease in taxes (all data in this paragraph are from Steinmo 1993, 5).

A Relational Approach to Debates on Government

Under capitalism, the capitalist class normally has enormous influence and control over government. This is another way of saying that class relationships affect political relationships. The relational approach has produced hundreds of detailed studies of the two-way interaction between politics and economics. All Marxian political economists agree that the capitalist class influences the government, but there have been vast debates over both the mechanisms of control and the degree of control. Most Marxian writers emphasize the qualifications on economic control given above. The Marxian relational method emphasizes that the political process also affects the economic process, contrary to the picture of one-way causation painted by Soviet Marxism.

Although there is an area of basic agreement, Marxian and other radical economists have recently spent a great deal of time debating a proper theory of government because (1) Stalinism distorted and prevented reasonable discussion on the left for many decades; (2) government is becoming much more powerful in the United States, Japan, and Western Europe; (3) dictatorship still prevails in many underdeveloped capitalist countries; and (4) dictatorship also prevailed in all of the so-called socialist countries. These debates are discussed briefly here, but they are discussed in more detail with great clarity in Carnoy 1984.

Instrumentalism

The simplest Marxian view is *instrumentalism*. This view sees government as a direct instrument of the ruling class, which uses government for its own benefit. This is an economic reductionist view when it is stated in an extreme form. It argues that capitalist wealth is used to gain many of the key positions in the government for members of the capitalist class. Since this is a very simplistic view, no known Marxian or radical scholar in the United States or Western Europe admits to owning it.

It is sometimes alleged that William Domhoff (1967) held this view because he traced the interrelationships of the ruling class in various spheres of activity and argued that there is indeed only one ruling class. Domhoff, however, specifically stated that he was not an instrumentalist because he did not focus solely on the role of the capitalist elite. Rather, he saw the political sphere as one of class conflict and said that this was basic to his analysis. As one example, Domhoff analyzed labor laws in this perspective and saw a complex three-way relation between labor, business, and government. Although there are many criticisms of his analysis, all of Domhoff's early work was extremely useful in terms of detailed description.

Domhoff and many other radicals have described how capitalist wealth is used to influence government. First, capitalists give money to candidates. Of course, a capitalist such as the billionaire Ross Perot may use the money for his own political campaign. The more normal pattern, however, is for capitalists to give money to professional politicians, who then vote for capitalist interests. The very rich do often participate personally at the cabinet level in U.S. government (usually in return for contributions), and millionaires have constituted 20–25 percent of the U.S. Senate in recent decades.

Second, capitalists give money to parties, either directly or through political action committees. Of course the middle class also contributes money, but the amount of contributions naturally declines as income declines. Third, the capitalist class owns and controls the media. In the United States, anyone has the right to own a television network or newspaper chain, but only big business has the money to buy one. Fourth, big business issues propaganda through the media and advertising. Moreover, under U.S. law much of this propaganda expense is legally deductible from taxes. Fifth, the wealthy contribute to schools and universities, so they have some influence over education. This is particularly evident if one examines the lists of trustees and regents of universities. For example, the regents of the University of California are appointed by the governor from among his or her friends. Although there have been some exceptions in recent decades, the regents have tended to be white, male, elderly, and very rich.

Sixth, wealthy capitalists and corporations use lobbyists to influence politicians. This creates spectacular scandals when the lobbying takes the form of bribes and corruption, but it is a very minor part of the whole political process. Seventh, far more important is the fact that as income declines so does political participation. The reason is simply that poor people have less time to themselves, less information about politics, and a greater feeling of helplessness and resignation.

Thus, half of the eligible voters in the United States do not vote in presidential elections, while participation in local elections and primary elections is often very low. Eighth, part of the reason for the feeling of helplessness and uselessness of political participation among much of the population comes from the fact that people take for granted that the economic status quo is the only possible system and cannot be changed. Polling data have often shown that people are not converted to being procapitalist by politicians and the media, but they do get the feeling that nothing can be changed.

Domhoff's early work argues that U.S. institutions are democratic in form but not in content, because of differences in economic power. Thus, a millionaire who owns a newspaper chain has only the same formal political rights as an unemployed worker, but surely their actual political influence is very different. Domhoff discusses

> the existence of a national upper class that meets generally accepted definitions of social class . . . that this upper class owns a disproportionate amount of the country's wealth and receives a disproportionate amount of its yearly income, and that [its] members . . . control the major banks and corporations, which . . . dominate the American economy . . . that [its] members . . . and their high-level corporation executives control the foundations, the elite universities, the largest of the mass media, . . . the Executive branch of the federal government . . . regulatory agencies, the federal judiciary, the military, the CIA, and the FBI. (Domhoff 1967, 10–11)

The hypothesis is that class interests play a major role in political behavior through some degree of domination by the capitalist class. This hypothesis may be called a more sophisticated version of the instrumentalist hypothesis.

Gramsci

To understand how the strong Marxian reaction against instrumentalism has evolved, one must begin with Antonio Gramsci (1971, written in the 1920s). Gramsci argues that the most important weapon of capitalist dominance is the "hegemony" of bourgeois values and ideology. He sees the state as a key factor in supporting capitalist hegemony. Soviet Marxism often stressed that the state is nothing more than an instrument of violence. Gramsci said that the state is much more than that. Gramsci's spotlight here is on thought—on how thought affects and is affected by the state. Thus, he disowns any simplistic economic reductionism and is thoroughly relational in approach. Since Gramsci, Marxian writers have used the term *state* to include not only the government and organs of repression but also mechanisms used by the ruling class to legitimate the status quo and control the media and other avenues of cultural domination.

According to Gramsci, it is through the culture (or social process) that the ruled come to accept a conception of the world put forth by the rulers. And it is this conception that keeps the rulers in power. This emphasis on spelling out the importance and the details of the ideological process is Gramsci's most vital contribution.

Structuralism

Althusser (1971) argues that political economy should study social structures, not human psychology. The function of government is to reproduce and protect the relations of production. The government has a repressive apparatus, which includes the armed forces, the police, the courts, the prisons, and so forth. Yet the government also has ideological functions (as Gramsci argued). The government operates to support capitalist ideology through the educational system, political parties, trade unions, the legal system, churches, the media, and the cultural system (even though most of these are formally separate from the government).

Poulantzas's early work ([1969] 1975) is also structuralist, arguing that the government is part of the class relations of production. The government, through its use of laws and ideology, isolates workers as separate individuals to prevent a working-class consciousness from developing. The government also uses patriotism to instill a national consciousness, partly as a barrier to class consciousness. The capitalist government is both a product and a determinant of class conflict, but it is not itself a site of class conflict. Poulantzas's later work ([1978] 1980) argues that class conflict also takes place within the government apparatus (for a different, fascinating view of class and government, see Miliband 1973, 1977).

There have been further contributions to the debates by U.S. and Western European Marxists (the contributions of Poulantzas, Miliband, E. Atwatter, Claus Offe, and James O'Connor are reported in detail in Carnoy 1984). One may summarize the literature by saying that the long decades of Soviet domination and stultification of Marxian theory of government have suddenly given way to a blossoming of discussion in Western Europe and the United States. The debates are still under way to shape a new independent Marxian or radical view of government, but no overall agreement has been reached.

If there is any consensus within contemporary Marxism, it is the view that under capitalism the interests and views of the capitalist class, the working class, and other classes clash in the media of propaganda, in the churches, in the education system, in the legal system and the courts, and in the legislative and executive branches of government. In all of these institutions capitalist interests tend to be dominant. There is, however, more or less pressure from and expression of the interests of the working class and other classes. Depending on the circumstances and the level of organization, there are differing degrees of success by the nondominant classes.

In the debate the instrumentalists emphasized that there are innumerable ways in which the economic power of big business is translated into political power, such as control of the media, churches, universities, candidates, and political parties through the direct use of wealth. The structuralists have emphasized that the structure of capitalism forces all politicians, regardless of ideology, to follow the interests of capital. For example, when the Chrysler Corporation was on the verge of bankruptcy in the late 1970s, labor and liberal members of Congress supported a government bailout because it was the only way to protect jobs. Thus, organized labor was forced to support a welfare handout to a large capitalist corporation because of the constraints of the capitalist economic structure. Perhaps the best synthesis would be to say that capitalism influences social and political institutions through both the ways described by instrumentalists and the ways described by structuralists; but as Gramsci emphasized, ideological dominance is often the key to government control, and control of the government is used to ensure control of the economy.

The Degree of Democracy

One specific issue clarified in the debate was the degree of democracy present in different socioeconomic systems. It is certainly true that under capitalism, in some circumstances and to some extent, universal suffrage can make possible the expression of working- and middle-class views as against those of the capitalist class. To put it another way, if there is no formal democracy with universal suffrage, then working-class views will not be represented. This was the case in Hitler's Germany, as it has been in all fascist and all military dictatorships. Thus, universal suffrage and formal democracy are necessary conditions for a wide degree of political democracy. Another necessary condition, however, is a high degree of equality in income distribution so that everyone has an equal opportunity to participate.

There is still controversy over whether public, or at least cooperative, ownership of most productive property is a necessary condition for a reasonable degree of equality in income and power. With universal suffrage, but with a continued concentration of wealth and power in a few capitalist hands, there can be only a limited amount of democratic control of workers and the middle classes.

Under either capitalism or socialism one cannot say that democracy does or does not exist. Democracy exists *to some degree*. Where there is formal democracy but capitalist ownership, the degree of democracy for most people is pretty low. There are "democratic" struggles among factions of the capitalist class, but there is a relatively small amount of outside pressure exerted by farmers and industrial and professional workers. Only in crises, such as the Great Depression or the civil rights struggle of the 1960s, are wide-ranging reforms enacted.

On the other hand, where there is government ownership but no formal democracy, and where the universal vote is only allowed for the purpose of endorsing a single party, the degree of democracy for most people is infinitesimal. This was the case in the Soviet Union before Gorbachev, though some pressure was always exerted by the nonruling groups in various ways. A high degree of democracy requires both a formal democratic process and a high degree of equality of income, wealth, and economic power. Public or cooperative control of much of the economy may be required to ensure that equality.

In the 1970s and 1980s there was a complex controversy among Marxian theorists over just how autonomous the government under capitalism is from the capitalist class. Theda Skocpol vigorously attacked the economic reductionist position that pictures the state as a mere reflection of "socioeconomic forces and conflicts" (1979, 25). Her work shows in detail how control of political power is used in revolutionary periods to help shape events, as the relational view has always emphasized.

Skocpol also has contributed to the discussion of how major reforms are made even when capitalists have dominant control of the government. She shows how the extensive New Deal reforms of the 1930s were not given away freely by farsighted capitalists, though there were a few such. Rather, the reforms were conceded in response to working-class pressure (1980). She thus stresses the importance of organized movements on the political-economic matrix. Those Marxian political activists who understand in their hearts as well as their minds that nothing can change without organized activity, no matter what impersonal economic circumstances may occur, have a thoroughly relational attitude rather than an economic reductionist one.

Skocpol's work on revolution also illustrates the fact—emphasized by many Marxian historians—that the relationship of the political system to the economic system varies extremely from one society to another. Thus, no single description of the relationship between economics and politics holds true in all cases, either in normal times or in times of revolutionary crisis. This is an important point in refuting economic reductionism.

The later works of G. William Domhoff similarly stress that "Marxian analysis of the state in democratic societies . . . creates a tendency to downplay the importance of representative democracy. For many Marxists, representative democracy is an illusion that grows out of the same type of mystification that is created by the market place" (1990, 8). Like Skocpol, he is criticizing the economic reductionism of the old Stalinist Marxism, but he is stating a position that is compatible with most of contemporary, critical Marxism. The view of most Marxian social scientists is that popular illusions about democracy do exist, but the illusions are based on the exaggeration of an important aspect of reality. In other words, democratic representation is vital but is very much affected by the economic power of the capitalist class.

The Conflict between Capitalism and Democracy

Conservatives argue that capitalism is an excellent foundation for democracy. Perhaps the best answer to that argument is provided in a book by Bowles and Gintis (1986). They point out that capitalism means the rule of a small elite in the economy and that capitalism keeps spreading to new realms, such as preparation of food by restaurants and fast-food places rather than by the family. On the other hand, they point out that democracy means the rule of all the people and that democratic processes also keep spreading to new realms, such as suffrage for women or workers' control of enterprises. Control of an enterprise by a capitalist is dictatorial because the capitalist can hire and fire people (and make other vital decisions) regardless of the wishes of the workers or the community. But democratic control of the enterprise by workers or by the community excludes capitalism. Thus there is a conflict between capitalism (control by a small elite) and democracy (control by all the people).

Bowles and Gintis find that the conflict has been reflected in the

fear expressed by the rich that in a democracy the propertyless majority might vote to take over the economy and the wealth. Thus, in the
nineteenth century most countries with "democracy" restricted voting
to those people who held a certain amount of property. Also, the U.S.
system of checks and balances was partly designed to prevent rash actions by the democratic majority.

Bowles and Gintis further point out that economic wealth gives
power over jobs, investment, and the media, which leads to extra political power for the elite. Moreover, since capitalists control investment,
they can have a capital strike or threaten one unless policies favorable
to capital are enacted. For example, corporations have threatened to
leave California unless strict antipollution laws are repealed.

So far, two main areas of conflict between capitalism and democracy have been noted. First, in each enterprise there is either dictatorial, undemocratic control by capitalists or democratic, noncapitalist
control by workers and/or the community. Second, as long as capitalism continues, there will be inequality and concentration of wealth,
which means disproportionate, undemocratic power over the political
process by the wealthy.

The conflict between the economic power of the capitalist class and
the formal right to vote of the other classes is expressed by Bowles
and Gintis as follows: "Liberal democratic capitalism is a system of
contradictory rules, empowering the many through . . . citizen rights
—and empowering the few through property rights" (1990, 39).
They define *citizen rights* as the formal freedoms fought for by the
working class, women, and minorities and *property rights* as the legal
reflection of the actual economic power used by the capitalist class.
They show that the history of capitalist democracies is the history of
conflict between citizen rights and property rights. The result has been
formal equality, as in the civil rights acts of the 1960s, but actual continuing inequality for workers, women, and minorities.

Bowles and Gintis stress the clash between "two fundamental historical tendencies. The first is the expansionary logic of personal
rights, progressively bringing ever wider spheres of society . . . under
at least the formal . . . rubric of liberal democracy. The second tendency concerns the expansionary logic of capitalist production, according to which the capitalist firm's ongoing search for profits progressively encroaches upon all spheres of social activity" (1986, 29).
On the one hand, working-class parties extended the suffrage to all
U.S. white males, regardless of property, in the early nineteenth century, the women's movement extended suffrage to women in the early
twentieth century, and the African American civil rights movement

extended effective suffrage to minorities in the late twentieth century. On the other hand, corporations grow larger and larger and have more power over government, as was shown in the counterrevolution of the Reagan years, which rolled back many previous reforms.

Like the later Domhoff, Bowles and Gintis attack "Marxists" for paying too little attention to democratic rights, concentrating only on class exploitation. They call on the Left to push for extension of citizen rights, from the political sphere to the economy, a call for economic democracy. They make the point that capitalists exert undemocratic—unelected—power. They argue that all socially important economic authority should be by virtue of democratic elections.

When Bowles and Gintis attack "Marxists," they are actually attacking the economic reductionism of the old Soviet Marxism. All contemporary, non-Soviet Marxian political economists, however, would agree with their attack on Soviet Marxism, so they are speaking the prose of present-day Marxism whether they care to use that term or not. All non-Soviet Marxian writers are profoundly committed to democracy. There are, of course, many differences among Marxian theorists about *(a)* the tactics needed to achieve political and economic democracy and *(b)* the detailed characteristics of a future political and economic democracy.

Moreover, Bowles and Gintis's actual political program is no different from that of other Marxian political economists, that is, democratic socialism, which they call "economic democracy." One writer points out that economic democracy is "something qualitatively different from socialism . . . only . . . if one accepts the curious notion that [socialism] . . . is inherently undemocratic. . . . [But isn't] the extension of democratic rights to the economy precisely what socialism is all about?" (Goodwin 1990, 138, 143). Socialism is defined in this book to be political democracy and economic democracy. (The specifics of economic democracy or socialism are discussed in part IV.)

It is certainly true, as Bowles and Gintis argue, that the fight for economic democracy (or socialism) takes the form of a conflict between liberal democracy and capitalism. For example, it is democratic for the majority to control the environment in order to eliminate pollution. But that means telling automobile corporations how they must build their cars in some respects. To tell a corporation how to produce its product is contrary to capitalism. It is also the case, however, that this fight is "grounded in the contradiction between the material interests of workers and capital" (Goodwin 1990, 142). Thus, the political struggle appears to be a struggle between different ideologies, but its content continues to be one level of class conflict.

The fact that politics is an arena of class conflict does not mean that it is not also an arena of racial and gender conflict. All present-day Marxism, including the book by Bowles and Gintis, stresses the crucial importance of racial and gender conflicts in our society. The civil rights movement, including all minority organizations and minority theorists, showed with great clarity that racial conflicts shape and are shaped by politics and class conflict (see the extensive discussion of the literature in Sherman 1987). The women's movement, including organizations and theorists, has shown with equal clarity that gender conflicts shape and are shaped by politics and class conflict (see, e.g., Hartsock 1985, as well as Sherman 1987). These contributions by women and by African Americans and other minorities have been incorporated into the heart of contemporary, democratic Marxism.

The Effect of Politics on the Economy

There is a huge Marxian literature on how the economic process shapes the political process, but there is relatively little on how the political process shapes the economic process, perhaps because of a lingering residue of economic reductionism. But in a relational view, it is certainly important to specify how the government affects the economy, and vice versa. This influence can be stated only briefly here, but it is presented at length in Sherman 1987, 203–22.

First, the U.S. government emphasizes "law and order," which translates into protection of private property. This entails laws, courts, police, and prisons. It is almost always the poor who land in prison, because white-collar crimes are seldom prosecuted.

Second, closely related is external "law and order," which translates into military forces designed to kill people from other countries and other ethnic groups. Military spending has been the largest single stimulus to the U.S. economy ever since the Second World War. Military spending led to long economic expansions in the Vietnam War and in the military buildup of the 1980s.

Third, the U.S. government has used higher taxes to ward off inflation and lower taxes to stimulate the economy in order to reduce unemployment. But there is no consensus on what to do if the U.S. economy is faced by both inflation and unemployment. An expanding economy always causes taxes to rise, while a declining economy causes taxes to fall. The overall effect on income distribution of all the different types of taxes in the United States, each of which has a different effect on income distribution, has usually been very slight.

When, however, President Reagan lowered taxes on the rich in 1981, it did significantly increase U.S. income inequality.

Fourth, education has mixed effects. To some extent it helps prepare an educated work force for the economy. It is a road to upward mobility for some people, but numerous studies have shown that (1) the percentage of students going to college increases with income and (2) most students end up at the same general level of income as their parents did (see Bowles and Gintis 1975).

Fifth, the government provides some welfare to both the rich and the poor. The total amount going to the poor is a very small percentage of national income. There are also subsidies to rich farmers, including tobacco farmers. And there are numerous other subsidies to business.

Sixth, the U.S. government's macroeconomic fiscal policy has never done much to stimulate the economy, though that goal is often discussed. The goal of cutting the deficit has been set above the goal of stimulating the economy and reducing unemployment. In practice, this means cutting those programs that give something to the poor and the middle class. It is worth noting that the deficit has been countercyclical. In expansions, government spending rises very slowly, while taxes rise much faster, so the deficit declines. In contractions, government spending always jumps because of the automatic increases (such as unemployment compensation), while taxes tend to decline because their sources decline, so the deficit rises.

Conclusions

Under capitalism the government is an integral part of the political and economic system: the government process and the economic process are entwined. Thus, Marxian scholars do not reduce social explanation to either politics or economics, but use a relational view of the two aspects of society. Each government in history has been affected by the type of class relations in that society, so each type of government is historically specific. There are no eternal laws of movement of the governmental process. Rather, the evolution of government has been an integral part of the evolution of the class relationships of society. At the moment, the focal point of Marxian research in this area is the conflict between capitalism and democracy. In the chapter on policy (14), some reforms are discussed that might reduce the effect of wealth on the political process, but the wealthy will always have disproportionate political power as long as capitalism exists.

T E N

The Rise and Fall of the Soviet Union

The purpose of this chapter is to show, first, that the former So-viet Union had unique relations of production that could not be called capitalist but certainly could not be called socialist within a rigorous Marxian framework; and second, that the spectacular rise and fall of the Soviet Union can best be under-stood within the framework of the relational-historical ap-proach of Marxism. There is an immense literature on the details of each of the sections in this chapter. Only the highlights can be covered here, but the details may be found in Sherman 1987; and Zimbalist, Sherman, and Brown 1988.

A Historical Approach to the Rise of the Soviet Union

In tsarist Russia, before the 1917 revolution, the forces of production were mostly very backward. Most production was rural and agricul-tural, using rather primitive technology. There were a few advanced factories in the cities, but they were islands in the vast sea of back-ward agriculture.

The most important relation of production was the continued eco-nomic power of the noble landlords over the peasants. Serfdom was abolished in 1861, but under conditions that favored the landlords and left the peasants enmeshed in debt and poverty. In the cities there were some very large factories, with a small elite of capitalist owners facing thousands of workers, who worked for low wages under poor conditions. About a third of Russian industry was foreign-owned.

The most important political institution was the absolute power of the tsar. After the revolution of 1905 a parliament was added, but with very limited powers. Only very tame political parties were allowed; those that fought for democracy and socialism were outlawed, with many people sent to Siberian exile for what they did or said. Russia was a prison of nations, with attempts to suppress all cultures except Russian and to keep all power among Russians. Women had few rights, and their husbands had all of the authority. Very few peasants —who constituted the majority of the population—could read or write; and very few women of any class were allowed to get an education.

The ruling ideology was that of the Greek Orthodox Church, which was in favor of religion and of the tsar as the father of his people. The ruling ideology strongly supported the power of the noble landlords in the countryside. There were, however, opposing ideological trends. The small group of intellectuals produced a liberal-oriented literature that became famous all over the world (with names such as Tolstoy or Dostoyevsky). There was also a small, illegal socialist literature; one socialist newspaper was edited by Lenin in exile in Switzerland.

When the First World War imposed enormous hardship and defeat on Russia, elements of class conflict immediately rose to the surface. In the countryside there was mounting peasant violence, which reached a revolutionary level by 1917. In the cities workers were starving and began to organize in *soviets,* a Russian word meaning "councils." In 1917 the army also organized into elected soviets, and the soldiers often would not move unless their soviet agreed with the officer's orders. In February 1917 a revolution tossed out the tsarist regime in favor of democracy and capitalism. But the soviets continued because there was no peace for the soldiers, there was no bread for the workers in the cities, and no land was given to the peasants. Finally, in October 1917 another revolution tossed out the government in favor of a Soviet government led by what became the Communist Party, dedicated to peace, giving land to the peasants, worker control in the factories, and political democracy. Lenin, who led the Soviet government, claimed that this revolution was the result of a frozen class structure (semicapitalist in the cities and semifeudal in the countryside) that stood in the way of economic progress and improvement in the forces of production.

A Historical Approach to the Soviet Transition, 1917–1928

The brief period from 1917 to 1928 was vital because it set the basic parameters for the rest of Soviet history. What were the forces of production? In 1917 the new Soviet regime inherited a very backward, mainly agricultural economy with low productivity. From 1914 until

1921 that backward economy was subject to world war and German invasion, revolution, a three-year bloody civil war, and foreign intervention by sixteen capitalist countries, including the United States. The economy was devastated; production in 1921 was only about 10 percent of what it had been in 1914. There was a very slow recovery from 1921 to 1928.

How did the class relations of production evolve? Everything was chaotic and in transition, so class relations kept changing. Much of the landed nobility, the capitalist class, and some of the professionals and intellectuals fled the country. In tsarist Russia the old middle class had been tiny, but war and revolution reduced it further. In the countryside, the peasants took over the land and redistributed it, with the blessings of the Soviet regime (which had little choice in the matter). Most farms remained tiny, and there were 26 million private farms by the late 1920s, most with extremely low productivity. In the countryside, a small class of more affluent peasants slowly climbed toward middle-income levels and dominated their neighbors, often buying or leasing their land and employing them.

In the cities, the main enterprises that survived were run by state-appointed managers, with the help of the head of the local Communist Party and the head of the local trade union. Early experiments in control by the workers in the plants disappeared as more power was taken by the central government. In the period 1914–21 many of the old organized workers were killed in the wars or forced by hunger to return to the countryside. During the slow recovery of the 1920s, a new working class grew up of former peasants, who were more pliant than members of the old working class under the control of Communist Party bosses.

The Rise of the Soviet State and Dictatorship

The rise of the Soviet state—the Soviet government plus its police and armies—provides a clear example of the determinants of political institutions. Soviet Marxism contended that the Soviet state represented the working class and was therefore a democracy. But all the world knows—and it was admitted by the Soviet leadership under Gorbachev—that the Soviet state was a dictatorship from about 1928 to 1988. It was a personal dictatorship under Joseph Stalin from 1928 to 1953; then it became a collective dictatorship of the Party leaders until about 1988, when democratic reforms began.

What brought about this long-lasting dictatorship? Psychological reductionists, including some Soviet writers, say it was the personality of Stalin, while some technological reductionists say it was the initial low level of Soviet technology. Both of these have some validity, but a relational picture is more complex, with the Soviet class process at its center.

In prerevolutionary Russia, as noted above, the country was ruled by an autocratic tsar and a landed nobility, so there was very little democratic tradition. The country was 80 percent agricultural with an illiterate and poor peasantry, who were concerned with survival and getting ownership of land, not political democracy. There was a small working class and a small middle class; hence, the class basis for the usual democratic development was missing.

As also noted above, the Russian revolution of 1917 was made during a world war, followed by a lengthy and bloody civil war, with much foreign intervention. This was not the best atmosphere for the initial development of democracy. The revolutionaries belonged to a political party that had spent most of its life as a small, persecuted, highly disciplined, underground group, not the best training ground for democratic politics. Moreover, the former working class, which had learned socialist and democratic ideals, was largely killed off during the unremitting warfare. The new Communist Party was largely filled with recruits from the peasantry, who had little background or training in politics, and with many opportunists.

In this situation, the Party leadership was all-powerful. While the leadership was split in the 1920s, there was room for debate. There was a left wing, led by Leon Trotsky, which wanted a purely publicly owned economy with central planning. There was a right wing, led by Nicolai Bukharin, which wanted slow development based on an alliance with an affluent peasantry, who would privately own the land. Stalin led a center faction that vacillated between Right and Left. By 1928, after Stalin had defeated both the Left and the Right, he held sole power. We shall see below why the dictatorship continued so long and what its class basis was.

Soviet Ideology

An example of how ideas are shaped by the social environment may be found in the early history of Soviet thought. In the earliest period of the Soviet revolution, when it still had the power of a mass movement, there were strikingly new thought patterns in many different areas. There was a militant feminism. There were new schools of art, including the extreme abstract art of Kandinsky and the surrealism of Marc Chagall. There was innovative thinking in education, in criminology, in philosophy, and about economic planning techniques.

There was also a fascinating debate on economic development, with many new ideas that have had an impact ever since in the Third World (for a detailed discussion of that debate, see Zimbalist, Sherman, and Brown 1988). The right wing, under Bukharin, argued for a very slow, balanced growth of industry and agriculture with a large amount of aid to private farmers, leading to rapid growth of agriculture. Government-owned industry would grow only slowly, as the tax base grew, and each enterprise would be ruled by the market, even though profits would go to the government. A large area of small business would remain.

An opposite viewpoint was put forward by the left wing of the Communist Party under Trotsky. Members of this wing said that it was necessary to appropriate the agricultural surplus in order to have rapid industrial growth. They visualized large-scale cooperative farms with high technology and farmers moving into them voluntarily. They wanted rapid growth of government enterprises in industry, and they began the discussion of how to plan industry centrally. The vision was of a country with rapid development, with industry run democratically by a government representing all of the people.

When Stalin took sole political power in 1928 the debate was declared over. The government under Stalin exiled Trotsky and then took what has been called a Super Left position. The decision was made to have rapid, all-out industrialization. The resources were to be taken by force from the peasantry, who were pushed into so-called collective farms. The peasants did not join them voluntarily, and the farms were not democratically run. A *collective farm* was a very large agricultural establishment. In theory, collectives were cooperatively run, with the farmers all having equal control. But in practice, a manager was designated by the government (by means of a phony election) and told what to produce. The collective farms had to deliver the produce to the government at the price set by the government. The collectives were a mechanism to remove most of the agricultural surplus and invest it in industry. The argument in favor of such farms was that (1) they could make better use of technology than tiny private farms and (2) they could produce and send to the cities a large amount of goods for export (to buy machinery abroad), to feed the workers in industry, and to provide raw materials for industry.

The upshot was that for many years the peasantry were unable to raise their standard of living because their entire surplus was taken away from them. Since the peasantry were the overwhelming majority of the population, this was a war on the majority and left no room for

democratic majority control. In brief, a forced march for industrialization was decided by a small, ruling minority and carried out in an
underdeveloped country without agreement by the majority. As we
shall see, there emerged a new ruling class whose interest was tied to
the rapid industrial development, who kept the development going
and maintained the dictatorship. So this decision in favor of rapid industrialization had immense ramifications for the development of Soviet political institutions, productive forces, and class relations.

What led to the decision was only partly the personality of Stalin,
which had been determined by his own previous life experience. More
importantly, the type of Soviet political institutions that had evolved,
the class relations that had emerged, and the level of development of
the productive forces all led to the decision to force the peasants into
collective farms, to use central planning for the whole economy, and
to have an all-out industrialization drive. These structural changes led
to the emergence of the Stalinist or Soviet Marxian ideology, which
defended it. Thus, Soviet thought was shaped by Soviet political institutions, class relations, and productive forces. The ideology in turn
helped to shape Soviet political and economic decisions. To sum up,
by 1928 there was a political dictatorship, and that dictatorship decided that it would have complete control of Soviet industry through
a mechanism of central planning and collective farms.

The Political Institutions, 1928–1988

In the Soviet Union in the period 1928–88 the political and the economic could not be separated. In theory, all means of production were
owned jointly by the Soviet people. In practice, this meant that production decisions were centralized in Moscow under the authority of
the Soviet political leadership. While economic planning was done in
detail by a central planning agency, the central planners were subordinate to the political leadership for all tactical and strategic decisions.
In its unity of politics and economics, the Soviet economy resembled
feudalism more than capitalism. Under feudalism the nobles automatically had both political and economic control, whereas under capitalism the economic ruling class attempts with varying success to control
the political process. In brief, the Soviet framework in that period
amounted to: (1) government control of production, plus (2) dictatorial control of the government. We shall see below that the Soviet ruling class included the Party leaders, government leaders, and top economic planners (and, to a lesser extent, the top military).

The combination of Soviet central planning and political dictatorship must be explained. The reasons for the political dictatorship were explained above. What were the reasons for the emergence and continuance of central planning? First, ideology had some small effect. Marx made many references to planning, but they were quite vague since he did not believe in utopian dreaming. Second, Lenin in his *State and Revolution* and many other Soviet leaders in various works discussed the need for planning. They were not clear what planning meant, since they had no experience in it. And they were unclear whether control of production would be in the hands of local workers or of a central body.

In this ideological context, new political institutions affected the view of planning. The wars and civil war devastated the forces of production. At first the Communists had supported local workers' control of enterprises. As the war went on, however, the Communist political leadership, which had a monopoly on political power, felt that it was necessary to centralize control in order to win the civil war and to drive out the foreign armies. Munitions and food were desperately needed, but the decentralized economic apparatus was not fulfilling the task. It should be remembered that most countries, including the United States, have given the central government practically unlimited economic powers in times of war.

When the civil war ended, in 1921, the Soviets instituted the New Economic Policy, which decentralized control of economic decisions to each government firm. When Stalin seized political control, however, he wanted rapid growth and felt that rigorous central planning and state control of resources was the only way to do it. The government attempt to take resources from the farmers was not popular, so it further removed the possibility of political democracy as well as economic decentralization. Thus, the extreme central control and planning resulted from the drive to industrialize a previously backward agricultural country in the face of resistance by most peasants. The central planners took the limited resources and funneled them all into industrialization. The new classes that emerged in the Soviet Union did so within this framework.

Soviet Forces of Production, 1928–1988

As noted above, the tsarist Russian economy was extremely backward, then war and revolution destroyed much industry, so production fell to an extraordinary low point by 1921 and only very slowly recovered until 1928. After that, there was all-out industrialization at an unprecedented pace from 1928 to 1940. This successful attempt to industrialize a previously backward country must be counted as a major achievement of central planning. There are many arguments in the literature about the exact speed of Soviet industrialization, but all of the experts concede that it was very rapid development.

In the Second World War, from 1941 to 1945, a third of Soviet industry and buildings were destroyed, so production was again very low by 1945. Yet central planning could concentrate all resources on heavy industry, so it allowed a very rapid recovery in the period 1945–50. In the fifties and sixties the Soviet Union became the world's second largest industrial power and advanced far more rapidly than the United States. Yet, in the seventies and eighties the rate of growth slowly diminished and led to a crisis. Why that crisis occurred is a major focus of the rest of this chapter.

A Class Analysis of the Former Soviet Union

During the Cold War, orthodox U.S. sociologists found no antagonistic classes in the United States. Also during the Cold War, official Soviet Marxian sociologists found no antagonistic classes in the Soviet Union. The official Soviet Marxian dogma claimed that there were no exploiting or antagonistic classes in the Soviet Union, only workers divided into nonantagonistic strata—manual workers, intellect workers, and farm workers, none of whom exploited one another.

Classes were defined exclusively in terms of legal ownership of the means of production. Since all ownership was public, the Soviets pretended that there were no classes in the former Soviet Union. Aside from the collective farms, all means of production were owned by the Soviet government. The Soviet government therefore planned the whole economy. The Soviet elite amassed all of their economic power as agents of the government.

A small group of people held political power in the former Soviet Union, while most people had little or no political power. But that fact by itself is of little help in analyzing Soviet class structure, since it was equally true of many very different times and different countries, for example, the small group who had political power in Hitler's Germany. Classes are not defined by political power, though one can analyze which class holds the ruling power.

Let us examine the facts, all factual statements here referring to the former Soviet Union in the period 1928 to 1988, that is, the period of extremely centralized ownership and planning. In that period it was a fact that *(a)* the means of production were owned by the Soviet government and *(b)* the Soviet government was controlled by a relatively small group. Given the Soviet system of that period, it follows that those who exercised political power automatically exercised economic power as well.

But class is not defined by either legal ownership or political power; rather, class must be defined as a relation. In the Soviet Union, from 1928 to 1988 at least, there was a ruling class that controlled the economy, extracted the surplus, determined the use of the surplus, and told workers what to do. On the other side, there was a working class that worked for money income, doing industrial, agricultural, or professional work. The working class was told what to do and produced a surplus that was appropriated from it. The exploiting class was also the political ruling class. So the basic relation of exploitation existed as it did in the United States, but its mechanisms were totally different and were historically specific to the Soviet Union, particularly the extreme unity of economics and politics.

In the former Soviet system, wages and salaries were set by political decree, not by the market. Therefore, the elite with political and economic power set their own wages and salaries or had a major impact on setting those salaries. In official Soviet theory, all wages and salaries were paid according to the labor that was done, so there was no exploitation. But it would be naive to think that the people at the top set their own salaries so as to just equal their labor expenditure. In practice, the elite group gave themselves salaries far above the value of the labor they expended.

It was also the case—even according to official Soviet analysis— that the average Soviet worker had extracted from his or her labor expended a certain amount of *surplus labor,* that is, labor expended above the necessary labor going to produce his or her own individual consumption of goods and services. This does not prove exploitation; it must be true of any modern economy. According to the official view, the surplus labor extracted from the Soviet working class was supposed to go to *(a)* creation of new means of production to expand the economy and *(b)* collective consumption by the whole population, such as parks. Marxian political economists, beginning with Marx, have always said there must be some such surplus under socialism.

Whether or not there was exploitation depends on who controlled the surplus. There is no doubt that a relatively small ruling group—or class—controlled the Soviet surplus. To say that the surplus went to all of "the people" would mean, at the very least, that the Soviet Union had a democratic process of decision making, which it did not. The Soviet ruling class exploited the surplus from workers in government enterprises and then distributed it in two ways. First, part of the surplus labor of workers went to provide the very large salaries (and extraordinary fringe benefits) of the Soviet ruling class. Those salaries and fringe benefits were far beyond remuneration for labor. This mechanism of exploitation was rather similar in form to the mechanism that gives some of the surplus to top corporate executives in the United States. U.S. corporate executives may earn $5–10 million in so-called salary and fringe benefits. One knows, however, that most of the corporate executive's enormous salary was surplus value or profit in disguise. In the U.S. corporation the top executives set their own salaries; similarly, in the Soviet Union the top officials set their own salaries and those of the rest of the ruling class. Thus, in both cases what was called salary was mostly surplus value extracted from workers.

Second, the ruling class of the former Soviet Union controlled expenditures on new investment and collective consumption. In the United States it is obvious that new investment comes out of the surplus value of the capitalist class in order to increase that surplus value in the future. In the Soviet case the ruling class acts through the government to make use of the surplus in the form of profits to the government. It uses government profits to make new investments that will increase the surplus in the future. Legally, the Soviet ruling class did not own the new investments, but it did control the additional surplus coming from the new investments. Each member of the Soviet ruling class might also benefit individually if the investment increased the industrial empire under his or her control. Collective consumption, such as roads or education, would serve both a common function for all citizens and a function of ensuring further profit and power for the ruling class. Thus, education was necessary for everyone, but the content of Soviet education was shaped by the Soviet ruling class to spread its ideological views.

It has been noted that the people at the top of Soviet society set their own salaries. These salaries had three components. First, the official salary itself was several times the average wage. Second, there were many important fringe benefits, including chauffeurs and automobiles, specialized health treatment, special luxury stores, and summer homes in the countryside. Third, there were large additional, secret sums of money. In the Gorbachev period enough of the secret data were leaked to prove that the top Soviet leaders did receive the surplus labor of others as part of their own remuneration. Since they received surplus labor, their own remuneration was far above what their own labor produced. That surplus labor was extracted through the exploitation of the Soviet working class.

Quantitatively, the total amount of surplus labor transferred directly from Soviet workers to individuals of the Soviet ruling class was relatively small. The larger amount of surplus labor was that which the Soviet ruling class directed to new investment and collective goods. Of course a large part of the so-called collective goods consisted of military production. Before Gorbachev, the Soviet population never voted either directly or indirectly on whether their surplus labor should go to hospitals or to nuclear bombs. The Soviet ruling class decided that their military must be at least as large as the enormous U.S. military. Since the Soviet economic product was much smaller than the U.S. product, this meant that the percentage going to the military was much larger (though the absolute amount may have been about the same). Thus, in the case of the Soviet Union, the mechanism of exploitation inextricably bound together the economic process and the political process. This is also true in the United States, but to a much lesser degree than it was in the Soviet Union.

The forms of surplus labor extraction depended on ruling-class control of the Soviet political process and political control of the means of production. For this reason, the Soviet system may be considered a unique mode of production. It was certainly not capitalist. On the other hand, the existence of surplus labor extraction or exploitation reflects one type of class society. The Soviet ruling class was defined by its position as an exploiting class, but the form of exploitation was different than in any other society on record.

There were four main hierarchies in the former Soviet Union: the Communist Party, the government apparatus, the economic pyramid, and the military. Within the Communist Party, the top functionaries (such as in the Politburo) had enormous power and were appointed rather than elected. There were only phony elections after the real decision was made. There was also a political pyramid composed of powerful officials in the government, such as the Council of Ministers and their deputies. The economic pyramid was ruled by a small group of economic planners at the top (responsible to the government and Party leaders) plus some powerful directors of sectors and very large enterprises. The military was completely hierarchical, with the top generals also being Party leaders in most cases.

In each of the four hierarchies, orders flowed downward, while some information flowed upward. At the top were fifty to two hundred people who controlled all four hierarchies and frequently transferred from one to the other. These people received high salaries, huge fringe benefits, and probably enormous secret income. Their income level in the Soviet society was equivalent to those of the capitalist class in the United States, when we consider how far the elite income was above the average wage. Thus, the top levels of each of these four hierarchies constituted subgroups of the ruling class, each of which contributed to the extraction of surplus labor in different ways.

Below the very top Soviet group, there were another 100,000 to 200,000 Soviet officials who had high salaries and huge fringe benefits (with perhaps some illegal income). The total income, however, of each of these high Soviet officials was still far below that of most U.S. capitalists, both absolutely and relatively. One U.S. study finds that the Soviet elite were only 0.2 percent of all gainfully employed Soviet citizens, or only 220,000 people (Bergson 1984, 1085). The elite were defined in this study as those who received at least 3.1 times the average wage or at least 5.7 times the minimum wage. These 220,000 included most enterprise directors, party officials, government officials, top military officers, and some professionals.

Compared with the U.S. capitalist class, the members of the Soviet ruling class probably had less income (both absolutely and relative to the average wage) but far more power over social decision making. They made decisions about jobs, investment, and allocation of goods and services. This is because the Soviet leaders directly controlled all of the levers of political and economic decision making, and economic decisions were highly centralized. As a group, U.S. capitalists do control jobs, investment, and allocation of resources in the private sector, but the decisions are more decentralized (though a fairly small number of capitalists control the thousand largest corporations that own a majority of the U.S. assets). U.S. capitalist control of political decisions, such as military spending, is more indirect and is limited in certain ways.

The members of the U.S. ruling class are more secure in their economic power than the members of the Soviet ruling class were, both for themselves and for their children. If a U.S. capitalist loses or gives up an executive job, he or she retains wealth and status. In the Soviet Union, on the other hand, power and wealth adhered to a particular official position. If you lost the position, then you lost all your power. If your power was lost, then your income disappeared.

The children of the top twenty thousand Soviet leaders did not hold the same jobs and were not usually at the same rank as their parents (see Nove 1975). If one examined the top 10 percent of all Soviet income receivers, however, one would find that their children were also usually somewhere in that category. Thus, it can be concluded that even though the very top leadership positions were not hereditary, most officials, managers, and more highly placed professionals

did give their children enough cultural and monetary advantages—
and good connections—to enable them to land jobs that would put
them among the top 10 percent of income receivers.

The Soviet working class represented a wide spectrum of income
and status, since it included workers from highly paid artistic and
sports stars to very poorly paid menial workers. Thus, in 1981 the
top 10 percent of Soviet wage and salary workers earned three times
what the bottom 10 percent earned (Bergson 1984, 1063). By comparison, in the United States in 1975 the top 10 percent of wage and
salary workers earned four times what the bottom 10 percent earned.
So there appeared to be somewhat less inequality within the Soviet
working class than within the U.S. working class. The main differences in income inequality between the two countries came, however,
in the much greater wealth of the U.S. elite. One overall estimate,
based on considerable guesswork and limited data, found that a standard measure of inequality (the Gini coefficient) for the pre-tax income of all households in the United States was .376 in 1972 (Bergson 1984, 1070). The same measure of inequality for the pre-tax
income of all urban households in the Soviet Union was only .288 in
1972–74. Small changes in this coefficient are very important, so the
difference between the two reflects significantly less inequality in the
Soviet Union (see Zimbalist, Sherman, and Brown 1988).

The Fall of the Soviet Union

The rise and fall of the Soviet Union is well worth an analysis because
it begins in revolution and ends in revolution within the twentieth
century. It is therefore a well-documented example in which the relational-historical method of Marxism may be tested. For lack of space,
only the highlights of the fall of the Soviet Union can be discussed
here to show how the method is applied (for more concrete detail in a
Marxian framework, two excellent pioneering studies are Callinicos
1991; and Kotz 1992b).

The first Soviet revolution took place in 1917. It resulted from the
inability of the weak tsarist socioeconomic system to meet either economic or military needs. Specifically, the class relations of production
were frozen into a mold in which the landed aristocracy retained most
political power, a few giant capitalist firms monopolized parts of a
small industrial base, and one-third of industry was foreign-owned.
The peasantry were scattered and had little power, a small number of
industrial workers worked at low wages, and there was no middle
class. These class relations impeded and held back progress in both

agriculture and industry, so Russia remained at a very low level of productivity by international standards.

This tension between the class relations and productive forces led to class conflict and eventually revolution. The relatively weak capitalist class took power in the revolution of February 1917 but could not improve performance enough to solve Russia's problems. In the revolution of October 1917 the working class and intellectuals in the Communist Party (called Bolshevik at that time) took power. The revolution abolished capitalism and claimed that the new system would be democratic and socialist, with Lenin envisioning an eventual end to all state coercion.

It appeared that the Russian revolution of 1917 followed the exact prescription of Marxism: class relations held back forces of production, leading to class conflict and a democratic, socialist revolution. Unfortunately, the revolution took place in an underdeveloped country, whereas Marx's prescription for socialism assumed an advanced capitalist country that had converted to socialism. As a result of Soviet underdevelopment (combined with world war and intervention), the Soviet Union emerged as a poverty-stricken country unable to build a democratic socialism but in need of an all-out drive to industrialize. Thus, as detailed above, the Soviet revolution of 1917 resulted in a dictatorial political regime and an extremely overcentralized planned economy.

The second Soviet revolution took place in 1991, after rapid deterioration in the late 1980s. If nothing else, it should demonstrate to conventional social scientists that real, revolutionary changes can and do take place. It also demonstrates that major revolutionary changes in the socioeconomic system may be largely peaceful rather than violent.

What exactly led to this second Soviet revolution, or counterrevolution? From the 1950s to the 1990s the tension slowly worsened in the former Soviet economy between the vast potential of its forces of production and the straitjacket of the Soviet central planning institutions and frozen class relations in a repressive political environment. In the 1960s that exact tension—or contradiction, if one prefers—was discussed in several outstanding books by Isaac Deutscher (see, e.g., Deutscher 1965a, 1965b, 1971). The fact that Soviet class relations held back economic growth was reflected in the slow decline of the economic growth rate from the 1950s to the 1990s.

The Soviet class relations and their reflections in political and economic institutions held back growth in several ways. First, the overcentralized direction resulted in incorrect and inefficient orders to local enterprises. Second, the system of incentives under dictatorial central planning resulted in the wrong motivations for Soviet managers and Soviet workers, pushing them in directions counter to socially optimum actions. For example, stating a plan target purely in terms of weight may result in extraheavy bridge girders or extralarge and extraheavy nails, with no small ones.

Third, there was frequent shifting of managers to prevent corruption, so targets and bonuses were paid by the month rather than any longer period. The frequent shifting of personnel and the one-month time horizon for profitability resulted in a short-term vision. Specifically, it caused resistance to technological improvements because these improvements were costly and might pay off only over a longer period (see Zimbalist, Sherman, and Brown 1988 for details). The lack of technical innovation, in spite of constant verbal encouragement, eventually became the greatest weakness of the Soviet system.

The lack of innovation was partially due to the excessive central planning, which led to a policy treating managers as easily replaceable, putting the emphasis on following orders promptly month by month, and discouraging local decision making and risk taking. Excessive central planning also meant that a manager who did something innovative could not count on getting supplies from other firms, since other firms could not change their plan without central authorization. Moreover, because the central planners tried to push the economy as fast as possible—actually faster than possible—it was impossible for managers to get enough supplies of most things and enough skilled labor. It was a shortage economy. This is hard for people living in capitalist countries to understand because our problems are so different, usually being a lack of demand rather than of supply, and unemployment rather than a lack of labor. The Soviet system was not viable in the long run in an industrialized economy, but it was very different from capitalism, with different laws and different problems.

Yet excessive central planning was not the only cause of the problems. Political dictatorship, especially when it is combined with central planning, can also hold back economic growth. A repressive political dictatorship does not allow the free development of science, which is crucial in the modern world. A repressive political dictatorship does not allow the ordinary citizen—or any lower-ranked employee—to criticize the actions of powerful managers and economic planners. Thus, incredible mistakes could be made over a long period of time, with no criticism within a firm or in any of the media. Only after things got so bad that a powerful official was finally removed and disgraced was a torrent of public criticism allowed. Furthermore, a repressive political dictatorship is not the proper environment to encourage an ambitious manager to take risks. The road to survival and advancement lay through being very careful and agreeing with superior authorities. Only at the very top could major changes be considered, and that is far too high a level for making local technological decisions.

The Soviet system accomplished much in its early years, when the problem was initial development. Planning and dictatorship ruthlessly took resources from the whole economy, used them at full employment in heavy industry, and achieved a remarkably high rate of industrial growth. The combination of excessive central planning and repressive dictatorship, however, was not viable in the long run in a modern industrialized economy.

From the 1960s through the 1980s, such problems led to slower and slower Soviet growth, shortages, and rising prices. One result was deep resentment by the population and many conflicting reform ideas among the ruling class. The ruling class wanted rapid growth, but it also wanted to keep its privileged position. This basic contradiction between two goals led to conflict. One reason for the population's resentment was the success of one aspect of the old ideology. Soviet ideology condemned any religious notion of an afterlife, so it emphasized that an economic system should deliver the goods here and now. Furthermore, it was emphasized that the Soviet government ran the whole system collectively and was the only source of good things, there being no private entrepreneurs. But if immediate growth was so important, and if the Soviet government was the final decision maker, then the population also condemned the Soviet government as soon as growth fell very low or even became negative. Such a situation was completely counter to all the expectations raised by Communist propaganda, so it hit the population with immediate and violent effect. U.S. citizens reacted with equal vehemence to the Great Depression, but at least private entrepreneurs and the "inevitable working of the economy" could be blamed, rather than the government (though the government was also blamed).

The resentments and conflicts of ideas led to an almost total collapse of belief in the old dominant so-called socialist, or official, Marxian ideology. The ideological chaos and the poor growth were reflected in class conflicts, which were evidenced by vast political changes, including quite open elections, defeat of a large percentage of official candidates, vehement parliamentary debates, militant unionism in the coal industry, an attempted coup, violent protest demonstrations, and an upsurge in nationalism. The nationalism and ethnic prejudice of each group was stirred up by desperate politicians who needed an easy scapegoat to deflect the citizens' anger from their own failings. Finally, a quick revolution put an end to the old Soviet Union.

The final outcome of this new Russian revolution is still in doubt, but it now looks like capitalism will result. Since the reforms started out to revitalize and democratize the so-called socialism of the Soviet Union, how did those reforms turn into a rush down the road to capitalism? In a fascinating article, David Kotz (1992b) answers this question with a Marxian type of class analysis. He cites the polling data that show that most of the working-class population of the Soviet Union still tend to support public or cooperative ownership, but because of a lack of organization and a lack of information, their views have been only slightly reflected in the political arena. Kotz cites external capitalist pressure but shows that it has played only a very subordinate role.

Kotz argues that some pressure has come from the former black-market entrepreneurs, who have now become legalized, but notes that all of small business is still a very small force in Soviet politics. He gives somewhat more weight to those intellectuals who expect to receive much higher relative salaries in a capitalist milieu but again acknowledges that the intellectuals are too weak to make a revolution by themselves, though they may supply its oratorical form.

Since sufficient pressure for capitalism did not come from any of the strata of the working class or from the intellectuals or the new entrepreneurs, Kotz concludes that a part of the old ruling class led this procapitalist revolution. In support of that view, it was shown above that none of the groups within the old Soviet ruling class were as secure as members of the capitalist class in the United States. Their power and income resided solely in their official positions, so they could not automatically hand them to their children. And if they lost their positions, they had no reserve of private capital ownership to retreat to. The Gorbachev economic reforms were aimed at decentralizing economic decision making and power to lower levels of local management. Since the reforms implied that many would lose their powerful positions, most of those who belonged to the intermediate levels of the ruling class responded to the initial reforms with panic and by slowing down and sabotaging the reforms.

The majority of the ruling class prevented reforms that might have led to a democratic socialism, but they did realize that drastic change must occur to save the Soviet economy. Therefore, a large part of the Soviet ruling class decided to allow a return to capitalism and to use their official positions to gain private ownership of assets and go into business. Many of them have done that, and the rest wish to take the same road, so they are now supporting the transition to capitalism. Thus, the crisis was created by the fact that the Soviet class relations, in the form of central planning and dictatorship, caused a severe reduction of economic growth and innovation. The crisis led to a class conflict in which masses of people wanted a better system to improve their lives. At the same time, it forced the ruling class to recognize that its old mechanisms of exploitation would no longer work, so they hunted for new mechanisms. International capitalist ideology told them that only one road was open: market capitalism. They chose to make use of capitalist ideology and capitalist methods of exploitation rather than follow the ideology of democratic socialism, which was completely alien to their thoughts, their life style, and their interests.

Such a transformation of part of the old ruling class into a new ruling class has occurred several times before in history, so it would be a surprise only to those who held a rigid and simplistic version of the Marxian view of revolutions. Seen in this light, the Soviet experience strongly reinforces a belief in the usefulness of the historical method.

Conclusions

Psychological reductionists explain Soviet history on the basis of Stalin's personality and that of a few other leaders, while economic reductionists see Soviet history strictly in terms of technology. Nonreductionist Marxian researchers begin, using the relational approach, with the class relationships dominant during the Soviet period. The Soviet ruling class consisted of the Party officials, the government officials, the economic planners and managers, and the top military personnel. The Soviet middle classes included experts and professionals, managers of small enterprises, lower-level Party officials, and lower-level government bureaucrats. The working class included industrial workers and agricultural workers. The Soviet ruling class exploited the other classes through the economic mechanism of government ownership and central planning, combined with the political mechanism of repressive dictatorship. This exploitation was resented, not only for the obvious material reasons but also because it was in direct conflict with some Marxian aspects of Soviet ideology, which promised an end to all exploitation. Although it was exploitative, nevertheless it was not capitalism. Thus, the problems faced by Soviet society were mostly very different from the problems faced by a capitalist society.

These problems included in the economic sphere the misallocation of resources, the inefficient use of resources, shortages of capital goods and of labor, and lack of innovation. The causes of the problems may be traced back to the Soviet class structure and its dominant institutions of central planning and political dictatorship.

The Soviet experience did not prove either the uselessness or the usefulness of central planning because it was so intertwined with political dictatorship that one cannot say which of them caused the problems. The Soviet experience does not tell us that central planning is not an effective tool. Central planning probably was a big help in early Soviet development, and it did eliminate unemployment. But almost all observers would agree that excessive central planning was one cause of the declining growth rate. A moderate amount of central planning combined with a thoroughly democratic political system might yield a result very different from the Soviet result.

Using the historical approach of Marxism, this chapter has shown that the First World War exposed the very weak ability of the old Russian giant to deliver food to the cities or ammunition to the soldiers. This failure of the rigid political and economic system was defended by the Russian ruling class, so it led to the Soviet revolution of 1917. The revolution revealed the class power of the peasants, industrial workers, and intellectuals.

In the 1980s the Soviet class relations similarly failed to allow a successful economic system. That situation led to class conflict between the Soviet rulers and the middle and working classes. The Soviet ruling class backed away from confrontation but also backed away from the economic reforms necessary to build a socialist society. The Soviet ruling class interpreted reform to mean a forced march to capitalism, with parts of the Soviet ruling class turning up as capitalists.

This analysis does not show the failure of a Marxian viewpoint, because that viewpoint was never followed in the Soviet Union. On the contrary, the analysis shows the power of the critical approach of Marxism as a tool for understanding not only capitalism but also the unique noncapitalist, nonsocialist mode of production that emerged in the Soviet Union.

If the Soviet Union was not socialist, because there was exploitation and the economy was not controlled by the people, then what would be the road to a democratic socialism? That question is discussed in the last chapter of this book.

PART THREE

The Critical Method

ELEVEN

Dialectics as a Critical Method

Many practicing political economists, and certainly many other social scientists, think of methodology as a waste of time, some abstruse cogitations that do not concern them or their work. This attitude can be a costly mistake. All social science requires methodological decisions at every turn in the road. If one does not consciously and explicitly consider methodology, one still makes these decisions. If the decisions are made unconsciously, then they are usually made with the most popular methodology, which is often taken for granted.

Many Marxian writers have emphasized the central importance of methodology in Marxian thought. For example, Georg Lukács argued that one could violate every specific proposition of Marxism and still take a Marxian approach because "orthodox Marxism refers exclusively to method" (quoted in Ollman 1992, v). Similarly, Leon Trotsky stated that "Marxism is above all a method of analysis" (quoted in Ollman 1992, v). One radical writer asks why radicals should be interested in methodology. He answers that "methodology is for the mainstream, a point of both weakness and discomfort, and student dissatisfaction with methodology has often been the beginning of interest in non-mainstream approaches" (Stewart 1991, 149).

The lowest, or most concrete, level of methodology involves problems using mathematical or statistical methods. Everyone knows that this level must be studied, and studied carefully, in order to avoid pitfalls. The intermediate level of methodology comprises the general approaches to society, discussed in part I of this book. There it is shown in ample detail why the choice of approach is important. The highest, or most abstract, level of methodology concerns the following difficult questions: Is there anything worth keeping in the concepts of dialectics? How can one compare paradigms? What is meant when something is said to determine something else? What is the relation of ethics to science? In each case, a relational-historical approach will be used to clarify the question.

Is Dialectics Important or Useless?

Soviet Marxism contended that dialectics states the laws of motion of the universe, that it is a logic of change, and that it is the methodology of Marxian social science. The importance that some Marxian writers have attached to dialectics cannot be overstated. Antonio Gramsci wrote that "the dialectic . . . [is] the very marrow of historiography and the science of politics" (quoted in Ollman 1992, v). Finally, the Marxian political scientist Bertell Ollman says in a provocative book devoted entirely to dialectics: "Yet it is just here, with Marx's dialectical method, that any serious attempt to recover what is of value in Marx's contribution toward remaking our world must begin" (quoted in Ollman 1992, 1). Thus, Ollman contends that rethinking Marxism must begin with rethinking dialectics.

Critics of Marxism have also written an enormous amount on dialectics, arguing that dialectics is a nonsensical and useless piece of unscientific baggage. Some members of the school of Analytic Marxism have similarly argued that dialectics is nonsense and that dialectics is not a useful methodology in the social sciences. Thus John Roemer writes that "there is [no] specific form of Marxist logic or explanation. Too often obscurantism projects itself behind a yoga of special terms and privileged logic. The yoga of Marxism is 'dialectics.' Dialectic logic is based on general propositions which have certain inductive appeal but are far from being rules of inference that things turn into their opposites, and quantity turns into quality. . . . In Marxian social science, dialectics is often used to justify a lazy kind of teleological reasoning" (1986, 191). If one substitutes *the old Soviet Marxism* for *Marxism,* then Roemer is certainly correct. My contention is that the old Soviet interpretation of dialectics was exactly the kind of sloppy thinking that Roemer criticizes.

To fully understand the argument, one needs to trace the evolution of the concept of dialectics, which is presented in some detail in appendixes 11A to 11D. The insights of the early Greeks are presented in appendix 11A; G. W. F. Hegel's system is discussed in 11B; the Soviet view of the universal laws of dialectics is presented in 11C; and the Soviet view of dialectics as a logic is in 11D.

Dialectics as a Relational-Historical Method

According to Bertell Ollman, "The subject of dialectics is change . . . and interaction" (1990, 27). The term *interaction* should remind the reader of the discussion of the relational, or holistic, method, which was designed to consider interactions within all of society treated as one organism. The term *change* should remind the reader of the discussion of the historical, or evolutionary, method. Thus, the relational-historical method, developed at length in part I, would appear to be at the heart of any dialectics seen as a method.

One must give up the notion that the dialectic approach provides answers or universal laws in some magical fashion. Rather, it should be viewed as providing some of the questions one needs to ask in order to understand and change society.

Note that the relational-historical method was considered a tool in the social sciences; it said nothing at all about research methods in the natural sciences. Frederick Engels did discuss the dialectics of nature, and Soviet Marxism followed his lead. Clearly, some general issues of methodology, such as the relations of facts to theories, are similar in both the natural and the social sciences. On the other hand, many particular points of method have quite different applications in the two areas. Most of the methodology developed by Marx and later Marxian social scientists has been concerned primarily with society. The terminology of dialectics, such as *conflict,* seems to apply to human behavior; it would have a very different meaning (if any) if it were applied to trees and rocks. At any rate, the method put forth here is designed strictly for the social sciences. One reason for that limitation is that a good method grows out of good practice in an area, so a social scientist can only speak authoritatively about the social sciences.

Whereas Soviet Marxism viewed dialectics as a set of laws about how the world evolves, most non-Soviet Marxists see it only as a method. Dialectics as used here states no laws, gives no answers, and makes no predictions, but merely suggests questions. Since it deals with society, the method of dialectics is interpreted here simply as a critical method of political economy or social science. If this interpretation is correct, then the reader already knows a great deal about dialectics, which might also be called the *critical method* or even the relational-historical method, because they all have the same definition. What must be demonstrated is that dialectics as it is defined here is a useful method for all radical political economists.

When dialectics is treated as a method of political economy, the usual criticisms of it do not apply. A method is not falsifiable by confrontation with any facts; it is not "testable" in the usual scientific way because it does not assert any facts. It grows out of our empirical knowledge of the way social scientists behave. But it does not consist of statements about their behavior; that is the job of the history of the sciences. Rather, it tries to provide political economists—or anyone else—with a useful way to approach social problems.

The test of a method is not whether it is true with respect to facts (since it says nothing factual) but whether it is useful. In other words, is it fruitful in terms of questions for research? Does it add anything to the practice of political economy? If it is useful for radical social scientists, the method is a good one; if it is not, it should be discarded.

Exactly what is meant by a *useful* method? A method is most useful if it (1) directs us to choose the most important problems; (2) helps us to select the facts that are most relevant for solving those problems; and (3) helps provide a framework for interpreting the facts so that we may solve the problems, formulate new theories, and lead to better social practice. A method does not explain or predict anything, but it may be judged on its success in leading to theories that do explain and predict.

If dialectics can be proven a useful method in these terms, then it is very important to all political economists and all people interested in social analysis, particularly radicals, who must understand the world in order to change it. Yet many Soviet Marxists did not think this was enough; they wanted an all-knowing system that told the *truth* without any factual investigation. As Ollman correctly observes: "Nothing is more difficult in writing about Marx than to keep the dialectic on the 'common place' level to which I have assigned it. The temptation among friends and foes of Marxism alike is to use the dialectic as a means of proving and predicting things. For it to perform these functions they endow it with a body and content it does not have. . . . The classic result is the construction of a rock ribbed triad of thesis, antithesis, and synthesis, whose strict lines allow prediction even before the facts have been gathered" (1973, 509).

The anti-Marxian critics complain that dialectics as an omniscient system (or as a logic of contradiction) attempts to do things that are impossible for any science. Yet when the critics are told that non-Soviet Marxism sees dialectics only as a method, they make the opposite complaint. One critic of dialectic method says that "it does not appear to tell one any more than one already knows" (Gregor 1965, 69). A similar complaint could be made against mathematics, statistics, or logic, none of which provide any new content; they do provide ways of learning things more easily or more precisely. Dialectics, like logic, is merely a common-sense approach made explicit. One can think or practice science without knowing the explicit rules of logic or dialectics, but such knowledge may make some things easier.

By way of analogy, consider that people managed to eat for thousands of years before dieticians existed, but people may now eat better and more healthful diets with the help of dieticians. In the same way, "men thought dialectically long before they knew what dialectics was, just as they spoke prose long before the term prose existed" (Engels [1878] 1966, 156). The point is that one can practice political economy without any conscious method, but a correct method may make it easier to formulate and solve problems even though it does not unearth any facts or solve any problems by itself.

The Relational Approach

According to the dialectic method, the approach to problems of political economy should be relational or holistic. Operationally, this means that a social scientist should never try to treat a problem in isolation, but rather in its relation to the rest of society. The basic question that a radical political economist should always ask is, What are the interconnections of this problem to all of society? One should never assume that a particular social phenomenon, such as drug pushing or suicide or the Gulf War or unemployment, is accidental or isolated; one should ask how it is related to the entire social, political, and economic environment surrounding it. Although one may analytically separate a single phenomenon from the whole for study, no valid policy conclusions can be drawn until the possible relations to the rest of the social system are also studied.

Specifically, one should always ask questions about how ideologies and social or political institutions are related not only to each other and their own internal past development but also to the class relations of production and the forces of production. Conversely, when investigating the class relations or the forces of production, one should not only consider their internal development but also ask questions about the influence of ideology and of social and political institutions (such as laws) on the economic process.

In the Marxian relational approach the social world cannot be considered an accidental collection of unrelated individuals or groups ripped out of context. On the contrary, society must be investigated as a connected whole in which each separate individual or group is part and parcel of a single social process.

The analogy may be made with a relational orientation to ecology. If we take a walk through a forest, for example, we will see many different animals, and any relation between them strikes us as purely accidental. Further study, however, reveals that if any one species of animal is removed from the forest, the whole balance of nature may be upset, for the animals it fed on multiply so greatly that they crowd each other as well as other species for living room, while the animals that fed on it must now go hungry.

Similarly, when people pollute the ocean or the air, they do not "merely" kill a few fish or give bronchitis to a few children, but rather upset a whole ecological web, so that the destructive effects travel on in ever-widening circles of desolation. When the U.S. Air Force defoliated many areas of Vietnam in the colonial war there, it not only removed a few hiding places but automatically destroyed much of the wildlife (both plant and animal) and created many other kinds of ecological chaos.

Some anti-Marxian critics have thought that the relational method tells us to look at everything at once and have attacked it on these grounds: "The argument for the inseparable inter-connectedness of all phenomena, so that the knowledge of one thing requires knowledge about all other things, has a paralyzing effect" (Dworkin 1961, 53). This may be a valid objection to some extremist statements of some Marxian theorists, but it is a misunderstanding of the normal use of the Marxian relational approach, which emphasizes that one must often look at a social phenomenon or a single relationship separately for purposes of analysis. The method merely insists that we should keep in mind that a single process or relationship can be fully understood only in terms of the whole social environment of which it is a part. Thus, the more we study its relations to other phenomena, as well as to the whole, the better we will understand it.

It would be truly paralyzing to assert that one could not get any knowledge of a thing without analyzing all its connections. It is very different to say that we may sometimes learn some of it in isolation but that as we examine more of its connections to the rest of the social universe, we will modify and improve our original conception of it. Any isolated conception will be misleading, because a thing can only be defined as part of a relationship. If one examined an individual drug dealer and followed all of his or her relations to those who buy the drug and those who sell the drug, that might be quite sufficient for a criminal prosecution, but it would reveal little or nothing about drug dealing as a social phenomenon. So one step is to view each facet of a social problem separately. Another step is to integrate the separate phenomena into a meaningful whole. For example, one must integrate drug dealing into a society in which some people are unemployed, where many people feel alone and threatened economically or by violence, where the economic system is based on exploitation, where money is God, and so forth. The new integration is the basis for further detailed research.

A reasonable relational, or holistic, approach to political economy does not consist in reducing everything to the statement that everything is related to everything else. That statement is either a truism or it is meaningless. As a truism, it simply asserts that any action will affect all society. That is surely true, but some actions have a negligible effect on many other events. For example, the failure of the coup against Gorbachev in 1991 may have affected decisions on which crops to plant in southern Bolivia, but surely the effect was negligible. Belief in this view, however, may be an obstacle to understanding if we try to say nothing until we can say everything. The whole point of good political economy is to decide which relationships are important and to emphasize those, while ignoring the negligible effects of other relations. Parts I and II spell out the relations considered of importance by most contemporary Marxian political economists.

The Historical Approach

According to the historical approach to political economy, problems should be treated dynamically wherever possible; one should not be content with a static picture. A Marxian investigator, therefore, should ask, Is the social system changing? Specifically, what changes are going on in its ideas, institutions, productive relations, and productive forces? What are the specific historical features of this period? What kind of society preceded this one, and how did this one evolve from it? What kind of structural changes have occurred in the political economy since the previous stage?

Some critics of dialectics have asked whether there is a contradiction between a relational approach and a historical, or process, approach. Actually, the two are closely related and depend on each other. Bertell Ollman even says that "the terms 'process' and 'relation' each express, with only differences of emphasis, what is ordinarily meant by both" (1986, 44). A historical process is composed of certain relationships; any particular society has relationships that lead to change in a historical process. In any concrete case, one must look at both aspects, but may emphasize one or the other depending on the issues. The important point for Marxism is to perceive, not isolated, static things, but processes and relations, such as when we speak of capital and labor or of production and environment.

Another widespread confusion about the historical method is the notion that history will stop when we reach the utopia of pure communism. But the historical approach does not assume that history stops at any given point. Of course if we conceive theoretically of the perfect society, one may ask why it would ever change any further. But a perfect society is only something to be seen in science fiction. Even if we had a society with the specific relations suggested by socialists, that would solve some major problems, but others would surely remain.

Part I explored in detail how the historical approach explains evolutionary and revolutionary changes. Such changes are seen as the result of internal conflicts within various socioeconomic processes. The questions asked about conflict in the contemporary relational-historical approach probably were influenced by the old dialectic laws, which have now been rejected.

Rejecting and Replacing the Law of the Unity of Opposites

The so-called law of the unity and struggle of opposites says that each pair of opposites is inseparable but is always in conflict. As an example, the two poles of a magnet are said to be in conflict. But any such example in nature is misleading. The poles of a magnet are *not* like two groups of feuding humans (this is the mistake of anthropomorphizing nature, or treating it as if it were human). The prime example given is class conflict; for example, slaves and slave owners are said to be opposite parts of an inseparable relation and always in conflict.

The examples are often thought-provoking, but appendix 11C shows that the law itself is meaningless, so ambiguous that it will apply to any relationship. If we completely reject this so-called law, then we may replace it with the relational method, which provides no laws or answers but does suggest questions about the conflicts and the unifying relations among groups of people.

Marxian socialists were attracted to the concept of a unity of opposites because it seemed to support and explain the set of relations dealing with class conflict. But even with respect to class conflict, the law tends to mislead the analysis. First, it appears to be universal and inevitable. This alleged inevitability tends to prevent careful investigation of real situations.

Second, concepts such as plus and minus are opposites, but in what sense are social groups opposites? Workers and bosses may love or hate each other and may struggle or work together, but the term *opposite* does not apply. Only on the incorrect assumption of just two classes, who are always locked in combat, would the term seem appropriate. When Marx himself begins his systematic study of classes in the last chapter of volume 3 of *Capital,* he states that there are three important classes in mid-nineteenth-century England. So which are the opposites? Taken as a description of classes in all societies, the law does not hold.

Nevertheless, Marxists have certainly contributed a great deal to the analysis of class and class conflict, as well as its relation to other types of conflict. In any society in which classes exist, one can certainly ask questions about the relations between the various classes. As noted in chapter 6, these class relations are a subcategory of all social relations, so such questions make the relational approach more concrete. Furthermore, Marxian social scientists have explored conflicts of class, race, and gender, asking questions about both cooperation and conflicts between groups. If the so-called law of unity and struggle of opposites helped sensitize and interest Marxian theorists in these conflicts, it was helpful. At any rate, the questions about class and class conflict do constitute an important part of the critical method of Marxism. They may be taken as one set of the questions that may be substituted for the alleged law of the unity and struggle of opposites.

For the meaningless law of the unity of opposites Marxian research has substituted the relational method and class analysis. We have rejected all universal laws and omniscient answers. We have replaced this all-encompassing law with a set of concrete questions that are useful for research in the social sciences.

Specifically, one may always ask, What are the opposing forces in this socioeconomic process? How are they related? What kinds of conflicts exist, and in what direction are they moving? A Marxian analysis should ask (and not assume that he or she knows the answers), What are the opposing interests of different classes? What holds the opposing classes together in the relative unity of the present system? Which classes are growing in numbers or power and which are declining? What tensions and disharmonies exist in the present evolutionary stage between ideologies, political and social institutions, class relations, and productive forces? Many of the same types of questions can be asked about race and gender relations.

As another example of the relational method, regarding the macroeconomic aspect of political economy, it pays to ask, In a period of apparent prosperity, what disproportions are accumulating between demand and supply, revenues and costs, consumption and production, savings and investment, and so forth? Examples of the relational approach to conflict in this book included the interactions between social process and economic process, the treatment of class and other types of conflict, and the tension between frozen socioeconomic institutions and rapidly changing technology. In each case, however, it was emphasized that the critical method asks questions but does not give answers before the actual research is done.

Rejecting and Replacing the Law of Quantity and Quality

The so-called law of quantity changing into quality, and vice versa, says that gradual, incremental changes eventually cause a drastic, revolutionary change. A revolutionary change is the beginning of new quantitative trends. One example would be the geological tensions that slowly build up to a volcanic eruption. But nature is not included in this discussion of dialectics. Another example would be the tensions that slowly build up to a revolution.

If the statement that quantitative changes lead to qualitative ones is interpreted as a law of the universe giving specific answers, then it may be criticized as in Appendix 11C. Briefly, the so-called law does not specify any exact meanings for its terms, nor does it specify any exact time durations. If it did specify those aspects, it would apply to only one period and one type of society, so it would no longer be a general law. The law in its old version must be rejected. It can be replaced by the historical method developed in chapter 4. Since most of the useful insights in the literature on this so-called law were discussed there, only a few additional points need to be highlighted here. These points are not answers, as in the rejected law, but questions, as in the earlier explanation of the historical method.

When a socioeconomic process shows a discontinuity or qualitative jump, one should ask, What continuous, quantitatively measurable, incremental evolution led it to that point? When a social or economic process shows only continuous, quantitative, incremental change for a long period, one should ask, What discontinuities or qualitative leaps may occur in the future? The critical political economist should ask (and not assume that he or she knows the answers), What are present quantitative, incremental trends in ideologies, institutions, classes, and productive forces? Will these trends eventually create a sufficient level of class conflict to cause a revolutionary change? In what direction is that change likely to be? Will it be good or bad from the viewpoint of the oppressed classes? For example, is there increasing economic concentration, and has it brought qualitative changes in the operation of the economy? Is there increasing government economic activity, and has it brought qualitative changes in the operation of the economy? Similarly, do the long-term trends in race or gender conditions point toward some radical change in the near future?

Long-term trends, with tiny, incremental changes each year, can lead to a situation where a major change is ripe and waiting to happen, so that it appears sudden to a casual observer. "The Russian Revolution shook the world in ten days, and the U.S. Constitution was hammered out in a few weeks" (Platt 1970, 4). But the sudden change did not come out of nowhere; it was prepared by incremental changes over a long period of time. Similarly, to understand the causes of the First World War in 1914, it is not sufficient to look at immediately prior events, such as the assassination of Archduke Ferdinand in Serbia. It is necessary to ask serious questions about the social changes that took place in the decades leading up to 1914. By asking these questions, one may find that once social tensions had reached a certain point, any incident or "accident" might set off a war.

As another example, looking at the Great Crash of 1929 strictly in terms of the sudden panic of the stock market does little to aid the understanding of the basic economic processes that led to the Great Depression. Political economists ask detailed questions concerning how the long and prosaic course of trends in prices, production, and income distribution in the period before 1929 led to the Great Depression.

Similarly, a journalist may consider Gorbachev's revolutionary changes in Russia to have come out of nowhere or to have come from Gorbachev's powerful personality. But a political economist must ask how the underlying tensions in the Soviet Union built up bit by bit to the breaking point. Some of the problems began in the 1920s or 1930s, but most of the quantifiable trends were observable from the 1950s through the 1980s.

Another example illustrates some specific interactions of quantitative and qualitative changes and some of the questions to be asked about them. In the United States from the 1870s to the 1890s there were quantitative economic improvements from better machinery, better-trained labor, better transportation and communication, and so forth. These quantitative or incremental changes eventually led to qualitative changes in business, such as trusts and other forms of monopoly power, in the 1890s and early 1900s. These qualitative changes led in turn to new quantitative trends in the size of corporations, as well as different types of industrial research, that laid the ground for a new round of qualitative changes in business forms, especially vertical integration with suppliers and dealers in the 1920s.

A Marxian approach should encourage questions about both gradual evolution and rapid revolution. A flamboyant writer in the turbulent 1930s said, "In the history of evolution, Marx also discovered revolution. He found . . . that instead of the superstructure being always gradually, by small increments, remodelled by man's daily activity, there were periods when the superstructure, as if by explosive force, was rapidly shattered and transformed" (Caudwell [1938] 1971, 149). In more prosaic terms, this process, together with the questions that arise from it, is described as the historical approach in this book. Finally, in the words of a non-Marxian economic historian studying the Neolithic and industrial revolutions: "Each 'Revolution' had its roots in the past. But each 'Revolution' created a deep break with the very same past" (Cipolla 1962, 32).

The questions and suggestions of the historical method are all grounded in past empirical research and the practice of political economists. Yet the method does not presume to make statements of any sort, only to direct the political economist to ask certain questions. Therefore, criticisms concerning the truth or even vagueness of these suggestions or questions are inappropriate. The only test of this method is whether it leads social analysts in fruitful or useful directions.

Rejecting and Replacing the Law of the Negation of the Negation

The so-called law of the negation of the negation says that every process leads to its own end but that some of its forms reappear at a higher level. The usual example states that a seed is ended when it becomes a tree but that the tree produces many seeds. A social example might be that classless, primitive societies evolved into class-divided societies that will one day evolve into classless communist societies. This alleged law is, as appendix 11C shows, a mystic-sounding generalization with no real content. It must be rejected.

The few additional insights that emerged from the tedious Soviet debates on this meaningless law can easily be incorporated in and replaced by the relational-historical description of how methodology itself develops.

The Process of Model Building

The development of methodological rules is a never-ending process in which we learn from practice, formulate a set of rules to guide practice, and then eventually learn more from practice to develop better rules. In order to explain and use the rules, each paradigm or worldview creates particular scientific concepts and categories in which to express them. As more is learned from practice, the rules change, and so do the definitions, concepts, and categories. Of course the definitions and categories are treated as fixed at any one time.

Hegel turned this process upside down. He saw certain categories, such as Being and Nothing, or Quantity and Quality, as absolute ideas that develop from their own inner movements and conflicts. According to Hegel, the natural and social worlds of human beings merely reflect this ideal development of categories. Most contemporary Marxian scholars, on the other hand, see the categories of method as reflections of the process of development of human knowledge. And the process of human knowledge in turn reflects the processes of natural and social development.

If the process of developing concepts and categories is viewed as one of trial and error in human scientific experience, a relational or dialectic approach to categories can be helpful. The relational approach tells us never to think of things as isolated objects, but as related processes. So this approach may help resolve some of the sterile disputes of those who see rigid dichotomies between isolated, unrelated categories. If one wishes to use Hegel's terminology (but with a different content), then when a political economist runs across totally conflicting extreme views of methodology, she or he should ask, Is there a way that both the opposites, thesis and antithesis, can be negated (or deconstructed) and replaced by a new synthesis? Note that a synthesis should not be just an eclectic mixture of the old opposites, but some new way of putting things that removes an old and false dichotomy. As an example, a non-Marxian anthropologist mentions the false dichotomies in anthropology: "past and present, static and dynamic, system and event, infrastructure and superstructure, and others of that intellectual dichotomous ilk" (Sahlins 1985, xvii).

Examples of the relational (or dialectic) approach to method, which negates false dichotomies and searches for new syntheses, include all of the major themes of this book:

Chapter 2 discusses the erroneous notion that one must choose between psychological reductionism and economic reductionism. Chapter 3 shows, however, that in a relational, or holistic, approach psychology and economics are related facets of society, and each affects the other, so it is not necessary to choose either reductionist position.

Chapter 4 demonstrates that it is incorrect to think of the world as either in a purely static equilibrium or changing so fast that there is no structure at all. Chapter 4 also explains a synthesis, namely, the historical, or evolutionary, method for asking the proper questions about both continuity and change.

Chapter 5 shows that it is false that one must choose between starting from isolated individuals (and ignoring structures or collective groups) and starting from a social structure with collective groups (and ignoring individuals). Chapter 6 explains the viewpoint of class analysis, which synthesizes the individualist and structural, or collectivist, approaches.

Chapter 12 examines the traditional conflicting views of truth: positivist and rationalist. Chapter 12 also attempts a synthesis based on Thomas Kuhn's notion of dynamic paradigms and John Dewey's relational approach to knowledge.

Chapter 13 shows that the notion of free will is incorrectly set in opposition to a predetermined, or fatalist, view. Chapter 13 also attempts to provide a synthesis allowing for human beings to make decisions within a given set of conditions.

Chapter 14 shows that "ethical values" are said to be opposed to "value-free science," as if one cannot be both ethical and scientific. Chapter 14 also attempts to show that if social science is viewed as an ongoing process in which the ethical and the factual are both aspects, the mystery disappears.

The following are a few additional false dilemmas commonly found in the social sciences: relative truth versus absolute truth, accident versus necessity, freedom versus necessity, inspiration versus technique, intuition versus science, principle versus flexibility, skepticism versus utopianism, uniqueness versus universality, practice versus theory, and form versus content. The point is that these are not absolute fortresses sitting on isolated mountaintops glaring at each other. All of these concepts are merely different aspects of the process of research practice in the social sciences. In the course of that practice, one finds that each of the two apparently opposite concepts are only artificially held to be absolutely distinct from each other. As one learns from mistakes in doing actual research, one eventually learns a proper melding of each of these pairs of apparent opposites into a new and different synthesis.

The Method of Successive Approximations

One example of the application of a dialectic approach to method is the Marxian approach to the problem of realism versus abstraction. In order to be realistic, one should analyze a subject in all of its concrete complexity. But to be clear, one needs to use simple abstractions. The method known as *successive approximations* acknowledges that in research one cannot know everything at once, so one must approach the problem in a set of stages, gradually moving closer to a general theory. Similarly, in exposition not everything can be explained at once, so one must approach the explanation in stages that gradually add to our understanding.

The process of research and the process of exposition can both use successive approximations, but the places from which they begin are completely different. Research starts with a vast mound of concrete data (and some preconceived notions) and tries to extract, by successively broader generalizations, some abstract principles to be used in all future cases. In contrast, an exposition of previous research can start from statements of the principles in the most abstract and simple case, using many heroic and unreal assumptions. The exposition should then proceed, by successive approximations, to more and more concrete cases by gradually adding the more realistic assumptions.

Michael Harrington makes clear the difference between successive approximations in research and exposition by using Marx as an example: "*Das Kapital* begins its study of existential reality behind capitalist economic categories with dry-as-dust definitions. . . . This is because the book proceeds from the abstract to the concrete. On the face of it, that is a preposterous order to follow, since it is obvious that thinking always moves from the concrete to the abstract. . . . But there is method in Marx's apparent madness. . . . Marx, like everyone else, actually begins [his research] with the 'chaotic whole' of immediate experience, but in his masterpiece he follows a logical rather than experiential order" (Harrington 1970, 86–87). So research goes from concrete to abstract, while exposition goes from abstract to concrete.

As one example, research on business cycles begins with large amounts of undigested facts, which may have been gathered in many areas over many years. Only after a long while can one put things together into simple-looking models. Yet an exposition of the business cycle (see, e.g., Sherman 1991) begins with the simplest possible case, assuming negligible government intervention, negligible foreign relations, no explicit discussion of monopoly, no explicit discussion of the role of money and credit, and so forth. Each of these unrealistic assumptions is then changed in successive approximations to reality.

Conclusion: Questions, Not Answers

The old notion that dialectics provides a magical key to the world and provides all the answers has been rejected. The view that dialectics is simply nonsense has also been rejected. Marxism should use a new synthesis that insists that if dialectics is viewed as a set of questions to guide social research, it can be very useful. Thus, interactions in society may be investigated in terms of the questions asked by the relational, or holistic, method. Social change may be investigated in terms of the questions asked by the historical, or evolutionary, method. Class relations may be investigated in terms of the questions asked by both the relational and the historical methods, which are aspects of dialectic method.

The so-called three laws of dialectics were found to be empty of content, so they were rejected. Instead of the three laws, the dialectic method as described here includes (1) the relational method, (2) the historical method, (3) the relational-historical approach to the resolution of false dilemmas and construction of better methodology, (4) the use of successive approximations in a relational-historical context, as well as other applications of the relational-historical method (such as the study of conflict). Rather than laws or answers, this concept of the dialectic method results in questions that are used as a guide to research.

Finally, the critical method (the term is used here somewhat differently than it was by the Frankfurt school) encompasses the four aspects treated in part III: the dialectic method; the Marxian theory of knowledge; the Marxian understanding of determinism; and Marxian humanist ethics.

Appendix 11A: The Early Evolution of Dialectics

In the face of the wildly conflicting claims about dialectics, it is best to begin by determining what people have meant by *dialectics*. Remember Bertell Ollman's brief definition: "The subject of dialectics is change . . . and interaction" (1990). Most writers would agree that dialectics has something to do with change and interaction, but no brief definition can remove the controversies over just what it is. The dialectic method did not appear from outer space nor even spontaneously from the head of Marx. Dialectics has a long history, which is worth noting, and one must apply the historical approach to dialectics as to any other concept. Only by using a historical approach to trace the evolution of the dialectic method can one understand how it has come to its present situation.

Plato in his discourses (in which Socrates is the protagonist) tried to reach the truth through a process—a dialogue or dialectic—of confrontation of opposing viewpoints. Socrates offered his students and his opponents the choice of two positions, taking for granted that these were the only two positions possible. Socrates then pushed the other person to the extreme implications of that position in order to reduce it to absurdity. Through this clash of extreme opposite positions, he tried to teach what he saw as truth. This was one of the earliest meanings of dialectics; it is still useful as a dialectic of teaching.

Many of the early Greek philosophers of the Eleatic school, such as Heraclitus, considered the world to be in constant motion because of strife and opposition within it (see Russell 1945, pt. 1). Some of these early Greeks were so preoccupied with the idea of constant flux that they denied any possibility of scientific classification or scientific laws because of the constantly changing situation. Thus, Heraclitus is supposed to have said that one cannot step in the same river twice because it will have changed and that perhaps one cannot even step into the same river once since it will have changed by the time one's foot hits the bottom.

Aristotle fought against the extreme form of this position in his attempt to classify many kinds of things and to lay down rules for scientific method. Aristotle's classification tended to be static, though he did not deny that further scientific advances may lead to more dynamic systems.

In the Middle Ages the scholastic philosophers interpreted Aristotle in a very narrow way, making rigid his tentative classifications in order to proclaim a static world for all eternity. At any rate, most people in the medieval period assumed that the world never changed. That static view of the world was dominant through at least the seventeenth century.

Appendix 11B: G. W. F. Hegel, Nineteenth-Century Pioneer of Dialectics

Not until the eighteenth- and nineteenth-century discoveries of empirical evidence of evolution in geology, astronomy, and biology did the concept of change reappear in philosophy. The greatest advance was made by G. W. F. Hegel ([1873] 1950), who developed a very insightful and comprehensive view of a changing universe, in which all of the changing processes were interconnected. Hegel called this process of change, as well as our understanding of it, *dialectics*. Hegel's extremely important achievement was to end the total dominance of the medieval philosophy of static, unchanging, isolated objects.

In addition to presenting an analysis of change and evolution, Hegel had a relational approach at the core of his thought. For Hegel, an entity only existed in relation to its "other," or opposite. A thing can only be defined by its other, or opposite, which makes clear what it is and what it is not. Thus, a slave can only be defined in relationship to a slave owner. Economics can only be defined with respect to the noneconomic, such as politics. Society must be defined in its relation to nature. One must understand how society differs from nature, but one must also understand what its close ties are to nature. For Hegel, an entity can have no prior existence independent of such relationships.

In addition to his historical, or evolutionary, approach to change and his relational point of view, Hegel stresses that all change is caused by conflict. Because of his contributions to the historical approach to change, the relational approach to all processes, and the central role of conflict, many Marxian writers have found Hegel to be fascinating. He had an important impact on Marx and on the whole Marxian tradition through these contributions to the dialectic approach.

Yet the Hegelian and Marxian approaches to dialectics are fundamentally different. Hegel's universe is a universe of ideal concepts or absolute ideas, not our familiar material or social universe. For this reason, Marx spoke of Hegel as an *idealist*, one who sees reality as determined by ideal concepts. Marx contrasted his own philosophy as *materialist*, beginning with the prosaic facts of the known material and social world.

Thus, Hegel begins his *Science of Logic* with the categories Being and Nothing, which Hegel considers to be real entities. Hegel does not give us a simple, unchanging, Aristotelian definition of these two categories. This is in part because he assumes that people know these concepts intuitively and in part because he explains them in the development of his argument. He tells us that Being and Nothing are opposites and that every concept is only defined by its opposite. So Being and Nothing are defined by Hegel in relation to each other. He literally argues that one cannot understand the concept of Being without understanding Nothing, while one cannot understand Nothing except in relation to Being. Thus Hegel begins with a relationship, but it is a relationship of two abstract concepts. He shows us immediately a dialectic method, but dialectics is part of a mystic or idealist approach.

Hegel then argues that the developmental process of our thought must move us beyond these two concepts of Being and Nothing. The apparently absolute conflict between Being and Nothing is resolved at the next level. The resolution of the conflict between these two concepts is Becoming. So we see that Hegel moves his argument forward by stressing conflicts or contradictions at each level. We also note that Becoming, evolution, or historical change is a basic part of Hegel's system from a very early point. But it is still a mystical or idealist system in that the real things in it are abstract concepts, not the usual social or natural reality.

Hegel asserts that all opposites, such as Being and Nothing, are really identical and become unified in their synthesis, in this case Becoming. Hegel always emphasizes conflict and change (or Becoming), as in this typically mystic-sounding statement: "Identity is only . . . dead Being, while Contradiction is the root of all movement and life, and it is only in so far as it contains a contradiction that anything moves and has impulse and activity" ([1873] 1950, 103). In its turn, Becoming is confronted with its opposite, producing a new synthesis, and so on until we reach Hegel's final category, the Absolute. The Absolute perhaps stands for God, but according to Frederick Engels, Hegel says absolutely nothing about the Absolute.

Hegel's contributions to a systematic analysis of dialectic method are brilliant. Most Marxian philosophers do not agree with his mystical, theological, and very complex system of categories. It was Hegel's impressionistic description of conflict in a changing or evolving world that captured their imagination. For example, Lenin commented: "There is much mysticism and empty pedantry in . . . Hegel, but the basic idea is one of genius; that of the universal, all-sided, vital connections of everything with everything" (quoted in Selsam and Martel 1963, 334). Note that Lenin is here describing a version of a holistic, or relational, approach. Hegel's basic ideas of interconnection and change through internal conflict influenced not only Marxian thought but many related nineteenth- and twentieth-century methodologies. These include Bergson's emergent evolution (see Russell 1945, 791–810), Whitehead's organic-process approach (see Whitehead 1929), Korzybski's oddly phrased but interesting "non-Aristotelian" general semantics (see Korzybski 1933; and Rapoport 1948), and even some gestalt psychology (see Wertheimer 1959).

Marxian Dialectics versus Hegelian Dialectics

Marx never wrote a full-length treatise on dialectics, though his own work is an example of its applications. He did mention his intention, never accomplished, to write his own explanation of dialectic method, contrasting it to the Hegelian version: "I shall very much want to publish two or three papers which will render the rational element of the method, which Hegel both discovered and turned into a mystery, accessible to common sense" (Marx to Engels, January 14, 1858, in Marx and Engels 1934). Marx did indicate two main ways in which the "common sense" Marxian dialectics should differ from the mysterious Hegelian dialectics. The Marxian dialectic method should be (1) materialist rather than idealist and (2) an open-ended method rather than a closed system of laws.

In his first point Marx claimed that Hegel's dialectic method is idealist in the sense that its subject matter is the development of disembodied, abstract ideas. Marx's dialectic method is materialist in the sense that its subject matter is the development of human beings in a material world. Marx attempts to ground his concepts on human experience in the changing material and social world. Marx wrote: "My dialectic method is not only different from the Hegelian, but its direct opposite. To Hegel, the life-process of the human brain, i.e., the process of thinking (which, under the name of 'the idea,' he even transforms into an independent subject) is the demiurge [the creator] of the real world—and the real world is only the external phenomenal form of 'the idea.' With me, on the contrary, the ideal is nothing else than the material world reflected by the human mind and translated into forms of thought" ([1872] 1965, afterword). Marx says that his method is opposite to Hegel's because Hegel sees the interconnections of the real world as mere reflections of the connections among abstract ideas, whereas Marx starts from the real world and sees ideas as reflecting that world.

It must always be remembered that "a central focus of Hegel's was to defend Christianity against the ravages of science. . . . He proposed to do that by reinterpreting religion so as to make it immune to criticism by science" (Schmidt 1989, 445). A major criticism of religion was directed against the claim that God made the universe and keeps it moving. It was claimed that the scientific method produced a more persuasive explanation for the movements of the universe than did religion. To overcome this criticism of religion, Hegel got rid of a transcendent God who makes everything behave as it does. Instead, Hegel pictures God (the Idea) and the world as one.

The critics of religion had also asked, If God is good and all-powerful, why is the world so evil? Hegel attempts to solve this paradox by describing a process of becoming. Both God and the world must pass through a set of stages. "Weakness thus is a move toward power; error is a step toward knowledge; evil is a step toward the good" (Schmidt 1989, 445). So Hegel makes use of dialectics to show how everything unfolds according to divine plan. Since Marx's dialectic method is merely an aspect of scientific method in a material world, the two conceptions of dialectics are utterly different.

The second difference between Marx and Hegel is that Hegel puts forth dialectics as a system of laws. It is a totally known picture of the whole universe, that is, an ontology (though Hegel claims that dialectics is also a logic and a method in some sense). Marx's dialectics does not claim to be a complete and closed system; it is not meant to be a picture of the universe (an ontology) or dogma or set of laws of any sort. It is designed to be a flexible tool of analysis. Marx's dialectics can be developed into a nondogmatic method of approach to problems of science or politics or everyday life. Marx's dialectics emphasizes the need to ask useful questions as a guide to new, open-ended research. Hegel's idealist scheme of dialectic development is thus very different from the method advocated by Marx.

In contrast to my interpretation, Jacques Maritain claims that Marx's materialism is in opposition to his idealist dialectics. Maritain claims that Marx's dialectics states the laws of movement of the universe without having proved these laws by the usual scientific methods (1964). Actually, as shown above, Marx's materialist dialectics is the opposite of Hegel's idealist dialectic and its preconceived knowledge of the universe. Marx's own dialectic method is materialist in the sense that it is best interpreted, not as a system of laws, but as a set of questions for research, derived from experience and practice in the world.

Appendix 11C: Soviet Marxism: Dialectics as a System

Unfortunately, Soviet Marxism did not see dialectics merely as a part of scientific method. The Soviets preferred to see it as an omniscient system explaining the whole universe, following the Hegelian tradition in this respect. For the political dictatorship of Stalin, it was useful to have such an omniscient system of answers, framed vaguely so that they could be changed at will. It is true that Soviet Marxian philosophers no longer talked about Hegel's abstract, disembodied ideas. Soviet Marxism did, however, see dialectics as a systematic statement of the most general laws of the universe (see Cornforth 1971a; Gollobin 1986; Somerville 1946; and Stalin 1940). It is also true that Soviet Marxian philosophers asserted in general rhetoric that dialectics was not a system or dogma but a method. In practice, however, they applied dialectics as a finished product or a closed system of fully known laws.

Part of the blame lies with Engels, who wrote about the laws of dialectics in his books *Anti-Dühring* and *Dialectics of Nature*. He himself usually applied dialectics as a flexible method or approach with some important insights into social processes. Yet he stated dialectics in an ambiguous manner that allowed Soviet Marxists to see it in terms of his loose phrase about the "most general laws of movement."

Thus, Soviet Marxism continued to view dialectics as a typical nineteenth-century philosophy of nature or philosophy of history, as if pure philosophical contemplation could reveal the detailed laws of biological or social evolution. One awful example of the official use of dialectics as a philosophy of nature was Stalin's patronage of the crank biologist Trofim Lysenko, who thought he could make plants inherit characteristics that were acquired and not genetically transmitted. Lysenko's confused biology was defended by some Soviet writers as an example of dialectics in action.

Yet Engels frequently warned against such speculative uses: "Today, when one needs only to comprehend the results of natural scientific investigation dialectically . . . natural philosophy is finally disposed of" (Engels [1888] 1941, 353). Engels is equally vehement in his critique of those who would explain social events by a priori philosophy. "The philosophy of history . . . has consisted in the substitution of an interconnection fabricated in the mind of the philosopher for the real interconnection to be demonstrated in the events" (Engels [1888] 1941, 353).

In spite of the warnings by Engels, the official line in the Soviet Union under Stalin transformed Marx's flexible methodological rules into three rigid laws within a universal system (see Stalin 1940). It is true that Engels did discuss the alleged three laws of movement of dialectics, but he was ambiguous about their status. Official Soviet Marxism stated unambiguously that these three laws were laws of the movement of the universe as well as statements of method. As late as 1986 a Marxian analysis by Ira Gollobin states that there are three laws of dialectics: "Each is a very general law of a thing's self-movement, an exemplification of certain universal interconnections in nature, society, and thought" (185). Each of these three "laws" is considered here in the form given them from Stalin to Gollobin.

Unity of opposites. According to Soviet Marxists the first "law" was the Unity and Struggle of Opposites. This law states that everywhere in the natural and social universe, "opposites" interpenetrate each other. The term *opposite* is unclear and is given many different meanings. Common examples are the two poles of a magnet, the productive relations versus the productive forces, and worker versus boss. Opposites are said to be unified at any given time, but in the long run their strife produces change. Therefore, in this view, social conflict is basic, with social harmony being a rare phenomenon. According to Stalin, "Contrary to metaphysics, dialectics holds that internal contradictions are inherent in all things . . . and that the struggle between these opposites . . . between that which is dying away and that which is being born . . . constitutes the internal content of the process of development" (Stalin 1940, 11).

Note that Stalin, like Hegel, finds that contradictions are "inherent in all things." This view of *contradictions* was widespread in Soviet and Chinese Marxism (see, e.g., Mao Tse-tung [1937] 1985). We shall see that as a law or a statement about the universe, the unity of opposites and the related concept of contradiction are either meaningless truisms or misleading.

Quantity into quality. The second "law" is that quantitative change becomes qualitative change; that is, small marginal changes eventually produce major jumps or leaps in any process. According to Stalin, "Contrary to metaphysics, dialectics does not regard the process of development as a simple process of growth, but as a development which passes from insignificant . . . quantitative changes to . . . fundamental qualitative changes; a development in which the qualitative changes occur not gradually, but rapidly and abruptly . . . they occur not accidentally, but as the natural result of an accumulation of . . . quantitative changes" (Stalin 1940, 8). Note that Stalin regards dialectics as a system of laws inherent in the natural universe, and not merely in society.

Negation of the negation. The third "law" has the mysterious title Negation of the Negation (see Gollobin 1986). This law states that a new stage of any developmental process repeats many features of the previous stage, but at a "higher" level, as in an ascending spiral. This law is sometimes stated as the clash of a thesis (the first stage) with an antithesis (its opposite) to produce a synthesis (a higher stage). Again, this so-called law is criticized below.

A Critique of the Three "Laws"

Just as Hegel's idealist—but dynamic and rich—writing on the dialectic may stir one's imagination, these Soviet Marxian statements of universal laws convey certain insights. The trouble is that they claim too much. They claim to present a comprehensive and omniscient knowledge of all of the past, present, and future history of the natural and social universe. This is obviously absurd. It implies that its users already know all about social development without any research. "In Soviet Marxism, the dialectic has been transformed from a mode of critical thought into a universal 'world outlook' . . . and this transformation destroys the dialectic" (Marcuse 1961, 122). The problem is that Soviet Marxism viewed dialectics as a set of known, universal laws of motion, not as a set of questions for research. It must be emphasized that the notion of dialectics as a set of universal laws solving all problems (similar to a religion) was very widespread among Communists (see, e.g., Mao [1937] 1985).

Although Marx sometimes uses Hegelian terminology in a playful manner, Marx never spoke of universal laws or universal patterns, since the concept has no precise meaning. "The problem of tracing the design of the world, or of finding out the nature of the universe as a whole, or of specifying the essential patterns and forms of things to which particular things must conform, is found to be unanswerable because it rests on a misunderstanding" (Cornforth 1965, 273–74). The misunderstanding is the idea that human beings, including scientific researchers, can know something about the world before experience or practice. Yet the official Soviet Marxian version of dialectics, as shown above, provided just such a priori laws.

Using the critical method of the relational-historical approach, contemporary Marxian scholars view a law as nothing more or less than a constancy or regularity, learned through experience via the research process, always defined precisely within exact constraints in a certain range, and always open to revision on the basis of new evidence. For example, one may state a law of the behavior of aggregate consumption for a given class in a given stage of capitalism. Such a law comes from experience and may yield specific predictions in a given situation, though as a probability rather than a certainty.

The Soviet Marxian philosophers claimed that their dialectic laws were not mere speculation but scientific propositions. Yet they fit none of the criteria one should follow in any materialist research. First, these laws did not arise from practice or experiment, but from the abstract contemplation of various philosophers. Second, each of these so-called dialectic laws is expressed as an absolute applying always and everywhere. Yet meaningful laws in materialist research are always constrained within some range because that is the range that has been explored. If one can state absolutely the future of the whole universe, then there is no need for empirical research. Such absolute statements imply that the person who states them (such as Stalin) is omniscient and perfect.

Third, the critical method of Marxism—and all consistent method—demands that propositions be precisely defined and usable in an operational way in the social and material world. But Soviet Marxism did not state the so-called dialectic laws in a meaningful way. For example, when Soviet Marxism claims that quantitative changes always lead to qualitative ones, it does not give an exact and operational definition of the terms such that one could pin down the specifics. Moreover, there is no statement of the exact time duration of this change. The vague nature of these so-called laws makes them immune from criticism. How can one use or test a "law" whose terms and time of application are not precisely stated? Thus, quantitative changes in an embryo may cause it to be born in nine months, but quantitative changes in a volcano may cause it to erupt in nine thousand years. If one predicts for long enough that prosperity will produce a depression under capitalism, it will finally occur. But one loses faith in the predictor who predicts the occurrence every single year for twenty years. If he or she merely keeps saying that it will happen someday, how are we to know what *someday* means? Precise and identifiable statements are necessary for any research program that intends to increase our understanding rather than just make dogmatic statements. Only precise propositions are open to criticism and revision.

The anti-Marxian critic Planty-Bonjour (1967) argues that the law that quantity changes into quality is so ambiguous that it provides no precise prediction. Another critic, Gerald Dworkin, argues that the law of quantitative and qualitative change "gives us no way of predicting in each case what the necessary quantity will be" (1961, 56). Clearly, these attacks are correct if they are applied to the old Soviet approach but have no relevance to contemporary Marxian research methods.

This point has been clearly expressed by Bertell Ollman, who comments that dialectics does *not* "provide a formula that enables us to prove or predict anything, nor is it the motor force of history." Instead, Ollman emphasizes that dialectics is merely an approach to the world: "Dialectics restructures our thinking about reality" because it replaces an approach that views the world as a set of static, isolated objects with an approach that views the world in terms of relations and processes and asks questions about change and interaction (Ollman 1992, 10, 11).

Appendix 11D: Dialectics and Logic

Logic has its systematic beginning with Aristotle's formal rules for consistent thinking from precise premises. The formal logic descended from Aristotle and taught in universities around the world today was criticized by some Soviet and Chinese Marxian philosophers on the grounds that it could only deal with a static situation, whereas dialectic logic deals with change. Ping-yuan, a Maoist Chinese philosopher, stated: "The laws of the movement, change, and development of things, reflected in men's consciousness, constitute the dialectical laws of thought; the laws of fixity, inactivity, and stability within the process of movement, change, and development, reflected in men's consciousness, constitute the laws of thought of formal logic" (Ping-yuan [1969], 30). Thus, formal logic was relegated to a small subset, or "lower stage," of dialectic logic.

The Soviet and Chinese Marxian philosophers restated the three "laws" of dialectics as logical laws in contrast with those of academic logic:

Academic, or Formal, Logic

  1. *Identity:* Any true proposition is true.

  2. *Noncontradiction:* No proposition can be both true and false.

  3. *Excluded middle:* Every proposition is either true or false.

Dialectic Logic as Stated by Soviet Marxism

  1. *Unity of opposites:* Because each thing is interconnected with and changing into its opposite, every proposition is both true and false.

  2. *Quantity into quality:* Because everything is changing, sometimes slowly and sometimes by leaps, every true proposition is slowly or rapidly becoming false, and vice versa.

  3. *Negation of the negation:* Because every stage is negated but returns at a higher level, every proposition becomes false but then returns to truth at a higher level.

The formal logic presented by academic logicians discusses consistent ways of dealing with propositions. The "logic" presented by some Soviet and Chinese Marxists, such as Ping-yuan, confused statements about propositions with statements about the material world. The logic of propositions does not deal with the truth or falsity of the factual content of a proposition; logic only deals with the forms of propositions and their relations. Statements in logic (or mathematics) are statements with blank spaces (variables) in them. The statements are such that any particular content may be inserted in the blank spaces, so long as it is the same content throughout, and the statement will necessarily hold true. For example, any one X plus any other of the same X equals $2X$. The consistent use of propositions certainly does not rule out discussion of change and interaction.

Yet the Maoist Chinese philosopher Ping-yuan attacked this view, saying, "The position that in reasoning we only ask whether the syllogism is valid or not, and do not ask whether the statements are true or false—is an expression of . . . idealist logic . . . also called imperialist logic" ([1969], 88–89). On this basis he treated all academic, or formal, logic as a continuation of the medieval view of a static world, while he claimed that all dynamic propositions must be in a broader dialectic "logic." As mentioned above, this argument confuses two different categories of statements: statements about change in the world and statements about the formal connections of propositions.

Another defender of the old Marxian position emphasized that formal logic is wrong because real contradictions exist: "Someone who accepts that there are true contradictions, and therefore that some things are both true (A) and false (A-) is hardly going to accept the unargued assumption of [formal] logic that truth and falsity are mutually exclusive" (Priest 1989–90, 392). The problem is that a contradictory logic leads to inconsistent thinking, so everything is true and everything is false. As one Marxian philosopher observed: "The laws of logic are the laws of consistency. To advocate ignoring or breaking them is to advocate inconsistence . . . dialectics advocates nothing of the kind" (Cornforth 1968, 76). There is no conflict between logic and dialectics, because a correct version of dialectics does not assert that two contradictory statements can be correct at the same time and in the same place and aspect of a phenomenon. Similarly, a Marxian philosopher states: "One will look in vain for examples of logical contradictions in the material world" (Marquit 1981, 323). The view that one cannot accept logical contradictions eventually became the dominant view even in Soviet Marxism (see, e.g., Schaff 1960, 131), but there are still some confusions.

The Hegelian Marxian philosopher Sean Sayers agrees that rules of noncontradiction must apply to propositions: "In a purely formal and deductive system or argument, where the only concern is for consistency and formal validity, the law of non-contradiction holds true. A contradiction, the assertion of P and not-P, ... in these circumstances is invalid and cannot be accepted." On the other hand, he still asserts the Hegelian view that "the minute the content of what is being said is also taken into account the situation changes. ... in concrete circumstances one may well have good reasons for asserting both sides of a contradiction. ... all concrete things are contradictory and a unity of opposites. ... all things are in a process of change ... and ... contradiction is the root of such change" (1981–82, 425–27).

Thus, Sayers extends the Marxian view of human conflicts to the mystical statement that all things are contradictory in the material world, though he admits that logical contradictions between propositions cannot be accepted. In the material world, can one speak of contradictions? What does it mean to say that there is a contradiction between the two poles of a magnet? What is the contradiction within a rock? It often appears that such theories are speaking anthropomorphically, that is, that they are attributing human characteristics to inanimate objects. Richard Norman emphasizes that the dialectic concepts of conflict may be appropriate to society but "cannot be applied to natural processes without thereby subscribing to an anthropomorphic, animistic view of nature" (Norman and Sayers 1980, 145). Inanimate objects do not have conflicts. The two poles of a magnet have a particular relation, but it is wrong to picture it as if it were a human conflict. Certain geological disproportions lead to volcanic eruptions, but it is a misleading metaphor to speak of volcanoes resulting from the conflict of opposing sides of a battle. Of course, some ancient peoples did view volcanoes as the result of fights among the gods, but that is not a view that most geologists would defend today.

The term *contradiction* is sometimes used to describe a love-hate relation between two individuals or a relation of conflict between classes. This use of the term is misleading, however, because these are not logical contradictions. They are processes of change among individuals or groups involving certain conflicts. Marxian social scientists must be bound by formal logic (consistent thinking) in their investigation of such conflicts and processes.

TWELVE

The Conflict of Paradigms

The medieval period in Europe was a period of religious super-stition and idealist mystification. The term *idealism* in this con-text means the notion that reality is not material, but is a set of absolute ideas or an idea of God. It should be noted that the statement that someone is an idealist about reality has no rela-tion to the statement that someone is idealistic in moral terms. In the medieval, or idealist, view, the road to knowledge consisted in revelation from God or argument by authority, such as the authority of Aristotle or Aquinas.

There was a long period of struggle against superstition and ideal-ism, led by British and French philosophers such as Locke and Diderot. Marxian materialism represents an evolution from these early materialists. The simplest meaning of the *materialist* approach is that one accepts no supernatural explanations and no arguments by authority, only the knowledge that comes from experience and exper-iment.

Once science and materialism became stronger among intellectuals than religion or idealism, two differing methods emerged for conduct-ing research: *empiricism* (or *positivism*) and *rationalism*. In brief, an empiricist (or positivist) holds that one only needs to collect facts in order to prove or disprove any hypothesis. Rationalism holds that be-fore collecting facts, it is necessary to set up a framework of defini-tions and concepts, so one starts with theory rather than facts. Marx-ism rejects both empiricism and rationalism, proposing a different solution. In order to unravel and explain all of these positions more clearly, let us review and evaluate the empiricist and rationalist tradi-tions in some detail.

Empiricism

In the Middle Ages, as noted above, it was common to believe that all truth comes from authorities, such as Aristotle or Aquinas, or from direct revelations from God. On the basis of assumptions given by the authorities, philosophers would then reach correct conclusions by careful syllogistic reasoning. In early capitalism, the need for scientific understanding of the world led to the overthrow of argument by authority or revelation and the beginnings of various forms of scientific method.

The empiricist approach specifies that all scientific research must begin with the facts from patient observation and experimentation. It should be noted that what is called *empiricism* in this chapter has gone by many names, especially *positivism,* but also *logical positivism, logical empiricism,* and *emperio-criticism.* The term *empiricism* will be used to cover the whole broad tradition, except where a subschool differs on some important point relevant to this chapter.

Empiricism was publicized by Auguste Comte in the mid-nineteenth century but reached its peak in some ways with the founding of a philosophical circle in Vienna in 1922 to pursue a philosophy of science. Its announced aim was to rid both natural and social science of all traces of metaphysics, speculation, and idealism (see the excellent description of the history of empiricism and its impact on economics in Caldwell 1982; see also the clear and charmingly written history of this complex debate in Diesing 1991).

The Vienna circle divided all statements into *factual* and *analytic.* Analytic statements are definitional identities, such as "one plus one equals two." They are best known for their early empiricist view that, for factual statements, "a statement has meaning only to the extent that it is verifiable. Verifiability implies testability" (Caldwell 1982, 14). Thus, those who accepted a rigid empiricism argued that concepts such as atoms in physics or value in economics were not testable and therefore were useless metaphysical concepts. A perfect scientific language was to be built using statements of fact and identities only. Their method taught that science came only by stating rigorous hypotheses, testing them against the facts, and thereby reaching a new scientific conclusion.

Empiricism continued to have a very strong influence throughout the period from the 1920s through the 1950s. As it came under increasing criticism, however, it became more and more aware of dilemmas arising from its basic assumptions. For example, if only facts and identities are allowable, then what about the statements explaining the empiricist method itself? Such statements of method did not seem to be either facts or identities.

Another paradox arose from the notion that one looks only at "facts," but how does one identify the relevant facts? It was shown that facts are always viewed within some theoretical framework. The empiricists attempted to deal with the paradox—that is, that a theory is needed to interpret facts—by a more sophisticated empiricism. The new empiricism acknowledged that one must look at a whole theory in order to evaluate it, not just one isolated hypothesis, and that theories may contain some elements that are not easily provable.

Another paradox and a still more sophisticated empiricism were proposed by Karl Popper. Popper pointed out that hypotheses cannot ever be fully proven. The problem is that any inductive generalization from facts may always be shown to be false by a new fact tomorrow. Take, for example, the following: "I have seen a large number of white swans; I have never seen a black one; therefore, all swans are white" (example in Blaug 1980, 15). It is always possible that someone will discover a black swan in the future.

For a more relevant example of the problem in political economy, suppose someone argued that all unemployed white men show a lack of confidence, and suppose that a survey found that 100 percent of unemployed white men did lack confidence. That would not prove the hypothesis fully because an unemployed white man might be found tomorrow who was very confident. Thus, Popper concludes that no number of facts can ever fully prove the truth of a hypothesis.

Popper maintained that hypotheses could not be proven to be true but might be proven to be false. For example, if our hypothesis is that all swans are white, then if one black swan is discovered, the hypothesis is proven to be false. The earlier empiricists said that a hypothesis is scientific only if it is possible to verify it. Popper says a hypothesis is scientific only if it is possible to falsify it. Popper does not want to falsify a hypothesis to replace it with another. He merely wants to know if it is possible to devise a way to test it so that it might be falsified. If a hypothesis is stated in such a way that it cannot be tested and falsified, then in Popper's view it is not a valid scientific hypothesis. Suppose, for example, it is claimed that all wars are caused by an aggressive supernatural demon that lodges within people and is undetectable. Popper would say that such a hypothesis is not testable and therefore is not a valid scientific hypothesis. So the possibility of falsification became the mark of a scientific hypothesis. Popper has had enormous influence in economics and other social sciences.

One economist who reflected the prevailing opinion was Milton Friedman, who wrote that "the ultimate goal of a positive science is the development of a theory or hypothesis that yields valid and meaningful predictions. . . . The only relevant test of the *validity* of a hypothesis is comparison of its predictions with experience. The hypothesis is rejected if its predictions are contradicted" (Friedman, quoted in Diesing 1982, 1). Friedman emphasized the basic point of this school that no amount of factual evidence can "prove" a hypothesis; it can only disprove or falsify it (or fail to disprove it). Friedman's basically empiricist position was fairly typical of this period, though debates about Friedman's view immediately became widespread. Friedman was a bit unusual only in that he emphasized testing predictions to the exclusion of testing assumptions, a twist that was rejected by many economists. Nevertheless, Friedman reinforced Popper, so that the accepted approach in economics was to (1) formulate a hypothesis that is falsifiable, (2) test it against the facts to see if it is falsified, and (3) if it is not falsified, accept the hypothesis for the time being.

In the 1960s a new variety of empiricism emerged, after which empiricists no longer attempted to construct a whole new language of science but did try to answer and reconcile the puzzles that had come to characterize empiricist philosophy. It looked analytically at the problems of the philosophy of science, so it was called *analytic philosophy*. It still tried to construct a single optimal method for science, though it relied more on the idea that science (especially physics) already displayed most of the analytic method found to be optimal by the philosophers. This method continued to include the model of a hypothesis, factual testing, and conclusions. It added, however, a strong emphasis on use of the axiomatic method in order to gain a clear analysis. The axiomatic method emphasizes that one should not state any position casually, but should do so by a rigorous set of propositions or axioms as part of a clear sequence of analytic reasoning.

The 1960s saw not only the emergence of the analytic form of empiricism but also a successful critique of empiricism on the grounds that it was contradicted by the actual history of science (see Kuhn 1962). This critique (plus the paradoxes seen by the analytic philosophers) began a whole new discussion that led to the rapid decline of empiricism (or positivism) among philosophers of science and experts in methodology in the social sciences. By the early 1970s an orthodox economics methodologist could say that "virtually all of the positivist program has been repudiated. . . . Positivism today truly belongs to the history of the philosophy of science" (Frederick Suppe, quoted in

Caldwell 1982, 37). Alas, the news has never spread to most practicing economists or to writers of introductory economics texts (see McCloskey 1985).

By the mid-1980s, methodologists in orthodox economics had backed away from the empiricist position to a considerable degree. An entire conference on Karl Popper mostly agreed that his method fit economics even less than it did the natural sciences. In economics there are so many variables for which the definitions are controversial and the data unreliable that nothing ever is definitely falsified. The decline of empiricism, including the decline of Popper's influence in economics and the rise of other views, such as Kuhn's (1962), was well documented in a conference of orthodox economists (see De Marchi 1988).

Problems of Empiricism

It is worth looking more rigorously at the question, What is the problem with the fundamental empiricist position that one merely tests a hypothesis by gathering facts, which then leads to a new theory? Why have so many orthodox methodologists declared it a failure? The general answer is that no economist or other social scientist can do any factual research without definitions, concepts, and a whole theoretical baggage. Specifically, three reasons have been emphasized.

First, one must decide what problem is worth studying. That decision is not based on facts, but occurs prior to fact gathering. For example, should one study the best ways to speed up workers, or should one study the causes and amount of unemployment in the United States? The researcher will make this decision based on some theoretical and ethical viewpoint.

Second, if a social scientist has chosen a problem, how does he or she decide which of the infinite number of available facts should be collected? For example, if an economist studies unemployment, should he or she stand on a corner and ask people whether they are employed, or should the economist study the historical record from 1800 to the present—or some other set of facts?

Third, once a social scientist has chosen a problem and has decided which facts to gather, how should these facts be interpreted? Facts do not speak for themselves. For example, suppose an economist found that unemployment rose to 11 percent during the Reagan administration. Does that show that Reagan's policies were bad because they led to such high unemployment? Or does it show that his policies were good because otherwise unemployment would have been higher (and because he held down inflation)? Only with a theoretical framework can the facts answer such questions.

Paul Diesing claims, in an examination of Milton Friedman's work, that "frequently when social scientists claim to be testing hypotheses, they are actually interpreting or adjusting data" (1985, 63). In fact, Diesing surveys all of Friedman's own work from 1945 to 1973 to show in great detail that when Friedman claims to test hypotheses, he is almost always just reinterpreting or adjusting the data to fit his theory, not actually testing.

In other words, suppose someone asks the question, Why is it not enough to merely gather facts, without worrying about theory? In practice, this outlook just means that the researcher takes for granted that the dominant theory is correct. This often results in a crude use of neoclassical theory in economics or a similar crude use of the dominant paradigm in other social sciences. In each case the researcher is more or less unconsciously using the most simplistic version of a dominant theory to decide what problem to study, what "facts" to collect, and how to interpret the "facts." Most economists still think of research as nothing but hypothesis testing, but research always involves (1) selection of exact projects by the use of theory, (2) gathering and selection of facts with the help of theory, and (3) interpretation of many complex facts with the help of theory.

It should be noted that even such defenders of empiricism as Karl Popper and Marc Blaug (see Blaug 1980, 17, 18) admit that testing and falsifying hypotheses is not so easy. Thus Blaug discusses the Duhem-Quine theorem, which says that one can never conclusively falsify a single hypothesis because it is always embedded in auxiliary hypotheses. For example, Galileo's law of falling objects assumes a vacuum, so in any real case one must have some hypothesis about air resistance. Popper himself says: "In point of fact, no conclusive disproof of a theory can ever be produced; for it is always possible to say that the experimental results are not reliable, or that the discrepancies which are asserted to exist between the experimental result and the theory are only apparent and they will disappear with the advance of our understanding" (quoted in Blaug 1980, 18). Blaug and Popper, however, would both maintain that falsification must remain the aim of science and that only that which at least in principle can be falsified is science.

Warren Samuels observes that "the dependency of observation upon a theoretical pre-perception is a view which [Karl] Popper himself accepts, but this means that it is impossible for a theory to be falsified by the facts, as facts themselves are always tied to a theoretical discourse" (1990, 222). Similarly, Wilbur and Jameson summarize the argument by stating that "contrary to the logical positivist position of standard economics, empirical tests seldom resolve theoretical disputes" (Wilbur and Jameson 1983, 149). Thus, disputes continue about the exact nature of the consumption function in economics, and no amount of testing reduces the controversies by much. Even within a single framework or viewpoint, there are seldom conclusive tests in economics.

Wilbur and Jameson note some of the reasons why tests do not end disputes: (1) it is hard to specify the variables precisely in any agreed way; (2) there are many leads and lags that complicate the argument and are themselves hard to specify; (3) cause can usually not be distinguished from effect; and (4) there are disputes over the many ways to collect the data. One could add (5) the lack of the practical possibility of controlled experiments as a reason for continued unsettled disputes. And one must also consider (6) how vested interests may keep alive some disputes; for example, the dispute over the impact of lower taxes on capital gains is not a mere academic dispute, but involves powerful class interests.

A Postmodernist Critique of Empiricism

This is not the place for a full-scale discussion of postmodernism, but for those who want more on it, there is a good postmodernist history of postmodernism in Martin 1992. There are favorable discussions of postmodernism from a Marxian viewpoint in Amariglio 1990 and in D. Harvey 1989, while there is a very hostile discussion from a Marxian viewpoint in Wenger 1994. There is no agreement on what postmodernism means among various writers in various disciplines, so this section concentrates on one self-identified postmodernist in one discipline.

The most important postmodernist in economics has been Donald McCloskey (1985). McCloskey contrasts modernism to postmodernism. He says that the modernist "credo of scientific methodology is ... positivism" (5). As to its origin, modernism "is the program of Descartes ... to build knowledge on a foundation of radical doubt" (5). Modernism became dominant in the nineteenth century, when faith in science replaced faith in religion. McCloskey contends that modernism still holds sway among most economists, even though most philosophers have deserted its banner. He says that Milton Friedman is a modernist and that "a watered-down version of Friedman's essay of 1953 is part of the intellectual equipment of most economists" (9).

McCloskey begins his critique by demonstrating—with numerous examples throughout the book—that economists do not actually follow the rigorous empiricist standards of modernism. Even the orthodox neoclassical economist Marc Blaug says that economists often merely appear to do empirical testing, but "instead of attempting to refute testable predictions, modern economists all too frequently are satisfied to demonstrate that the real world conforms to their predictions, thus replacing falsification, which is difficult, with verification, which is easy" (1980, 256). In other words, merely showing that X correlates with Y is as easy and as useless as playing tennis without a net. Yet Blaug still supports Popper's notion of falsification and wants economists to practice what they preach.

McCloskey not only faces the fact that falsification is impossible in the usual case but also argues that economists should not even try to follow any set of rigid rules devised by philosophers. All empiricist rules, such as hypothesis testing and falsification, limit the ability of the economist to use whatever method is appropriate to the problem. He charges, for example, that modernists in economics have ruled out the use of questionnaires because they consider them to be too subjective. He claims that for the methodologist: "The proper business, if any, is an anarchistic one, resisting the rigidity and pretension of rules" (1985, 21). The spirit of McCloskey's comment is surely correct; note that this book does not suggest any hard and fast rules, only a set of questions that might be useful to political economists. In that sense, one main theme of this book might be a postmodernist approach.

McCloskey says, "Facing facts, we all agree, is good" (22). The problem is that there is no single correct way of gathering facts or of looking at and interpreting facts. He argues that modernism is therefore intolerant, without sufficient reason, when it tosses out psychoanalysis and Marxism because they are not empiricist or positivist. He claims that by the same criteria of rigid empiricist rules one should also toss out most of neoclassical economics, much of history, and even much of physics. Thus he comments that a strict empiricist in physics would not hunt for quarks.

McCloskey argues that modernist or empiricist methodology claims to be "a universalization from particular sciences to a science of science in general" (25). But such generalizations over and above science are impossible, and the practical effect of such attempts is merely to limit what is considered to be legitimate debate. He says that "methodology and its corollary, the Demarcation Problem (What is science? How is it to be distinguished from non-science?), are ways of stopping conversation by limiting conversation to people on our side of the demarcation line" (26).

McCloskey's point is a good one in that writers do try to argue that their opponents are not really "scientific," a rhetorical ploy used, for example, in the writings of Roemer and Elster (discussed in chapter 5). But McCloskey allows his rhetorical purpose to push him to an untenable extreme when he seems to say, in the above quote, that *all* methodology tries to limit discourse. Surely, he would claim that is not true of his own methodological discourse, and it is not useful to pretend that his own discussion of rhetoric is something other than a version of methodology. Marxian scholars must develop a useful, operational methodology (call it something else if you will) that does not in any way try to put blinders and limits on discourse.

With respect to the criticism of empiricism or positivism, "postmodernism and deconstruction are not opposed to—but allied with—Marxism" (Gottlieb 1992, 194). On the other hand, McCloskey gives just as harsh a criticism of the declarations by some Soviet Marxists that Marxism was an objective "science" above all other science. Marxian political economists should agree with McCloskey on this point. Some contemporary Marxian social scientists have explicitly affirmed and supported his postmodernist view of the social sciences (see, e.g., the useful articles by William Milberg [1991] and Jack Amariglio [1987, 1990]).

The one major point on which Marxian writers have criticized Mc-Closkey is that although McCloskey exposes all the rhetoric of neoclassical economics, he does not relate its rhetorical manipulations to the vested interests of those classes that support the dominant role of neoclassical economics. Thus, from a Marxian viewpoint, Mc-Closkey's delightful and often charming yet sophisticated and subtle analysis often sounds a little naive because it lacks a sociology of class.

Many Marxian social scientists also worry that some postmodernists take their critique to an extreme where they have no theory of social science knowledge, only a theory of literary discourse. These issues are discussed below with respect to the false dilemma that asserts that we may have absolute knowledge or no knowledge.

Rationalism

As noted in the previous section, most neoclassical economists and other conventional social scientists tend to use the empiricist method.

They accept the dominant approach as a conscious or unconscious assumption. Yet some conventional social scientists, such as Talcott Parsons in sociology or Ludwig von Mises in economics, go to the other extreme, called rationalism. *Rationalism* means that one begins with a few abstract definitions and assumptions and then deduces an elaborate theoretical scheme before considering empirical research.

In conventional economics, for example, the assumptions are often very unrealistic and untested notions about individual psychology. Economists following a rationalist method assume that their fundamental assumptions are basically or essentially true and that their definitions are the only rational ones. E. K. Hunt makes it clear that "the rationalist tradition in science (in contrast to the empiricist or positivist position) is built on the belief that ... a definition ... may ... be true or false" (1983, 332). Some rationalists distinguish *essential* from *accidental* qualities of a thing. For the rationalists, "if a definition includes all of the essential qualities or features of a thing, it is a true definition" (Hunt 1983, 332).

Most Marxian theorists, using the relational approach, contend that definitions, concepts, and theories can only come out of our experience and knowledge of the world. How can one know the most basic, or *essential*, qualities of anything, such as a social process, before investigating it? To believe that there are true or essential definitions independent of human experience is to follow the same idealist philosophy as Hegel and is therefore subject to all of the same criticisms. The main point is that human beings create definitions and concepts as tools of communication. Humans develop their linguistic tools over a long period of human experience and long practice in communicating with each other. We develop the definitions, so they do not precede our experience.

Our definitions must always be limited, because our knowledge is limited; no one can ever reach a perfectly true definition. Marx wrote a wonderfully sarcastic description of how a definition is declared essential or true above and beyond the material world: "If from real apples, pears, strawberries and almonds I form the general idea, 'Fruit,' if I go further and imagine that my abstract idea 'Fruit,' derived from real fruit, is an entity existing outside of me, is indeed the true essence of the pear, etc., then—*in the language of* speculative philosophy—I am declaring that 'Fruit' is the 'Substance' of the pear, apple, almond, etc." (quoted in Hudelson 1990, 114).

Definitions must change over time as new knowledge is acquired and new problems are addressed. For example, what is the "true definition" of the rate of profit? The most useful definition depends on what question is asked. For example, if the question is, What is the best place to invest? then it is the ratio of profit to investment. But if the question is, How efficient is the enterprise? then the best definition may be the ratio of profit to output. So definitions are neither true nor false, but they are useful or not with respect to particular questions.

Typical of the rationalist approach, in the 1870s the famous neo-classical economist Leon Walras maintained that economics could only use the mathematical method, which he said was "not an *experimental* method; it is a *rational* method. . . . the pure theory of economics ought to take over from experience certain real-type concepts, like those of exchange, supply, demand. . . . the pure science of economics should then abstract and define ideal-type concepts in terms of which it carries on its reasoning. The return to reality should not take place until the science is completed" ([1874] 1969, 71). Thus, according to Walras, economic reasoning is to be rational but need not use empirical studies, except as a secondary and inferior application of the science.

In the 1930s, Lionel Robbins wrote a methodological treatise that had enormous influence in neoclassical economics for a long time. In discussing the basic postulates of economics, he said: "We do not need controlled experiments to establish their validity; they are so much the stuff of our everyday experience that they have only to be stated to be recognized as obvious" (1935, 79). He claimed the postulates came from experience, yet there was no need to specify them by exact experiments or even observations. For example, Robbins specifically rejected the extensive empirical research on business cycles by Wesley Mitchell as unnecessary (113).

Soon after Robbins wrote, he was attacked from the empiricist, or positivist, position, and most economists have tended to be empiricists ever since (see Caldwell 1982, 106–17). Economic theorists, however, still usually use a rationalist method. One of the most important modern neoclassical theorists is Gerard Debreu. His *Theory of Value* states a set of axioms (see the Marxian discussion of Debreu by W. H. Locke Anderson 1987; see also Resnick and Wolff 1987). Debreu makes no attempt to show that these axioms are empirically true, but he uses them to prove that his "economy" (that is, the economy described by the axioms) reaches an optimal equilibrium.

Debreu's argument is a typical rationalist argument, not an empirical one. According to Anderson, "General equilibrium theory does not make even conditional predictions in the ordinary sense. . . . Insofar as it makes any substantive statement at all, it merely argues that [its model of] competitive capitalism is essentially ordered and efficient. But it does not imply observations or experiments by which we might distinguish essential order from disorder, essential efficiency from inefficiency" (1987, 42–43). The theories of some of the greatest neoclassical theorists, such as Debreu, tend to sound rather strangely out of touch with the real world. The reason is their implicitly rationalist methodology, which allows them to begin with unrealistic postulates, manipulate the postulates in very complex and sophisticated mathematical models, and arrive at conclusions that apply only to those unrealistic assumptions.

The Dilemma and the Road to a Solution

The materialist position of most Marxian theorists is opposed to both empiricism and idealist rationalism. "If for Marx idealism is the typical fault of philosophy, empiricism is the endemic failing of commonsense. Marx sets himself against both the idealist ontology of forms, ideas . . . with its conceptual (or religious) totalities and the empiricist ontology of given atomistic facts" (Bhaskar 1989, 135). If Marxism is opposed to both rationalism and empiricism, what does it propose as a materialist solution?

There appears to be a dilemma. On the one side, it seems that social scientists must know the facts before they can formulate any theories or definitions. On the other side, they cannot investigate the facts until they have some theory and definitions. How can one get out of this dilemma?

The Soviet Marxian philosophy of *dialectical materialism* always answered that the two categories (facts and theories) must form a unity of opposites, so one begins with a synthesis of theory-and-fact. But that only puts a name on the problem. Now let us begin to spell out a solution to the apparent dilemma.

Materialism as a Relational-Historical Method

Marxian materialism is not a theory of what the universe is "really" like "beyond" science, though Stalin's (1940) explanation of it could be interpreted that way. Marxian materialism is merely an affirmation of a method of approach. What is that approach?

The previous section posed the apparent dilemma whether one must begin the study of society by *(a)* looking at the "facts" with no theory or *(b)* designing a theoretical framework before looking at the facts. Both seem to have strong arguments in their favor, and both have traditions of widespread support among Marxian as well as non-Marxian writers.

One way to remove the dilemma is to approach scientific research as a set of relationships (of which human beings are a part) evolving within a historical process. This approach ends the static either/or situation expressed in the question, Which comes first, the chicken or the egg? Which comes first, fact or theory?

One concrete example of a relational-historical approach to the development of facts and theories is Thomas Kuhn's work (1962) on the history of science. The enormous literature discussing Kuhn's work, including Kuhn's later modifications, all points to a concrete process of change, which occurs in the interrelated whole of theory-and-fact. It is argued below in some detail that Kuhn's pioneering work is relational in that it does not view theory and fact as isolated from each other, but as part of one whole. The whole that contains theories and facts and methods is called a *paradigm* by Kuhn. It is also argued in detail that Kuhn's work is historical in that its entire focus is on the evolution of paradigms, never on a static comparison of two paradigms.

One reason this argument is so important is that the social sciences are in a period of methodological strife between various traditional and more radical paradigms. The conflict between paradigms in the social sciences will not be easily resolved, because each paradigm is related (in very complex ways) to class viewpoints and class interests; includes different basic assumptions; has different methods and approaches; and has different statements of the main "facts." Thus, there are no simple experiments that could settle the conflict.

Moreover, it is usually impossible to conduct controlled experiments in the social sciences. The observed facts, however, can easily be made to fit different paradigms because of the differences in method and definition. The apparently abstract philosophical issue of how to resolve differences over facts and theories is identical with the very practical issue of determining which paradigm is "correct."

Normal Science

Thomas Kuhn defined *paradigms* as "universally recognized scientific achievements that for a time provide model problems and solutions to a community of practitioners" (1962, x). Kuhn points out that included in each paradigm are certain accepted facts, theories, and methods. In the normal course of their work, called "normal science" by Kuhn, scientists using that paradigm assume the truth of the paradigm and only add or modify it in small increments. So most analysts of society take for granted a given paradigm most of the time and do not doubt or challenge it.

Kuhn has described the whole process of the development of science throughout history. He emphasizes that scientists normally work within some general framework, or "paradigm," which is taken for granted for a long period of time. One example would be Newtonian physics, in which physicists took Newton's general framework for granted, while working to extend it, to tidy up some of the loose ends left by Newton, to explain some new facts encountered, and to clarify puzzles arising from the attempts to fit new facts into the theory. According to Kuhn, "In so far as he is engaged in normal science, the research worker is a solver of puzzles, not a tester of paradigms" (143). So not only are tests between paradigms difficult or impossible but hardly anyone ever attempts such tests.

Thus, the ordinary Newtonian physicist worked within Newton's paradigm and did not question it but assumed that his or her job was to amplify its details. Similarly, the neoclassical economist does not question his or her paradigm, but strives only to apply or extend it. He or she looks for new issues to conquer, but always within that framework. For example, an economist formulates a new hypothesis suggested by the paradigm, which would be an amplification or slight modification of the accepted paradigm. Then the economist gathers the facts suggested by the paradigm. On the basis of the new facts, the economist then amplifies or modifies the paradigm.

Normal science should not be defended or condemned for its limitations; it is a necessary part of research. The reason it is necessary is that people like Marx or Veblen or Keynes made scientific revolutions in economics, but their work was pioneering. It is impossible for any human to contribute a pioneering work that is also fully polished, so new paradigms are always rough-edged in some respects. Their followers spend decades polishing and amplifying their work. For example, in the physical sciences, Einstein created a revolutionary paradigm, but others applied it to a whole host of problems, resulting in further theoretical and practical contributions, which made the paradigm more useful for practical applications.

Kuhn describes the usual textbook view of the history of science (before he wrote) as a smooth, linear growth. "One by one, in a process often compared to the addition of bricks to a building, scientists have added another fact, concept, law, or theory to the body of information supplied in the contemporary science text" (1962, 139). Kuhn demonstrates that while this purely incremental, quantitative picture of growth is correct for normal science, it is totally wrong as a description of historical evolution because there are also extraordinary or revolutionary periods in science.

The process of normal science and revolution is presented clearly but amusingly by Barbara Ehrenreich: "There is an iron law of scientific development . . . that science will bumble along for decades, doing things like studying the thought processes of nematodes as a function of sunspot activity, and then—POW!—a new paradigm emerges; quantum theory, relativity, the genetic code!" (1991, 59). She also clarifies, in her own delightful way, what happens after a paradigm change: "For a few months, the scientific community bubbles with creativity.... Then inevitably comes the next phase, in which thousands of lesser minds pick over the paradigm, looking for bits and pieces which can be turned into grant applications, journal articles and lectures tedious enough to dim the minds of the competition. This phase [is] known technically as 'nerd science'" (259).

Revolutions in Science

Kuhn is interesting because he discusses not only the slow, incremental, or quantitative, advances made in scientific knowledge under a given paradigm but also the violent shifts to a qualitatively new paradigm that sometimes occur in the history of science. Kuhn's historical approach emphasizes that the history of science is not continuous and cumulative, but shows qualitative jumps at the introduction of a new paradigm. According to Kuhn, the conflict or tension between the old paradigm and the facts of new discoveries impels the jump to a new paradigm. "Scientific fact and theory are not categorically separable, except perhaps within a single tradition of normal-science practice. That is why the unexpected discovery is not simply factual in its import and why the scientist's world is qualitatively transformed as well as quantitatively enriched by fundamental novelties of either fact or theory" (1962, 7).

Kuhn emphasizes the major jumps and qualitative changes that may occur in a scientist's view: "After a revolution, scientists work in a different world" (134). Yet he also emphasizes that the qualitative change in paradigms does not occur without lengthy preparation and follow-up; it is not all done at one blow by one genius apart from the whole process of scientific development. The assimilation of a new paradigm is "an intrinsically revolutionary process that is seldom completed by a single man and never overnight. No wonder historians have difficulty in dating precisely this extended process that their

vocabulary impels them to view as an isolated event" (7). Thus, on
the one side, he blasts those historians of thought who see only incremental, or quantitative, advances and deny revolutionary leaps. On
the other side, he blasts those historians who see only qualitative
leaps and deny the quantitative process of development leading up to
and through them.

Kuhn himself speaks of the parallelism between scientific and political revolutions:

> Political revolutions are inaugurated by a growing sense, often restricted
> to a segment of the political community, that existing institutions have
> ceased adequately to meet the problems posed by an environment that
> they have in part created. In much the same way, scientific revolutions
> are inaugurated by a growing sense, again often restricted to a narrow
> subdivision of the scientific community, that an existing paradigm has
> ceased to function adequately in the exploration of an aspect of nature
> to which that paradigm itself had previously led the way. (91)

According to Kuhn, the sense of a malfunction, if it is objectively
based, leads to a crisis, then to a revolution.

Kuhn's work on the dialectics of historical change within science is
immensely useful. In dialectic terms, the prerevolutionary situation in
a science could be described as an increasing conflict between the
given paradigm and changing social needs, perceived as conflict between facts and theory and reflected in increasing tensions between
two tendencies. The paradigm shift could be visualized as a qualitative jump resulting from a long, quantitative evolution.

Kuhn also paints the revolutionary conflict in the period just before
a qualitative jump in science. He shows that the new interpretation is
usually first voiced by a few individuals who have concentrated on the
problems that were most difficult to solve under the old paradigm.
"Usually, in addition, they are men so young or so new to the crisis-
ridden field that practice has committed them less deeply than most of
their contemporaries to the world view and rules determined by the
old paradigm" (143). Furthermore, Kuhn rightly points out that
whereas science normally proceeds with little attention to methodology, a prerevolutionary or revolutionary period is usually marked by
deep conflicts over the rules of the game because theories and methods are so closely tied together in the ruling paradigm. It is because
the old paradigm is so strongly ingrained in scientists (and because
they have an immense intellectual investment in it) that a new paradigm is always preceded by conflict and crisis and is often first enunci-

ated by "amateur" outsiders and first accepted by the younger scientists. Some of these features, such as the dispute over methodology, characterize the scene in the social sciences today.

It is worth emphasizing the practical importance of Kuhn's shift away from empiricism toward a relational-historical approach similar in direction to Marx's materialism. Empiricism was long used—by Karl Popper and others—to cast all of Marxism out into the netherworld of metaphysics. Since it was then alleged that Marxian arguments over such collective concepts as class were merely illegitimate constructs, there was no need to discuss them any further. Thus, an incorrect methodology is not harmless, but it may do immense damage by its narrow definition of the "proper" limits of "science."

A Criticism and Amplification of Kuhn

Thomas Kuhn's interesting and provocative views about paradigms, which appear to be an excellent application of relational and historical approaches by a non-Marxian historian, have been criticized from many points of view.

Some historians have argued that scientific revolutions are not as discontinuous as Kuhn painted them to be. It is true that revolutions differ in their degree of continuity. All scientific revolutions, however, have in common a long period of incremental, or quantitative, increase in perceived problems, followed by some kind of qualitative jump.

A more serious criticism is that in economics and several other social sciences there is no one "universally recognized" paradigm, but a continuous conflict between paradigms. (Kuhn recognized this point in the 1970 edition of his book, but the discussion here will not deal with all of the later modifications to his 1962 view.) The neoclassical paradigm is certainly dominant in economics, but it is challenged by critical and radical paradigms, such as the Marxian, institutionalist, and Post Keynesian paradigms, so this conflict has continued ever since the dissolution of the classical paradigm in the 1840s. Thus, in social science, conflict between paradigms is more usual than one universally recognized paradigm. Of course most social scientists continue to do normal science within a dominant paradigm.

A third criticism is that Kuhn does not discuss the relation between science and the rest of society. Kuhn's work tends toward psychological reductionism in that he concentrates on the psychology of scientists and attributes revolutions to the accumulation of subjective puzzles. In his preface, Kuhn notes that he will say little "about the role of technological advance or of external social, economic, and intellectual conditions in the development of the sciences" (1962, xii). Thus, although Kuhn does a magnificent job of pointing out the inner dialectics of a scientific revolution, Paul Sweezy (1961) has shown that Kuhn errs when he overlooks the external relations linking it to the rest of society. Sweezy uses a relational approach in which science is one integrated part of society, whereas Kuhn's relational approach operates only within the scientific community.

Kuhn himself acknowledges that "external conditions may help to transform a mere anomaly into a source of acute crisis . . . and may influence the range of alternatives available" (1962, xii). So it is perhaps fairest to say that he admits the importance of society's influence on science but does not choose to discuss it. A Marxian historian would emphasize that society exerts an important influence in the history of the social sciences as well as the natural sciences. For example, Galileo had to contend not merely against a preceding paradigm (and scientists committed to it) but against the overwhelming power of the church. And the church fought against his subversive notions about the real shape and movements of the earth not merely because of an intellectual commitment to a theological dogma but because that dogma was considered to be important in protecting the church's earthly power and vested interests.

Moreover, the new paradigm promoted by Galileo did not emerge by accident or merely due to a puzzle. Rather, it emerged partly because the growth of commerce demanded better ships and better navigation, which in turn depended on a better knowledge of physics and astronomy. Furthermore, the new paradigm did not triumph merely because Galileo gave better answers to "puzzles," but because of the whole Renaissance and Reformation, plus the rising power of the bourgeoisie and their concrete needs for better scientific knowledge. Similarly, the increased economic concentration and the atmosphere of Victorian complacency, as well as the contemporary mathematical techniques in physics, supplied the necessary background for the neoclassical revolution in economics in the 1870s and 1880s (much of its evolution is discussed in detail in Hunt 1992b; see also Mirowski 1989).

Thus, the external conditions giving rise to paradigm changes include (1) changing technological and economic conditions, and (2) the changing power of various classes with differing interests. These links of scientific revolutions to society obviously exist even more strongly in the social sciences than in the natural sciences. Kuhn's approach, modified to include the effects of society, has been applied to political

economy by many authors (see the provocative studies by Bronfenbrenner [1971] and Karsten [1973] and the comprehensive work by
E. K. Hunt [1992b]).

Revolution and Relativity

While all of the above criticisms have appeared in the literature on
Kuhn, the greatest storm of criticism resulted from his implication
that differences between paradigms could not be settled by empirical
tests, but only by conflict and revolution. Kuhn says that the choice
between competing paradigms "is not and cannot be determined
merely by the evaluation procedures characteristic of normal science,
for these depend in part upon a particular paradigm, and that paradigm is at issue. When paradigms enter, as they must, into a debate
about paradigm choice, their role is necessarily circular" (1962, 93).
Thus, one may be able to choose to some extent between two competing theories within the neoclassical paradigm with the help of empirical testing. But one cannot choose between the whole neoclassical paradigm and the whole Marxian paradigm by any set of empirical tests.

The strongest critic of Kuhn on this point is Karl Popper, who
claims, with evident horror, that "Kuhn's logic is the logic of *historical relativism*" (in Lakatos and Musgrave 1970, 55). Popper concentrates his attack on Kuhn's notion that scientists from two conflicting
paradigms cannot talk to each other in a meaningful way because they
start from different postulates and approaches. "The central point is
that a . . . comparison of the various frameworks is always possible. It
is just a dogma—a dangerous dogma—that the different frameworks
are like mutually untranslatable languages" (Popper, quoted in Caldwell 1982, 76).

But how does Popper know that it is "always possible" to compare
different frameworks or paradigms? For example, in economics many
debates between Marxian and neoclassical paradigms have sounded
surrealistic in the sense that their statements to each other are like
strangers who pass in the night without seeing each other. Kuhn's description of noncomparable paradigms appears to apply to many current controversies in the social sciences, which are impossible to resolve by any practical tests, even if we ignore the biases introduced by
the competition of vested interests. Kuhn sounds like he is describing
some of the history of economics when he says "that to the extent . . .
that two scientific schools disagree about what is a problem and a solution, they will inevitably talk through each other when debating the
relative merits of their respective paradigms" (1962, 108). If one ac-

cepts these descriptions by Kuhn, then simplistic empiricism is dead forever. Normal science may settle an argument within a paradigm by empirical tests, but struggles between paradigms cannot be settled by any number of empirical tests. In Kuhn's view, the decisive determination of which paradigm is more correct is made through conflict and evolution, with the survivor judged to be the fittest. Unfortunately, in the social sciences old paradigms never die, so the evidence with regard to which is the fittest is not conclusive. Since Kuhn finds that no empirical procedure can choose which paradigm is "correct," he has been criticized as too subjective or relativist, *relativism* meaning that truth is relative to a paradigm. The best-known critique of Kuhn and an alternative view were presented by Imre Lakatos (see, e.g., Lakatos and Musgrave 1970).

John Dewey and Instrumentalism

It is interesting that a postmodernist, Donald McCloskey, sees his rhetorical approach as being very similar to the pragmatic or instrumentalist approach of John Dewey. John Dewey wrote about *instrumentalism*, also called *pragmatism*, in the 1920s and 1930s (see, e.g., Dewey [1920] 1957). Dewey was attacked and discarded by the dominant empiricist (or positivist) tradition of that day. Following the work of Thomas Kuhn and the postmodernists, there has been some revival of interest in John Dewey (see e.g., Diesing 1991, 78; and Kaplan 1964).

Instrumentalism argues that one should always start from actual problems, not from ideal models, universal laws, or any rigid rules of research. Dewey's approach is pragmatic in the sense that it says that one should use the method that best suits the problem. His approach is instrumentalist in that it says that one must always ask exactly how the analysis acts as a tool for understanding the problem. Dewey starts with scientific practice; he says that it is legitimate to codify that practice for the sake of students but that any codification must be tentative and open to improvements. Like Marx, Dewey attacked speculative philosophy for trying to find eternally correct rules and for creating artificial problems. When philosophers ask how an observer, who is assumed to be isolated from practice in the world, is going to understand the world, they create an artificial problem. No one is isolated from practice in the world; or to paraphrase the words of John Donne, No human being is an island.

Dewey's aim is not to analyze the problem of the isolated observer and the absolute truth but to confront real problems and to change the world. "Truth for Dewey could not be the correspondence of theory to reality. The correspondence definition [of truth] assumes an external, unchanging world separate from us; it is part of the spectator theory of knowledge. But we are in the world, in a changing world, and want to participate in those changes to make it a better world" (Diesing 1991, 78). John Dewey is often quoted by the institutionalists, but it is obvious that he has much in common with the Marxism that uses the critical or relational-historical method.

Conclusion: Questions, Not Answers

Marxian materialism was born in the struggle to free people from supernatural and speculative theories of the universe. The rejection of idealism, rationalism, and empiricism leads Marxism to a position quite compatible with some important themes in the historical approach of Kuhn, the postmodernism of McCloskey, and the instrumentalism of Dewey (though there are also areas of disagreement).

Kuhn's work tells us that a paradigm is an integrated whole composed of facts, theories, and methods, a position that is surely compatible with the holistic, or relational, approach of contemporary Marxism. Kuhn's work also tells us that a change from one paradigm to another results from conflict within the discipline leading to a scientific revolution, a position that is compatible with the Marxian historical, or evolutionary, approach, but only with some important amendments. Marxian scholars amend Kuhn in two important respects. First, in the social sciences, conflicts over paradigms may continue indefinitely without resolution for many reasons, including vested class interests in a paradigm. Second, paradigm revolutions are caused not merely by accumulation of puzzles in a paradigm but also by socioeconomic change.

McCloskey's work shows the rhetorical and ideological influences within economics. It is also perfectly compatible with Marx's relational view—which situates science within the socioeconomic world—but with some amendments. McCloskey does not consider the importance of vested class interests in the rhetoric of economics, so one must amend McCloskey to include the environment of socioeconomic conflict. With that amendment, most radical political economy is also compatible with McCloskey's postmodernist critique of the rhetoric of orthodox economics.

Most Marxian social scientists also agree with the concept of John Dewey ([1920] 1957) that science is a process that involves researcher and world, practice and theory, at every moment. Dewey's instrumentalist approach tells us to ask the questions that are relevant to the particular problem at hand rather than trying to set out a rigid procedure for every possible use. Dewey's emphasis on using method as a tool or instrument, rather than a speculative dogma, is in accord with a central theme of this book, namely, that the method of Marxian social science should tell people the correct questions to ask but should not try to give universal or general answers.

The contributions of Kuhn, McCloskey, and Dewey are useful within the context of Marxism because they help supply us with a list of questions to be asked by radicals about the process of knowledge in the social sciences: First, what paradigm is dominant, and what paradigm is in opposition? Second, how do the facts, theories, and methods of each paradigm fit together? Third, what class interests benefit from each paradigm? Fourth, how has each paradigm evolved in the past, and what is its likely path of evolution in the future? Fifth, what are the inner dialectics of, as well as the socioeconomic influences on, paradigm change? Sixth, how are the specific views of a particular paradigm cloaked in the general and universal terms of the rhetoric in which it is presented? And seventh, what problems are we trying to solve, and, consequently, what paradigm or part of a paradigm is needed in the analysis?

Appendix 12A: Mathematics and Statistics as Rhetoric

Two Analytic Marxists charge that other Marxian social scientists make a mistake by not using mathematics and statistics. Jon Elster states a favorable view of these techniques and charges that "Marx went wrong largely because he believed he could discuss verbally problems that can only be handled by quantitative techniques" (1985, 52). In fact, Marx did use the quantitative techniques of his time, for example, in part 3 of volume 2 of *Capital,* and many Marxian social scientists do use the latest mathematical techniques.

John Roemer argues that Marxian social scientists should use math and statistics because they rise above ideology and may be neutral. "First of all, not all social science is ideological. Secondly, even the techniques that ideological social science uses may be generally useful by scientists of many different ideological persuasions. To be specific, two such techniques are statistical inference and formal modelling" (1989, 377). As to the first point, depending on your definition, it is certainly debatable whether any social science is nonideological. To be nonideological in the social sciences would be to deny Thomas Kuhn's view that every science is embedded in a particular paradigm and to deny Marx's view that every paradigm in the social sciences is closely linked to class interests.

Roemer's defense of the use of mathematics and statistics is in one sense a fight against ghosts. *All Marxian social scientists agree that mathematics and statistics are powerful tools of the social sciences and may be used wherever they are appropriate* (see the discussion of the literature on these issues in Ruccio 1988). The issue is not whether these powerful tools should be used but whether they are always used in the appropriate problems or sometimes used excessively and inappropriately as a kind of rhetorical device to pretend to be "scientific" and to cover up the lack of content in a thesis. Let us see exactly what the critics charge.

The Critics of Excessive Mathematics

First, the Marxian sociologist Eric Olin Wright comments that "many sociologists begin with a bag of technical tricks and then ask: 'What questions can I address with these methods?'" (1985, 71). Similarly, one may sometimes hear an economist say, "I have a wonderful new technique; do you happen to know some problem to which I could apply it?" Surely, any competent social scientist should recognize the myriad problems of our society and try to do something about them, using whatever techniques are available, without letting the choice of technique determine the problem.

Second, it has been charged that some social scientists do not even attempt to examine problems that are not easily quantifiable. In a critical survey of all the social sciences, Andreski comments, "Those who refuse to deal with important and interesting problems simply because the relevant factors cannot be measured, condemn the social sciences to sterility" (Andreski 1972, 123, in a chapter called "Quantification as Camouflage").

Third, it has been charged that quantification is sometimes motivated solely by the desire to resemble the physical sciences: "Quantification has become a status symbol for many social scientists. They envisage rows of equations with which they could compute the processes of social life. To others, however, quantification is . . . a specter: the rich texture of experience usurped by bloodless figures and formulas" (Brodbeck 1968, 573). One reason for excessive use of quantification is the notion that if it looks like science, it must be science.

Fourth, the critics charge that unreal assumptions are sometimes defended as the only road to rigorous quantitative analysis. Thus, John Kenneth Galbraith, in his presidential address to the American

Economic Association, made the insightful comment that "there will be fear that once we abandon present [neoclassical] theory, with its intellectually demanding refinement and its increasing instinct for measurement, we shall lose the filter by which scholars are separated from charlatans. . . . Those latter are always a danger, but there is more danger in remaining with a world that is not real" (1973b, 6).

The Neoclassical Establishment on Excessive Mathematics

The greatest use of mathematics and statistics in the social sciences has been in orthodox economics, especially since the birth of neoclassical economics in the 1870s. From the beginning, there have been worries over its excessive use even within the neoclassical establishment. Alfred Marshall, one of the founders of neoclassical economics, revealed: "I had a growing feeling . . . that a good mathematical theorem . . . was very unlikely to be good economics; and I went more and more on the rules: (1) Use mathematics as a shorthand language rather than an engine of enquiry. (2) Keep to them till you have done. (3) Translate into English. (4) Then illustrate by examples that are important in real life. (5) Burn the mathematics. (6) If you can't succeed in 4, burn 3. This last I often did" (letter, 1906, quoted in Skidelsky 1986, 223).

Perhaps the most persuasive attack on the neoclassical use of these techniques in graduate teaching has come from the American Economic Association (the complete report of the American Economic Association Commission is presented in Kreuger et al. 1991). Alan Blinder, an official discussant, sums up the commission's report: "Our surveys found widespread dissatisfaction with graduate education in economics—and a fairly consistent pattern of complaints. Both students and faculty find economics obsessed with technique over substance, or too theoretical, or too mathematical, or insufficiently connected with the real world, or too removed from policy and institutional context" (1990, 445).

Blinder's point is supported by vast amounts of quantitative findings (as one would expect in a report of the American Economic Association). For example: "Only 14 percent of the students report that their core courses put substantial emphasis on 'applying economic theory to real-world problems'" (1990, 445). Moreover, Blinder stresses that the problem is not the use or level of mathematics; "the problem is that we train our mathematical artillery on imaginary rather than real targets" (1990, 445). It appears that the American

Economic Association is reporting some of the same criticisms that the critics of neoclassical economics have long made, but it is predictable that little will change. As long as the basic paradigm remains psychological, individualist, and ahistorical, it is inconsistent with a more realistic approach to problems. The sometimes excessive and inappropriate use of quantitative methods is not the cause of the unreal landscape of economics, only a symptom of the problem.

Appendix 12B: Analytic Philosophy and Analytic Marxism

The ideas of dead economists often influence government policy, but the ideas of a dead philosophy may influence economists. Just at the time when empiricism and its offshoot, analytic philosophy, were beginning to die away, some Marxian theorists discovered analytic philosophy and began calling themselves Analytic Marxists.

One thing that Analytic Marxism took from analytic philosophy was the notion that there is only one good scientific methodology and that Marxism should follow it. Thus, one Analytic Marxist writes: "Analytic Marxists think all social science draws upon a common pool of methodology, and they deny the existence of a separate Marxist method" (Mayer 1990, 425; see also Carling 1990). Their assertion sounds strange since there clearly are different methodologies. The motivation for their incorrect argument that there is only one methodology was the desire to combat some of the mysticism that had crept into Soviet Marxism, which claimed that dialectics had all the answers.

One point that makes it obvious, however, that their assertion of a single methodology is wrong is the fact that the Analytic Marxists disagree among themselves on just what this single methodology is. For example, three Analytic Marxists write that "the methodology adopted by Marxists should be just good scientific methodology. But methodological individualism is *not* good scientific methodology" (Wright, Levine, and Sober 1992, 108). Since methodological individualism is at the heart of not only neoclassical economics but also the economics of some self-identified Analytic Marxists (such as Roemer and Elster), it is hard to see how they can speak of just one "good scientific methodology." The truth is that there are conflicting views about good methodology, and each paradigm has a different methodology.

Appendix 12C: Phenomenological Marxism

Since rationalism is in the idealist tradition, most Marxian writers have opposed it, and its followers have been largely conservatives. Yet some Marxian theorists are so opposed to empiricism (or positivism) that they have gone back to a rationalist method. The school called *phenomenological Marxism* goes back to the writings of two idealists, Edmund Husserl and G. W. F. Hegel. The basic point of phenomenological Marxism is the need for a rationalist approach to all problems. This means that research must begin with "true" definitions and concepts in all research. This kind of Marxism was particularly strong in the early 1970s but continues to survive to some extent. It is sometimes called Hegelian Marxism because it stresses that much that is good in Marx comes directly from Hegel (see, e.g., Pozzuto 1973 or Kojève 1970).

Like their mentors, Husserl and Hegel, the phenomenological Marxists concentrate their fire against empirical science, which they call scientism. One phenomenological Marxist writes:

> Marx's epistemology . . . exhibits a dynamic opposition to objectivist scientism . . . especially those . . . which elevate science to the primary position of THE tool which provides *objective truth*. . . . The sociological "need" is for a critical theorizing which points *beyond* the factual situation to which orthodox science is chained. . . . With Marx, man was no longer chained to the brutality of empirical fact but was seen as an actively creating, actively knowing . . . being. [Marxism] is anti-positivistic and anti-scientific. (Neill 1974, 39, 42)

It is true that most present-day Marxism is antipositivist, but it is misleading to call it antiscientific or disdainful of facts. Most Marxian social scientists spend a large amount of time collecting the brutal empirical facts of capitalism. While they retain its critique of positivism, most Marxian social scientists have *not* been attracted to this new form of idealism (one exception is the rationalist book by Hollis and Nell 1975; more typical of the usual Marxian view is the rejection of both empiricism and rationalism by Resnick and Wolff 1987, ch. 2).

Marx's materialism tried to integrate facts and theory. One of the many criticisms of Marx has resulted from the habit of critics who overlook this attempt. For example, Hyppolite attacks Marx because "he seems to start from certain *facts* which, however fruitful they may be, are nonetheless merely facts to which others may be opposed" (Hyppolite 1969, 155). Most Marxian scholars would say that he incorrectly portrays Marx as an empiricist. In contrast, most social scientist critics of Marx (such as Karl Popper [1959, 278]) argue that Marx commits the opposite sin. Popper argues that Marx starts from a priori theories and only collects a few facts for illustration. Whatever Marx may have thought, most contemporary Marxism attempts to present a large number of facts tightly bound together by a general theoretical framework; thus, most Marxism is neither rationalist nor empiricist.

THIRTEEN

Determinism and Predeterminism

There has been a long and confused debate about the age-old issue of determinism and free will in social processes. Part of the confusion stems from the notion that there are only two logically possible positions. One is *predeterminism*, that everything is rigidly determined by outside forces, such as "history" or God, so people are puppets. The political result of predeterminism is often fatalism. The second position is *free will*, that people are at liberty to do whatever they will. The political result of free will is voluntarism. A third position holds that both of the above views are inaccurate and one-sided. According to the third position, people make their own history, but under given relationships in a specific historical setting.

Predeterminism

Many religions of the world have considered the path of history to be predetermined by God or Fate. On this basis, many take a view called *fatalism;* that is, they believe that what will happen will happen, and they accept their destiny, whatever it may be, without a fight. This attitude is obviously deadly to any political action, and for centuries religious fatalism has stood as a barrier to any attempts to improve the world in which we live.

In the eighteenth and nineteenth centuries several philosophies developed that were not always explicitly religious but came to the same conclusions. For example, some historians explained the rise of American imperialism by the notion of "manifest destiny." Typical of this view was a statement by the historian Edward Cheney in 1927:

"These great changes seem to have come about with a certain inevitableness, there seems to have been an independent trend of events, some inexorable necessity controlling the progress of human affairs. . . . History . . . has not been the result of voluntary efforts on the part of individuals or groups of individuals, much less chance; but has been subject to law" (7).

The predeterminism or fatalism expressed by Cheney must be distinguished from what is here called *determinism*. The definition of fatalism has been stated clearly by the mainstream theorist May Brodbeck, who writes: "*Fatalism* is the view that everything is pre-determined, that what happens is not affected by what we do. . . . Everything . . . just happens to us, for nothing is the result of our own decisions" (1968, 671). By contrast, Brodbeck defines determinism very differently from fatalism: "*Determinism* is the view that everything occurs lawfully. That is, for any event there is a set of laws or regularities connecting it with other events" (1968, 671). In other words, Brodbeck's determinism merely asserts that there is nothing supernatural or inherently mysterious, that everything may be described and explained.

Predeterminists and determinists use the term *law* very differently. Cheney, a predeterminist, uses the term *law* to mean an inevitable change caused by some force beyond human control. Brodbeck, a determinist, uses the term to mean simply an observable regularity of human behavior. Is there any room in Brodbeck's "set of laws" for human beings and their choices? Brodbeck answers the question quite clearly: "With respect to human conduct, this implies, first, that there are circumstances—in our constitutions, background, environment, and character—that are jointly sufficient conditions for our behavior, including the choices we make. It implies, second, that these choices have causal consequences. . . . In contrast to fatalism, it follows that our choices sometimes make a difference" (1968, 671). Where fatalism or predeterminism rejects human choice, moderate determinism incorporates it. Humans are not puppets of history, but their choices may be understood in light of their conditions.

Brodbeck thus defines the essential difference between predeterminism or fatalism and determinism. *Determinism* means explaining events in the matrix of relationships and regularities of human behavior. But unlike the fatalists, a social scientist should include human beings and their decisions among the factors causing any social event. Of course, our behavior is conditioned by our social and biological inheritance and environment.

John Stuart Mill pointed out that it is one thing to say that social change is determined by "laws" or regularities and quite another to say that "*therefore,* human actions have no effect on history." The *therefore* simply does not follow. Similarly, Mill argues that there is a great difference between the belief in causation, the existence of "laws" or regularities of human social behavior, and fatalism, the belief that individuals or even governments are helpless to influence history. Mill gives a striking concrete example of this difference: "If any one in a storm at sea, because about the same number of persons in every year perish by shipwreck, should conclude that it was useless for him to attempt to save his own life, we should call him a Fatalist; and should remind him that the efforts of shipwrecked persons to save their lives are so far from being immaterial, that the average amount of those efforts is one of the causes on which the ascertained annual number of deaths by shipwreck depend" ([1872] 1959, 99–100). In other words, in the case of any observed social regularity, such as the trend in divorces or births, one of the causes is human choice.

Mill also attacks one of the most persistent variations of the fatalist argument, the notion that "human nature" cannot be changed. The argument about human nature assumes fixed psychological attitudes as well as fixed physical parameters. The argument that "human nature" cannot be changed has been used against every proposal to improve society. The argument is even used to deny that any major social changes ever could have taken place or ever will—except those changes somehow predetermined by "human nature." Mill argued, in contrast, that "human nature can no longer be regarded as the final and most general cause of historical progress; if it is constant, then it cannot explain the extremely changeable course of history; if it is changeable, then obviously its changes are themselves determined by historical progress" ([1872] 1959, 84). Most Marxian social scientists believe that human psychology or human nature does change as its social and natural environment changes.

Predeterminism and Soviet Marxism

In the official propaganda of Soviet Marxism under Stalin, the idea of inevitable laws of historical change was used to show that it is impossible to resist the march of socialism, so the official Soviet propaganda had a vested interest in keeping the argument about inevitability. This type of fatalism or predeterminism "insists that there are comprehensive laws of the social process that are wholly independent of actions of individuals. Men's choices do not and cannot affect these large-scale, collective historical developments. . . . Pre-determinism is not only different from scientific determinism, it is inconsistent with it" (Brodbeck 1968, 671).

Whereas the predeterminism of medieval theologians referred to the decisions of God, the predeterminism of Soviet Marxism referred to general historical or economic forces. These forces were considered to operate regardless of human psychologies or actions. Thus, Stalin concludes his discussion of the laws of dialectics by declaring that on the basis of these universal laws "it is clear that revolutions . . . are . . . natural and inevitable phenomena" (Stalin 1940, 14). This view makes very nice propaganda because everyone likes to be on the side of the inevitable winning cause. The major drawback, however, is that fatalism leads to neglect of political struggle. If the revolution is inevitable, why do we have to work for it?

Yet, the Stalinists and the Communist parties of the world professed to be strongly in favor of organization, political struggle, and revolution. Therefore, they also strongly attacked the views of fatalism found in some earlier socialist movements. Since inevitability leads to fatalism, however, their position is an inconsistent merger of two contradictory views. One cannot assert both that all of history is predetermined by nonhuman forces in an inevitable progression and also that there is a need for human political action. These two views contradict each other in a formal, logical sense. The attempt to combine a predeterminist view of history with an activist political view fails. It is not convincing merely to define their eclectic joining as a "higher, dialectic synthesis," as numerous Soviet critics have done. The non-Soviet Marxian answer to this contradiction is to discard predeterminism.

A Critique of Soviet Predeterminism

The confusions of Stalinist Marxism have been exploited with enthusiasm by every critic of Marxism. For example, Lewis Feuer says that if Marx sees a necessary progression of history, he cannot also believe in any human intervention in history (1969, 302–41). Similarly, Murray Wolfson bases virtually his entire anti-Marxian book on a predeterminist interpretation of Marx. He claims that for Marx to be correct, it is not enough to show that socialism is a desirable alternative to capitalism: one must also show that "capitalism *has* to decline" (1966, 6). He thus sets up a straw man who argues that the inevitable laws of history must make capitalism come to a final and automatic doom, regardless of human action. Wolfson then demolishes his own straw man and believes that he has thereby demolished Marx.

Finally, the most often quoted critic of Marxism is Karl Popper, whose works form the basis for that of most other critics. Popper calls the Stalinist Marxian view *historicism,* which he defines as "the claim that the realm of social sciences coincides with that of the historical or evolutionary method, and especially with historical prophecy" (1952, 106), and he attacks all Marxists for holding that view. By the *historical method* or *historical prophecy* Popper means unconditional and unsupported statements of what will happen over the next decades or centuries, as one finds in the writings of the biblical prophets or in the predetermined history of Stalinist Marxists. Popper specifically uses the example of the prediction that slavery always evolves to feudalism, feudalism always evolves to capitalism, capitalism always evolves to socialism, and socialism always evolves to communism. Popper is correct that this was the viewpoint of the official propaganda of Soviet Marxism (as may be seen in Keiusinen 1961, quoted in chapter 4 above). Popper claims that this is the viewpoint of all Marxian writers, but that claim is false.

Popper is correct in his attack on predeterminism, or "historicism," and he is also correct that it is distinct from ordinary scientific prediction. He points out that "ordinary predictions in science are conditional" (1959, 278). For example, a physicist may say that *if* the temperature of water in a kettle is raised sufficiently, then the water will boil. The statement is conditional in the sense that it assumes that the water is confined to a kettle and that its temperature is raised; it does not say unconditionally that all water will soon boil. Similarly, an economist may say that if there is a deficiency of supply relative to demand, and if there is price control, then a black market is likely to develop. But economists would not say that any price system will automatically develop a black market.

Popper admits that "unconditional scientific predictions can sometimes be derived from . . . conditional scientific predictions together with historical statements which assert that the conditions in question are fulfilled" (1959, 279). He gives the example of a doctor who knows that if there is scarlet fever, a rash will develop. If the doctor then diagnoses scarlet fever in a patient, the doctor may unconditionally predict that there will be a rash. The doctor combines conditional statements with the known condition of the patient.

Popper, however, claims that Marxian social scientists do not derive their historical prophecies from conditional scientific statements and from known facts. He says that Marxian writers claim unconditionally that capitalism must lead to poverty, which leads to a socialist revolution. He admits that Marxism has demonstrated that the conditional laws of capitalism plus the facts of capitalism may lead to poverty, yet he claims that Marxism does not show at all that poverty will lead to a socialist revolution.

Although Popper's attack on Stalin's predeterminism is basically correct, his argument does not apply to most contemporary Marxian social scientists. There are exceptions, however; for example, the position of G. A. Cohen (1978) does tend to support an inevitable sequence of societies based on an inevitable sequence of technology.

Popper correctly argues that there is no predetermined or unconditional law of biological or socioeconomic evolution. Yet, he sometimes exaggerates by rejecting all determinist and conditional laws of evolution, along with predeterminist laws and unconditional prophecies. Popper states that his attack on predeterminism holds "not only for the evolution of man, but for the evolution of life in general. There exists no law of evolution, only the historical fact that plants and animals change, or more precisely, that they have changed" (1959, 280). In his enthusiastic opposition to Marx he also gets rid of Darwin.

Contrary to what Popper says, there certainly is a "law of evolution" for animals. First, biologists make conditional statements about regularities, or "laws," concerning the process of selection and adaptation. Second, biologists study the actual conditions of the past or the present. Third, on the basis of their conditional statements and of their facts, biologists can explain the past or predict the future. Popper contradicts himself, because this explanation of the evolutionary process is exactly the same as Popper's explanation of how the doctor can predict the course of scarlet fever.

Similarly, the "laws of evolution" of society can be stated by Marxian political economists. Just as in biology, the socioeconomic process has certain regularities on the basis of which conditional scientific explanations and predictions can be made. First, political economists make conditional statements about regularities, or "laws," concerning the process by which societies adapt and change. Second, they study the actual conditions of the past or the present. Third, on the basis of their conditional statements and of their facts, political economists can explain the past or predict the future to the extent that their laws and factual assumptions are correct.

Thus, as Popper admits, even unconditional historical predictions can be made on the basis of conditional statements plus factual knowledge of conditions. For example, if a Marxian social scientist had examined the Soviet Union in 1988 and combined the factual knowledge of Soviet conditions with the knowledge of Marxian relational-historical theory, he or she might have been able to predict the Soviet collapse in an unconditional statement.

Free Will and Voluntarism

Opposed to the fatalists are those who deny any determinism in history. They point out that men and women make decisions, that they have the "free will" to do what they will. One can choose to vote for candidate X or for candidate Y. They therefore conclude that human actions are not determined in any way, that each of us has the free will to do as he or she pleases. The political consequence of this type of thinking is *voluntarism,* the notion that one has merely to decide something and it will be done. If tomorrow most Americans decide that all goods and services will be free and that people will work simply for the good of society without wages, then that will be so.

There are those who believe that any recognition of necessary scientific laws of nature and society is opposed to human freedom. Engels countered this argument by noting that "freedom is the recognition of necessity. . . . Freedom does not consist in the dream of independence from natural [and social] laws, but in the knowledge of these laws, and in the possibility this gives of systematically making them work toward definite ends" (Engels [1878] 1966, 125). The ignorant person is imprisoned by his or her ignorance, unable to achieve the things that would be possible with knowledge. Human freedom is increased by an understanding of the "laws," or behavioral regularities, that enable us to control fire, build computers, and plan for full employment.

The voluntarist (or extreme free-will) view, that people can make any choice regardless of their circumstances, plays a major role in conservative social thought. For example, President Ronald Reagan asserted in many speeches that anyone who really wanted a job could get one. Conservatives argue that people freely choose whether to be employed or unemployed (with the frequent assumption that there is no involuntary unemployment). Milton Friedman says that consumers are completely "free to choose" what to purchase. Voters are free to choose how to vote. And so forth.

In opposition to the free-will position, both John Stuart Mill and Karl Marx pointed out that one can find regularities of human behavior, that on the average we do behave in certain predictable ways.

This behavior also changes in systematic ways, with predictable trends, in association with changes in our technological and social environments. At a simpler level, the regularities of human behavior are obvious in the fairly constant annual number of suicides and divorces, although these also show gradual, systematic trends. If humans did not generally behave in fairly predictable ways, not only social scientists but also insurance companies would have gone out of business long ago. Any particular individual may make any particular choice, but if we know the social composition of a group, we can predict, with a given probability, what it will do. Thus, on the average, most large owners of stock will vote in favor of preferential tax rates for capital gains.

In addition to socioeconomic interests affecting our choices, there are obvious biological and physical constraints on what humans can do, in spite of their freedom of decision. An imaginative example of constraints was given by Plekhanov: "The combination of conditions that are necessary to cause an eclipse of the moon does not . . . include human action; and, for this reason alone, a party to assist the eclipse of the moon can only arise in a lunatic asylum" (1959, 141). Plekhanov's constraints on moving the moon may someday be overcome by a fantastic increase in human technology, but he is correct until then.

Existentialist Marxism

The existentialist school of Marxists revived the free-will argument against fatalism. Immediately after the Second World War, people such as Jean Paul Sartre felt that more consideration must be given to ordinary human problems than to the allegedly "inevitable" sweep of history. The existentialists attacked official Stalinist Marxism for neglecting problems such as human alienation and human freedom. They attacked it for seeing an "inevitable," almost fatalistic, march of history to preordained ends. The existentialists argued that people are not puppets of historical forces but free individuals with responsibility for their actions and the ability to make choices.

A historian, Howard Zinn, sympathetic to existentialism, wrote: "Existentialist-Marxist thought . . . emphasizes . . . the freedom of man to act. . . . Many philosophers and historians have rebelled at the idea that men are ruled by 'laws' or 'patterns' of historical development" (1970, 279). There is a confusion here in the belief that "the freedom of man to act" is opposed or limited by the regularities, laws, or patterns observed in men's and women's choice of how to act.

How can observations of how we usually act restrict our freedom to act? This confusion between observations of lawlike regularities by social scientists and laws enforced by governmental power, is quite common.

By the early 1960s, Sartre and others had begun to form the existentialist Marxian movement, which achieved some popularity later in the decade. While the earlier Sartre was anti-Marxian, he later made a major contribution to Marxian social science. In *Search for a Method* (1968) he violently attacks the economic determinism of Soviet Marxism but upholds the importance of historical materialism for an understanding of society. For example, in explaining the views of a politician or a poet, he shows that it is quite insufficient to cite his or her class background as the only determining factor. Frederick Engels was the son of a factory owner and later supported Marx from the factory's profits, but this did not make Marx and Engels supporters of capitalism. Sartre correctly points out that to understand an individual, it is necessary to dig deeper than the official Stalinist two-class analysis. It is necessary to examine specific historical complexities and to investigate in detail the individual's biography, beginning with his or her family and childhood. There is certainly nothing un-Marxian about going beyond a simplistic two-class view or examining personal psychological motivation. This more sophisticated approach is obvious in many Marxian works, such as Marx's very rich historical analysis of Napoleon III ([1852] 1963).

Determinism as a Relational-Historical Method

So far this chapter has shown why both the free-will and the predeterminist position must be rejected. Marxian social analysts must understand both human decision making and the circumstances that constrain it.

Marxian and institutionalist scholars have written extensively on how human ideas ("human nature") arise from given structures and conflicts in socioeconomic institutions. Yet most institutionalists and most Marxian writers also avoid economic or technological determinism by emphasizing that human beings, guided by their own ideas, are the makers of institutions and events at a given time. There is a reciprocal interaction. As Marx wrote, "Men make their own history, but they do not make it as they please; they do not make it under circumstances chosen by themselves, but under circumstances directly encountered, given and transmitted from the past" ([1852] 1963, 16).

Thus, the Marxian view of determinism is built on a relational-historical approach. It is relational, or holistic, in that human ideas and behavior are an integral part of the whole matrix of society. Much of the confusion about the concept of free will comes from thinking about human beings as separate from society; one can then ask silly questions about whether society determines individuals or individuals determine society. The totality of individual human beings is society. Even the Marxian notion of relations of production is a concept about nothing more nor less than human relationships in the economic sphere. If political economists are careful not to reduce relationships to psychology or technology, then one must include human beings and their ideas within a relational picture of society.

Similarly, when a historical, or evolutionary, view is stated carefully, it emphasizes that human beings make history. It was shown that ideas and decisions form a crucial part of the process of change. Seen as a process, human decisions are part of that historical process, not external to it. The notion of a matrix of human relations moving as a process through time should serve to resolve the endless controversies over so-called free will by isolated human beings versus a predetermined history of society.

The Concept of Determinism

Neither the dogmatic view called predeterminism nor the equally dogmatic view called free will is defensible. A radical or critical or Marxian determinism must oppose both, while using the grain of truth in each. Remember that predeterminism is defined as the claim that humans are puppets of Fate, God, economic forces, or whatever, an argument that was shown above to be incorrect. Remember also that the free-will position is defined as the claim that history is accidental, there are no laws, and humans can do anything, an argument that was shown above to be incorrect. What, then, should be the determinist view of Marxian political economy?

A Marxian determinist position simply asserts that everything in society is explainable on the basis of observed relationships, *including the existing psychology and behavior of humans*. In this view, humans make their own history; that is, humans can make their own decisions on the basis of their own ideas and psychologies, but under given natural and social constraints. "Scientific determinism is the view that every event occurs in some system of laws. . . . This frame of reference includes, as it consistently must, human actions which, therefore, can be the object of scientific study" (Brodbeck 1968, 669). The fact that human actions and human choice can be studied and explained does not reduce human freedom of action. On the contrary, such knowledge allows people to act more rationally.

The term *laws* as used here by Brodbeck, merely means the observed regularities or patterns of behavior in society. One must distinguish the actual laws or regularities of society from those observations or "laws" stated by scientists. Laws stated by scientists reflect the actual behavior of society only to the extent of our present knowledge, so they are always imperfect and subject to revision.

Of course, we can never know all of the laws of the universe or the complete state of the universe at a particular time, so our explanations and predictions must always be partial, although we may hope that they will improve as we learn more laws. Furthermore, "laws" are not absolutes given forever, as religious truths claim to be. On the contrary, laws are merely our best description of certain regularities or patterns as presently known. The future will take place in some particular way, but our knowledge of social "laws" and our predictions based upon them are always limited. We are constrained at any given time by (1) the extent of known facts; (2) the analytic theories available (including restricted mathematical knowledge); (3) our imperfect reasoning power; (4) the time available to research a problem; and (5) the fact that we are part of the social process and therefore have limited or biased views of it (see Kemeny 1959, 78). Marxian social scientists know *something* about social patterns and regularities at any given time, but they obviously do not know everything.

One skeptical view argues that political economy cannot be determined because social situations are not recurrent; that is, they are not repeated in exact detail down to the last individual thought or action. This view concludes that social scientists can make no precise, unconditional predictions. This claim, however, is not a telling argument against a moderate determinism; it is simply another limitation of our ability to predict. Even in the natural sciences, none but the very simplest situations can be exactly repeated in the laboratory. Outside the laboratory, natural situations also do not repeat themselves down to the last molecule.

Both natural scientists and social scientists base "laws" on what is common to many situations. The fact that each situation or individual is unique does not mean they have nothing in common. For example, every business cycle is unique. That does not mean, however, that there can be no valid theory of business cycles. Some patterns and regularities are found in every business cycle under capitalism. A business cycle theory simply must include those sequences and processes that are common to every cycle, while they must ignore—in the general theory—those things that are unique to just one cycle.

Thus, Marxian social scientists can formulate laws, but they are limited by the degree to which each new individual or situation includes the common aspect on which the law is based. This variability limits predictive power for both the natural and social sciences, so the difference is only one of degree.

Marxian determinism has always emphasized that human beliefs and actions must be included as a dynamic determining factor of social analysis. Certainly, humans are "free" in the sense that they may make any decision they care to make and may act upon it. "The individualist truth that people are the only moving forces in history—in the sense that nothing happens behind their backs, that is, everything that happens, happens in and through their actions—must be retained" (Bhaskar 1989, 81). On the other hand, humans are "determined" in the sense that their decisions are part of a whole social matrix, but their decisions are "free" in the sense that the social matrix is composed of individuals and their decisions in certain relationships. The fact that weather is inanimate, or nonconscious, while human beings are conscious does not prevent them from having in common the characteristic of showing certain regularities of behavior. In both cases, these regularities may be stated as conditional statements or laws. It is worth repeating in this context that human freedom of choice is not limited by the fact that humans may follow certain regularities of behavior and may sometimes be predictable within limits. This is not the same as saying that there are universal laws of human behavior. The laws or regularities of socioeconomic behavior are always limited to specific socioeconomic systems.

Human ideas and psychological states are determined for each individual by his or her experiences from birth, as well as his or her inherited physiology. Knowing a group's history and environment, social scientists can understand the group's behavior (within the limits stated above), but that does not make the group or the individual member any less free or their actions any more predetermined by some outside plan. Of course, humans can carry out their decisions only within biological, physical, and socioeconomic conditions inherited from the past. Humans make their own history, but under given ("determining") conditions and in predictable ways, although our predictive powers are limited for the reasons stated above. The fact that we behave in somewhat predictable ways only means that we behave somewhat rationally with respect to conditions, not that we are coerced.

It is thus perfectly consistent to be determinist in the sense that social scientists may investigate and discover the interconnections and patterns of socioeconomic history, while acknowledging free will in the sense of urging individuals to participate in political struggles to affect history. We cannot change history, in the sense that there is no predetermined history to change, but we can make history, in the sense that history is always made by human beings acting under certain social and natural conditions. Even the existentialist Jean Paul Sartre (1968) agreed that humans make history on the basis of certain given conditions. These include our present (1) technology and capital; (2) resources and natural environment; (3) social, economic, and political institutions; and (4) ideas, including each individual's psychology.

Human beings are free to make (or not make) a revolution, but our actions are understandable given a knowledge of present and previous conditions, *including our psychologies,* and the laws or regularities of human behavior under these conditions. "To say that the revolution is inevitable is simply (in Marx's scheme) to say that it will occur. And it will occur . . . not in spite of any choices we might make, but because of choices we will make" (Addis 1968, 335). The prediction of socialist revolution, however, must always be limited and uncertain because of our limited knowledge of natural and economic conditions, details of human psychology, and the regularities or laws of society.

Cause, Effect, and Overdetermination

The Marxian determinist view may be used to clarify the relations of cause and effect. In the popular view, cause and effect seem quite opposite, and it appears to be clear which is which. For example, it seems clear that high profits cause capitalists to invest. Yet it is also true that a high level of investment causes a booming economy, which causes high profits. In an interconnected social system every cause is also an effect. Lenin pointed out that "cause and effect are merely aspects of the many-sided inter-connections of the social system" (1963, 337). This approach is basically similar to the relational approach already discussed in this book.

This is one case where Karl Popper agrees with Lenin, but he adds the caution that this view of causality as interconnection is not a description of the whole universe, but merely a methodological rule: "It is the simple rule that we are not to abandon the search for universal laws and for a coherent theoretical system, nor ever give up our attempts to explain causally any kind of event we can describe" (1959, 287). In other words, an interactive, or relational, approach to determinism does not make it impossible to state laws, but any given "law" must be viewed as dealing with only a part of the whole process.

Lenin would also agree with Popper that, while science aims for "universal laws," any particular hypothesis or law must always be treated as a very tentative statement. Lenin emphasizes the nondogmatic nature of this methodological rule by noting that "every law is narrow, incomplete, approximate" (1963, 334).

This methodological view that scientific laws are tentative approximations to the causal interconnections of society is acceptable to the radical Lenin and the liberal Popper, but it is not acceptable to some conservative economists. William Grampp argues that "a certain type of economic behavior . . . cannot be examined by the methods of science. . . because that kind of behavior is the expression of autonomous choice. . . . It is not motivated, or determined, influenced or governed in any way and therefore has no 'cause' in the usual sense of the word" (1970, 14). This is the ultimate defense of consumer preferences as causing economic activity but not being caused by anything else. If one truly believes that consumers are not "influenced" by anything else (such as income or advertising or the media), then not only Marxism but also almost all conventional sociology, anthropology, political science, and even business administration is destroyed!

Somewhat similar to Lenin and Popper is the approach of Resnick and Wolff (see, e.g., Resnick and Wolff 1987), who say that "no one process in society . . . can be understood as *the* cause of . . . other social processes" (25). They are particularly concerned with attacking the theory of economic reductionism (or, as they call it, economic determinism or economic essentialism) in exactly the same way as that theory is criticized in chapter 2 above. The reason that no one social process can be the exclusive cause of another social process is that "the truth is the whole, the totality . . . this true totality encompasses a mutual interaction of each process . . . with all others" (Resnick and Wolff 1987, 65). In a somewhat different language, they are saying the same thing as Lenin and Popper.

A similar point is made strongly by Bertell Ollman, who contends that "in any organic system viewed over time, each process can be said to determine and be determined by all others" (1992, 36). The rhetoric of Resnick and Wolff goes further along these lines to use the word *overdetermined* for these interconnections (perhaps an unnecessary rhetoric). They note that to say a social process "is an overdetermined process . . . is to say that its existence, including all its properties or qualities, is *determined* by each and every other process

constituting that society" (Resnick and Wolff 1987, 2). If one inter-
prets this definition of *overdetermined* as meaning the same thing as a
methodological view of interconnection, multiple causation, and a
matrix of relations, then their rhetoric is a dramatic way of emphasizing the usual Marxian relational-historical approach.

Critics of Resnick and Wolff have complained, however, that because of their zeal to combat economic reductionism or determinism,
their rhetoric is exaggerated in its lack of structure because "everything determines everything else." Their view is best interpreted, however, as saying that there is no simple, single cause and effect. They
would agree with Lenin and Popper that one can reach tentative conclusions without knowing *all* the causes of a phenomenon (because
they do so throughout their book), but they would emphasize that we
should never stop looking for additional influences.

Social science (including political economy) is the art of picking
out the most important connections in society, which will depend on
the paradigm used by the researcher. One does not have to say that
other connections have no effect in order to say that these are the
most important connections to examine (in my paradigm). Of course
all systems of simultaneous equations are only partial explanations
because they leave out many connections (see Resnick and Wolff
1987). Any model in political economy leaves out many connections
but may still be very useful as a first approximation. This is why good
political economists use a method of successive approximations, first
stating a simple model and then increasing the level of reality and
complexity in later models. The complexity of social science should
not paralyze us or prevent any social science, so long as we remember
that any given model is a tentative, imperfect approximation to social
connections.

For a more detailed discussion of cause and effect, see Wright,
Levine, and Sober 1992. For an extremely detailed discussion of what
Marx and Engels had to say on determinism, including cause and effect, see the book by Joseph Ferraro (1992), with an excellent introduction by John B. Foster.

Conclusion: Questions, Not Answers

If one takes seriously the notion that determinism is not a picture of
the universe but a nondogmatic methodology for understanding issues (as both Lenin and Popper agree), then it does not provide ultimate answers but does direct us to ask some crucial questions. Concretely, how do human ideas and decisions affect social and political

institutions, class relationships, and the forces of production? How do social and political institutions, class relations, and the forces of production affect human ideas and decisions? As part of the historical process, how do human ideas affect reforms and revolutions? How do reforms and revolutionary changes affect human ideas and decisions?

As an example, consider the fact that a student assassinated Archduke Ferdinand of Austria in Sarajevo on the eve of the First World War. It is legitimate to ask how this event influenced the other events leading to the war. But one must also remember that millions of other human decisions were made at that time and that they all affected events, so any one decision or behavior by an individual tells only a small part of the whole story. Moreover, it is also legitimate to ask what social factors affected that student's decision.

In conclusion, when the confused controversy over the free-will position versus the position of predeterminism is replaced by a series of operational questions about relations and historical change, the confusion disappears. Understood in this light, the relational-historical approach is determinist but not predeterminist. The determinist approach of Marxism is relational in the sense that the questions asked about cause and effect are about, not one isolated thing affecting another, but relationships within a social matrix. The Marxian determinist view is historical in that the questions asked about social change do not assume universal and inexorable laws, but ask the same type of questions that biologists ask about biological evolution. The concept of determinism as this set of questions then becomes a very useful method for understanding socioeconomic institutions and changing the world.

FOURTEEN

Marxian Humanism and Liberal Humanism

What is the relation of social science to ethics? Is Marxian political economy a social science, an ethical view, or both? To answer these questions, this chapter first examines the viewpoint that the social sciences are all science with no ethics, the viewpoint that the social sciences are all ethics with make-believe science, and finally, the viewpoint of most Marxists and institutionalists, that the social sciences are, and should be, both scientific and ethical.

The Myth of Value-Free Social Science

Neoclassical economics and most orthodox social science make a rigid distinction between *science* and *ethics*, or *facts* and *values*, or *positive* and *normative* statements. When this distinction was first made, it constituted a major advance in scientific method. In the Middle Ages, science and theology were all mixed together. In economics, according to the philosopher Thomas Aquinas, the price of a commodity could not be merely average: it had to be "just" on theological grounds. Monarchy wasn't merely useful; it was divinely ordained.

The philosopher David Hume first emphasized the positivist view, favored ever since by conventional social science, that ethics should get its nose out of science. No accumulation of facts can lead to an ethical value judgment; no value judgment tells us anything about actual relationships. The scientist should keep his or her ethical values separate from science. This view, called *positivism*, helped liberate science in capitalist society from the grip of feudal theology.

Now, however, the logical distinction has been extended to an apologetic defense of conventional social science as pure, unbiased, and value-free. Conventional social science "argues that it is value free. . . . It bases its case on Max Weber's overworked sophism that there is no logical relation between the Is and the Ought" (Albert Szymanski, quoted in Colfax and Roach 1973, 103).

The positivist view of orthodox social science confuses (1) the logical separation of fact and value argued by Hume and Weber and (2) the extension to the claim that orthodox social science is not influenced by ethical values in its actual practice. The former is true; the latter is not. "Logically, Weber's position is . . . impeccable. . . . As in most sophisms, the trick is in the posing of the problem. . . . The problem is not one of the formal-logical relation between the Is and the Ought. It is rather a problem of the mental patterning" (Szymanski, quoted in Colfax and Roach 1973, 104).

There is an intimate psychological relationship between conventional social scientists' ethical values and practice in "factual" social research. Whether their values and their "factual" research are related is an empirical question to be answered by examining the practice of conventional social science.

Orthodox social science claims to be value-free. It will be shown that in practice any social scientist is forced to make decisions involving ethical judgments at every step of his or her research. First, some particular material must be selected for study, while other possible facts are ignored. For example, does the social scientist investigate styles of dress in the nineteenth century or why African American unemployment rates today are twice as high as white unemployment rates? Both the focus and policy results are quite different. The choice of topic is not determined by science, but by ethical values.

Second, which "facts" does the social scientist choose to collect from the infinite available ones? For example, a conservative social scientist might interview the unemployed in order to show that they lack confidence, tending to put the blame for their unemployment on them. A radical social scientist might collect facts showing that lack of confidence is one result of unemployment. The choice of facts is based in part on ethical biases.

Third, the social scientist must determine which "facts" are fully supported and which are merely false interpretations of the data. For example, women quit jobs more often than men in the aggregate; but if we look at any specific job, women quit less often than men. The reason for this pattern is that women generally are employed in less interesting, lower-paid occupations, in which everyone tends to quit more often. So are women reported to be more or less responsible than men? Different writers may interpret the same data differently, depending on their ideological and ethical views.

Fourth, even in the statement of supposed "scientific" conclusions, some sort of evaluation and some policy suggestions will always be implied. Thus, if one describes incredible human misery on a pre–Civil War plantation, it is hardly necessary to explicitly recommend abolition of slavery. Conversely, if the plantation is described as a joyous place of happy, singing slaves, the opposite implication is clearly present.

Orthodox Economics and Ethical Values

My tentative hypothesis is that most orthodox economists sincerely believe in the slogan "value freedom," yet their supposedly objective, value-free analyses tend to favor the status quo because of their fundamental assumptions. Most of these biased practices are unconscious, based on acceptance of a particular paradigm (an interesting example of unconscious bias is examined in an incisive article by Paul Burket [1992]). The evidence that the assumptions of orthodox economics bias it toward the status quo is presented in detail in appendix 14B.

Alternative Marxian Views of Ethics

There are at least three different positions in Marxian ethics: (1) that Marxism is solely an ethical outlook, with no scientific contribution; (2) that Marxism is a positive science, with no ethical view; and (3) that Marxism combines science and ethics (see Kain 1988). Each of these views is examined here, the goal being a consistent radical outlook. What Marx may have said is not considered here, but it is stated in great detail in Kain 1988 and is discussed extensively in many other references given in this chapter.

The Value-Only Position

Frequently, radical and Marxian social scientists become fed up with the hypocrisy of those theorists who proclaim value freedom while practicing value bias. In reaction some of these radical or Marxian writers proclaim *humanism* an approach to problems based exclusively on emotions and ethical values. They end up with the mystics, who denounce all efforts at objective knowledge as "scientism."

The most careful and insightful statement of the ethical, value-only position was in a very interesting book by the radical historian Howard Zinn (1970). Zinn begins by attacking the method of traditional historians. He summarizes the traditional methodology in five rules: (1) "carry on 'disinterested scholarship'"; (2) "be objective"; (3) "stick to your discipline"; (4) "to be 'scientific' requires neutrality"; and (5) "in order to be 'rational' avoid 'emotionalism'" (9–14).

Zinn then shows that traditional historians are in reality very biased. He shows that all writing of history involves selection and interpretation according to some set of values. The French Revolution is not selected as a topic at random, but for what it "can tell us about revolutions today, about the behavior of people today" (Zinn 1970, 332). Similarly, Zinn says, "I can choose, by the way I tell the story, to make World War I seem a glorious battle between good and evil, or I can make it seem a senseless massacre. There is no inherently true story of World War I . . . there is only the question of which version is true to which present purpose" (275–76). While Zinn has a good basic point, his conclusion is overstated. Because the facts can be interpreted in two directions, it doesn't follow that we cannot, within a given paradigm, increase our knowledge about the First World War.

Zinn urges historians and other social scientists to sharpen their perceptions of the miseries of the oppressed, expose the pretensions of governments to neutrality or good deeds, expose ideological apologia for the going order, and recapture those few past moments that showed "the possibility of a far better way of life than that which has dominated the earth thus far." Moreover, he says, "we can show how good social movements can go wrong, how leaders can betray their followers, how rebels can become bureaucrats, how ideals can become frozen and reified" (Zinn 1970, 51).

By his emphasis on values and relevancy and his neglect of the need to understand past social processes, he tends toward, though he does not quite reach, an extreme relativist position. Relativism denies any possibility of any understanding of history, even within a given paradigm. This tendency leads him to pose a false dichotomy: one can either learn relevant lessons or learn to understand social processes, but one cannot do both. He claims that good history is only what moves the reader in the direction of radical change. He tends to oppose any attempt, even within a radical paradigm, to derive a consistent approach to the process of social change. He seems to claim that any understanding of historical processes is impossible because our knowledge is always limited and biased. Specifically, he criticizes the Marxian historiography of Eugene Genovese, saying:

Even if one replaced (as Genovese is anxious to do) the economic determinism of a crude Marxism with "a sophisticated class analysis of historical change," discussing class "as a complex mixture of material interests, ideologies, and psychological attitudes," this may or may not
move people forward toward change today. That—the total effect of
history on the social setting today—is the criterion for a truly radical
history. (Zinn 1970, 50)

Zinn appears to say that political relevancy is the only criterion of
truth for radicals. He tends toward the view that it doesn't matter
what methodology we use or what facts we look at; what matters is
whether our interpretation helps or hinders social progress, defined
according to his ethical values. He says that a historical interpretation
is "true" if it contributes "to the practical needs for social change in
our day. . . . If the 'political ends' . . . are those humanistic values we
have not yet attained, it is desirable that history should serve political
ends" (Zinn 1970, 51).

Zinn thus sets ethics against science. If carried to its logical extreme, this position, which puts relevant ethical values above science, would destroy any attempts to understand the world. But if we
couldn't understand the world, we wouldn't know how to change it;
we could only sit and contemplate "good" values and raise our own
consciousness. It follows that we should go through every work of
political economy, such as Marx's *Capital,* and toss out every statement that merely tries to understand the world, leaving only purely
moral exaltations. The absurdity of this view when it is taken to an
extreme results from the fact that Zinn and others speak as if one
could separate out moral statements from statements of scientific understanding. In this absolute dichotomy, he agrees with the neoclassical economists. But they choose to leave only the "scientific" statements, while he chooses to leave only the "moral" statements.

Zinn wrote in 1970, but his ethics-only view continues to have
some life, as may be seen in a 1990 book by a self-identified Analytic
Marxist, R. G. Peffer. Peffer's framework is psychological, individualist, and static, or ahistorical. Within that framework, he argues that
Marxism does have a morality or ethical standard but that it is, of
course, an individualist and ahistorical ethical standard. He finds that
Marxian ethics are just like those of the liberal John Rawls. In other
words, like the liberals John Rawls and John Locke, Marxism is supposed to believe in absolute individual rights. Peffer writes, "I am
principally concerned with what we minimally owe one another as
free and moral beings in a social context" (1990, 15). Whatever else
this is, it is not relational, historical, and class-oriented Marxism;

rather, it is like the eternal and individualist perspective criticized in chapters 2 and 4 above. The conflict between liberal ethics and Marxian ethics is discussed in detail below. Here the only point to be made is that Peffer seems to think that ethics and understanding are so separate that one can combine a liberal, individualist view of morality with a Marxian understanding of society.

The "Purely Scientific" View

Many Marxists reject an ethical humanism that reduces Marxism to ethics. For example, the French philosopher Althusser claims that Marxism is anti-humanist. He explains this startling statement by saying that Marxism has made a "radical criticism of the theoretical pretensions of every philosophical humanism. . . . This rupture with every philosophical . . . humanism is no secondary detail; it is Marx's scientific discovery" (1969, 227). Althusser appears to define humanism as speculative ethical thinking designed to defend the status quo (see the critiques by Davis [1990] and Hartsock [1991]). Another self-proclaimed anti-humanist is Donald Hodges, who claims that "Marxism not only has no ethical foundations, but there are no Marxian foundations of ethics" (1964, 234–35). According to his interpretation, Marxism says "that moral ideas are ideological expressions of class antagonisms; that Communism will abolish morality along with religion by undermining their economic and social foundations" (232). Finally, Allen Wood (in Cohen, Nagel, and Scanlon 1980) believes that Marxism has no ethics, no morality, and no views based on rights and justice. He argues that Marxism shows how economic relations completely determine the notion of justice as written into civil and criminal laws. Wood states that Marxism condemns capitalism on the basis of its "theory of the historical genesis, . . . and the progress of the capitalist mode. . . . this is not itself a *moral* theory" (in Cohen, Nagel, and Scanlon 1980, 40).

By contrast, John Elliott (1986) divides the arguments that Marxism has no morality into three types and then argues against each of them. The first type argues that Marxism is a predeterminist outlook and, if everyone's actions are predetermined by historical forces, there is no moral choice. Elliott, however, points out that a scientific analysis of why people act as they do does not contradict the ability to make moral choices. The second type argues that Marxism attacks all of the usual eternal and transhistorical assumptions of most moral philosophers. Elliott says that is correct, but he shows that Marxism has a different view of morality, not a lack of morality. The third type argues that Marxism exposes all orthodox morality as being based in ruling-class interests. Elliott agrees that most morality supports the status quo. That does not mean, however, that the morality of Marxism is based on ruling-class interests. As shown below, the fact that Marxism bases its morality on the interests of the exploited majority does not make it invalid or purely relativist. Thus, most Marxian writers reject the notion of science without ethics, just as they reject the notion of ethics without science.

Is Marxism Contradictory?

Karl Popper emphasized the strong ethical position of Marxism, saying, "Marx's condemnation of capitalism is fundamentally a moral condemnation" (1952, 199). Popper explains that Marxism does not have the usual morality: "Marx avoided an explicit moral theory, because he hated preaching" (1952, 199).

Popper's main theme is that Marxism does have an absolute ethical view but that it is completely contradicted by its "historicist" view of the inevitable laws of history and its class, or relativist, views of ethics. According to Popper, Marxian writers distinguish two ideas: "The one is the idea of 'justice' as the ruling class understands it, the other, the same idea as the oppressed class understands it" (1952, 202). Popper concludes that since different classes have different views, there is no absolute standard here, only a relative one: "This theory of morality may be characterized as historicist because it holds that all moral categories are dependent on the historical situation; it is usually described as *historical relativism*" (1952, 202). It will be shown below that Marxism is not purely relativist in ethics; in fact it rejects such a view.

Popper concludes that Marx sees the proletariat as the winning side and that he believes that the social scientist should go with the "inevitable" development. He says that Marx defends socialism, not as ethically desirable, but as historically inevitable: "Historicist moral theory . . . is not based on any moral consideration . . . but on a scientific historical prediction" (1952, 205). This conclusion is subject to several criticisms.

First, one's taking sides is certainly not proof that one lacks ethics; rather, one takes sides because of one's ethics. Nor does taking sides preclude a scientific analysis. For example, one's ethics may lead one very strongly to take the side of raped women against rapists, but one can also examine the problem in terms of the theories and facts that explain it. In fact if one understands the social factors leading to the crime of rape, it will be easier to fight against it, and a commitment against rape may motivate one to study it as carefully as possible.

Second, although present-day Marxian social scientists may predict that some historical change is likely to occur, that does not mean that such a change would be ethically good. For example, just because one predicts a high level of rapes and other crimes this coming year, that does not mean that one desires that result. Similarly, a Marxian social scientist in Germany in 1929 might have predicted German fascism, but that would not mean that he or she thought fascism was a good thing.

Third, Popper misinterprets Marxian historical determinism as a kind of fatalist predeterminism (a view thoroughly refuted in chapter 13 above). Critical Marxian writers have emphasized that socialist revolutions are not inevitable, but will occur only under certain conditions. Marx stresses the necessity of two "material elements" as conditions for revolution: (1) a certain level of productive forces and (2) a "revolutionary mass" of people dedicated to the overthrow of the existing system (see Marx and Engels [1885] 1970, 59). Marxism is thus anything but fatalist: it does not assume that revolutions occur because of "history"; rather, it assumes that they occur because of human actions under certain specified conditions, which is exactly the same as the combination of laws and facts that Popper requires for scientific prediction.

Many others, such as Jacques Maritain (1964) and Allen Buchanan (in Cohen, Nagel, and Scanlon 1980), have claimed that there is a contradiction in Marxism between science and ethics. Steven Lukes (1985) investigates this alleged contradiction in Marxism. On the one side, Marxian writers state their case with great moral indignation at existing injustices and calls for a better world. On the other side, Marxism appears to say that all morality is ideological bias and that all statements of the so-called rights of man as eternal truths are supernatural nonsense. Lukes points out that the hypocrisy of ruling-class moralism has led many Marxian theorists to what sounds like an attack on all morality. For example, the right to freedom of the press has been seen to be nothing but the right of rich capitalists to publish newspapers. Lukes resolves the apparent contradiction by pointing out that Marxism has attacked only those moralistic statements of eternal rights that actually limit rights exclusively to the wealthy but that Marxism does argue for a morality of emancipation of the working class. (Lukes's thesis is discussed in great detail in several papers in the collection on Marx and morality by McLellan and Sayers [1990].)

Marxian Humanism as a Relational-Historical Method

The dominant view in critical Marxism is that all social science, including Marxism, must and should combine both science and ethics (see Davis 1983, 1987, 1990; Elliott 1987; Kain 1988; and Mandel 1971). Perhaps it should be emphasized again here that, as was discussed at length in chapter 12, the term *science* does not imply some absolute, unquestioned truth or "the facts," but only means an attempt to understand the world.

The Marxian position is presented as an answer to three questions. First, what shapes the ethics of a society? Second, is social science (including political economy) purely positive, purely normative, or a synthesis of both? Third, if social science is to have a normative (as well as positive) outlook, what should be its ethical criterion?

What Shapes Ethical Views?

Ethics are a form of ideas. Like all ideas, they are shaped by their relation to all social and political institutions, by class relationships, and by their relationship to the forces of production. Their form is affected by previous ethical ideas. For example, in the U.S. South before the Civil War, the ethics of the slave owners were strongly affected by the institution of slavery. Their ethics defended slavery (1) by the racist argument that African Americans were inferior beings and (2) by the theological argument that God had commanded some people to be slave owners in order to take care of their (inferior) slaves. The religious institutions of the South preached that theological argument to all who would listen. The political institutions of the South declared that it was right and proper to use maximum force and violence against slave uprisings or even against lazy slaves. The sexual mores of the slave owners were also affected by the fact that male slave owners could freely exploit slave women sexually as well as economically. On the other hand, slave owners considered it proper to put to death any male slave who had mutually desired sex with a woman of the slave-owning class. Even technology and medicine affect sexual ethics, as may be seen in the case of the birth control pill or the control of sexually transmitted diseases.

Ethics, however, do not remain static, but change and evolve as society changes. For example, after the end of slavery in the South, leftovers of the old racist ideology remained for a long time. Those leftover ethics were bolstered by the sharecropping system, in which African Americans remained economically inferior. But the civil rights movement of the 1960s forever changed the legally and socially accepted behavior and slowly changed ethical attitudes.

Thus, ethics should be seen within a given relational situation and a given historical framework in order to know what questions are to be asked. Some key relationships in the matrix from which ethics are distilled have included class, racial, ethnic, and gender conflicts. In other words, the contemporary Marxian explanation and description of current ethical attitudes and behavior is historically specific and relative to a given socioeconomic system. This does not mean that Marxian ethical criteria are "relativist." For example, a Marxian scholar may explain the attitudes and behavior of slave owners or of capitalists in terms of the systems in which they live, but that does not mean that he or she approves of those attitudes.

Should Political Economy Have Ethical Standards?

It was shown above that a political economist cannot practice positive science alone because in the process of choosing and conducting a research project and interpreting the results, every social scientist must apply some ethical framework. That framework may be humanist or anti-humanist, in sympathy with the oppressed and exploited groups or in sympathy with the elite, but some ethical viewpoint must guide the researcher.

It was also shown above, however, that if a political economist with no understanding of social processes tries to follow a humanist ethics, then it is merely a vague aspiration. The goals may be commendable, but they are no help in understanding the real world or in changing that world.

A Marxian (or a radical institutionalist) scholar should attempt to incorporate a conscious ethical view into social science for several reasons. First, as shown above, every social scientist must select problems, select facts, and interpret the "facts" according to some criterion. If a social scientist were merely doing science for the sake of science, the choice of problems would be random and aimless, resulting in mostly useless activity and neglect of major problems. In fact, every social scientist chooses to select and interpret facts in some ethical framework for some reason. Therefore, in practice, all social scientists are forced to include in their work, either explicitly or implicitly, an ethical viewpoint of some kind, and it is far less confusing for both the reader and the researcher if that ethical standard is made explicit.

Second, every Marxian social scientist (or radical of any kind) should select problems according to a criterion of social relevancy and should interpret them in the light of ethical values rather than some other values. Third, the goal is to build a theory that will help us understand society, combined with an ethical goal to change society. Thus, Marxists hold that in practice all social scientists combine theory, fact, and ethics and that in principle they should do so.

If Marxian social scientists clearly acknowledge that their discipline is *both* a social science of class struggle *and* a humanist ethical view, then it is possible both to understand the world and to change it in an ethically desirable and factually possible direction.

What Should Be the Marxian Ethical Standard?

The answers to the first two questions, then, are (1) that ethics must be explained to some degree by the socioeconomic system and (2) that social science theory and ethics must be combined. What about the third question, What ethical standard should Marxism follow? One might start from the humanist slogan of Marx that "nothing human is alien to me." But a generalized humanism is not sufficient: Marxian humanism must be distinguished from utilitarianism, or liberal humanism.

Utilitarianism, the Standard of Liberal Humanism

Liberal or individualist humanism arose in the eighteenth and nineteenth centuries as a reaction by some members of the early capitalist class to feudal religious ethics. The church supported feudalism with an ethical system that was said to be ordained by God. This view of ethics stated that the serf should serve his or her master. The noble master was obligated to take care of the serf in a paternalistic way, while rendering service to the king, who was divinely chosen.

When the most advanced liberals of early capitalist culture discarded their faith in God in the late eighteenth and early nineteenth centuries, what was left as a basis or standard of ethics? The only possible answer is humanity itself. Jeremy Bentham's utilitarianism stated the principle of the "greatest good for the greatest number" of human beings. If there is nothing above humanity, then some version of humanism, but not necessarily the utilitarian version, must be accepted as an almost tautological statement of the self-interests of humanity.

The tremendous contribution utilitarianism made in its day and age cannot be overemphasized. It was used to argue for all kinds of progressive causes. It was used to attack monarchy, feudalism, and serfdom. It was used to argue for equal rights for women. This ethical standard of liberal humanism was a weapon against every reactionary argument. Yet it had its limitations, and those limitations allow it to be used in the present period to justify the status quo. What are these limitations?

First, liberal humanism in its utilitarian form bases itself on psychological preferences, its standard being the subjective feeling of pleasure or pain. This standard has sometimes been used by modern conservatives to argue against progressive action by citing the sensitivity of the elite to pleasure and pain. For example, they argue that the pain of capital gains taxes for capitalists may be greater than the pleasure that revenue gives to most of the public.

Second, liberal humanism in its utilitarian form is ahistorical, so that policies are usually judged in terms of eternal psychological goals rather than in terms of the specific conditions of a given social formation. If we are to understand the effects of a given policy, we cannot consider in the abstract, but in terms of the specific historical situation. Suppose one were to argue to a German who lived under the fascist dictatorship of Hitler that one should always limit political efforts to legal and peaceful democratic action rather than underground violence and revolution. This would merely be a good way of getting that German liberal killed in a futile manner.

Third, liberal humanism in its utilitarian form is always individualist and does not recognize oppression or exploitation by class or group. Conservatives make use of this blind spot to picture all individuals on an equal playing field. If all individuals are equal in power, then there is no need for affirmative action by race or by gender. If all individuals are equal in power, then each individual worker can negotiate equally with the owner of a corporation, so unions are neither necessary nor desirable. If all individuals are equal in power and can allocate their wealth as they please, then it is perfectly democratic to allow everyone to spend as much as they wish in an election campaign.

In general, individualism is used by liberals to argue for full formal equality before the law. However, individualism is also used by conservatives to argue that formal equality means real equality. For example, in a court case between a rich landlord and a poor tenant, conservatives use an individualist approach to maintain that the law will be fair. Thus, conservatives may manipulate utilitarian arguments to argue for policies that they pretend are in everyone's interests but in fact are only in the interests of the capitalist class.

One very conservative twist resulted in the neoclassical economic concept of Pareto optimality, which says that society should make only those changes that help at least one person but hurt no one. This

is an example of superindividualism. It rules out the greatest good for
the greatest number of humans because it assumes that one cannot
add up subjective utilities. Thus, Pareto optimality does not balance
the utilities of all individuals to find the greatest good for the greatest
number, but protects the rights of each individual. Individual rights,
however, are protected only on the basis of the status quo. Since nothing can be changed that harms even one individual, Pareto optimality
concludes in favor either of the status quo or, at best, of small marginal reforms designed to help everyone in a harmonious world. Unfortunately, any major change benefits some classes and harms others.
For example, the way to improve slavery for the oppressed majority is
to end slavery, but that does harm to the slave owners. Similarly, redistribution of income from one billionaire to thousands of poor people may do much good for most people, but the billionaire is harmed.
Therefore nothing can be changed.

As another example of liberal individualist ethical reasoning,
Richard Miller, following the viewpoint of the liberal humanist John
Rawls, attacks the notion that class interests have anything to do with
ethics: "Morality is distinct from . . . class interests" (Miller, in Pennock and Chapman 1983, 4), which, of course, is true from a purely
individualist viewpoint. In contrast to a view of class interests, Miller
argues the usual liberal view that the standard of ethical rules he advocates is obvious, without evidence, to all thoughtful individuals:
"Anyone who rationally reflects on relevant facts and arguments will
accept these rules if he or she has the normal range of emotions"
(4–5). Miller is forced, however, to slip in a very significant assumption: that the society he is discussing is one "in which cooperation
benefits almost everyone" (5). This assumption makes sense from the
individualist viewpoint. But the reality is that class divisions have
meant that cooperation does not benefit everyone in slave, feudal, or
capitalist societies. Does cooperation by slaves in a slave society benefit the slaves?

Marxian Humanism and Liberal Humanism

Marxian humanism does not negate the liberal humanist standard of
"the greatest good for the greatest number," but it emphasizes that
this standard is a completely abstract and empty beginning to the discussion. What must be added to make the standard usable from a
Marxian viewpoint is related to the three main differences between
liberal humanism and Marxian humanism. First, liberal humanism reduces ethics to a psychological principle of minimizing individual

pain and maximizing individual pleasure. Marxian humanism, in contrast, begins with the holistic, or relational, view that the psychology of individuals is part of the organic whole of social relationships and may not be considered apart from those relationships.

Second, liberal humanism talks in terms of abstract, universal, and eternal rights. Marxian humanism, in contrast, is always historically specific in its determination of what is good and bad. Third, liberal humanism is individualist, whereas Marxian humanism is class-oriented. Each of these differences must be explored in some detail.

A Relational Approach to Ethics

Marxian humanism rejects a psychological, individualist view of ethics in favor of a relational, holistic view. John Dewey called this approach *social utilitarianism,* to distinguish it from individualist utilitarianism. It means that one must approach the good of humanity, not from the purported viewpoint of an isolated individual, but from that of society as an integrated set of human relations.

Suppose a woman with four children is on welfare. A psychological reductionist approach finds that she is guilty of promiscuous sex without responsibility and of not trying hard enough or being unwilling to accept the going wage (many conservative economists would claim that she is voluntarily unemployed). It follows, and this is a very common view in the United States, that the woman is morally at fault because *(a)* she has sex without worrying about the consequences and *(b)* she is too lazy to work. A relational view sees this woman very differently. According to this view, she is an integral part of a society and the society has problems. The society is ethically at fault for not providing childcare so that she can at least look for a job. The society is ethically at fault for allowing unemployment.

Similarly, if a person steals a loaf of bread, a psychological reductionist approach says the person could have chosen to earn the money for it, so stealing was unethical. A relational approach asks what social conditions led this person to steal a loaf of bread. Likewise, using a psychological reductionist approach, the average member of the capitalist class considers that beggars are ethically at fault because they choose to beg. A relational approach, however, asks why society put beggars in the position where they must beg, so it concludes that society must be changed. Thus, both views may claim to follow a standard of the greatest good, but they come to diametrically opposed conclusions because of their different approaches to the factual situation.

The Historical Specificity of Ethics

Unlike liberal humanism, Marxian humanism is historically specific and allows for historical evolution. The static approach of liberals assumes that the present social relations are universal and eternal, though they admit the possibility of incremental reforms. Thus, liberals can reach the conclusion that in no society should one person be allowed to steal private property from another individual. One problem is that this rule assumes that private property must exist in all societies. If there is no private property (as in some primitive societies), then the rule is either meaningless or misleading.

Even in a given social formation with private property, the rule against stealing goods or services only makes sense if one assumes that private property rights are the only possible set of rules. For example, in the present U.S. society it is illegal to force a private hospital to care for a moneyless person about to die because that violates the private property rights of the hospital. But what if society decided that all hospitals must take in anyone who needed medical care? Then the crime would be reversed: it would be illegal for a hospital to refuse to care for someone.

The most abstract humanist ethical standard—the greatest good for the greatest number of human beings—appears to be universal and eternal. But the truth is that it is a truism; it is acceptable to all nonreligious people because it has no specific content. As soon as any specific content is added to it, as one must do for any actual ethical decision, then it applies only to one specific historical social formation.

On the other hand, Marxian humanists are not pure relativists. Unlike Stalin, they do not merely look at historical evolution, expect the result inevitably to be socialism, and say that future might makes right. On the contrary, they work actively for a democratic socialism because they believe, based on the criteria of Marxian humanist ethics, that it will be a better society. What are those criteria? While they do not disagree with the abstract and meaningless truism of the greatest good for the greatest number of human beings, they emphasize that ethical decisions must be made on the basis of awareness of (1) the unity of social relations, (2) the evolution of society, and (3) class relations and class conflicts.

Is the Marxian humanist ethical standard absolute or relative? This depends on whether ethics is viewed as a static, eternal decision or as one that is historically specific. As pointed out above, if one thinks only of the simplistic and abstract utilitarian standard of the greatest good for the greatest number, it appears to be absolute. But that standard has no actual content, and liberals and radicals interpret it in a completely different way. The Marxian humanist ethical standard could be called historically relative in the sense that it leads to different appropriate policies relative to different circumstances.

The same act may be good in one circumstance and not be good in another. So the empty, abstract standard appears absolute, but the application of the standard must always be relative to the given historical, class relations. For example, it is impossible to be simply against violence in all circumstances. If a lynch mob attacks an African American, a radical should use whatever means are necessary to prevent this violence. The means should be nonviolent if possible but may include violence if absolutely necessary. Even many liberals have ethics that are actually relative to situations, even though they are very ambiguous and confused about it. For example, a liberal may believe murder is always bad, but in the event of a war the same liberal may find that murder by a soldier of his or her country is heroic and ethical.

Arguing for historical specificity, Engels takes the example of the commandment Thou shalt not steal, which appears to be an eternal truth in our society. Engels notes that the commandment is meaningless in some situations. If we lived in a society in which all goods were free, only a mad person would steal, so this apparent eternal truth is in reality limited to certain social relations. In this context, Engels reaches the conclusion that we "reject every attempt to impose on us any moral dogma whatsoever as an eternal, ultimate, and forever immutable moral law. . . . As society has hitherto moved in class antagonisms, morality was always a class morality; it has either justified the domination and the interests of the ruling class, or, as soon as the oppressed class has become powerful enough, it has represented the revolt against this domination and the future interests of the oppressed" ([1873] 1963, 253).

Note that Engels is attacking all the supernatural, eternal truths of religions; he is saying that the interpretations of these eternal truths are always manipulated in an ideological manner relative to class interests. An interesting book by Cornel West—who describes himself as an African American, Christian, socialist—shows that "the quest for philosophic certainty and the quest for philosophic foundations is an ahistorical vision" (1991, 3; see also "Symposium on Cornel West's *Ethical Dimensions of Marx's Thought*" 1993). In other words, aside from the contentless truism of the greatest good for the greatest number of human beings, there are no eternal, God-given standards that can be applied in every case. Ethical decisions are made on the basis of the class interests of a given period.

But Engels, Cornel West, and many others have made clear that the critique of absolute, eternal truths does not mean the rejection of all ethics. It does not mean the acceptance of a pure relativism, which says that anything convenient is alright. Almost all Marxian writers oppose both the pure absolute and the pure relativist positions (see the useful survey by Tool [1983]). Marxian humanists do not accept the false dichotomy that there are either absolute ethics or no ethics.

Engels's critique of absolutist, eternal ethics does not repudiate the Marxian imperative that humanity must be the highest standard for humanity; indeed, he reaffirms it. The hypocritical uses of so-called eternal truths by the ruling class are rejected by Engels on the basis of Marxian humanist ethics. Engels recognizes that the use of a bad means usually produces a bad end; he is merely exposing the historical specificity and class bias of existing ethical systems, not arguing against any ethics.

Which Side Are You On?

The relation to be taken as an entry point to ethics is the class relation, though one must also immediately consider racial and gender relations in most societies. Examination of issues from the viewpoint of class, race, and gender is the heart of a Marxian form of social utilitarianism. This approach ensures that one cannot assume harmony between classes or groups, but must examine actual conflicts in making ethical statements. This means that we must make choices between opposing sides. We must answer the central ethical question, Which side are you on?

For example, in examining slavery, it is perfectly possible to reach the conclusion that slavery should be abolished. This conclusion may be reached in Marxian humanism even though it hurts some slave owners (and thus would not be allowed under the rules of the individualist standard of Pareto optimality). If there are social conflicts, then we must choose: California farm workers versus California corporate farm owners; Arab women versus Arab sheiks; Chinese bureaucrats versus Chinese democratic students; minorities versus racists; and so forth.

Marxian humanists emphasize the socioeconomic reality of the conflict between the interests of various groups and classes in society. On this basis, Marxian humanism rejects the assumptions of the social harmony view and recognizes the necessity to take sides. If humanist ethics considers these group interests, then social scientists must admit that the expansion of freedom or happiness for one group may reduce that of another. If a social scientist wishes to improve the life of millions of workers in the United States, then it will be necessary to attack the monopoly power of a few. It may be necessary to end the ownership by a billionaire (such as Ross Perot) of the means of production no matter how much his subjective utility suffers. Similarly, the freeing of the slaves in the Civil War meant a reduction of wealth and power and subjective utility for the slave owners. If it had been a requirement that slaves could be freed only if their being freed would not hurt the interests of the slave owners, the slaves would have had to wait forever.

Utilized properly and carefully, the class approach can make all political issues concrete. For example, from a class viewpoint, there is neither an abstract right of revolution nor an abstract right to defend the government. Marxian humanism obviously does not believe in God-given or eternal "natural rights." On the other hand, it is consistent with Marxian humanist criteria to say that everyone in a good society should have a legal right to a job.

Every time a government makes a decision about its budget, it makes ethical decisions, which are dependent on relative class power. As one routine example, a newspaper article in June 1994 explained that Governor Wilson of California "once again successfully protected prisons and the state's businesses in this year's budget. But the poor, college students . . . and the education system took another recession-era hit" (Smith 1994). The article does not ethically condemn Governor Wilson, but it seems to take these interests for granted and is concerned only with their political effects. A Marxian humanism that is relational, historical, and class-oriented certainly can condemn the governor's ethics.

The present government in the United States (like the government in the former Soviet Union) represents and belongs to a ruling class, who will defend it and resist all change. Other classes may find that the present government oppresses them and will fight for reform or for revolutionary change, as the slaves fought against slavery. Given this reality, Lenin defines Marxian humanism as follows: "We repudiate all morality derived from non-human and non-class concepts. . . . *Our* morality serves the purpose of helping human society to rise to a higher level and to get rid of the exploitation of labor" (Lenin [1918] 1945, 257).

Unfortunately, Lenin's definition of Marxian ethics (and similar phrases by other leading Marxists) was ambiguous enough to allow two different interpretations, which have influenced two opposing Marxian views of ethics. On the one side, Stalin emphasized that all means that contributed to the goal of working-class triumph were good. Over and over again, Stalin stated explicitly that the will of the working class was represented by the Communist Party, and he implied that the will of the Communist Party was represented by him. Since he claimed that workers were the overwhelming majority in the Soviet Union, it followed that whatever Stalin did—such as murdering thousands of people—was ethical and represented the greatest good for the greatest number of Soviet citizens. Stalin added to that claim that socialism was "inevitable," so what was done to achieve it was also inevitable and good according to him.

Outside of the remaining Communist countries, most Marxian writers reject these notions as a mockery of Marxian ethics. As we have seen, nothing is inevitable on the basis of history; nothing happens without human choice. We have also seen that even if something is inevitable, it is not necessarily good. Furthermore, we have seen that the dictatorial mechanisms of Soviet society refuted the claim that the Communist Party necessarily represented the working class. Finally, even if we assume in any society that there are only two classes, it does not follow that every action (such as Stalin's executing someone) must be completely beneficial to one class (such as the working class). This is illogical and is an attempt to defend unethical decisions by a perversion of class analysis.

In the interpretation by Paul Sweezy, when Lenin says that we should "help human society to rise to a higher level," this means that Marxists should *not* try to perpetuate conflicts and social divisions, nor should Marxists narrowly favor the short-term interests of one class or group. In the reality of class conflict, Marxists should, according to their ethics, fight for the oppressed, but with the eventual goal of a classless society: "Marxism . . . is quintessentially the body of thought which identifies the *long-term* interests of the *whole* population and provides a goal to their realization. These long-term interests do not coincide with the short- or medium-term interests of any existing class or stratum, even the proletariat, since their essence is precisely the elimination of *all* existing classes and other social divisions which generate conflicts of interest" (Sweezy 1974, 11).

In the short term, therefore, one cannot avoid taking sides in the reality of class conflict. The long-term goal, however, is not the victory of one class but the elimination of all classes. Moreover, critical Marxian writers such as Sweezy make clear that one must properly choose those means that really do benefit the majority of human beings. Killing thousands of people in the name of class struggle was not the proper means to achieve the greatest good for Soviet society.

Of course there can be conflicts between subjective interests and objective interests. Subjective interests of a class or a group may be shaped by propaganda and habit, for example, the notion that there is no alternative to the present society. Another widespread subjective notion asserts that it is ethical to support one's own country whether it is right or wrong. Objective interests are defined by one's actual situation in a class or any other group, such as a gender or racial group. It is not up to Marxian theorists, however, to dictate to people what their objective interests are; it is up to people themselves in the democratic process to reach their own conclusions, and Marxian activists only have the right to attempt to persuade according to their own ethical viewpoint. Any dictatorship, including a so-called Marxian dictatorship, is wrong according to critical Marxian ethical standards because democracy has been proven to be the only means to a better society no matter how long the road may be (see chapter 10 above on the Soviet Union).

The Marxian humanist approach does not start with isolated individuals, but with people in classes, as discussed above. Ethical decisions are affected by the fact that existing class relations may cause the interests of a majority and a minority to conflict. Marxism sees the goal of democratic socialism as a good world, with no class conflicts, and therefore a good life. According to Marxism, the good life entails the fullest development of the potential of each human being.

Conclusion: Questions, Not Answers

What causes ethical attitudes and behavior? According to Marxism, in trying to understand ethical viewpoints one should always ask, From where did this view come? Which class has this view? What class interest does the view serve?

What is the relation between social science (including political economy) and ethics? Marxian humanism is also quite clear that *(a)* it is impossible to do social science without an ethical outlook and *(b)* one should do social science with an ethical outlook. As argued at length above, there is nothing contradictory in this methodological directive.

What is the ethical standard of Marxian humanism? If one were to accept an absolute standard, it would have to be the greatest good of the greatest number of human beings, because only the good of humanity is the ethical standard of humanity. But any absolute ethical standard must be so abstract, in order to apply to all societies, that it is lacking in content. This follows from the historical specificity and class divisions in each society. Therefore, it is more useful to think of ethics as a method that tells us what questions to ask rather than attempting any abstract, eternal standard.

The methodological directive of Marxian humanism tells a social scientist to look very critically at the status quo. Moreover, the social scientist should strive to explain all of the facts of the present situation from the viewpoint of the oppressed working class, women, minorities, and other oppressed groups and in terms of the long-term interests of humanity. Marxian humanism is an ethics of the exploited and the oppressed.

In every investigation, the social scientist must decide what problem to tackle, what "facts" to select, how to interpret the facts, and what policies to support. Therefore the social scientist is forced to choose an ethical position, consciously or unconsciously, implicitly or explicitly, in every case. That ethical position must answer the question, Which side are you on—that of the exploiter or that of the exploited, that of the oppressor or that of the oppressed?

The Marxian humanist method approaches each issue from the view of the oppressed and exploited group, so it has an interest in exposing the true situation. Ordinarily, therefore, it should lead to a closer approximation to reality than does the view given by an apologetic defense of the status quo. The reason is that the "interest group" chosen is the vast majority and the goal is an end to classes. Therefore, the Marxian humanist directive always encourages the social scientist to expose the reality (as he or she sees it), even if it is a corrupt labor leader or a corrupt socialist leader or a distorted "socialist" society.

It must be emphasized once more that Marxian humanism does not offer any answers, but directs attention to certain questions. It suggests asking questions about the ethical decisions that are necessary to social science from the viewpoint of the oppressed. It suggests asking those questions within the methodological framework of a relational, historical, and class analysis. Since the whole point is to ask these questions from the viewpoint of the oppressed, the exploited, the nonrulers, it follows that the Marxian humanist method directs attention to questions of the utmost importance for radicals. Of course this means that the radical or critical method is of no use to anyone who wishes to defend the status quo. Thus, the methodology offered in this book, and especially the ethical methodology, is not a universal methodology because a universal methodology is impossible. It is, it is hoped, a very useful methodology for all those who wish to change the status quo.

Appendix 14A: Institutionalism and Ethics

Institutionalism and Marxism have some ethical positions in common and some that are different, so much is to be learned from the comparison of institutionalist and Marxian ethics. Two main propositions of Marxian humanist ethics are in complete agreement with the viewpoint of the institutionalist followers of Veblen. Those propositions are (1) a relational, or holistic, approach that ensures the unity of scientific analysis and ethical values; and (2) a historical, or evolutionary, approach that entails the rejection of pure relativist as well as pure absolutist ethical standards.

Both groups agree that there can be no divorce between facts and values, so any statement of political economy must be both factual and ethical. Wisman and Rozansky note that "with perhaps few exceptions, institutionalists have claimed that the positivist theory/value distinction is untenable" (1991, 725). Institutionalists have long criticized neoclassical economics for its separation of "positive, objective science" from normative ethical values. Institutionalists argue strongly for the combination of objective analysis and ethical values both as what happens in practice and as what should happen in practice.

Given their historical, or evolutionary, approach, both Marxian and institutionalist writers agree that there is no basis for either a purely absolute ethics or a purely relative ethics (on this point, see the excellent article by the institutionalist Marc Tool [1982]). A correct ethics must properly combine a clear moral standard with the appropriate understanding relative to specific circumstances. Institutionalists call such a specific and concrete approach to problems an *instrumentalist* method, stemming originally from John Dewey (see Tool 1982).

Institutionalists rely heavily on John Dewey's approach, saying, for example, that "Dewey's analysis . . . demonstrates the inadequacy of any fixed or *a priori* views of [ethical] valuation as a static process" (Sheehan and Tilman 1992, 199). If one views ethical judgments in a historical, or evolutionary, manner, then ethics must be specific to each historical situation. Although Dewey rejects all general or a priori ends or goals, he does believe that some generalized statements of ethical ends may be useful. The problem is that if *no* goals are stated, then the approach becomes purely relativist; that is, anything goes.

The institutionalists answer this criticism by arguing that what is "good" for Dewey is what is most efficient for the resolution of a particular problem. Again, this sounds relativist, but Sheehan and Tilman argue that Dewey's view, although it is called pragmatist or instrumentalist, is not purely relativist. They argue that institutionalists must combine instrumentalism with Veblen's insistence that the end of our endeavors must be "the fullness of life." The fullness of life does not sound all that different from Marx's fullest development of all human beings. Both are statements of a social utilitarianism, as opposed to a purely individualist utilitarianism.

One area of disagreement between Marxian humanists and liberal institutionalists is the application of class analysis to ethical decisions. Liberal institutionalists are completely opposed to class analysis. On the other hand, the old Soviet Marxism tolerated nothing but a crude class analysis. Marxian humanists still have a class analysis, but with all of the qualifications indicated earlier, including the reality and importance of racial and gender conflicts.

Radical institutionalists have done in-depth studies of corporate power that bear some resemblance to the complex class analysis of contemporary Marxism. Since radical institutionalists and Marxian humanists both repudiate any individualist or absolute ethics, they do not interpret humanism on the basis of an assumed harmonious world built on an eternal "human essence," but in the light of concrete conflicts in a specific historical situation. The only difference between these two schools is the exact nature of the conflicts.

Radical institutionalists usually discuss these conflicts in terms other than class. In the Marxian humanist view, class affects ethics in two ways: first, class interests reveal the origins of ethical views, which does not necessarily make them right or wrong. Second, class division is a fact to be considered in making ethical judgments. Institutionalists would agree with the view that conflicts among groups (not just classes) give rise to various ethical views and that some ethical views are a thinly veiled reflection of group interests.

Appendix 14B: Conservative Biases in Orthodox Economics

What are the main points of the paradigm that lead to conservative biases? First, psychological reductionism has a conservative bias because whatever happens, from unemployment to discrimination to drug use, can be blamed on the psychological preferences of voters, workers, and consumers, not on the socioeconomic system.

Second, a static equilibrium approach has a conservative bias because it tends to prevent discussion of crises in the system and does not ask where the evolution of the system is heading. It also ignores the question whether there could be an alternative to capitalism.

Third, the individualist approach makes it impossible to discuss class conflict because only individual interests exist.

These are only tendencies and need not follow in every case. Many neoclassical economists are liberals, but they are always trying to escape the consequences of their basic paradigm in order to argue for reforms. There are even radicals, such as John Roemer (1994), who use neoclassical assumptions to reach conclusions in favor of socialism. Using neoclassical assumptions, however, the argument for democratic socialism is always difficult to make because it runs counter to the basic framework of neoclassical economics. The assumptions of psychological axioms, individualist methodology, and an equilibrium technique make it easy to find that the alleged optimal resource allocation is found by the use of the capitalist market and that the alleged optimal way to produce incentives is capitalism. These are the conclusions of so-called welfare economics in the neoclassical tradition. For a detailed and penetrating critique of neoclassical welfare economics, see Hahnel and Albert 1990.

The equilibrium approach is ideal for examining how a market adjusts until it reaches the best possible position. An individualist approach makes it easy to conclude that each individual needs the incentive structure given by capitalism. If a liberal neoclassical economist wishes to argue that national health care is a good idea for dealing with millions of people who have no health care, he or she must argue against the notion that the market brings an optimal solution and that any interference with the market must mean a move away from the optimal solution. If a liberal neoclassical economist wishes to argue for environmental protection against pollution, or for affirmative action against widespread racial or gender discrimination, or for help to create jobs for millions of unemployed, then he or she must always fight uphill to prove that it makes sense to interfere with the market. Obviously, any brave soul who wishes to argue for some degree of democratic economic planning will feel the full force of the neoclassical market analysis.

The neoclassical theory that each factor of production receives its marginal product is built on the assumption that individuals freely exchange their services in a market of voluntary exchanges based on psychological preferences and choices. Although the modern form of this marginal productivity theory is rather carefully phrased, millions of students get the message that each person gets what he or she deserves. The rhetoric of marginal productivity is very strong. As Heilbroner (1988, 192) points out, all economists know that physical capital and capitalists are two different things, yet they often speak as if a machine will not perform unless it is motivated by a private profit.

The rhetorical approach to consumer demand based on psychological preferences also has made powerful propaganda. The theory that consumer preferences rule the economy and voter preferences rule the state asserts that the capitalist class does not rule. The refusal to study the formation and change of preferences hides the effects of advertising and other social conditioning, while it supports the myth of consumer and voter sovereignty.

One fascinating rhetorical device is the neoclassical definition of profit. According to the neoclassical definition, profit is revenue minus every kind of cost, and cost includes interest paid and imputed interest on an owner's capital. Thus, in the long run, since the costs are defined so as to equal the revenue, the profit should be zero. A conservative propagandist may therefore argue that entrepreneurs take nothing from society in the long run. Another rhetorical device is the notion that there is free and equal exchange in the capitalist market. But this notion ignores the reality that the power of a single worker and the power of a large corporation are not equal. Neither is the power of a single consumer equal to that of a large corporation.

The well-known neoclassical economist George Stigler boasts that economic training brainwashes all young economists into conservatism and denial of the possibility of major changes: "He is drilled in the problems of all economic systems and in the methods by which a price system solves these problems. . . . He cannot believe that a change in the form of social organization will eliminate basic economic problems" (Stigler, quoted in Lekachman 1973, 302). Thus, suppose a neoclassical economist (assumed to be male by Stigler) has liberal sympathies and initially looks favorably on a specific welfare program, such as national health care. The saturation training in the need for markets makes the neoclassical economist uncomfortable and suspicious of a change to a nonmarket form. Because of his or her training, the neoclassical economist takes it for granted that a nonmarket program, such as national health care, must be inefficient.

Neoclassical economics is certainly the most elegant and elaborate of the social sciences. From the radical viewpoint, "the only trouble is that it amounts to an ideology inherently hostile to significant change and implicitly friendly to all handy status quos" (Lekachman 1973, 307). A survey of economists in Shelton 1985 (pt. 4, p. 3) found that most neoclassical economists assume, as a fundamental and unchallengeable fact, that the market price system is a desirable and effective social choice mechanism. Therefore, any government intervention in the economy, such as health care, should be rejected. As noted above, liberal neoclassical economists do support much government intervention, but they are always on the defensive against the free-market view.

A 1993 article in an official journal of the American Economic Association begins by saying that "the predominant theory of markets, namely the Walrasian or Arrow-Debreu model of general competitive equilibrium, implies that unemployment never appears and that economic policy never has universally good effects . . . it postulates that the supply and demand by price-taking agents equilibrates in the market for any commodity, including labor" (Silvestre 1993, 105). In other words, contemporary orthodox economics assumes (as did Say's law) that in the aggregate economy any level of supply of goods automatically calls forth an equal level of demand, so the economy will always reach equilibrium at the full-employment level of supply. No argument can be a better defense of the status quo, since it implies that the system is perfectly stable and that all apparent unemployment is a voluntary choice of the worker, who prefers to choose idleness rather than the going wage. Remember the argument of Robert Lucas, cited in chapter 8, that workers choose the activity of unemployment for many reasons, though the reasons may be difficult to discern. If there is no involuntary unemployment, there is no need for government macroeconomic intervention to cure unemployment.

Paul Samuelson takes the more "liberal" view that involuntary unemployment does exist. But his argument is constrained within the neoclassical equilibrium approach. He argues that involuntary unemployment is due to the fact that workers maintain wages that are too high for market equilibrium. Specifically, the widely used and relatively liberal textbook by Samuelson and Nordhaus claims that "unemployment arises because wages are not flexible enough to clear markets. . . . inflexible wages lead to involuntary unemployment" (1992, 577). The average student concludes from this analysis that the system of capitalism is not to blame for business contractions and unemployment but that workers are to blame for unemployment.

Some Further Evidence on Bias in Economics

Far more detailed evidence of the biases in neoclassical economics has been given by many authors. There is not room here to consider all the evidence, but each of the following authors has surveyed a huge amount of literature. Only their conclusions are stated, but the interested reader will find each of them to be very useful on this subject.

First, the liberal economist Gunnar Myrdal concludes that "valuations are always with us. Disinterested research there has never been and can never be. . . . Our evaluations determine our approach to a problem, the definition of concepts, the choice of models, the selection of observations and . . . in fact, the whole pursuit of study from the beginning to the end" (Myrdal 1981, 41).

Second, the conservative economist Joseph Schumpeter concluded after his massive study of economic thought that "analytic work begins with material provided by our vision of things, and this vision is ideological almost by definition. It embodies the picture of things as we wish to see them, and . . . the way we see things can hardly be distinguished from the way in which we wish to see them" (1949, 358).

Third, the liberal economist Benjamin Ward concludes that the positivist picture of objective scientists testing hypotheses without preconceived notions "cannot be sustained in the face of what is now known about the nature of language, not to mention what is known about the actual practice of scientists" (1972, 115).

Fourth, the liberal economist John Kenneth Galbraith concludes that neoclassical economics "tells the young and susceptible and the old and vulnerable that economic life has no content of power and politics because the firm is safely subordinate to the market and to the state and for this reason it is safely at the command of the consumer and citizen. Such an economics is not neutral" (1973b, 11).

Fifth, the radical economist Stephen Marglin concludes that "the opinions that masquerade as ultimate truth are closely tied to fundamental values and beliefs. . . . our values and beliefs are closely tied to our stake in the existing order" (1989, 88).

Sixth, for an in-depth discussion of the biases of the most famous conservative economist, Milton Friedman, in all of his work from 1957 to 1982, see the elegant and careful discussion in Diesing 1985.

Seventh, for an excellent discussion of the biases in neoclassical economics from an institutionalist view, see Dwyer 1982.

How Biases Are Shaped in Economics

Economists are affected by the power of dominant class interests both directly, through their jobs, and indirectly, in the ways that all citizens are affected. A lengthy but delightfully written article by Edward Herman spells out the ways class interests and professional mechanisms cause conservative biases in economics by affecting the "choice of problem, . . . the predetermination of the correct answer, and . . . the processes of mustering support for *a priori* truth" (1982, 277).

Herman points out that the biases in the dominant economics are class biases, because they lend support to the existing class system (as shown in the examples given above). He emphasizes how mechanisms such as university tenure systems, increasing employment of economists by government, employment of economists by private industry, and grants from foundations (most of which are conservative) tend to make it dangerous to attack the status quo but safe to spin totally unrealistic economic models.

As an example of how biases are inculcated into students, a survey of economics graduate students by Colander and Klamer (1990) found, through in-depth interviews, two interesting facts about changes in student behavior. First, most students who enter as activists or radicals finish the graduate program as liberals committed to working as conventional economists within the system. Second, many liberal students come to graduate economics to pursue policy issues but eventually accept economics as a game played with mathematics. These results suggest that during the supposedly value-free education of graduate students, they are conditioned in certain political directions, depending on the university.

The importance of different biases in economic education was demonstrated by the finding that University of Chicago students were far more conservative on all questions than students at other universities. The more conservative view at Chicago is explained partly by conservative student selection of a known conservative department but partly by conditioning through the conservative biases of the graduate program at Chicago. Harvard and most other top universities conditioned their graduate students to a far more liberal viewpoint, as reflected in their scores on various questions (all data from Colander and Klamer 1990).

A Postmodernist Critique of Neoclassical Biases

An article by Milberg (1991) points out that postmodernists and poststructuralists have dissected (or deconstructed) neoclassical rhetoric in great detail. What they have found is that neoclassical economists claim to be objective and to represent the interests of everyone. Milberg writes, "The poststructuralist approach views ideology as that dimension of language that poses the discourse as universal, completely general, that is, objective" (95). In reality, however, postmodernist economists find that neoclassical economists use loaded emotional rhetoric to prove their views and represent special interests. In poststructuralist terminology, "Ideology hides the particularity of the discourse" (Milberg 1991, 95). The most complete critique of neoclassical rhetoric and its biases to date is that of Donald McCloskey (1985), discussed in chapter 12.

Some postmodernists have pointed out that Milton Friedman especially claims that he is objective, testing each thesis empirically, and claims that he follows Karl Popper's method of falsification. Actually, however, Friedman often advances a theory that could not possibly be falsified because its assumptions are not testable; yet Friedman then uses the rhetoric of the trial lawyer to defend every bit of his argument, making it appear that he is testing, when he is only defining and adjusting data (see the thorough critique of Friedman in Diesing 1985).

PART FOUR

A Radical Program for the Twenty-first Century

FIFTEEN

Reinventing Socialism

A book on Marxism should not end without a programmatic statement. That would violate Marx's demand that we must not only understand the present society but produce a better one. "The philosophers have only interpreted the world in various ways; the point, however, is to change it" (Karl Marx, thesis number 11 on Feuerbach, 1845, reprinted in Engels [1888] 1941, 248). Advocacy of a program is part of both the Marxian integration of positive and normative judgments and the Marxian attempt to unite theory and practice. Thus, the version of Marxism given in this book has been proven useful for criticizing the U.S. capitalist system as well as the former Soviet system, but it must also be shown to be useful in building a vision of a better future.

Before stating a program, it will be useful to summarize (1) the paradigm of Marxism as stated in this book, (2) the lessons of Soviet and Yugoslav history for a radical program, and (3) the lessons of U.S. history for a radical program.

The Paradigm of Marxism: A Weapon for Radical Political Economy

A paradigm in the social sciences may be divided into four parts. They are (1) the basic theory of society, stated in part I above; (2) the empirical details and theories dealing with specific issues, stated briefly in part II; (3) the methodology of the social sciences, stated in part III; and (4) the program for social change, stated here.

Contemporary Marxian social scientists, not to mention all radicals, are amazingly heterogeneous and engage in controversies among themselves on every single issue. Therefore, it is worth stressing once more that when the terms *radical* and *Marxian* are used in this book to describe an element of a paradigm, this usage expresses my own view of each controversy. It may also represent the majority opinion of all radicals, but no survey has been done to assure that the majority back a specific view. Rather than a survey of radical views (though there is some of that), this book focuses on what would be an optimal paradigm for radicals. The question asked in every case is, What tool will best enable radical analysts to help change the world in the direction dictated by the interests of the oppressed and exploited of the world? So what follows is a brief outline of a radical paradigm, using the Marxian social theory and method developed in this book as the best tool for constructing a radical program.

1. A Marxian Approach to Society

Part I above presents a new and reinvigorated Marxian historical materialism as follows:

A. A relational, or holistic approach, meaning that it views society as a whole, as an integrated set of relationships, not a bunch of separate phenomena.

B. A historical, or evolutionary, approach, considering how society may evolve over time.

C. A class approach, meaning that the key set of relations for beginning social analysis is class relations, which change in each historical era.

In order to be nondogmatic and allow for all of the historically specific situations, each of these three approaches is stated as a set of questions rather than as answers.

2. Marxian Factual Assumptions and Specific Theories

The substance of Marxian political economy, as reconsidered in Part II, stated:

A. Workers are exploited in capitalism as a result of the class relations of capitalism, but there is no agreement on one theory of value to explain the mechanics of exploitation.

B. The government under capitalism is an arena of class conflict. The government is not run simply by the ruling class, but there is no agreement on the exact relation of class and government.

C. There is vast discrimination against women and minorities caused ultimately by capitalism, but there is no agreement on the exact mechanism.

D. Depressions are caused by capitalist class relations when declines in the profit rate cause declines in investment, but there is no agreement on the mechanism that causes profit rates to decline at times.

E. The capitalist market is characterized by a high degree of monopoly power, but there is no agreement on how much monopoly power exists.

F. Under capitalism, there is psychological alienation of human beings, as well as objective exploitation, but there is no agreement on the relative importance of exploitation and alienation.

G. The goal is a society that is democratic in both polity and economy, nonexploitative, nondiscriminatory, nonalienating, and peaceful, but there is no agreement on how to get there.

Only some of these specific issues of political economy are discussed in detail in part II. The other issues are discussed in detail with plentiful citations in Sherman 1987 and Sawyer 1989. Details of the radical paradigm in political science, sociology, history, and so forth, plus a full guide to the literature, may be found in Ollman and Vernoff 1982, 1984, 1986.

3. Marxian Methodology

Part III presents a restructured Marxian methodology as follows:

A. A new view of the dialectic method as a set of questions rather than a set of answers.

B. A materialist approach, which says that we can understand society. It recognizes, however, that knowledge is never absolute, but is achieved with difficulty through controversy and the conflict of paradigms.

C. A determinist view, which understands the individual as part of society and society as the sum of individual actions but rejects both predeterminist fatalism and a free-will notion of voluntarism.

D. A Marxian humanist view, which claims that every statement of political economy involves both facts and ethical values; finds actual ethical views affected by class relations and the whole political economic system; and sees the needs of humanity as the basic ethical standard, while recognizing that humanity is at present class-divided.

Lessons of Soviet History

It is useful to begin with the Soviet experience because its collapse has been claimed as the final evidence to destroy socialism and Marxism. The view of this book is that the old doctrines of Soviet socialism and Soviet Marxism *have* died—and good riddance! A new socialism and Marxism, however, have been revitalized and may be far more successful than before the Soviet collapse, provided that we learn the lessons of Soviet history.

From approximately 1928 to 1988 the Soviet Union was characterized by (1) complete governmental ownership of industry and detailed central planning of all industry and (2) control of the government by a small ruling class through the mechanism of a one-party dictatorship. The result was *(a)* repression and dictatorship over the working class and everyone else and *(b)* strong economic growth in the early years, followed by spectacular inefficiency and stagnation in the later years. The Soviet Union began as an underdeveloped economy characterized by poverty, illiteracy, and backward technology. So the rapid rate of development in its early years may offer some positive lessons for the developing countries. This chapter, however, is limited to lessons for the future of the advanced capitalist countries.

For the United States and other developed countries, Soviet history does provide political as well as economic lessons. In the political sphere, the results of one-party dictatorship are completely opposed to the vision of a free society held by Marx, as well as by modern radicals and socialists. The fuzzy notion was put forth that a better society could easily dispense both with ideological arguments in public discussions and with all political parties. Are the only alternatives a benevolent dictatorship or a completely nonstructured, anarchic political life? Both the dictatorial and the anarchist alternatives must be rejected by the Left for the foreseeable future. The absence of parties and political discussion just disguises control by the new ruling class. Thus the Left must give all-out support to democratic forms, maximum free speech, and a multiparty system. This political mechanism is crucial for the working class as well as for the middle classes.

What are the economic lessons of the Soviet Union? The extreme inefficiency was probably due partly to excessive central planning but also partly to political dictatorship. So far no country has had a democratically run system of central planning. In the Soviet mode of production, the political leaders of the dictatorship made all the final economic decisions, with no independent criticism. Free speech was repressed, including much scientific free speech. Political repression and corruption reached into every enterprise, tending to stifle innovation, while putting much ingenuity into political manipulation.

For these reasons, we cannot disentangle the negative effects of excessive central planning from political dictatorship. Assuming a totally democratic political framework, would a high degree of central planning be good or bad for the growth and efficiency of the economy? We do not know from Soviet experience.

There is a consensus that Soviet planning was much too centralized and much too detailed at the microeconomic level. Yet, we also know that at the macroeconomic level the Soviet system performed at full employment and used 100 percent of resources. Therefore, in its sixty-year history the Soviet system was never subject to cyclical unemployment. We may conclude that democratic central planning of the macro economy is a necessary tool for ending unemployment and business cycles. Soviet full employment appears to be an argument for central planning, but Soviet inefficiency is an argument against central planning and dictatorship. As Ralph Miliband put it, "It is by now generally agreed on the Left that the state cannot possibly plan every detail of economic activity, or at least that it cannot do so in ways that are satisfactory. But this is very different from saying that a democratic state, mandated by popular will freely expressed after due debate and deliberation, should not determine economic and social priorities, and plan for their fulfillment" (Miliband 1991b, 386). This leaves open the issue of what should be the exact relation between market and planning. The appropriate border will depend on time, place, and circumstance.

Although Soviet labor incomes were very unequal, the Soviets did reduce inequality by an extensive use of free and highly subsidized goods and services. These included health care, education, subsidized public transit, and subsidized food. In the Soviet case, the success of these practices was limited because of the repressive dictatorship, the inefficient and excessive planning, and the low beginning level of economic development. But Western Europe followed many of these directions with success, so they are worth considering.

Finally, radicals should learn from the Soviet experience that it is necessary to emphasize the term *democracy* in every programmatic statement. There are two reasons for this emphasis: the tactical and the theoretical. In terms of tactics, it should be emphasized that the word *socialism* has been tainted by the Soviet experience. In the United States, at least, radicals might be well advised to downplay the word *socialism* in favor of *democracy*. Supporters of capitalism should not have sole possession of the word *democracy*, because one can build a case for socialism solely in terms of extension of democratic rights.

It must be emphasized that socialism has sometimes been defined, from an economic reductionist view, as simply a particular form of ownership. The definition of socialism as public or collective ownership is, however, too narrow a definition to catch the real flavor of socialism. A far clearer picture of socialism is provided if it is defined as the combination of political democracy and economic democracy. This definition stresses that the object of socialists is to go beyond the formal definition of democracy in the political sphere and to extend democracy to the economic sphere. Economic democracy has a class content and automatically reveals the relationship of economics and politics.

The term *economic democracy* has sometimes been used to mean a few very mild reforms, but there is no reason why it could not be used to describe a complete socialist program. Socialism is defined as the democratic control of the economy by the people. The Soviet case teaches us that radicals must be second to none in fighting for political democracy, whether under capitalism or under something called socialism. Furthermore, a better economic system will establish the conditions for a more democratic political system; that is, greater economic equality means greater equality of political power.

The Soviet evolution from workers' control at the plant level to central planning indicates that economic democracy may be explored in two avenues. First, there can be planning by a democratically elected government at the federal, state, and local levels. That alternative was advertised but not actually followed in the Soviet case. Second, however, there can be democratic control at the level of the enterprise. Control by workers in the enterprise was the claim made by the former Yugoslavia.

Lessons of Yugoslav History

By 1950 Yugoslavia had workers' councils in most enterprises, maximizing through the market the income of the workers in the enterprise, which was the sum of the enterprise profit and wages. Until the mid-1960s, however, the central government taxed away the whole surplus and used it to make new investments. Under that system, there was a high rate of growth but no real control by workers in the enterprise. Reforms in the mid-1960s greatly increased firm autonomy and firm control, exercised by a workers' council, over investment. From then until the end of the Yugoslav "self-management" system in 1989, Yugoslavia suffered from inflation, cyclical unemployment, lower growth rates, and increasing inequality. All of these are typical problems of capitalism but were largely absent when Yugoslavia had central planning.

Yugoslavia's workers' councils were elected councils that controlled the Yugoslav firm. The councils existed in the context of a mainly market economy (at least after 1965) and a one-party political dictatorship. This model was a failure, but was the failure due to use of the market, dictatorship, or workers' control? We do not know for sure, but the unemployment does seem to have come in with the market, while both the dictatorship and the market contributed to the inequality, the alienation, and the "take what you can for yourself" psychology. Workers' control of the enterprise did seem to create a less alienated atmosphere within the firm and did seem to increase the productivity of workers, but workers' control does tend to set the interests of workers in one enterprise against the general interest.

There was always some friction in Yugoslavia between enterprise decision making and governmental decision making. Economic democracy, which is the rule of the people over the economy, can be achieved either through the government—federal, state, or local—or through democratic institutions within the enterprise. If a society of political and economic democracy tries to use both mechanisms of control, there is bound to be conflict in many areas. For example, to attain macroeconomic stability, it would appear that the government rather than the enterprise should control the aggregate level of new investment. In the case of environmental protection, what if individual enterprises, even under workers' control, choose to pollute the environment in order to maximize profits? What if workers choose to use enterprise monopoly power to get high profits by using high prices to gouge the rest of the population? These problems—unemployment and instability, environmental pollution, and monopoly and inequality—all were present under Yugoslavia's system of worker-managed firms and pervasive use of the market. Some experts commented that there was less planning in Yugoslavia than in France.

All of these problems with the market indicate the need for a high degree of democratic planning, even when there is democratic workers' control of firms. The Yugoslav experience leaves us with an open question on the reasonable border between workers' enterprise control and democratic central planning. Since the little central planning there was in Yugoslavia was conducted under a one-party dictatorship, and since the workers' control of firms was also limited by the one-party dictatorship, we really have no very good answers from

Yugoslavia on the performance of workers' control in a democracy or on the best relationship between workers' control of enterprises and democratic central planning.

The Yugoslav experience does indicate that workers' control of enterprises works at least as well as other forms of management and control within the enterprise. But given the political dictatorship, with poor and limited planning, it does not tell us anything else. Thus, there is still much uncertainty about the proper use of market and planning mechanisms in a democratically owned economy. Perhaps the most one can say is that some mixture will be necessary.

Lessons of U.S. History

If one had any doubt about the need for radical and Marxian analyses after the collapse of the Soviet Union, the state of the U.S. political economy would surely be proof. The economy has suffered from significant recessions and weak recoveries for two decades, the environment is being degraded and polluted, racial and gender discrimination remain at unacceptable levels, and there is increasing violence (including child and wife abuse). Let us examine the U.S. political economy in a historical framework.

Workers and women and minorities have won many reforms in U.S. history through the use of democratic forms, including the rights to free speech, to demonstrate, to strike, and to vote. Many of these reforms greatly expand the democratic process. For example, the right of women to vote was won by the suffrage movement. The right of African Americans to vote was won through the Civil War as well as the civil rights movement. The rights of free speech were won by the Left over a long period of time, culminating in the anti-McCarthy civil liberties movement of the fifties and sixties.

The Marxian analysis emphasizes that these reforms to extend democracy were always won against the resistance of the capitalist class, which values property rights above democratic human rights. The capitalist class and its allies have often defeated or greatly limited democratic reforms. For example, the right to strike was won in the 1930s but was severely limited by restrictive labor laws in the forties and fifties that greatly weakened labor. And the Equal Rights Amendment was defeated, weakening the position of women and leaving them open to attack by a reactionary Supreme Court. The Left needs to strengthen democracy as a tool to end oppression. "The establishment of institutions for the democratic control of the rulers is the only guarantee for the elimination of exploitation" (Popper 1952, 139).

The capitalist class uses the power of wealth to limit democratic change. Wealth operates through (1) control of jobs, (2) control of the media, (3) control of much political advertising, and (4) legal and illegal contributions to compliant political candidates and parties. The wealthy can even use direct expenditures for their own campaigns, as in the case of the billionaire Ross Perot's political campaign in 1992. Thus democracy may play an important role in capitalism, but capitalism severely limits political democracy.

The limitations of political democracy under capitalism lead to a high degree of political dominance by the interests of the capitalists. The influence of capitalism may even work through the representatives of labor or reform parties, for example, when capitalists threaten to move their businesses to another state or another country. These limitations also cause very low participation in U.S. elections—50 percent turnouts in presidential elections and turnouts of as low as 20 percent in some primaries. These limitations also mean frustration by groups with less political power, for example, the frustration that led to the Los Angeles riots in 1992, which were set off by the failure to convict the four police officers who beat Rodney King, an African American. Neither workers nor women nor minorities can attain full democratic rights as long as the economic basis of capitalism is intact.

The interactions of race and class are apparent in the causes of the Los Angeles riots of 1992. King was both poor and an African American. Fifty percent of all African American males in southwest Los Angeles were unemployed at the time of the riots. Police beat people both because they are African Americans and because they are poor, since in most cases these groups do not have the power to retaliate in the legal system. People rioted against discrimination, poverty, and unemployment; thus, race and class are closely connected.

Moreover, when conservative politicians attack "welfare mothers," they are attacking and stereotyping both the poor and women (and often African Americans). Similarly, educational opportunities are restricted by income as well as by discrimination against minorities and women, so race, gender, and class are closely intertwined. Thus, many of the political needs of women and minorities are not specific to the group; they are the same needs for jobs, equality of income distribution, and economic democracy that all workers have.

A tiny elite controls the U.S. economy and extracts profits from it. That must be changed if we are to (1) extend and strengthen political democracy; (2) end discrimination by race and gender; (3) end unemployment caused by capitalism; and (4) democratize the economy in order to end exploitation. Bowles, Gordon, and Weisskopf define a democratic economy in part by the right of all groups to participate "in making the economic decisions that affect their lives, either directly or through their representatives" (1990, 187). When workers themselves control the economic process through some type of democratic mechanism, then they cannot be exploited.

The Historical Perspective: A Program for the Left

Since the collapse of the Soviet Union has forced some careful rethinking of Marxism and socialism, there has been an outpouring of interesting radical and Marxian ideas for both short-term and long-term programs. For a very detailed statement and defense of a short-term program, see Bowles, Gordon, and Weisskopf 1990, pt. 4; the program discussed there is very similar to the immediate program discussed below but gives the interested reader more detail. For more detail on the long-term program, see the very useful, militant, and enthusiastic discussion of the technical mechanisms and advantages of democratic, market socialism by John Roemer (1994). Also see the excellent set of articles on long-term systemic changes that appeared in a special issue of *Science and Society* (1992). This issue included an article on workers' and consumers' participation in the planning process by Michael Albert and Robin Hahnel (1992); an article on economic democracy, workers' control, and market socialism by David Schweickart (1992); a careful weighing of the advantages of planning and markets for socialism, with an argument for a significant level of democratic planning, by David Laibman (1992); and a thorough analysis of the failure of the Yugoslav experiment in workers' control and self-management by Diane Flaherty (1992). I make considerable use of all of these contributions in the following programmatic proposals.

If a program fails to specify the time horizon for changes, then it causes utter confusion, so this chapter examines a short-term, a medium-term, and a long-term program. These are, respectively, the program of the Left for radical reforms within capitalism, for which immediate implementation might be feasible; the program in which radicals argue for a qualitatively better society in the near future; and the radical vision of the further future, which is a utopian vision under present circumstances.

This set of programs is designed specifically for the social formation of the United States. It is hoped that much of it will be applicable to other advanced capitalist countries. Of course, on the world scene no issue is more important than the development of the Third World countries. That issue, however, presents an entirely different set of specific, substantive questions. The project of this book is already ambitious enough. Issues of Third World development must be left for another book (see, e.g., Sherman 1987, ch. 9, for an introduction to the literature on this subject).

An Immediate Program for the Left

Each program must include both proposals to increase political democracy and proposals to increase economic democracy, including an end to exploitation.

Political Democracy

The chief lesson of both U.S. and Soviet history is that political democracy must be expanded. A few incremental steps may be specified for the United States.

1. Rights of minorities and women

Proposal: Equal rights and equal representation of women and minorities, including, but not limited to, the following:

A. the Equal Rights Amendment, to ensure equal rights in all areas for women;

B. the Freedom of Choice Act, which would ensure women's right to choose or not to choose abortions;

C. prevention of discrimination by banks and insurance companies against minorities and women;

D. drastic changes in police forces, such as more recruitment of minorities and women;

E. equal rights to full employment, as discussed below.

Comment: Democracy cannot survive unless it is democracy for everyone, including minorities and women.

2. Voting rights

Proposal: Automatic voting registration of all citizens at birth, effective at age eighteen.

Comment: One form of class control in the United States is the achievement of scandalously low rates of voting participation, especially among low-income workers and unemployed workers. So the Left must support every possible expansion and easing of restrictive registration procedures.

3. Public financing

Proposal: Prohibition of private political contributions, replaced by public financing.

Comment: The extreme corruption of the election and legislative process by the wealth of the capitalist class must be ended if a more democratic process is to exist. This art of using money to buy votes in elections was brought to its absurd extreme in 1992 by the billionaire Ross Perot, who used his wealth to buy his way into the election and came uncomfortably close to buying the presidency. Of course, it is perhaps even worse to have the influence of lobbyists day after day in every legislative body because legislators must continually be gathering money if they are to win elections.

4. The media and political discourse

Proposal: Encouragement (through subsidies and tax credits) of nonprofit media.

Comment: The capitalist-owned media always strive to run spectacular stories about politics. These are usually personal mudslinging charges rather than stories about issues; the reason is that they wish to maximize their sales in order to maximize their profits. Moreover, capitalist-owned media may endorse liberal reform proposals, but they will always be biased against radical proposals or radical candidates. Their influence is enormous, even though most Americans claim to be skeptical of their veracity. It is possible to have some alternative, nonprofit media even under capitalism. One type is the cooperative controlled by its subscribers, such as the radio stations KPFK in Los Angeles and KPFA in Berkeley. Another type is the Public Broadcasting System, which operates under rules designed to ensure some measure of fairness and equal time, as well as encouragement to discuss the issues.

5. Political advertising

Proposal: Free political advertising (proportionate to votes) in the media and prohibition of private political advertising.

Comment: The biggest expense of candidates is for political advertising. This advertising should not be determined by wealth, but only by the previous votes received by a party or a candidate. Contrary to a Supreme Court ruling, there is no reason to allow individuals to buy political advertising just because they have the money to do so. One would have to design rules that did not give incumbents a built-in advantage.

Economic Democracy

On the economic side, democracy means control of the economy by democratic means in one of two ways. As noted earlier, one means of democratic control is through local, state, or federal government. Another is through the workers in the enterprises. And, of course, it is possible to have a mix of both types of economic democracy. Therefore, economic democracy implies, in terms of immediate reforms:

1. Full employment

Proposal: A minimum condition of economic democracy is that everyone have the right to a job. Specifically, full employment in the private sector is promoted by monetary and fiscal means. But if the private sector cannot provide enough jobs, then involuntary unemployment must be reduced to zero by public sector jobs for all the unemployed.

Comment: It is impossible to have economic democracy unless every worker who wants a job can get one. An unemployed person is left out of any form of economic democracy. The details of a full employment guarantee are discussed in an outstanding study by Philip Harvey (1989), which spells out all you ever wanted to know about the desirability of a program for full employment, with careful and detailed discussion of its benefits and costs.

2. Public investment

Proposal: Additional public investment in many areas, including roads and bridges, parks, education, health care, transportation, mail service, and environmental quality.

Comment: To achieve full employment involves not only the usual monetary and fiscal policies but also fiscal spending on well-planned public investments, beginning with the infrastructure. Well-planned public investment is the only way to eliminate unemployment and inflation, as shown in Sherman 1991. David Kotz (1992a) emphasizes that the use of the market must be limited because it inevitably means instability, inflation, and unemployment. A high degree of democratic planning of public investment is crucial to full employment.

3. Public housing

Proposal: Local, state, and federal government construction of a great deal of low-cost, high-quality public housing.

Comment: That there are homeless in a rich country is a scandal against human integrity. There should be extensive public housing of high-quality construction at very low rents.

4. Free goods and services

Proposal: Inclusion of the following in this sector of the U.S. economy:

    A. free public health care for all;

    B. free public education at all levels;

    C. free, improved roads and bridges;

    D. free, improved local, state, and national parks.

Comment: There is a very large measure of support in U.S. society for an extensive nonmarket area. The support is passionate in the health and education sectors. The Left must lead the charge for these nonmarket areas. Radical political economists must do far more than they have so far done toward explaining and justifying these reforms in economic terms. Radical economics is especially needed, since all of these reforms violate the market fetishism of neoclassical economists and their political allies. If a strong argument is built for the economic logic of nonmarket goods and services in the areas where a majority of Americans strongly agree, it will be possible to set the stage for further nonmarket reforms in the future. This is the easiest road to a democratic economy, which may be deemed socialism and even communism without the use of those words.

5. Public control and worker control

Proposal: In all public enterprises, such as the post office, strong worker representation in many aspects of management.

Comment: In those economic sectors controlled by the "public," what should be the democratic mechanism? In every case of local, state, or federal ownership discussed above, democracy means the greatest possible participation by citizens and their representatives in all major planning decisions. Democracy also means, however, participation in many management decisions by workers in the enterprise, whether it be a factory, hospital, or university. Two-thirds of respondents in a 1975 poll said they would prefer to work in an employee-controlled company (Bowles, Gordon, and Weisskopf 1990, 231).

Exactly which decisions are made by all citizens of the governmental unit and which decisions are made by workers in an enterprise will differ in every case. For example, in the University of California, average salary increases and public investment in new structures are determined by the state legislature and the board of regents, which are supposed to represent the general public. But all programs and courses are determined by faculty decisions, and all hiring, firing, and promotions of faculty are heavily influenced by faculty decisions (with input by students). That is one model, but each sector will evolve differently.

6. Worker control

Proposal: Worker control of many private enterprises.

Comment: Many U.S. enterprises are presently under employee cooperative control; for example, Avis rental cars is employee-owned. The present rules for employee takeovers are not very conducive to that economic form. The rules need to be changed so that they actively encourage employee ownership of firms as one form of economic democracy. If employees own the business, even within a capitalist society, exploitation will be greatly reduced, if not eliminated.

7. Taxation and profits

Proposal: Government revenue should come from strongly progressive income taxes, as well as profits of government enterprises (though some profits may go to workers in the enterprise). Of course, government finances will also benefit from a large reduction in military spending.

Comment: In the United States, the Right has gotten rid of much progressive taxation by means of the false argument that it would reduce everyone's taxes. In reality, most tax breaks have gone to the rich. Most people in the United States want greater fairness in the tax system, so the argument for progressive taxes must be made on fairness grounds.

The above immediate economic program is a long way from utopia, but it will reduce exploitation, alienation, poverty, and unemployment. That is a good beginning.

A Medium-Term Program for the Left

The intermediate goal for radicals should be to further strengthen political democracy while extending economic democracy throughout much more of the economy and eliminating most exploitation.

Extending Political Democracy

Proposal: In the medium-term period, consideration of somewhat more radical reforms of politics:

A. Congressional election of the president;

B. Abolition of the U.S. Senate;

C. A form of proportional representation with a minimum requirement of X percent for a party to be represented.

Comment: These reforms will increase the fairness of representation and will also tend to make political parties clearer reflections of programmatic divisions in the population. Specifically, Congress's electing the president will strengthen political parties and help to avoid gridlock between Congress and the president. The U.S. Senate serves no earthly purpose except to block progressive legislation. Some form of proportional representation would also help increase the responsibility of the parties and the clarity of party messages. To prevent the legislature's being paralyzed by the existence of too many parties, no party would be allowed representation unless it received at least 10 percent, perhaps 5 percent, of the vote.

Economic Democracy

Economic democracy could be expanded in the medium time frame to the extent that it could be considered a new economic system, called either *economic democracy* or *democratic socialism*.

1. Public, cooperative, and private ownership

Proposal: That the largest one hundred corporations be publicly owned and subject to democratic planning; that the next nine hundred largest corporations be employee-owned; and that the rest of the economy remain in private hands, unless already public or cooperative. These would be mixed rather than pure economic forms. Employees would have certain rights in public enterprises and in private firms, and the public would have certain rights in cooperative and private firms.

Comment: This proposal would result in a three-tier set of businesses. The very largest—the top one hundred—should be put under public ownership, which would mean that the public would have the right to control the level of aggregate output, employment, and investment. Of course workers would have rights in certain areas of management. The exact division between workers' rights and public rights depends on the situation in each industry.

The most important reason for public control of these enterprises is that it would allow effective control of the business cycle. There would not only be indirect economic influence through fiscal and monetary policy but direct control of much investment in important sectors. Only such direct control of investment in the top corporations, plus direct control of investment in infrastructure, would give a democratic planning agency the ability to ensure full employment once and for all (see Sherman 1991).

Conservatives will object that public control and democratic planning of the one hundred largest corporations would make these corporations inefficient. But that is impossible because these giant firms, such as IBM, are already inefficient. They all exert enormous oligopoly power, so all economic theory agrees that they are likely to be inefficient. Public control would determine aggregates, such as total investment and total production, but would leave as much autonomy as possible to local enterprise. Even if this arrangement resulted in slightly more inefficiency than there is at present, it would be worth the cost if it ended the cycle of boom and bust.

The second tier—the next 900 largest corporations—would all be employee-owned businesses. As noted earlier, even in employee-owned businesses the public must also have certain rights, such as in the areas of safety and the environment. Why is that necessary? It is not written in concrete that ownership of General Motors by the automobile workers would assure adequate attention to pollution control. Democratic control of the automobile industry by the workers would tend to increase worker incentives and productivity, as well as an end to exploitation within a firm. Cooperative firms would still have many problems, as the history of Yugoslavia makes clear, but they would be a major improvement over capitalist firms and they would be far more feasible politically than any public firm.

Finally, the bottom tier would consist of smaller private enterprises. This third tier would supply those goods and services that can best be produced by small business. The third tier might not survive forever, but it should be emphasized that its demise would only be voluntary. Even in the private sector, however, there must be the right of public control of safety and environmental issues, as well as worker rights on some other issues.

2. Public utilities

Proposal: Public ownership at the local level of public utilities, as occurs now in many U.S. cities and in many European countries.

Comment: Providers of gas, water, electricity, and phone services are natural monopolies with little competition, so they should be owned by local governments and there should be regional coordination.

3. Free goods

Proposal: Gradual expansion of the nonmarket area of free goods and services. Everyone should be eligible for a minimum amount of low-cost, public housing and a minimum amount of food.

Comment: The extension of free goods and services is a complex issue with many problems, but it is worth debating in the future for a possibly very favorable effect on society. The extension of these services in the not too distant future does not appear technically impossible, but one would also have to consider large resource allocation to the present underdeveloped countries. As long as the expansion of free goods and services is done very, very gradually and begins with necessities, there should be few if any negative effects on incentives (see the last two chapters of Sherman 1987 for a detailed discussion). Moreover, if the increase of free goods and services is limited to no more than the yearly increase of output, then there need be no problem of excess demand or inflation. To ensure rational allocation as the free goods sector expands, planning agencies must either calculate prices based on known resources and needs (called shadow prices) or simulate the market through an iterative process with workers and consumers (see Albert and Hahnel 1992; and Sherman 1987).

A Long-Term Program for the Left

Humans need the dream of a future utopia or at least a vision of the road to travel.

1. World government

Proposal: World government, with reduction of armies, police, and prisons.

Comment: It is reasonable to expect that if everyone were fully employed, working shorter hours at good pay, most crime would die away and most frictions of race, gender, and national or ethnic type would end. If such frictions were mostly gone, a world government would be possible. Moreover, the government might "wither away" (as Frederick Engels predicted), but only in certain aspects. If crime and war were greatly reduced, then it might be possible to have an enormous reduction of police, armies, prisons, and similar vehicles of violent government action.

There would, however, continue to be world, national, state, and local governments. In fact, there would also be much more for those governments to do in the areas of health, education, economic planning of free goods and services, as well as macroeconomic policy and control of public investment. All of this would require strengthening the peaceful, constructive, administrative side of government with an extensive net of lively, participating democratic communications and public debate on the widest scale, probably via interactive television and computer networks.

In other words, if there were a wide range of public and cooperative ownership as well as considerable free goods and services, class distinctions and exploitation might be largely eliminated; however, many other differences of interest and opinion would always remain and require democratic articulation. Lenin is wrong to say that the withering away of the state would mean the withering away of democracy. The only aspects of government that might "wither away" are the violent, class-related, aspects. The peaceful, administrative aspects of government—which Lenin mentions briefly but mostly ignores—must expand, so democracy must continue to expand and strengthen its hold on society.

2. The future of private enterprise

Proposal: Allow the voluntary withering away of private enterprise.

Comment: If the social sector (composed of public and cooperative firms) gradually grows and proves to be better fitted for the modern technological environment than the private sector, then the fittest will survive. Having taken the commanding heights of finance and the largest corporations, the Left should *never* advocate the forceful takeover of the rest of the private sector. The private sector of small business may die on the vine (or wither away) as the economy evolves, when it is no longer needed for its present useful functions, and when the public and cooperative sectors are more attractive to everyone. Thus, the market and small private enterprise are utilized as long as they have a function, so democratic planning is never suddenly overloaded or excessive relative to its environment, but very gradually expands.

3. Workers' control and democratic planning

Proposal: Maintain both worker control and democratic planning.

Comment: In each area, people will slowly work out the proper balance of local worker control versus local, regional, national, or world levels of democratic planning. This mix will be different in different places for an indefinite period and will evolve over time in ways we cannot foresee.

4. Free goods and services

Proposal: Further expansion of free goods and services.

Comment: The area of free public goods and services may very gradually be expanded as the market "withers away." The directions in which free goods and services will be substituted for the market are not easily predictable. One principle is that the sector of free public goods should begin with necessities and only gradually move toward other goods and services. Because of this incremental expansion, work incentives would never be lowered, because this shift never proceeds faster than popular psychology allows. Of course, better technology gives more degrees of freedom (more options), so some of increased productivity would go toward leisure, some toward more free goods, and some toward abolishing the dirtiest jobs (and helping the environment). If hours of work are greatly reduced, the incentive problem becomes easier.

Conclusions

Now that the Soviet Union is off the world stage, people may be able to think more clearly about socialism and perhaps be more open to its argument. In the United States and some other countries, the word *socialism* has a bad odor. Therefore, for both tactical and theoretical reasons, the Left should always define socialism in terms of both political democracy and economic democracy (in its socialist version, spelled out above). Political and economic democracy really do sum up what socialists have always advocated. Of course economic democracy must entail the main socialist goals: ending exploitation, enough democratic planning to guarantee full employment, and a widespread system of free goods and services.

There has often been confusion on the Left about exactly which policies make sense at present in the short term and which must be postponed. Therefore, this chapter has spelled out the meaning of economic democracy (alias socialism) for the short term, for a medium term, and for the more distant future. This historical approach to the achievement of socialism—or political and economic democracy—exemplifies the critical method proposed throughout this book.

References

Ackerloff, George, and Janet Yellen. 1986. *Efficiency Wage Models of the Labor Market*. Cambridge: Cambridge University Press.

Addis, Laird. 1968. "The Individual and the Marxist Philosophy of History." In Brodbeck 1968, 335–49.

Ahmed, S., B. W. Ickes, P. Wang, and B. S. Yoo. 1993. "International Business Cycles." *American Economic Review* 83 (June): 335–59.

Albert, Michael, and Robin Hahnel. 1978. *Unorthodox Marxism: An Essay on Capitalism, Socialism, and Revolution*. Boston: South End.

———. 1992. "Participatory Planning." *Science and Society* 56 (spring): 39–59.

Alchian, Armen. 1969. "Information Costs, Pricing, and Resource Unemployment." *Western Economic Journal* 7 (June): 107–29.

Almond, Gabriel. 1960. "A Functional Approach to Comparative Politics." In Almond and James Coleman, *The Politics of the Developing Areas*, 83–97. Princeton: Princeton University Press.

Althusser, Louis. 1969. *For Marx*. London: Allen Lane.

———. 1971. *Lenin and Philosophy and Other Essays*. New York: Monthly Review.

Amariglio, Jack. 1987. "Marxism against Economic Science: Althusser's Legacy." *Research in Political Economy* 10:159–94.

———. 1990. "Economics as a Postmodern Discourse." In *Economics as Discourse*, edited by Warren Samuels, 15–46. Boston: Kluwer Academic Publishers.

Amariglio, Jack, Antonio Callari, and Stephen Cullenberg. 1989. "Analytic Marxism: A Critical Overview." *Review of Social Economy* 47 (winter): 415–32.

Amin, Samir. 1990. "The Future of Socialism." *Monthly Review* 42 (July–August): 10–29.

Amin, Samir, Giovanni Arrighi, Andre Gunder Frank, and Immanuel Wallerstein. 1990. *Transforming the Revolution: Social Movements and the World System.* New York: Monthly Review.

Anderson, W. H. Locke. 1987. "Apologizing for Capitalism." *Monthly Review* 39 (March): 37–48.

Anderson, W. H. Locke, and Frank Thompson. 1988. "Neoclassical Marxism." *Science and Society* 52 (summer): 215–28.

Andreski, Stanislav. 1972. *Social Sciences as Sorcery.* New York: St. Martin's.

Arestis, Philip. 1990. "Post-Keynesianism: A New Approach to Economics." *Review of Social Economy* 48 (fall): 222–46.

Arestis, Philip, and Thanos Skouras. 1985. *Post Keynesian Economic Theory.* Armonk, N.Y.: M. E. Sharpe.

Aristotle. 1941. *Politics.* In *The Basic Works of Aristotle,* edited by Richard McKeon, 1127–1324. New York: Random House.

Ashton, T. H., and C. H. E. Philpin, eds. 1985. *The Brenner Debate: Class Structure and Economic Development in Pre-Industrial Europe.* New York: Cambridge University Press.

Avineri, Shlomo. 1968. *The Social and Political Thought of Karl Marx.* Cambridge: Cambridge University Press.

Babic, Ivan. 1966. "Blanshard's Reflections on Marxism." *Journal of Philosophy* 63 (December): 233–59.

Balbus, Isaac. 1972. "The Negation of the Negation." *Politics and Society* 3 (fall): 24–41.

Balinky, Alexander. 1970. *Marx's Economics.* Boston: D. C. Heath.

Bandyopadhyay, Pradeep. 1971. "One Sociology or Many?" *Science and Society* 35 (spring): 1–26.

Baran, Paul. 1959. "On Marxism." *Monthly Review* 11 (June): 1–12.

———. 1960. *Marxism and Psychoanalysis.* New York: Monthly Review.

Barbalet, J. M. 1992. "Class and Rationality: Olson's Critique of Marx." *Science and Society* 55 (winter): 446–68.

Bardan, Pranab, and John Roemer. 1992. "Market Socialism: A Case for Rejuvenation." *Journal of Economic Perspectives* 6 (summer): 101–16.

Baron, Harold. 1985. "Racism Transformed." *Review of Radical Political Economics* 17 (fall): 10–33.

Becker, Gary. 1957. *The Economics of Discrimination.* Chicago: University of Chicago Press.

Berger, Peter, and Thomas Luckman. 1966. *The Social Construction of Reality.* Garden City, N.Y.: Doubleday.

Bergson, Abram. 1984. "Income Inequality under Soviet Socialism." *Journal of Economic Literature* 22 (September): 1052–99.

Bhaskar, Roy. 1989. *Reclaiming Reality.* New York: Verso, 1989.

Blanshard, Brand. 1966. "Reflections on Economic Determinism." *Journal of Philosophy* 63 (March): 324–35.

Blaug, Mark. 1980. *The Methodology of Economics.* Cambridge: Cambridge University Press.

Blinder, Alan S. 1990. "Discussion of Report of AEA Commission on Graduate Education in Economics." *American Economic Review* 80 (May): 445.

Block, Maurice. 1983. *Marxism and Anthropology.* Oxford: Clarendon.

——, ed. 1975. *Marxist Analyses and Social Anthropology.* New York: Wiley.

Bluestone, Barry. 1972. "A Discussion of Capitalism and Poverty in America." *Monthly Review* 24 (June): 61–69.

Boddy, Raford, and James Crotty. 1975. "Class Conflict and Macro-Policy." *Review of Radical Political Economics* 5 (spring): 1–17.

Boger, George. 1991. "On the Materialist Appropriation of Hegel's Dialectic Method." *Science and Society* 55 (spring): 26–59.

Bonacich, Edna. 1980. "Class Approaches to Ethnicity and Race." *Insurgent Sociologist* 10 (fall): 9–24.

Boston, Thomas D. 1988. *Race, Class, and Conservatism.* London: Allen & Unwin.

Bowles, Samuel, and Herbert Gintis. 1975. *Schooling in Capitalist America.* New York: Basic Books.

——. 1981. "Structure and Practice in the Labor Theory of Value." *Review of Radical Political Economics* 12 (winter): 1–27.

——. 1986. *Democracy and Capitalism.* New York: Basic Books.

——. 1990. "Rethinking Marxism and Liberalism from a Radical Democratic Perspective." *Rethinking Marxism* 3 (fall–winter): 37–45.

Bowles, Samuel, David Gordon, and Thomas Weisskopf. 1986. "Power and Profits: The Social Structure of Accumulation and the Profitability of U.S. Postwar Economy." *Review of Radical Political Economy* 18 (spring–summer): 132–67.

——. 1990. *After the Wasteland.* Armonk, N.Y.: M. E. Sharpe.

Boyer, Richard O., and Herbert Morais. 1970. *Labor's Untold Story.* 3rd ed. New York: United Electrical Workers.

Braverman, Harry. 1974. *Labor and Monopoly Capital: The Degradation of Work in the Twentieth Century.* New York: Monthly Review.

Brodbeck, May, ed. 1968. *Readings in the Philosophy of the Social Sciences.* New York: Macmillan.

Bronfenbrenner, Martin. 1971. "The 'Structure of Revolutions' in Economic Thought." *History of Political Economy* 3 (spring): 140–51.

Brooks, Keith. 1973. "Freudianism Is Not a Basis for a Marxist Psychology." In *Radical Psychology,* edited by Phil Brown, 25–42. New York: Harper.

Brown, Bruce. 1973. *Marx, Freud, and the Critique of Everyday Life.* New York: Monthly Review.

Brown, Doug. 1992. "Postmodern Politics of Social Change." *Journal of Economic Issues* 26 (June): 545–52.

Brown, Phil. 1974. *Toward a Marxist Psychology.* New York: Harper & Row.

Burket, Paul. 1992. "The Bankruptcy of Mainstream Economics." *Monthly Review* 44 (October): 18–26.

Caldwell, Bruce. 1982. *Beyond Positivism: Economic Methodology in the Twentieth Century.* Boston: Allen & Unwin.

Callinicos, Alex. 1988. *Making History.* Ithaca: Cornell University Press.

———. 1991. *The Revenge of History.* University Park: Pennsylvania State University Press.

Carling, Alan. 1990. "Rational Choice Marxism." In King 1990, 1:371–408.

Carnoy, Martin. 1984. *The State and Political Theory.* Princeton: Princeton University Press.

Caudwell, Christopher. [1938] 1971. *Studies and Further Studies in a Dying Culture.* New York: Monthly Review.

Cheney, Edward. 1927. *Law in History and Other Essays.* New York: Harper & Row.

Chilcote, Edward, and Ronald Chilcote. 1992. "The Crisis of Marxism." *Rethinking Marxism* 5 (summer): 84–106.

Childe, V. Gordon. 1951. *Social Evolution.* London: Watts.

Cipolla, Carlo. 1962. *The Economic History of World Population.* Baltimore: Penguin.

Cohen, G. A. 1978. *Karl Marx's Theory of History.* Princeton: Princeton University Press.

Cohen, Marshall, Thomas Nagel, and Thomas Scanlon, eds. 1980. *Marx, Justice, and History.* Princeton: Princeton University Press.

Colander, David, and Arjo Klamer. 1987. "The Making of an Economist." *Journal of Economic Perspectives* 1 (fall): 95–111.

———. 1990. *The Making of an Economist.* San Francisco: Westview.

Colfax, R., and Jack Roach. 1973. *Radical Sociology.* New York: Basic Books.

Cornforth, Maurice. 1965. *Marxism and the Linguistic Philosophy.* New York: International Publishers.

———. 1968. *The Open Philosophy and The Open Society: A Reply to Karl Popper's Refutations of Marxism.* New York: International Publishers.

———. 1971a. *Dialectical Materialism.* New York: International Publishers.

———. 1971b. *Historical Materialism.* New York: International Publishers.

Coulson, Margaret, and David Riddell. 1970. *Approaching Sociology.* London: Routledge & Kegan Paul.

Danto, Arthur. 1965. *Analytical Philosophy of History.* New York: Cambridge University Press.

D'Arge, Ralph, and James Wilen. 1974. "Government Control of Externalities." *Journal of Economic Issues* 8 (June): 353–72.

Davis, John B. 1983. "Marx's Conception of the Status of Ethics in Capitalist Society." Ph.D. diss., University of Illinois, Urbana-Champaign.

———. 1987. "Marx's Conception of Ethics in Capitalist Society." *Research in the History of Economic Thought and Methodology* 5:51–90.

———. 1990. "Althusser's View of the Place of Ethics in Marx's Thought." *Social Science Journal* 27:95–109.

Deckard, Barbara Sinclair. 1983. *The Women's Movement.* 3rd ed. New York: Harper & Row.

De Marchi, Neil, ed. 1988. *The Popperian Legacy in Economics*. New York: Cambridge University Press.

DeMartino, George. 1993. "First Principles in New Macroeconomics." *Journal of Economic Issues* 27 (December): 1127–54.

Dennon, A. R. 1969. "Political Science and Political Development." *Science and Society* 33 (fall): 1–26.

Deutscher, Isaac. 1965a. *Stalin*. New York: Oxford University Press.

———. 1965b. *Trotsky*. 3 vols. New York: Vintage Books.

———. 1971. *Marxism in Our Time*. Berkeley: Ramparts.

Devine, James, and Gary Dymski. 1991. "Roemer's General Theory of Exploitation Is a Special Case." *Economics and Philosophy* 7:235–75.

Dewey, John. [1920] 1957. *Reconstruction in Philosophy*. Boston: Beacon.

———. 1939. *Logic, the Theory of Inquiry*. New York: Dover.

Diamond, Stanley, ed. 1979. *Toward a Marxist Anthropology*. New York: Mouton.

Diesing, Paul. 1982. *Science and Ideology*. New York: Aldine.

———. 1985. "Hypothesis Testing and Data Interpretation: The Case of Milton Friedman." *Research in the History of Economic Thought and Methodology* 3:61–89.

———. 1991. *How Does Social Science Work?* Pittsburgh: University of Pittsburgh Press.

Dietz, James. 1992. "Overcoming Underdevelopment: What Has Been Learned from the East Asian and Latin American Experience?" *Journal of Economic Issues* 26 (June): 373–84.

Dobb, Maurice. 1946. *Studies in the Development of Capitalism*. London: Routledge.

Dodge, Norton. 1966. *Women in the Soviet Economy*. Baltimore: Johns Hopkins Press.

Domhoff, G. William. 1967. *Who Rules America?* Englewood Cliffs, N.J.: Prentice-Hall.

———. 1990. *The Power Elite and the State*. New York: Aldine de Gruyter.

Donald, David. 1960. *Charles Sumner and the Coming of the Civil War*. New York: Knopf.

Draper, Hal. 1977. *Karl Marx's Theory of Revolution*. New York: Monthly Review.

Dray, William. 1964. *Philosophy of History*. Englewood Cliffs, N.J.: Prentice-Hall.

DuBoff, Richard. 1989. *Accumulation & Power: An Economic History of the United States*. Armonk, N.Y.: M. E. Sharpe.

Dugger, William. 1992. *Underground Economics: A Decade of Institutionalist Dissent*. Armonk, N.Y.: M. E. Sharpe.

———, ed. 1989. *Radical Institutionalism*. New York: Greenwood.

Dugger, William, and Howard J. Sherman. 1994. "Comparison of Marxism and Institutionalism." 1992. *Journal of Economic Issues* 28 (March): 101–27.

Dugger, William, and William Waller, eds. 1992. *The Stratified State.* Armonk, N.Y.: M. E. Sharpe.

Dupre, Louis. 1966. *The Philosophical Foundations of Marxism.* New York: Harcourt, Brace, & World.

Dworkin, Gerald. 1961. "Dialectics: A Philosophical Analysis." *Studies on the Left* 2:43–64.

Dwyer, Larry. 1982. "The Alleged Value-Neutrality of Economics." *Journal of Economic Issues* 16 (March): 75–106.

Ehrenreich, Barbara. 1991. *The Worst Years of Our Lives.* New York: Harper-Collins.

Eichner, Alfred. 1988. *Why Economics Is Not Yet a Science.* Armonk, N.Y.: M. E. Sharpe.

Elliott, John. 1979. "Social and Institutional Dimensions of Marx's Theory of Capitalism." *Review of Social Economy* 37 (December): 261–74.

———. 1986. "On the Possibility of Marx's Moral Critique of Capitalism." *Review of Social Economy* 44 (October): 130–45.

———. 1987. "Marx's Moral Critique of Capitalism." In *Annual Research in History of Economic Thought and Methodology,* edited by Warren Samuels, 321–39. Greenwich, Conn.: JAI.

Elster, Jon. 1985. *Making Sense of Marx.* New York: Cambridge University Press.

———. 1986. *An Introduction to Karl Marx.* New York: Cambridge University Press.

Engels, Frederick. [1873] 1963. "The Class Nature of Morality." In Selsam and Martel 1963, 251–53.

———. [1878] 1966. *Anti-Dühring.* New York: International Publishers.

———. [1888] 1941. *Ludwig Feuerbach.* In *Marx-Engels, Selected Works,* vol. 2, 218–353. New York: International Publishers.

———. [1888] 1972. *Origin of the Family, Private Property, and the State.* Introduction by Eleanor Leacock. New York: International Publishers.

Ferraro, Joseph. 1992. *Freedom and Determination in History according to Marx and Engels.* New York: Monthly Review.

Feuer, Lewis. 1965. "Causality in the Social Sciences." In *Cause and Effect,* edited by Daniel Lerner, 55–71. New York: Free Press.

———. 1969. *The Conflict of Generations.* New York: Basic Books.

Flacks, Richard. 1982. "Marxism and Sociology." In Ollman and Vernoff 1982, 9–52.

Flaherty, Diane. 1992. "Self-Management and the Future of Socialism." *Science and Society* 56 (spring): 92–108.

Fluehr-Labban, Carolyn, ed. 1987. *International Perspectives on Marxist Anthropology.* Minneapolis: Marxist Educational Project.

Foster, John B. 1994. *The Vulnerable Planet: A Short Economic History of the Environment.* New York: Monthly Review.

Frank, Andre Gunder. 1967. "Sociology of Development." *Catalyst* 3 (summer): 19–44.

Freud, Sigmund. 1969. "Anatomy Is Destiny." In *Masculine/Feminine,* edited by Betty Roszak and Theodore Roszak, 12–22. New York: Harper & Row.

Friedman, Milton. 1962. *Capitalism and Freedom.* Chicago: University of Chicago Press.

———. 1974. "Who Represents Whom?" *Newsweek,* October 14.

Gaffney, Mason. 1990. "Logos Abused." Report to Economics Department, University of California, Riverside, January 3.

Galbraith, John. 1973a. *Economics and the Public Purpose.* Boston: Houghton Mifflin.

———. 1973b. "Power and the Useful Economist." Presidential address to the American Economics Association. *American Economic Review* 63 (March): 1–18.

Gardiner, Patrick, ed. 1959. *Theories of History.* New York: Free Press.

Ginger, Ann Fagan. 1977. *The Law, the Supreme Court, and the People's Rights.* New York: Barron's Educational Services.

Gintis, Herbert. 1982. "The Resurgence of Marxian Economists in America." In Ollman and Vernoff 1982, 34–57.

Godelier, Maurice. 1974. *Rationality and Irrationality in Economics.* New York: Monthly Review.

Goldstein, Jonathan. 1985. "The Cyclical Profit Squeeze: A Marxian Microfoundation." *Review of Radical Political Economics* 17 (spring–summer): 103–28.

Gollobin, Ira. 1986. *Dialectical Materialism.* New York: Petras.

Goodwin, Jeff. 1990. "The Limits of 'Radical Democracy.'" *Socialist Review* 90 (March): 131–44.

Gorbachev, Mikhail. 1992. "Perspective on Communism." *Los Angeles Times,* February 24.

Gordon, David. 1971. "Class and the Economics of Crime." *Review of Radical Political Economics* 3 (summer): 122–47.

———. 1972. "American Poverty." *Monthly Review* 24 (June): 70–79.

Gordon, Wendell. 1973. *Economics from an Institutional Viewpoint.* Austin: University Stores.

Gottlieb, Roger. 1987. *History and Subjectivity: The Transformation of Marxism.* Philadelphia: Temple University Press.

———. 1992. *Marxism: Origins, Betrayal, Rebirth.* New York: Routledge.

Graaf, J. 1967. *Theoretical Welfare Economics.* London: Cambridge University Press.

Grampp, William. 1970. "Empiricism and the Progress of Economic Theory." Paper delivered at the annual meeting of the Western Economic Association, Davis, Calif., August.

Gramsci, Antonio. 1971. *Selections from Prison Notebooks.* New York: International Publishers.

Green, Francis. 1984. "A Critique of the Neo-Fisherian Consumption Function." *Review of Radical Political Economics* 16 (spring): 95–114.

Gregor, A. James. 1965. *A Survey of Marxism.* New York: Random House.

Gruchy, Allan. 1947. *Modern Economic Thought.* New York: Prentice-Hall.

————. 1973. "Law, Politics, and Institutional Economics." *Journal of Economic Issues* 7 (December): 619–33.

————. 1984. "Neo-Institutionalism, Neo-Marxism, and Neo-Keynesianism: An Evaluation." *Journal of Economic Issues* 18 (June): 545–61.

Grundman, Reiner. 1991. "The Ecological Challenge to Marxism." *New Left Review,* no. 187 (May–June): 103–20.

Hagen, Everett. 1962. *On the Theory of Social Change.* Homewood, Ill.: Dorsey.

————. 1966. "How Economic Growth Begins." In *Political Development and Social Change,* edited by Jason Finkle and Richard Gable, 175–92. New York: Prentice-Hall.

Hahnel, Robin, and Michael Albert. 1990. *Quiet Revolution in Welfare Economics.* Princeton, N.J.: Princeton University Press.

Hamilton, David. 1970. *Evolutionary Economics.* Albuquerque: University of New Mexico Press.

Harding, Thomas, David Kaplan, Marshall Sahlins, and Elman Service. 1960. *Evolution and Culture.* Ann Arbor: University of Michigan Press.

Harrington, Michael. 1970. *Socialism.* New York: Saturday Review Press.

Harris, Marvin. 1968. *The Rise of Anthropological Theory.* New York: Thomas Crowell.

————. 1974. *Cows, Pigs, and Witches.* New York: Random House.

————. 1977. *Cannibals and Kings.* New York: Random House.

————. 1979. *Cultural Materialism.* New York: Random House.

Hartsock, Nancy. 1985. *Money, Sex, and Power: Toward a Feminist Historical Materialism.* Boston: Northeastern University Press.

————. 1991. "Louis Althusser's Structural Marxism: Political Clarity and Theoretical Distortions." *Rethinking Marxism* 4 (spring): 10–40.

Harvey, David. 1989. *The Condition of Postmodernity.* Cambridge, Mass.: Blackwell.

Harvey, Philip. 1989. *Securing the Right to [Full] Employment.* Princeton, N.J.: Princeton University Press.

Hegel, G. W. F. [1873] 1950. *The Science of Logic.* Translated by William Wallace. London: Oxford University Press.

Heilbroner, Robert. 1988. *Behind the Veil of Economics.* New York: W. W. Norton.

Herman, Edward S. 1982. "The Institutionalism of Bias in Economics." *Media, Culture, and Society* 4:275–91.

Hill, Christopher. 1961. *The Century of Revolution, 1603–1714.* New York: W. W. Norton.

Hilton, Rodney, ed. 1975. *The Transition from Feudalism to Capitalism.* London: New Left Books.

Hodges, Donald. 1964. "Marx's Ethics and Ethical Theory." In *The Socialist*

Register, 1964, edited by R. Miliband and J. Saville, 231–47. New York: Monthly Review.

Hodgson, Geoffrey. 1986. "Behind Methodological Individualism." *Cambridge Journal of Economics* 10 (September): 211–24.

Hodgson, Geoffrey, Warren Samuels, and Marc Tool, eds. 1994. *Institutional and Evolutionary Economics.* Brookfield, Vt.: Edward Elgar.

Hokken, David, and Hanna Lessinger, eds. 1987. *Perspectives in U.S. Marxist Anthropology.* Boulder: Westview.

Hollis, Martin, and Edward Nell. 1975. *Rational Economic Man: A Philosophical Critique of Neoclassical Economics.* New York: Cambridge University Press.

Homans, George. 1967. *The Nature of Social Sciences.* New York: Harcourt, Brace, & World.

Horner, Jim. 1991. "The Case of DAT Technology: Industrial versus Pecuniary Function." *Journal of Economic Issues* 25 (June): 448–58.

Horowitz, David. 1971. *Radical Sociology.* New York: Harper-Collins.

Howard, Michael, and John King. 1989a. *History of Marxian Economics, Volume I, 1883–1927.* Princeton: Princeton University Press.

———. 1989b. "The Rational Choice Marxism of John Roemer: A Critique." *Review of Social Economy* 47 (winter): 392–414.

———. 1992. *History of Marxian Economics, Volume II, 1929–1990.* Princeton: Princeton University Press.

Hudelson, Richard. 1990. *Marxism and Philosophy in the Twentieth Century.* New York: Praeger.

Hunt, E. K. 1979. "The Importance of Veblen for Contemporary Marxism." *Journal of Economic Issues* 13 (March): 1–21.

———. 1983. "Joan Robinson and the Labor Theory of Value." *Cambridge Journal of Economics* 7 (September–December): 329–40.

———. 1992a. "Analytic Marxism." In *Radical Economics,* edited by Bruce Roberts and Susan Feiner, 91–107. Boston: Kluwer Academic Publishers.

———. 1992b. *History of Economic Thought: A Critical Perspective.* New York: Harper-Collins.

Hunt, E. K., and Jesse Schwartz. 1972. *Critique of Economic Theory.* New York: Penguin.

Hyppolite, Jean. 1969. *Studies on Marx and Hegel.* New York: Basic Books.

Jarsulic, Marc. 1988. *Effective Demand and Income Distribution: Issues in Alternative Economics Theory.* Cambridge: Polity.

Jones, Gareth. 1973. "History: The Poverty of Empiricism." In *Ideology in Social Science,* edited by Robin Blackburn, 96–118. New York: Vintage Books.

Kain, Philip J. 1988. *Marx and Ethics.* New York: Oxford University Press.

Kaplan, Abraham. 1964. *Conduct of Inquiry.* San Francisco: Chandler.

Karsten, Siegfried. 1973. "Dialectics and the Evolution of Economic Thought." *History of Political Economy* 5 (fall): 399–419.

Keiusinen, Otto, ed. 1961. *Fundamentals of Marxism-Leninism.* London: Lawrence & Wishart.

Kemeny, John. 1959. *A Philosopher Looks at Science.* Princeton: Van Nostrand.

Kesselman, Mark. 1982. "The State and Class Struggle: Trends in Marxist Political Science." In Ollman and Vernoff 1982, 82–114.

Keynes, John Maynard. 1936. *The General Theory of Employment, Interest, and Money.* New York: Harcourt, Brace.

King, J. E. 1990. *Marxian Economics.* 3 vols. Brookfield, Vt.: Edward Elgar.

Kojève, Alexandre. 1970. *Introduction to the Reading of Hegel.* New York: Basic Books.

Korzybski, Alfred. 1933. *Science and Sanity.* Lancaster, Pa.: Science Press.

Kotz, David. 1992a. Review of *The Business Cycle,* by Howard Sherman. *Journal of Economic Literature* 30 (September): 1511–12.

———. 1992b. "The Directions of Soviet Economic Reform: From Socialist Reform to Capitalist Transition." *Monthly Review* 44 (September): 14–34.

Kreps, David. 1990. *A Course in Microeconomic Theory.* Princeton: Princeton University Press.

Kreuger, Anne, et al. 1991. "Report of the Commission on Graduate Education in Economics." *Journal of Economic Literature* 29 (September): 1035–53.

Kuhn, Thomas. 1962. *The Structure of Scientific Revolutions.* Chicago: University of Chicago Press.

Laibman, David. 1992. "Market and Plan." *Science and Society* 56 (spring): 60–91.

Lakatos, Imre, and Alan Musgrave, eds. 1970. *Criticism and Growth of Knowledge.* New York: Cambridge University Press.

Larrain, Jorge. 1986. *A Reconstruction of Historical Materialism.* London: Allen & Unwin.

Lasch, Christopher. 1965. *The New Radicalism in America, 1889–1963.* New York: Knopf.

Leacock, Eleanor. 1982. "Marxism and Anthropology." In Ollman and Vernoff 1982, 242–76.

Lebowitz, Michael. 1988. "Is Analytical Marxism Marxism?" *Science and Society* 52 (summer): 191–214.

Lefcourt, Robert. 1971. "Law against the People." In Lefcourt, ed., *Law against the People,* 495–513. New York: Vintage Books.

Leftwich, Richard, and Ansel Sharp. 1974. *Economics of Social Issues.* Homewood, Ill.: Irwin.

Lekachman, Robert. 1973. "The Conservative Drift in Economics." *Transaction* 12 (fall): 301–15.

Lenin, V. I. [1894] 1943. "What the Friends of the People Are and How They Fight against the Social Democrats." In *Selected Works,* vol. 11, 185–214. New York: International Publishers.

———. [1918] 1945. "The Tasks of the Youth Leagues." In *Selected Works*, vol. 2, 222–63. New York: International Publishers.

———. 1961. *Collected Works*, vol. 38. London: Lawrence & Wishart.

———. 1963. "Philosophical Notebooks." In *Reader in Marxist Philosophy*, edited by Howard Selsam and Harry Martel, 325–64. New York: International Publishers.

Levine, Andrew, Elliott Sober, and Eric Olin Wright. 1987. "Marxism and Methodological Individualism." *New Left Review*, no. 162 (March–April): 67–84.

Lewis, John. 1957. *Marxism and the Open Mind*. New Brunswick, N.J.: Transaction Books.

Lichtenstein, Peter. 1983. *An Introduction to Post-Keynesian and Marxian Theories of Value and Price*. Armonk, N.Y.: M. E. Sharpe.

Lichtman, Richard. 1982. *The Production of Desire: The Integration of Psychoanalysis into Marxist Theory*. New York: Free Press.

Lindblom, Charles E. 1977. *Politics and Markets*. New York: Basic Books.

Los Angeles Times. 1986. "Strikers 'Totally Take Over' Hormel Gates." February 1, pt. 1.

Lucas, Robert. 1975. "An Equilibrium Model of the Business Cycle." *Journal of Political Economy* 63 (December): 1113–44.

———. 1986. "Models of Business Cycles." Paper delivered at the Yrjo Jansson Lectures, Helsinki, Finland, March. Mimeographed.

Lukács, Georg. [1923] 1971. *History and Class Consciousness*. Cambridge: MIT Press.

Lukes, Steven. 1985. *Marxism and Morality*. Oxford: Clarendon.

Lustig, Jeffrey R. 1982. *Corporate Liberalism: The Origins of Modern American Political Theory, 1890–1920*. Berkeley and Los Angeles: University of California Press.

Mandel, Ernest. 1971. *The Formation of the Economic Thought of Karl Marx*. New York: Monthly Review.

Mankiw, Gary, and David Romer. 1991. *New Keynesian Economics*. Cambridge: MIT Press.

Mao Tse-tung. [1937] 1985. "On Contradiction." In *The Essential Left*, edited by David McLellan, 265–306. Boston: Unwin Paperbacks.

Marcuse, Herbert. 1961. *Soviet Marxism*. New York: Vintage Books.

———. 1964. *One Dimensional Man*. Boston: Beacon.

Marglin, Steven. 1989. "Understanding Capitalism: Control versus Efficiency." In *Power and Economic Institutions*, edited by Bo Gustafsson, 85–99. Brookfield, Vt.: Edward Elgar.

Maritain, Jacques. 1964. *Moral Philosophy*. New York: Charles Scribner's Sons.

Markovic, Michailo. 1965. "Humanism and Dialectic." In *Socialist Humanism*, edited by Erich Fromm, 84–97. Garden City, N.Y.: Doubleday.

Markusen, Ann. 1985. *Profit Cycles, Oligopoly, and Regional Development*. Cambridge: MIT Press.

———. 1987. *Regions: The Economics and Politics of Territory.* Totowa, N.J.: Rowman & Littlefield.

Marquit, Edwin. 1981. "Contradictions in Dialectics and Formal Logic." *Science and Society* 45 (fall): 306–23.

———. 1990. "A Materialist Critique of Hegel's Concept of Identity of Opposites." *Science and Society* 54 (summer): 147–66.

Marshall, Alfred. 1920. *Principles of Economics.* 8th ed. London: Macmillan.

Martin, Bill. 1992. *Matrix and Line: Derrida and the Possibilities of Postmodern Social Theory.* Albany: State University of New York Press.

Martindale, Don, ed. 1965. *Functionalism in the Social Sciences.* Philadelphia: American Academy of Political and Social Science.

Marx, Karl. [1852] 1963. *The Eighteenth Brumaire of Louis Bonaparte.* New York: International Publishers.

———. [1857] 1964. *Pre-Capitalist Economic Formations.* New York: International Publishers.

———. [1858] 1973. *Grundrisse.* New York: Vintage Books.

———. [1859] 1904. *Contribution to the Critique of Political Economy.* Chicago: Charles H. Kerr.

———. [1867] 1965. *Capital.* Vol. 1. London: Allen & Unwin.

———. [1872] 1965. Afterword to the second edition of *Capital,* vol 1. New York: International Publishers.

———. 1907. *Capital.* Vol. 3. Chicago: Charles H. Kerr.

———. 1968. *Theories of Surplus Value.* Moscow: Progress Publishers.

Marx, Karl, and Frederick Engels. [1885] 1970. *The German Ideology.* New York: International Publishers.

———. 1934. *The Correspondence of Karl Marx and Friedrich Engels.* Edited by F. Adoratsky. New York: International Publishers.

———. 1968. *Selected Works in One Volume.* New York: International Publishers.

Mayer, Thomas F. 1990. "In Defense of Analytical Marxism." *Science and Society* 53 (winter): 416–41.

McCloskey, Donald. 1985. *The Rhetoric of Economics.* Madison: University of Wisconsin Press.

McLellan, David, and Sean Sayers. 1990. *Socialism and Morality.* New York: St. Martin's.

McMurtry, John. 1978. *The Structure of Marx's World View.* Princeton: Princeton University Press.

Mead, Margaret. 1971. *Sex and Temperament in Three Primitive Societies.* New York: Dell.

Means, Gardiner. 1972. "The Administered-Price Thesis Reconfirmed." *American Economic Review* 67 (June): 292–306.

Meek, Ronald. 1967. *Economics and Ideology.* London: Chapman & Hall.

Merrill, Michael, and Michael Wallace. 1982. "Marxism and History." In Ollman and Vernoff 1982, 242–76.

Milberg, William. 1991. "Marxism, Poststructuralism, and the Discourse of Economics." *Rethinking Marxism* 4 (summer): 93–104.

Miliband, Ralph. 1969. *The State in Capitalist Society.* New York: Basic Books.

———. 1973. "Poulantzas and the Capitalist State." *New Left Review,* no. 82 (March): 83–92.

———. 1977. *Marxism and Politics.* London: Oxford University Press.

———. 1990. *Class Struggle in Contemporary Capitalism.* New York: Oxford University Press.

———. 1991a. *Divided Societies: Class Struggle in Contemporary Capitalism.* New York: Oxford University Press.

———. 1991b. "What Comes after Communist Regimes?" In *Socialist Register, 1991,* by Ralph Miliband and Leo Panitch, 375–89. London: Merlin.

Mill, John Stuart. [1872] 1959. "Elucidations of the Science of History." In Gardiner 1959, 82–105.

Miller, Edythe. 1993. "Economic Imagination and Public Policy." *Journal of Economic Issues* 17 (December): 1041–58.

Miller, Eugene. 1972. "Positivism, Historicism, and Political Inquiry." *American Political Science Review* 66 (September): 800–822.

Mills, C. Wright. 1961. *The Sociological Imagination.* New York: Grove.

Mintz, Sidney, Maurice Godelier, and Bruce Trigger. 1984. *On Marxian Perspectives in Anthropology.* Malibu: UCLA Department of Anthropology, Undena Publications.

Mirowski, Philip. 1989. *More Heat Than Light.* New York: Cambridge University Press.

———, ed. 1986. *The Reconstruction of Economic Theory.* Boston: Kluwer-Nijhoff.

Mitchell, Wesley. 1937. *Backward Art of Spending Money.* New York: McGraw-Hill.

Modern Approaches to the Theory of Value. 1990. Special issue of *Review of Radical Political Economics* 21 (winter–spring).

Mongait, A. L. 1961. *Archaeology in the USSR.* Baltimore: Penguin Books.

Myrdal, Gunnar. 1981. "What Is Political Economy?" In *Value Judgment and Income Distribution,* edited by Robert Solo and Charles Anderson, 19–45. New York: Praeger.

Nef, John U. 1940. *Industry and Government in France and England, 1540–1640.* Philadelphia: American Philosophical Society.

Neill, R. B. 1974. "The 'New Materialism' and the Sociology of Knowledge." *Insurgent Sociologist* 4 (winter): 38–54.

Newlon, Daniel. 1991. "The Quality of Graduate Education in Economics." *Newsletter of the AEA Committee on the Status of Women in the Economics Profession,* spring, 4–5.

Nisbet, Robert. 1969. *Social Change and History.* New York: Oxford University Press.

Norman, Richard, and Sean Sayers. 1980. *Hegel, Marx, and Dialectic.* Atlantic Highlands, N.J.: Humanities.

North, Douglas. 1990. *Institutions, Institutional Change, and Economic Performance*. Cambridge: Cambridge University Press.

Nove, Alec. 1975. "Is There a Ruling Class in the USSR?" *Soviet Studies* 27 (October): 615–38.

Oelsner, Leslie. 1972. "Scales of Justice." *Daily Enterprise* (Riverside, Calif.), September 28.

Ollman, Bertell. 1971a. *Alienation*. New York: Cambridge University Press.

———. 1971b. "Is There a Marxist Ethic?" *Science and Society* 35 (summer): 148–63.

———. 1973. "Marx and Political Science." *Politics and Society* 3 (summer): 501–21.

———. 1986. "The Meaning of Dialectics." *Monthly Review* 38 (November): 42–55.

———. 1990. "Putting Dialectics to Work: The Process of Abstraction in Marx's Method." *Rethinking Marxism* 3 (spring): 26–74.

———. 1992. *Dialectical Investigations*. New York: Routledge.

Ollman, Bertell, and Edward Vernoff. 1982. *The Left Academy: Marxist Scholarship on American Campuses*. Vol. 1. New York: McGraw-Hill.

———. 1984. *The Left Academy: Marxist Scholarship on American Campuses*. Vol. 2. New York: Praeger.

———. 1986. *The Left Academy: Marxist Scholarship on American Campuses*. Vol. 3. New York: Praeger.

Peffer, R. G. 1990. *Marxism, Morality, and Social Justice*. Princeton: Princeton University Press.

Pennock, J. Roland, and John W. Chapman. 1983. *Marxism*. New York: New York University Press.

Peterson, Wallace. 1993. "America's Silent Depression." *Review of Social Economy* 11 (spring): 2–13.

Pheby, John. 1988. *Methodology and Economics: A Critical Introduction*. Armonk, N.Y.: M. E. Sharpe.

Piccone, Paul. 1971. "Phenomenological Marxism." *Telos* 9 (fall): 93–126.

Ping-yuan, Shen. [1969]. "A Discussion of Formal Logic and Dialectics." *Chinese Studies in Philosophy* 1 (fall): 73–91.

Pitelis, Christos. 1991. *Market and Non-Market Hierarchies: Theory of Institutional Failure*. Cambridge, Mass.: Blackwell.

Planty-Bonjour, Guy. 1967. *The Categories of Dialectical Materialism*. New York: Praeger.

Platt, John. 1970. "Hierarchical Growth." *Bulletin of the Atomic Scientists* 26 (November): 2–4, 46–48.

Plekhanov, George. 1959. "The Role of the Individual in History." In Gardiner 1959, 139–65.

Popper, Karl. 1952. *The Open Society and Its Enemies*. Vol. 2. London: Routledge & Kegan Paul.

———. 1959. "Prediction and Prophecy in the Social Sciences." In Gardiner 1959, 276–85.

Poulantzas, Nicos. [1969] 1975. *Classes in Contemporary Capitalism*. London: New Left Books.

———. [1978] 1980. *State, Power, Socialism*. London: New Left Books.

Pozzuto, Richard. 1973. "Pre-Marxian Marxism." *Insurgent Sociologist* 3 (summer): 50.

President's Commission on Law Enforcement and the Administration of Justice. 1968. *The Challenge of Crime in a Free Society*. New York: Avon Books.

Priest, Graham. 1989–90. "Dialectic and Dialetheic." *Science and Society* 53 (winter): 388–415.

Przeworski, Adam. 1985. *Capitalism and Social Democracy*. New York: Cambridge University Press.

Quinney, Richard. 1977. *Class, State, and Crime*. New York: David McKay.

Ransom, Roger, and Richard Sutch. 1977. *One Kind of Freedom: The Economic Consequences of Emancipation*. New York: Cambridge University Press.

Rapoport, Anatol. 1948. "Dialectical Materialism and General Semantics." *ETC* 3 (winter): 28–54.

———. 1954. *Operational Philosophy*. New York: Harper & Row.

Raskin, Paul, and Stephen Bernow. 1991. "Ecology and Marxism: Are Green and Red Complementary?" *Rethinking Marxism* 4 (spring): 87–103.

Reich, Michael. 1980. *Racial Inequality, Economic Theory, and Class Conflict*. Princeton: Princeton University Press.

Reichenbach, Hans. 1951. *The Rise of Scientific Philosophy*. Berkeley: University of California Press.

Reid, Herbert. 1973. "American Social Science in the Politics of Time and the Crisis of Technocorporate Society: Toward a Critical Phenomenology." *Politics and Society* 3 (winter): 201–44.

Reiman, Jeffrey. 1990. *The Rich Get Richer and the Poor Get Prison*. 3rd ed. New York: Macmillan.

Resnick, Stephen, and Richard Wolff. 1987. *Knowledge and Class*. Chicago: University of Chicago Press.

Riddell, David. 1970. *Approaching Sociology*. London: Routledge & Kegan Paul.

Rigby, S. H. 1987. *Marxism and History*. New York: St. Martin's.

Robbins, Lionel. 1935. *The Nature and Significance of Economic Science*. London: Macmillan.

Robinson, Joan. 1964. *Economic Philosophy*. Garden City, N.Y.: Doubleday.

Roemer, John. 1978. "Neoclassicism, Marxism, and Collective Action." *Journal of Economic Issues* 12 (March): 147–61.

———. 1982. *A General Theory of Exploitation and Class*. Cambridge: Harvard University Press.

———. 1986. "Rational Choice Marxism." In Roemer, ed., *Analytic Marxism*, 1–39. New York: Cambridge University Press.

———. 1989. "Marxism and Contemporary Social Science." *Review of Social Economy* 47 (December): 377–92.

———— 1994. *Future for Socialism*. Cambridge: Harvard University Press.
————, ed. 1986. *Analytic Marxism*. New York: Cambridge University Press.
Rose, Arnold. 1967. *The Power Structure*. New York: Oxford University Press.
Rotenstreich, Nathan. 1965. *Basic Problems of Marx's Philosophy*. New York: Bobbs-Merrill.
Ruccio, David. 1988. "The Merchant of Venice, or Marxism in the Mathematical Mode." *Rethinking Marxism* 1 (winter): 38–69.
Ruccio, David, and Lawrence Simon. 1986. "Methodological Aspects of a Marxian Approach to Development." *World Development* 14, no. 2:211–22.
Russell, Bertrand. 1903. *Philosophy of Mathematics*. New York: W. W. Norton.
————. 1945. *A History of Western Philosophy*. New York: Simon & Schuster.
————. 1959. "Dialectical Materialism." In Gardiner 1959, 285–94.
Ryle, Gilbert. 1937. "Categories." *Proceedings of the Aristotelian Society*, n.s. 38:453–77.
Sahlins, Marshall. 1985. *Islands of History*. Chicago: University of Chicago Press.
Samuels, Warren. 1977. "Technology vis-à-vis Institutions: A Suggested Interpretation." *Journal of Economic Issues* 11 (December): 867–95.
————. 1990. "Institutional Economics and the Theory of Cogitation." *Journal of Economic Issues* 14 (June): 219–27.
————. 1994. "Law and Economics." In Hodgson, Samuels, and Tool 1994, 8–12.
————, ed. 1979. *The Economy as a System of Power*. New Brunswick, N.J.: Transaction Books.
————, 1980. *The Methodology of Economic Thought*. New Brunswick, N.J.: Transaction Books.
Samuelson, Paul, and William Nordhaus. 1992. *Economics*. 14th ed. New York: McGraw-Hill.
Sapir, E. 1977. "The Status of Linguistics as a Science." In *Selected Writings of Edward Sapir in Language, Social Structure, and Personality*, edited by David Mandelbaum, 93–118. Berkeley and Los Angeles: University of California Press.
Sartre, Jean Paul. 1962. *Literary and Philosophical Essays*. New York: Collier Books.
————. 1968. *Search for a Method*. New York: Vintage Books.
Sawyer, Malcolm. 1989. *The Challenge of Radical Political Economy*. Savage, Md.: Barnes & Noble.
Sayer, Derek. 1987. *The Violence of Abstraction*. New York: Blackwell.
Sayers, Sean. 1981–82. "Contradiction and Dialectic." *Development of Science* 45 (winter): 409–36.
Schaff, Adam. 1960. "Marxist Dialectics and the Principle of Contradiction." *Journal of Philosophy* 57 (March): 127–41.

———. 1973. *Language and Cognition.* New York: McGraw-Hill.

Schlack, Robert. 1990. "Urban Economics and Economic Heterodoxy." *Journal of Economic Issues* 24 (March): 17–48.

Schmemann, Sergei. 1991. "Gorbachev Offers Party a Charter That Drops Icons." *New York Times,* July 26.

Schmidt, Richard. 1989. "The Materialist Dialectic." *Science and Society* 52 (winter): 441–455.

Schumpeter, Joseph. 1949. "Science and Ideology." *American Economic Review* 39 (March): 345–59.

———. 1950. *Capitalism, Socialism, and Democracy.* New York: Harper & Row.

Schweickart, David. 1992. "Economic Democracy." *Science and Society* 56 (spring): 9–38.

Schwendinger, Herman, and Julia Schwendinger. 1974. *Sociologists of the Chair: A Radical Analysis of the Formative Years of North American Sociology, 1883–1922.* New York: Basic Books.

Selsam, Howard. 1943. *Socialism and Ethics.* New York: International Publishers.

Selsam, Howard, David Goldway, and Harry Martel. 1970. *Dynamics of Social Change.* New York: International Publishers.

Selsam, Howard, and Harry Martel, eds. 1963. *Reader in Marxist Philosophy.* New York: International Publishers.

Semmler, Willi. 1982. "Competition, Monopoly, and Differentials of Profit Rates." *Review of Radical Political Economics* 13 (winter): 39–52.

Shaikh, Anwar. 1978. "An Introduction to the History of Crisis Theories." In *U.S. Capitalism in Crisis,* by Union for Radical Political Economies, 219–40. New York: Monthly Review.

Shaw, William H. 1978. *Marx's Theory of History.* Stanford: Stanford University Press.

Sheehan, Michael, and Rick Tilman. 1992. "A Clarification of the Concept of 'Instrumental Valuation' in Institutionalist Economics." *Journal of Economic Issues* 26 (March): 197–208.

Shelton, John F. 1985. "Economists Aren't Reagan Enemies." *Los Angeles Times,* March 19.

Sherman, Howard. 1968. *Profits in the United States.* Ithaca: Cornell University Press.

———. 1972. *Radical Political Economy.* New York: Basic Books.

———. 1979. "Technology vis-à-vis Institutions: A Marxist Commentary." *Journal of Economic Issues* 13 (March): 175–93.

———. 1984. "Contemporary Radical Economics." *Journal of Economic Education* 15 (fall): 265–74.

———. 1987. *Foundations of Radical Political Economy.* Armonk, N.Y.: M. E. Sharpe.

———. 1991. *The Business Cycle: Growth and Crisis in Capitalism.* Princeton: Princeton University Press.

————. 1992. Review of *Market and Non-Market Hierarchies: Theory of Institutional Failure*, by Christos Pitelis. *Review of Radical Political Economics* 24 (fall–winter): 229–30.

Sherman, Howard, and James L. Wood. 1989. *Sociology.* 2nd ed. New York: Harper-Collins.

Shils, Edward. 1966. *Political Development in the New States.* The Hague, Netherlands: Kluwer.

Silvestre, Joaquin. 1993. "The Market-Power Foundations of Macroeconomic Policy." *Journal of Economic Literature* 31 (March): 105–41.

Skidelsky, Robert. 1986. *John Maynard Keynes, 1883–1920.* New York: Viking.

Skocpol, Theda. 1979. *States and Social Revolutions.* New York: Cambridge University Press.

————. 1980. "Political Responses to Capitalist Crisis: NeoMarxist Theories of the State and the Case of the New Deal." *Politics and Society* 10 (winter): 63–81.

Smith, Dan. 1994. "Education, Destitute, Slapped by the Budget." *Press-Enterprise* (July 2) 1.

Smith, Tony. 1990. *The Logic of Marx's Capital.* Albany: State University of New York Press.

Soderbaum, Peter. 1990. "Neoclassical and Institutional Approaches to Environmental Economics." *Journal of Economic Issues* 24 (June): 481–91.

Somerville, John. 1946. *Soviet Philosophy.* New York: Philosophical Library.

Sraffa, Piero. 1960. *Production of Commodities by Means of Commodities.* Cambridge: Cambridge University Press.

Stalin, Joseph. 1940. *Dialectical and Historical Materialism.* New York: International Publishers.

St. Croix, G. E. M. de. 1981. *The Class Struggle in the Ancient Greek World.* London: Routledge.

Steinmo, Sven. 1993. "Higher Taxes Are More Myth Than Money." *Public Affairs Report* (Institute of Governmental Studies, University of California, Berkeley) 34 (May): 4–5.

Stewart, Hamish. 1991. Review of *The Popperian Legacy in Economics*, edited by Neil De Marchi. *Review of Radical Political Economics* 24 (summer): 146–50.

Stigler, George, and J. K. Kindahl. 1970. *The Behavior of Industrial Prices.* New York: National Bureau of Economic Research.

Stillman, Peter G. 1983. "Marx's Enterprise of Critique." In Pennock and Chapman 1983, 252–76.

Sweezy, Paul. 1961. "Toward a Critique of Economics." *Monthly Review* 21 (January): 45–62.

————. 1973. "Utopian Reformism." *Monthly Review* 25 (November): 1–10.

————. 1974. "The Nature of Soviet Society." *Monthly Review* 26 (November): 1–26.

———. 1992. "Base and Superstructure Revisited." *Monthly Review* 44 (June): 56–61.

"Symposium on Cornel West's *Ethnical Dimensions of Marx's Thought.*" 1993. With articles by John B. Foste, Alison Jaggar, Istuan Meszaros, Uillermo Bowie, Samir Amin, and Cornel West. *Monthly Review* 45 (June): 8–60.

Szymanski, Albert. 1973. "Marxism or Liberalism." *Insurgent Sociologist* 3 (summer): 45–62.

———. 1978. *The Capitalist State and the Politics of Class.* Cambridge, Mass.: Winthrop Publishers.

Taussig, Michael. 1980. *The Devil and Commodity Fetishism in South America.* Chapel Hill: University of North Carolina Press.

Terkel, Studs. 1970. *Hard Times: An Oral History of the Great Depression.* New York: Pantheon.

Thompson, E. P. 1963. *The Making of the English Working Class.* New York: Pantheon Books.

———. 1988. "Peculiarities of the English." In *The Poverty of Theory,* 14–29. London: Merlin.

Tigar, Michael, and Madeline Levy. 1977. *Law and the Rise of Capitalism.* New York: Monthly Review.

Tilman, Rick. 1992. *Thorstein Veblen and His Critics, 1891–1963.* Princeton: Princeton University Press.

Tool, Marc. 1982. "Social Value Theory of Marxists, Part I." *Journal of Economic Issues* 16 (December): 1079–1107.

———. 1983. "Social Value Theory of Marxists, Part II." *Journal of Economic Issues* 17 (March): 155–73.

———. 1990. *Evolutionary Economics.* 2 vols. Armonk, N.Y.: M. E. Sharpe.

Tullock, Gordon. 1971. *The Logic of the Law.* New York: Basic Books.

Turner, Jonathan H. 1974. *The Structure of Sociological Theory.* Homewood, Ill.: Dorsey.

Varian, Hal. 1992. *Microeconomic Analysis.* 3rd ed. New York: W. W. Norton.

Veblen, Thorstein. [1915] 1945. *Germany and the Industrial Revolution.* New York: Macmillan.

———. [1922] 1962. *Engineers and the Price System.* New York: Harcourt, Brace & World.

Wachtel, Howard. 1972. "Capitalism and Poverty in America." *Monthly Review* 24 (June): 49–60.

Walras, Leon. [1874] 1969. *Elements of Pure Economics.* Translated by William Jaffé. New York: Augustus Kelley.

Ward, Benjamin. 1972. *What's Wrong with Economics?* New York: Basic Books.

Weeks, John. 1981. *Capital and Exploitation.* Princeton: Princeton University Press.

———. 1989. *Critique of Neoclassical Economics.* New York: St. Martin's.

Weiss, Andrew. 1990. *Efficiency Wages.* Princeton: Princeton University Press.

Weisskopf, Thomas. 1982. "Radical Economics." In *Encyclopedia of Economics,* edited by Douglas Greenwald, 799–801. New York: McGraw-Hill.

Weisstein, Naomi. 1971. "Psychology Constructs the Female." In *Woman in Sexist Society,* edited by V. Gornick and B. Moran, 223–56. New York: Signet Books.

Wenger, Martin. 1994. "Idealism Redux: The Class-Historial Truth of Postmodernism." *Critical Sociology,* anthology 1, 20, no. 1: 53–78.

Wertheimer, Max. 1959. *Productive Thinking.* New York: Harper & Row.

West, Cornel. 1991. *The Ethical Dimensions of Marxist Thought.* New York: Monthly Review.

White, Leslie. 1949. *The Science of Culture.* New York: Grove.

Whitehead, Alfred. 1929. *Process and Reality.* New York: Macmillan.

Wilbur, Charles, and Kenneth Jameson. 1983. *An Inquiry into the Poverty of Economics.* Notre Dame, Ind.: University of Notre Dame Press.

———. 1990. *Beyond Reaganomics: A Further Inquiry into the Poverty of Economics.* Notre Dame, Ind.: University of Notre Dame Press.

Winnick, Andrew. 1989. *Toward Two Societies: The Changing Distribution of Income and Wealth in the United States since 1960.* New York: Praeger.

Wisman, John, and Joseph Rozansky. 1991. "Institutionalist Methodology Revisited." *Journal of Economic Issues* 25 (November): 709–38.

Wolff, Richard. 1990. "The Marxist Theoretical Tradition: One View." *Rethinking Marxism* 3 (fall–winter): 329–36.

Wolff, Richard, and Stephen Cullenberg. 1986. "Marxism and Post-Marxism." *Social Text* 15 (August): 126–35.

Wolff, Richard, and Stephen Resnick. 1986. "Power, Property, and Class." *Socialist Review* 16 (March–April): 97–124.

———. 1987. *Economics: Marxian and Neoclassical.* Baltimore: Johns Hopkins University Press.

Wolfson, Murray. 1966. *A Reappraisal of Marxian Economics.* New York: Columbia University Press.

Wood, Ellen Meiksins. 1989. "Rational Choice Marxism: Is the Game Worth the Candle?" *New Left Review,* no. 177 (September–October): 44–88.

———. 1990. "Explaining Everything or Nothing?" *New Left Review,* no. 184 (November–December): 116–28.

Wright, Eric Olin. 1985. *Classes.* New York: Verso.

———, ed. 1989. *The Debate in Classes.* New York: Verso.

Wright, Eric Olin, Andrew Levine, and Elliott Sober. 1992. *Reconstructing Marxism.* New York: Verso.

Zimbalist, Andrew, Howard Sherman, and Stuart Brown. 1988. *Comparing Economic Systems: A Political-Economic Approach.* 2nd ed. San Diego: Harcourt Brace Jovanovich.

Zinn, Howard. 1970. *Politics of History.* Boston: Beacon.

Subject Index

Business cycles, 152, 158, 161, 162

Capacity thesis, 61
Capitalism, 3, 12, 64, 72, 74, 83, 188
Capitalist class, 6, 325
China, 4, 14, 66
Class analysis, 87, 109, 200, 93, 101
Class conflicts, 70, 71, 73, 82, 93, 115, 116, 120, 141, 145, 171; ideological, 123; social-political, 121
Collectivism, 85, 86, 95, 105, 154–55
Communist party, 3–7, 77
Compatability thesis, 60
Contradiction thesis, 60
Cuba, 14, 35

Demand, effective, 168
Democracy, 18, 177, 186, 188, 321, 323, 324, 327, 330
Democratic planning, 323, 329
Determinism, 270–72, 278, 279, 282
Determinism, Relational-Historical Method, 278
Development, 82, 83
Development thesis, 60
Dialectics, 215, 216, 240; evolution of, 230; relational-historical; method, 217

Economic crises, 11, 158
Economic democracy, 322, 326, 332
Economic process, 18, 30
Economics, mainstream, 4, 22, 24–26, 36, 57, 74, 95, 152, 164

Economists, radical, 11
Egypt, 83
Empiricism, 243, 244, 245–51; postmodernist critique of, 249–51
England, 83, 84
Equilibrium mechanism, 308, 309
Ethical values, 288
Ethics; alternative Marxian views of, 288; historical specificity of, 300; relational Approach, 299
Evolutionary approach, 63
Exploitation: class theory, 136; historical approach, 140; relational theory, 136; technological Reductionist view, 134, 196; traditional Marxist Theory, 116, 133

Falling rate of profit theory, 157
Feudalism, 63, 66, 69, 84
France, 84
Free goods, 330, 334, 336
Free will, 276, 277
Full employment, 327, 329
Functionalism, 57

Germany, 34, 83
Greece, 84

Historical approach, 56, 66, 71–73, 125, 158, 180, 193, 221
Historical change; cohen and, 59–62; mainstream social science, 74, 75; and Soviet Marxism, 58, 59

Historical materialism, 20, 29, 38, 51, 59, 63, 72
Historical specificity, 62, 63
Holistic approach, 54
Human nature, 14, 15

Humanism: liberal, 296–98; Marxist, 294, 298, 299, 302, 306

Individualism, 85, 86, 94–97, 99, 106
Inequality, 10
Institutional approach, 54
Institutionalism, 54, 79, 80–82, 307; liberal, 9, 106; radical, 9
Institutionalist view, 10, 79, 106
Instrumentalism, 262, 182–86

Japan, 65, 83, 182

Keynesian period, 23

Labor theory of value, 130

Marxian class analysis, 87, 90, 92, 93
Marxian historical model, 63
Marxism: analytic, 8, 101–4, 216, 267; critical, 5, 7, 9, 23, 68; existentialist, 8, 277
Marxism, Phenomenological, 8, 268, 269; ethical standard, 288; methodology, 294, 318
Materialism, 254
Mathematics, 42, 43, 264; excessive, 265, 266
Media, 293, 328
Medieval views, 34
Middle class, 111–13
Model building, 227
Money and credit, 173

Negation of the negation, 226
Neoclassical approach, 9, 23
Neoclassical biases, 308, 310
Neoclassical economics, 309, 310
New classicals, 10, 24, 74, 78, 79, 100–102, 155
New institutionalism, 26
New Keynesians, 10, 26, 27, 74, 79, 101
Normal science, 255

Opposites, 222
Optimality thesis, 61
Overdetermination, 282
Ownership, public, Cooperative, and Private, 332

Paradigm, Marxism, 317
Paradigms, 42, 75, 243, 255
Philosophy, analytic, 267
Political advertising, 328
Political democracy, 325, 327
Post Keynesianism, 4, 10
Post-Marxian, 92
Postmodernist, 8, 27, 249, 313, 314
Poverty and inequality, 129,130
Pragmatism, 262
Pre-determinism, 270–75, 278, 279; Soviet Marxism, 273
Private enterprise, 335
Production, forces of, 47, 50, 52, 60, 70, 71, 193, 194, 199, 214; relations of, 47–49, 71, 185, 193, 195, 205, 219
Profit squeeze, 169–72
Public control, 330
Public financing, 328
Public housing, 330
Public investment, 329
Public utilities, 334
Purely science, 291–92

Quantity and quality, 224, 237, 240

Racial discrimination, 146–49
Racism, 51
Radicals, 11, 32, 318, 330
Radical institutionalism, 9
Radical political economy, 317
Rational choice theory, 102
Rationalism, 243, 251
Reductionism, 22, 39; economic, 6, 16–20, 22, 59, 95, 105, 158, 168, 178, 182, 185, 190, 191; political, 177; psychological, 13, 15, 16, 22, 45, 94, 104, 155, 177, 178, 195, 259, 299, 302; technological, 18, 21, 63
Relational approach, 29, 35–40, 51, 52, 54, 53, 73, 90, 115, 125, 150, 164, 182, 219
Relativity, 261
Reserve army, 165

mn
ort--

Revolution, 70, 257, 261
Revolution thesis, 61

Say's law, 152–55
Science, 207, 250, 251, 253, 255, 256, 260, 262, 286, 290; revolutions in, 257
Sexism, 51, 149–151
Sexist discrimination, 149–51
Slavery, 48, 64, 66, 69, 84, 146–47, 274, 302
Social process, 33, 34, 37, 38, 53, 54
Socialism, 190, 193, 272, 317, 321, 322, 332
Sociology of knowledge, 40
Soviet dictatorship, 195, 196, 320, 323
Soviet history, 193, 320
Soviet Marxism, 3, 5, 7–9, 12, 17–19, 30, 58, 59, 216–18, 235, 272, 273
Soviet Union, 3, 5, 6, 34, 50, 63, 66, 67, 72, 118, 178–81, 200, 205, 336
Structuralism, 36, 185, 186
Successive approximations, 172, 229

Taxation, 331

Underconsumption, 168
Unemployment, 10, 23, 76, 79, 101, 152, 153, 164, 167
United States, 6, 11, 14, 34, 35, 37, 49, 64, 67, 86, 180–84, 189, 191
U.S. history, 324
Utilitarianism, 296

Value, 134, 286; Sraffian theory, 145, 146
Value-free social science, 286
Value only, 288
Voluntarism, 270, 276
Voting rights, 324, 327

Wage cost, 165
Workers' control, 323, 330, 331, 336
Working class, 6, 113, 114
World government, 335

Yugoslav history, 322

Name Index

Ackerloff, George, 26, 157
Addis, Laird, 282
Ahmed, S., 155
Albert, Michael, 11, 21, 37, 100, 309, 326, 334
Alchian, Armen, 96
Althusser, Louis, 185, 291
Amariglio, Jack, 75, 104, 249, 251
Amin, Samir, 78
Anderson, Charles, 312
Anderson, W. H. Locke, 43, 44, 104, 253
Andeski, Stanislav, 265
Aquinas, Thomas, 243, 244, 286
Archibald, G. C., 77
Arestis, Philip, 10
Aristotle, 14, 231, 240, 243, 244
Ashton, T. H. , 69, 117
Atwater, E., 185
Avineri, Shlomo, 179

Balinky, Alexander, 93
Bandyopadhyay, Pradeep, 90
Baran, Paul, 15, 70, 148
Barbalet, J. M., 90, 91
Becker, Gary, 98, 99
Bentham, Jeremy, 296
Berger, Peter, 19, 20
Bergson, Abram, 204, 205, 233
Bernow, Stephen, 11
Bhaskar, Roy, 254, 281
Blanshard, Brand, 19
Blaug, Mark, 245, 248, 250

Blinder, Alan S., 266
Bluestone, Barry, 90
Boddy, Raford, 165
Bonacich, Edna, 146
Boston, Thomas D., 146
Bowles, Samuel, 122, 135, 137, 162, 188–90, 192, 325, 325, 331
Boyer, Richard O., 142, 143
Braverman, Harry, 138
Brenner, Harvey, 69, 117
Brodbeck, May, 265, 271, 273, 279, 280
Bronfenbrenner, Martin, 262
Brown, Doug, 92, 93
Brown, Stuart, 193, 197, 205, 207
Buchanan, Allen, 293
Bukharin, Nikolai, 196, 197
Burket, Paul, 288

Caldwell, Bruce, 244, 247, 253, 261
Callari, Antonio, 75, 104
Callinicos, Alex, 21, 37, 70, 91, 102, 124, 205
Carling, Alan, 267
Carnoy, Martin, 179, 182, 185
Castro, Fidel, 14
Caudwell, Christopher, 226
Chagall, Marc, 196
Chaplin, Charlie, 137
Chapman, John W., 298
Cheney, Edward, 270, 271
Chilcote, Edward, 8
Chilcote, Ronald, 8

Childe, V. Gordon, 67
Cipolla, Carlo, 226
Cohen, G. A., 16, 19, 59–66, 72, 92, 275
Cohen, Marshall, 291, 293
Colander, David, 42, 43, 314
Colfax, R., 109, 287
Comte, Auguste, 244
Cornforth, Maurice, 6, 17, 236, 238, 241
Coulson, Margaret, 57
Crotty, James, 165
Cullenberg, Stephen, 75, 92, 104

D'Arge, Ralph, 107
Dahrendorf, Ralf, 57
Danto, Arthur, 19
Darwin, Charles, 63, 275
Davis, John B., 291, 294
De Marchi, Neil, 247
De Martino, George, 27
de St. Croix, G. E. M., 116
Debreau, Gerard, 253, 254
Deutscher, Isaac, 206
Devine, James, 105
Dewey, John, 34, 56, 57, 89, 228, 262–64, 299, 307
Diderot, Denis, 243
Diesing, Paul, 244, 246, 248, 262, 263, 312, 314
Dobb, Maurice, 69
Domhoff, G. William, 183–88, 191
Donne, John, 262
Dostoyevsky, Feodor, 194
Draper, Hal, 179
Duboff, Richard, 162
Dühring, Eugen, 62
Dugger, William, 9, 10, 26, 54, 108
Dupre, Louis, 120
Dworkin, Gerald, 220, 239
Dwyer, Larry, 312
Dymski, Gary, 105

Ehrenreich, Barbara, 111, 257
Eichner, Alfred, 10
Einstein, Albert, 256
Elliott, John, 116, 291
Elster, Jon, 87, 102, 105, 251, 264, 267
Engels, Frederich, 5, 62, 71, 134, 217,

219, 233, 234, 236, 276, 278, 293, 301, 302, 317, 335

Ferraro, Joseph, 284
Feuer, Lewis, 13, 16, 273
Feuerbach, Ludwig, 317
Flaherty, Diane, 326
Foster, John B., 145, 284
France, Anatole, 46
Freud, Sigmund, 13, 14
Friedman, Milton, 97, 99, 246, 248, 249, 276, 312, 314
Fromm, Erich, 121

Galbraith, John, 42, 97, 106–8, 265, 312
Galileo, 260
Genovese, Eugene, 289, 290
Gintis, Herbert, 11, 122, 135, 137, 188–90, 192
Goldstein, Jonathan, 166
Gollobin, Ira, 6, 236, 237
Goodwin, Jeff, 190
Gorbachev, Mikhail, 6, 187, 195, 203, 221, 225
Gordon, David, 90, 162, 325, 326, 331
Gordon, Wendell, 94
Gottlieb, Roger, 72, 251
Graff, J. de V., 24
Grampp, William, 284
Gramsci, Antonio, 8, 184–86, 216
Green, Francis, 157
Gregor, A. James, 218
Gruchy, Allan, 80, 107
Grundman, Reiner, 11

Hahnel, Robin, 11, 21, 37, 100, 309, 326, 334
Hamilton, David, 56, 80
Harding, Thomas, 83
Harrington, Michael, 15, 229
Harris, Marvin, 4, 16, 17, 58
Hartsock, Nancy, 191, 291
Harvey, David, 249
Harvey, Philip, 329
Hegel, G. W. F., 5, 86, 216, 227, 231–35, 237, 252, 267
Heilbroner, Robert, 309
Heraclitus, 231
Herman, Edward S., 312

Hill, Christopher, 122
Hilton, Rodney, 69
Hitler, Adolf, 14, 34, 61, 64, 148
Hobsbawm, Eric, 63–64
Hodges, Donald, 292
Hodgson, Geoffrey, 157
Hollis, Martin, 268
Horner, Jim, 49
Horowitz, David, 75
Howard, Michael, 4, 105
Hudelson, Richard, 59, 252
Hume, David, 286, 287
Hunt, E. K., 4, 10, 26, 79, 80, 105, 252, 260, 261
Husserl, Edmund, 268
Hyppolite, Jean, 268

Jackson, Jesse, 138
Jameson, Kenneth, 9, 249
Jarsulic, Marc, 10
Jencks, Clinton, 144

Kain, Philip J., 288, 294
Kalecki, Michal, 10
Kaplan, Abraham, 262
Karsten, Siegfried, 261
Keiusinen, Otto, 58, 59, 274
Kemeny, John, 281
Keynes, John Maynard, 10, 23, 27, 42, 57, 76, 77, 97, 98, 154, 156, 157, 161, 165, 170, 173, 256
Khan, Genghis, 61
Khrushchev, Nikita, 7
Kindahl, J. K., 81
King, J. E., 104, 105
King, John, 4, 11
King, Rodney, 46, 325
Klamer, Arjo, 42, 43, 313
Kojeve, Alexandre, 268
Korzybski, Alfred, 273
Kotz, David H., 205, 209
Kreps, David, 20, 79, 145
Kreuger, Anne, 266
Kuhn, Thomas, 228, 246, 247, 255–64
Kuttner, Robert, 42

Laibman, David, 326
Lakotos, Imre, 261, 262
Larrain, Jorge, 21, 37

Lebowitz, Michael, 105
Lefcourt, Robert, 47
Leftwich, Richard, 165
Lekachman, Robert, 76, 100, 310
Lenin, V. I., 83, 194, 199, 282–84, 303, 304, 335
Leontief, Wassily, 42
Levine, Andrew, 21, 37, 60–62, 68, 102, 267, 289
Levy, Madeline, 45
Lewis, John, 143
Lichtenstein, Peter, 132, 146
Lichtman, Richard, 4, 82
Locke, John, 62, 243, 290
Lucas, Robert, 155, 311
Luckman, Thomas, 19, 20
Lukacs, Georg, 8, 215
Lukes, Steven, 293
Lustig, Jeffrey, R., 4
Luxemburg, Rosa, 8

Malthus, Thomas, 152
Mandel, Ernest, 8, 294
Mankiw, Gary, 26, 27, 29, 157
Mao, Tse-Tung, 14, 237, 238
Marcuse, Herbert, 8, 41, 238
Marglin, Steven, 78, 96, 312
Maritain, Jacques, 235, 293
Marquit, Edwin, 241
Marshall, Alfred, 75, 76, 81, 266
Martel, Harry, 233
Martin, Bill, 249
Martindale, Don, 57
Marx, Karl, 3, 5, 8, 13, 17, 19, 20, 29, 30, 36, 42, 44, 60, 89, 110, 116, 161, 165, 170, 171, 173, 232, 234, 235, 238, 252, 256, 269, 276, 278, 293, 321
Mayer, Thomas F., 102, 267
McCarthy, Joe, 144
McCloskey, Donald, 247, 249–51, 262–64, 314
McLellan, David, 293
McMurtry, John, 18, 20
Mead, Margaret, 33
Means, Gardiner, 81
Milberg, William, 251, 313
Miliband, Ralph, 116, 117, 185, 321
Mill, John Stuart, 271, 272, 276
Miller, Edythe, 26

Miller, Richard, 298
Mills, C. Wright, 62
Mirowski, Philip, 4, 75, 260
Mitchell, Wesley, 56, 70, 163, 170, 171, 253
Morais, Herbert, 142, 143
Mosca, Gaetano, 94
Musgrove, Alan, 261, 262
Myrdal, Gunnar, 311, 312

Nagel, Thomas, 291, 293
Neill, R. B., 268
Nell, Edward, 268
Newlon, Daniel, 43
Nisbet, Robert, 57
Nordhaus, William, 24, 156, 311
Norman, Richard, 242
North, Douglas, 26
Nove, Alec, 204

O'Connor, James, 185
Offe, Claus, 185
Ollman, Bertell, 12, 29, 36, 58, 90, 215–18, 221, 231, 232, 239, 240, 283, 319
Olson, Mancur, 90–92

Pareto, Vilfredo, 94
Parsons, Talcott, 36, 252
Peffer, R. G., 290, 291
Pennock, J. Roland, 299
Perot, Ross, 46, 66, 183, 325, 328
Peterson, Wallace, 163
Pheby, John, 10
Philpin, C. H. E., 69, 117
Ping-yuan, Shen, 240, 241
Pitelis, Christos, 26
Planty-Bonjour, Guy, 239
Plato, 231
Platt, John, 225
Plekhanov, George, 277
Popper, Karl, 59, 88, 90, 245, 247, 248, 250, 259, 261, 269, 274, 275, 282–84, 292, 293, 314, 324
Poulantzas, Nicos, 185
Pozzuto, Richard, 268
Priest, Graham, 241
Przeworski, Adam, 103

Ransom, Roger, 48, 69
Rapoport, Anatol, 233

Raskin, Paul, 11
Rawls, John, 290, 298
Reagan, Ronald, 124, 138, 192, 276
Reich, Michael, 146
Reiman, Jeffrey, 46, 47
Resnick, Stephen, 11, 21, 25, 37, 39, 47, 110, 116, 253, 267, 283, 284
Ricardo, David, 5, 22, 56
Riddell, David, 57
Rigby, S. H., 21, 71
Roach, Jack, 109, 287
Robbins, Lionel, 76, 77, 253
Robinson, Joan, 10
Roemer, John, 103–5, 136, 145, 146, 216, 251, 264, 265, 267, 309, 326
Romer, David, 26, 27, 79, 157
Roosevelt, Franklin D., 144
Rose, Arnold, 177
Rosenberg, Ethel, 14
Rosenberg, Julius, 14
Rozansky, Joseph, 307
Ruccio, David, 35, 265
Russell, Bertrand, 231, 233

Sahlins, Marshall, 227
Samuels, Warren, 9, 26, 32, 54, 81, 82, 106, 248
Samuelson, Paul, 24, 75, 156, 311
Sartre, Jean Paul, 8, 21, 37, 277, 278, 282
Sawyer, Malcolm, 10, 11, 77, 146, 319
Say, J. B., 152
Sayer, Derek, 21, 37
Sayers, Sean, 242, 293
Scanlon, Thomas, 291, 293
Schaff, Adam, 241
Schmemann, Sergei, 6
Schmidt, Richard, 234, 235
Schumpeter, Joseph, 20, 93, 94, 312
Schwartz, Jesse, 79, 80
Schweickart, David, 326
Schwendinger, Herman, 4
Schwendinger, Julia, 4
Seeger, Pete, 44
Selsam, Howard, 233
Semmler, Willi, 134
Shaikh, Anwar, 134
Sharp, Ansel, 165
Shaw, William H., 20
Sheehan, Michael, 307

Shelton, John F., 310
Sherman, Howard, 10, 11, 36, 70, 123,
   129, 130, 136, 152, 156, 158, 163,
   167–71, 173, 174, 191, 194
Silvestre, Joaqum, 311
Simon, Lawrence, 35
Sinclair, Barbara, 144
Skidelsky, Robert, 266
Skocpol, Theda, 45, 187, 188
Skouras, Thanos, 10
Smith, Adam, 5, 22, 74, 130
Smith, Dan, 303
Sober, Elliott, 21, 37, 60–62, 102, 267,
   284
Socrates, 231
Soderbaum, Peter, 99, 100
Solo, Robert, 312
Somerville, John, 6, 236
Sraffa, Piero, 10, 136, 145, 146
Stalin, Joseph, 6, 7, 17, 18, 58, 86, 87,
   195–98, 235–37, 239, 254, 273, 300,
   303, 304
Steinmo, Sven, 182
Stewart, Harnish, 215
Stigler, George, 81, 310
Stillman, Peter G., 5
Sutch, Richard, 48, 69
Sweezy, Paul, 7, 21, 37, 72, 107, 260,
   304
Szymanski, Albert, 179, 288

Terkel, Studs, 160
Thompson, Frank, 104
Tigar, Michael, 45
Tilman, Rick, 9, 307
Tolstoy, Leo, 194
Tool, Marc, 9, 302, 307
Trotsky, Leon, 196, 197, 215
Tullock, Gordon, 78

Turner, Jonathan H., 19, 93
Twain, Mark, 41

Varian, Hal, 24, 25, 78
Veblen, Thorstein, 9, 50, 79, 80, 82,
   83, 108, 256, 307, 308
Vernoff, Edward, 12, 58, 319
von Mises, Ludwig, 252

Wachtel, Howard, 90
Walras, Leon, 253
Ward, Benjamin, 312
Weber, Max, 36, 286, 287
Weeks, John, 75, 134, 158
Weiss, Andrew, 27, 157
Weisskopf, Thomas, 11, 162, 325, 326,
   331
Wenger, Martin, 249
Wertheimer, Max, 233
West, Cornel, 301, 302
Wilbur, Charles, 9, 249
Wilen, James, 107
Williamson, Oliver, 26
Winick, Andrew, 111, 130
Wisman, John, 307
Wolff, Richard, 11, 21, 25, 37, 39, 47,
   92, 110, 116, 253, 267, 283, 284
Wolfson, Murray, 19, 273
Wood, Ellen Meiksins, 21, 36, 37, 105,
   291
Wright, Eric Olin, 21, 37, 60–62, 101,
   102, 111–14, 119, 120, 124, 125, 265,
   267, 284

Yellen, Janet, 26, 157

Zimbalist, Andrew, 193, 197, 205, 207
Zinn, Howard, 4, 14, 87, 277, 289, 290

Sherman, Howard J.
  Reinventing marxism / Howard J. Sherman.
        p.   cm.
  Includes bibliographical references (p.   ) and index.
  ISBN 0-8018-5076-2 (acid-free paper). — ISBN 0-8018-5077-0 (pbk.: acid-free
    paper)
  1. Socialism.   2. Post-communism.   3. Communism.   4. Communism and social
  sciences. 5. Marxian economics.   I. Title.
HX73.S499 1995
335.4—dc20   95-11951

Printed in the United States
97444LV00003B/134/A